DICTIONARY OF
ACCOUNTING AND FINANCE

D1396411

INFORMATION AT YOUR FINGERTIPS

Up-to-date and comprehensive, Pitman Dictionaries
are indispensable reference books, providing clear,
crisp explanations of specialist terminology
in an easy-to-use format.

Dictionary of Advertising
Dictionary of Banking
Dictionary of Business Studies
Dictionary of Economics
Dictionary of Insurance
Dictionary of Law
Dictionary of Personnel and
Human Resources Management

DICTIONARY OF
ACCOUNTING
AND FINANCE

Raymond Brockington

School of Management
University of Bath

Pitman Publishing
128 Long Acre, London WC2E 9AN

A Division of Longman Group Limited

First published as *Concise Dictionary of Accounting and Finance* in 1986
Second edition 1993

© Longman Group UK Limited 1993

British Library Cataloguing in Publication Data
A CIP catalogue record for this book can be obtained from the British Library.

ISBN 0 273 60112 1

Printed in Great Britain by Bell and Bain Ltd., Glasgow

3 5 7 9 10 8 6 4 2

PREFACE

A great deal has happened in the world of accounting and finance and in the wider world since the first edition of this dictionary appeared in 1986. Comments I have received have indicated that this was well received but a need has become apparent both to update it and to make it more comprehensive. I was, therefore, delighted when my publisher invited me to prepare a second edition and endorsed my views on the form which this should take.

Like its predecessor this dictionary is intended as a work of reference for those studying the literature of Accounting and Finance and for the reader of the financial press. It seeks to define as many as possible of the terms likely to be encountered in these sources. A particular difficulty in this subject area is that many of its terms consist of words regularly occurring in everyday speech but with such specialist meanings in this context that the reader is unlikely to guess at their correct interpretation from general knowledge. This is particularly true, of course, for people to whom English is not a first language and it is hoped that the dictionary will be especially valuable to them.

Since the first edition I have more than doubled the size of the book so that over 2,500 terms are now defined. Some of the terms used are different in the USA from what they are in the UK and, where this is so, I have included both. The word 'leverage', for example, is used in the USA to mean what in the UK would be described as 'gearing'. Some terms have more than one meaning depending on the context. 'Stock' and 'apportionment' are examples of these and the alternative meanings are given. Sometimes a small change in the precise wording of an expression makes the meaning totally different. 'Cost of control', for example, does not mean the same thing as 'cost control'.

In the intensely commercial world in which we live many people find a need for a good understanding of the language of Accounting and Finance. These range from those studying for specialist qualifications through those to whom the subject is an important, if not central, part of their job, to those who wish, as citizens, to be fully informed on the events occurring around them. It is hoped that this new edition of the dictionary will be of value to them all.

January 1993   Raymond Brockington

A

abacus. A bead frame used for counting and other calculations. At one time widely used in Eastern countries, it has been rendered largely obsolete by the computer and electronic calculator.

Abacus. An academic journal on accounting and business studies produced in Australia. It is published by Sydney University Press.

abandonment value. The amount which could be recovered from an investment project if it were immediately to be abandoned. It is of importance in the field of CAPITAL BUDGETING (q.v.) as a concept relevant to the monitoring and review of ongoing capital projects. No decision to invest should be regarded as irrevocable, and if at any time the abandonment of a project is of greater value than its continuance then abandonment is indicated. The simple decision rule is that a project should be abandoned if its abandonment value exceeds the NET PRESENT VALUE (q.v.) of its projected cash flows.

EXAMPLE. A certain project, nearing the end of its useful life, is expected to last for 2 further years and to yield at the end of these years positive cash flows of £8,000 and £6,000 respectively. If abandoned now, the plant and equipment could be sold for £12,500. After 2 further years of use it will have no value. The COST OF CAPITAL (q.v.) is 10 per cent per annum.

Present value of future returns

Year	Returns	Discount factor	Present value
	£		£
1	8,000	0.909	7,272
2	6,000	0.826	4,956
Total			12,228

Since it is worth only £12,228 to continue the project, but £12,500 can be obtained by abandoning it, it should be abandoned. Failure to abandon is the equivalent of investing the £12,500 forgone into a project with a negative net present value.

abatement. A deduction which reduces the effect which some charge would otherwise have. The term is usually applied to an abatement of taxation which is given in special circumstances. Small companies, for example, receive an abatement of corporation tax by being charged at an especially low rate.

abnormal cost. A cost which has been incurred in connection with an activity but which would not normally have been expected to be incurred. It relates to some unanticipated and non-recurring event. In IAS 16 it was argued that in establishing the cost of a fixed asset, abnormal cost should be excluded.

abnormal wastage. Wastage leading to an unanticipated additional cost. Many industrial processes create a certain amount of waste material. When garments are cut out of cloth, for example, there will be pieces of material which cannot be used. The actual

1

amount of waste depends partly upon the care with which the process is undertaken but there will be an irreducible minimum which depends upon the technicalities of the process. Abnormal wastage is that amount by which actual wastage exceeds the irreducible minimum, known as NORMAL WASTAGE (q.v.) Its significance is that it represents a loss due to avoidable causes as opposed to a necessary part of the cost of production. For costing purposes it should be shown separately in the costing profit and loss account.

above the line. Included in the profit and loss account of the business. The 'line' is that dividing the PROFIT AND LOSS ACCOUNT (q.v.) from the APPROPRIATION ACCOUNT (q.v.). See also BELOW THE LINE.

abridged accounts. Accounts which, while covering the full financial period to which they relate, are not fully detailed financial statements. They may be used where a company wishes to give information of its financial affairs in a summarised form to those who may not be entitled to or require a full set of accounts, e.g. its employees. Where a company issues abridged accounts they must be accompanied by a statement which indicates:

(a) that they are not complete financial statements;

(b) whether or not full statements have been filed with the REGISTRAR OF COMPANIES (q.v.);

(c) whether or not the AUDITORS (q.v.) have reported on the full financial statements; and

(d) whether or not the AUDITORS' REPORT (q.v.) was QUALIFIED (q.v.).

abscond. To disappear, often taking property or money. An employee, for example, may abscond with the contents of the cash box.

absenteeism. The extent to which a workforce is absent from work because of sickness or other cause which requires that they still have to be paid. Absenteeism represents an important cost to any organisation and it should be minimised. This can be done by paying attention to the conditions in the workplace as a contented worker is less likely to be absent.

absentee landlord. A LANDLORD (q.v.) who does not live at or near the premises which he or she rents out. This sometimes make it difficult for a tenant to contact the landlord when this is needed.

absorb. To allocate or apportion an item of OVERHEAD (q.v.) to some unit of production or COST CENTRE (q.v.). Thus if fixed overhead is charged to production on, say, a MACHINE HOUR RATE (q.v.) it is said to have been absorbed on that basis.

absorption costing. That method of COSTING (q.v.) whereby all costs of production are attributed to identified units of production. The name is derived from the fact that the method requires some technique whereby OVERHEAD (q.v.) which is not directly attributable to these units is nevertheless absorbed by them, or added to directly attributable cost, after some process of APPORTIONMENT (q.v.). Absorption costing should be contrasted with direct or MARGINAL COSTING (q.v.) where only the fully attributable costs are taken into account.

ACA. The designatory letters of an associate member of the INSTITUTE OF CHARTERED ACCOUNTANTS IN ENGLAND AND WALES (q.v.).

ACCA. The designatory letters of an associate member of the CHARTERED ASSOCIATION OF CERTIFIED ACCOUNTANTS (q.v.)

accelerated depreciation. A method of calculating DEPRECIATION (q.v.) in such a manner that a larger proportion of an asset's value is written off in the early part of its life than in later parts. Examples of methods of applying accelerated depreciation are the REDUCING BALANCE METHOD (q.v.) and the SUM OF THE YEARS' DIGITS (q.v.) method. The STRAIGHT LINE METHOD (q.v.) is, by contrast, not a method of accelerated depreciation. Accelerated depreciation may be used either because it is believed that this reflects the actual pattern of the decline in value of the asset or because, as a general principle, it is regarded as more prudent to write off assets as quickly as possible.

acceptance. The action of signifying on the face of a BILL OF EXCHANGE (q.v.) that liability is accepted under it. An accepted bill of exchange is likely to be easier to negotiate than one which has not been accepted.

Access. The name of one of the two main CREDIT CARDS (q.v.) available in the UK. It operates within the Mastercard network.

accident insurance. Insurance which gives an indemnity for the consequences of an accident, e.g. extra expenses incurred, loss of income, but not for other sources of loss. Accidental death insurance carries a much lower rate of premium than full life assurance.

accommodation bill. A BILL OF EXCHANGE (q.v.) which has been drawn on and accepted by a reputable party for the purpose of giving value to the bill so that it can be discounted. There is no underlying trading transaction as would normally be the case for a bill of exchange.

account. 1. Any document or device whereby a record is kept of flows of value measured in money terms. A business will record all of its transactions in a set of accounts making up its LEDGER (q.v.). A cash account, for example, will show all cash received and paid. A fixed asset account will show purchases, sales and depreciation of fixed assets. The term may also apply to a record of dealings between contracting parties. Thus one may have an account with a shop from which one makes regular purchases or an account with a BANK (q.v.).
2. A period of time designated by the STOCK EXCHANGE (q.v.) during which all transactions fall to be settled at the same time. An account is usually of two weeks' duration, from a Monday until the Friday next but one, except where it embraces a public holiday, when it will last for three weeks. All the transactions within an account are due for settlement on SETTLEMENT DAY (q.v.) which is the Tuesday next but one after the end of an account.

accountability. The responsibility to explain actions involving financial matters to others. The directors of a company have accountability to their shareholders. This is discharged by the publication of annual accounts and by answering questions put at meetings of shareholders.

accountancy. The activity of preparing and auditing the financial records and statements of organisations.

Accountancy. The official journal of the INSTITUTE OF CHARTERED ACCOUNTANTS IN ENGLAND AND WALES (q.v.). It is published monthly and contains articles on accounting, auditing, taxation and other matters of professional interest. It also publishes the text of important statements such as FINANCIAL REPORTING STANDARDS (q.v.) and professional announcements. Members of the Institute are expected to make themselves aware of 'essential reading' contained in *Accountancy* and this is indicated by a red border to the pages containing this material. Less important 'official material' is printed on pages having a blue border.

Accountant's International Study Group. A body representative of accountants from a number of countries which considers a variety of topics and issues reports on them.

Accountants' Reporting Rules. A statement issued jointly by the main accountancy bodies setting out guidelines for accountants who have to report on the profit forecasts contained in company prospectuses.

accounting. The subject of the process of recording and analysing financial information so as to maximise the value of the information produced.

accounting bases. The various methods of constructing accounting figures which are available. There are, for example, several bases on which DEPRECIATION (q.v.) might be determined. From the available accounting bases any business has to make an appropriate selection which become its ACCOUNTING POLICIES (q.v.).

accounting concepts. The fundamental framework of ideas which underlie the preparation of accounts. There is no authoritative agreement on what these concepts are or ought to be although some attempts have been made by to codify them. *See also* CONCEPTUAL FRAMEWORK.

accounting date. A date marking the end of a period for which accounts are prepared. Thus if a business prepares accounts for periods which coincide with the calendar year its accounting date will be 31 December in each year.

accounting period. A period of time, say one year, for which accounts have been prepared.

accounting policies. The particular accounting bases judged by a business to be the most appropriate to its own circumstances and therefore the ones which it adopts. Accounting policies were required to be disclosed by SSAP 2 and this disclosure is now required by the Companies Act 1985. Accounting policies concern such matters as DEPRECIATION (q.v.), translation of foreign currency and stock valuation.

accounting principles. *See* GENERALLY ACCEPTED ACCOUNTING PRINCIPLES.

Accounting Principles Board. A standard setting body in the USA which operated from 1959 to 1973. The Board was set up by the AMERICAN INSTITUTE OF CERTIFIED PUBLIC ACCOUNTANTS (q.v.) to undertake a programme of research into the problems of financial reporting. It produced two series of publications. One series was called 'Opinions of the Accounting Principles Board' and the other was 'Statements of the Accounting Principles Board'. Thirty-one opinions were published and they became the ultimate source of authority for GENERALLY ACCEPTED ACCOUNTING PRINCIPLES (q.v.). The statements were less authoritative but were intended to provide helpful guidance in difficult areas. The Board, which was served by volunteer members, was superseded by the FINANCIAL ACCOUNTING STANDARDS BOARD (q.v.) from 1972.

accounting procedure. A clearly defined sequence of actions prescribed for the recording of a particular type of transaction. Each organisation is likely to have its own distinctive accounting procedures.

accounting rate of return. A crude arithmetical determination of the rate of return offered by an investment project. It should be contrasted with the theoretically more acceptable INTERNAL RATE OF RETURN (q.v.). Although an accounting rate of return may be calculated from information concerning a project which is completed, it is usually calculated on the basis of the estimated returns from a future project and is thus a method used for INVESTMENT APPRAISAL (q.v.).

EXAMPLE. Project X requires the immediate investment of £20,000 and promises to produce the following positive cash flows over the next 4 years:

Year	Cash flow
	£
1	8,000
2	7,000
3	6,000
4	5,000
Total	26,000

Calculation of accounting rate of return £

Total cash flow	26,000
Less initial investment	20,000
Total profit	6,000
Average profit	1,500 per annum
Average investment	10,000 (50% initial sum)

Accounting rate of return $\frac{1,500}{10,000} \times 100 = 15\%$ per annum

Accounting Review. The journal of the AMERICAN ACCOUNTING ASSOCIATION (q.v.). It is published quarterly and contains learned articles on accounting and on accountancy education. Articles are accepted only after independent reviewers have given a favourable opinion on their academic merit.

Accounting Standards. Short term referring to STATEMENTS OF STANDARD ACCOUNTING PRACTICE (q.v.) and FINANCIAL REPORTING STANDARDS (q.v.).

Accounting Standards Board. The successor to the ACCOUNTING STANDARDS COMMITTEE (q.v.). Unlike the Committee the Board issues standards under its own authority. It was formed in 1990.

Accounting Standards Committee. The standard setting body in the UK from 1976 until 1991. It superseded the Accounting Standards Steering Committee which had existed since 1970 and had now been itself superseded by the Accounting Standards Board of the Financial Reporting Council. The terms of reference of the committee required it to propose definitive standards for financial reporting to the councils of its constituent bodies. These bodies were:

Institute of Chartered Accountants in England and Wales
Institute of Chartered Accountants of Scotland
Institute of Chartered Accountants in Ireland
Chartered Association of Certified Accountants
Chartered Institute of Management Accountants
Chartered Institute of Public Finance and Accountancy

The standards, known as STATEMENTS OF STANDARD ACCOUNTING PRACTICE (q.v.), were then promulgated simultaneously to the membership of the participating bodies.

Accounting Standards Steering Committee. The standard setting body in the UK from 1970 to 1976 when it was reconstituted as ACCOUNTING STANDARDS COMMITTEE (q.v.).

accounting technician. One who works on accounting processes at a level above the merely clerical but below the level of operation of a fully qualified accountant. Thus an accounting technician might prepare the draft final accounts of a business but an accountant would be needed to complete these and to interpret them.

account payable. Synonym for CREDITOR (q.v.) commonly used in the USA.

account payee only. Words which written as a CROSSINGD (q.v.) to a cheque have the effect that the cheque may be paid only through a bank account in the name of the original PAYEE (q.v.). Such a cheque cannot be transferred to another person by ENDOR-SEMENT (q.v.).

account receivable. Synonym for DEBTOR (q.v.) commonly used in the USA.

account rendered. A term appearing against the opening item on a statement sent by a supplier to a customer. It signifies that this amount is brought forward from a previous statement from which full details may be obtained if required.

account sales. A detailed statement sent by an AGENT (q.v.) to his PRINCIPAL (q.v.) following the sale of goods by the agent on behalf of the principal. It accounts for the money received from the sales, stocks remaining and any expenses or COMMISSION (q.v.) retained by the agent out of the proceeds of sale.

accretion. An increase in value which takes place over a period of time.

accrual. A liability in respect of goods or services provided to a business in the form of a continuous supply, consumed up to an accounting date but not billed by that date. Common subjects for accruals are electricity, gas and telephone services. Accruals are required in order that MATCHING (q.v.) in the calculation of profit can be achieved. As well as being adjusted on the profit and loss account an accrual appears on the balance sheet as a CURRENT LIABILITY (q.v.). The accruals concept is one of the four fundamental principles embodied in the Companies Act 1985.

accruals basis. That basis of the preparation of the profit and loss which takes into account not merely amounts paid and received but also expenses accrued but not paid and for income accrued but not received. It is the normal basis of the preparation of accounts for commercial undertakings.

accrued benefits. Benefits which have accumulated up to the current point in time. A member of a pension scheme, for example, could refer to the accrued benefits of membership to the scheme.

accrued costs. Costs which have been incurred in the sense that their associated benefits have been consumed but where no payment has yet taken place because it has not formally become due. The cost of electricity consumed between a billing date and the end of an accounting period is an example of an accrued cost.

accrued interest. Interest which has been earned by money loaned or deposited but which has not yet formally become payable. If the interest on a deposit is payable on, say, 30 June and 31 December in each year, there will be accrued interest at any other date. The accrued interest by 30 September, for example, will be half of the amount actually payable on 31 December.

accumulated depreciation. The total amount of DEPRECIATION (q.v.) provided on a FIXED ASSET (q.v.) from its date of purchase to the present time. The figure will thus, normally, include several years' depreciation. Company law requires that a company's fixed assets are shown at cost, or valuation, less accumulated depreciation. Because both figures must be stated, a separate account for accumulated depreciation is required. When an asset is sold or otherwise disposed of it must be eliminated from both the account containing its original cost and from that containing its accumulated depreciation. The difference between the two figures is the net BOOK VALUE (q.v.).

accumulated fund. An item on the balance sheet of a NON-PROFIT MAKING ORGANISATION (q.v.) representing the net investment in the organisation of its contributing members. Such an organisation does not normally employ the concept of CAPITAL (q.v.) which is associated with proprietorial rights and with the earning of profit. The accumulated fund is, however, similar in function to a capital account as it represents members' EQUITY (q.v.) in the organisation and provides risk finance for the assets which are held and the operations which are undertaken. Very often, where no substantial assets are held, an accumulated fund represents the cumulative surplus of subscription over expenditure and contains no element of long-term funding provided explicitly at the organisations' inception or subsequently. It is then often quite small and represents merely the impossibility of matching revenues and expenditures exactly and the necessity to keep a small working balance of funds in hand.

accumulation. The process of allowing some value to grow. There will be an accumulation of interest in a deposit account where this is not withdrawn. There will be an accumulation of RETAINED PROFIT (q.v.) if a company pays a DIVIDEND (q.v.) which is regularly less than the profit.

accumulation units. Units in a UNIT TRUST (q.v.) where the income is reinvested in further units rather than being distributed in cash. Many unit trust managers offer their units on an accumulation basis at the option of the holder. Some are available in this form only. It is a useful feature where the prime intention of the investment is savings rather than to produce an immediate income. Even though reinvested, the income on accumulation units is regarded as part of total income for the purposes of determining liability to INCOME TAX (q.v.).

acid test ratio. The ratio which total liquid assets bear to current liabilities. It is so called because it is regarded as the ultimate test of a business's short-run ability to pay its debts. A synonym for the acid test ratio is the liquidity ratio.

For the purpose of determining the acid test ratio the liquid assets to be taken into account include CASH (q.v.), favourable bank balances, DEBTORS (q.v.) and readily realisable investments held as CURRENT ASSETS (q.v.). The calculation of the acid test ratio is:

$$\text{Acid test ratio} = \frac{\text{Liquid assets}}{\text{Current liabilities}}$$

An acid test ratio of approximately 1 (i.e. equality between liquid assets and current liabilities) is normally considered healthy. It implies that there are sufficient readily available funds from which all short-term commitments can be met. The business is not, therefore, in immediate danger of a shortage of liquid funds

ACMA. The designatory letters of an associate member of the CHARTERED INSTITUTE OF MANAGEMENT ACCOUNTANTS (q.v.).

acquisition. The amalgamation with a company's business of a previously independent business by the purchase of that business from its former owners. The consideration for the purchase may be cash or it may be shares in the acquiring company.

acquisition method. A method of preparing CONSOLIDATED ACCOUNTS (q.v.). The essential feature of the acquisition method of consolidation is that the PREACQUISITION PROFIT (q.v.) of the SUBSIDIARY COMPANY (q.v.) is unavailable to support dividends which will be credited to the profit and loss account of the HOLDING COMPANY (q.v.), for whom it has the status of capital funds. This is because the underlying assumption is that the holding company has purchased its controlling interest from those who previously owned it.

Until the Companies Act 1981, many authorities regarded the acquisition method as the only legal method of consolidation. Today it remains the method most commonly in use. The alternative MERGER METHOD (q.v.) may be used only in precisely defined circumstances.

EXAMPLE. Summarised balance sheets at 31 December 19X1

	Holding £000s	Subsidiary £000s
Fixed assets	520	320
Net current assets	260	280
Investment in subsidiary (80% of issued share capital) at cost	470	
	1,250	600
Represented by:		
Ordinary shares of £1 each	1,000	500
Profit and loss account	250	100
	1,250	600

Notes:
(a) At the date when Holding acquired its shares in Subsidiary the balance on that company's profit and loss account stood at £60,000.
(b) At that date all of Subsidiary's assets were fairly valued in its balance sheet.

The acquisition method requires the following calculation of GOODWILL (q.v.):

	£	£
Purchase price of shares in Subsidiary		470,000
Net assets acquired:		
80% share capital	400,000	
80% of profit and loss account at date of purchase	48,000	
		448,000
		22,000

The consolidated balance sheet of Holding and its subsidiary is then:

		£000s
Fixed assets		840
Net current assets		540
Goodwill[1]		22
		1,402
Represented by:		
Ordinary shares of £1 each		1,000
Profit and loss account:		
Holding	250	
Subsidiary	32	
		282
		1,282
Minority interest in subsidiary[2]		120
		1,402

1. SSAP 22 requires that goodwill be written off against reserves or amortised over the period of its effective life.

2. MINORITY INTEREST (q.v.) reflects the interest of the holders of 20 per cent of the issued capital not held by Holding.

across the board. Affecting every value equally. An across the board increase in salaries, for example, means that every employee will have a similar proportionate increase. An across the board reduction in prices means that all prices have been reduced.

ACT. Letters standing for ADVANCE CORPORATION TAX (q.v.).

active account. An account, usually with a bank, on which transactions are currently and regularly taking place.

active market. One in which there is a large amount of trading. Where there is substantial interest in a company and thus a great deal of buying and selling of its shares, there may be said to be an active market in those shares.

activity. 1. A particular direction in which a business applies its efforts. Thus a business may have a manufacturing activity and a selling activity.

2. A measure of the general level of business. Thus a business with a large TURNOVER (q.v.) may be said to be operating at a high level of activity.

activity-based costing. A method of ABSORPTION COSTING (q.v.) whereby INDIRECT COSTS (q.v.) are analysed in detail and each element is then associated with the activity from which it arises. This activity becomes the driver for that element of indirect cost. This means that it becomes the basis for charging the indirect expense to production.

act of bankruptcy. An action by a debtor which leads to a presumption of insolvency and therefore legally allows a creditor to instigate BANKRUPTCY (q.v.) proceedings. Acts of bankruptcy include assigning property to a trustee for the benefit of creditors, leaving the country with the intention of delaying payment to creditors and giving notice of the suspension of the payment of debts.

actual total loss. An insurance term meaning that the object insured has been completely destroyed or otherwise lost. The full amount of the insured value then becomes payable.

actuarial value. A valuation of contingent liabilities based on probabilities. It is most commonly used in the field of insurance and pension funds. A pension fund, for example, has an obligation to pay a pensioner an agreed amount for life. The value of that obligation cannot be determined exactly for an individual as the length of life cannot be known in advance. The value can, however, be assessed with reasonable accuracy for a group of pensioners by using statistics relating to the general pattern of mortality for the population of which they are a part. This latter would be an actuarial value.

actuary. A professional person concerned with assessing the financial implications of INSURABLE RISKS (q.v.). An actuary will probably be employed by an insurance company or a pension fund. The recognised professional bodies of actuaries in the UK are the Institute of Actuaries (in England) and the Faculty of Actuaries (in Scotland).

added value. The difference between the market value of the output of a business and the cost of the inputs required to produce that output.

additional premium. A PREMIUM (q.v.) charged in respect of an insurance policy where its terms are amended at the request of the insured after the original premium has been paid. The amendment may be of the risk insured against or of the value of the property insured.

additional voluntary contribution. An amount paid by an employee into an approved occupational pension scheme in excess of the amount required under the contract of employment. The purpose of making an additional voluntary contribution is to increase the amount of pension ultimately payable. It would, normally, be made only by a person entering the pension scheme midway through a career who could not otherwise accumulate a full pension entitlement. Provided that all pension contributions, compulsory and voluntary, do not exceed 15 per cent of income, full income tax relief is given in respect of them. This proportion is increased to 17½ per cent for persons close to retirement.

adjusted earnings statement. A statement of the profit of a business showing adjustments to exclude the amounts which have distorted the overall picture. This usually takes the form of excluding non-typical amounts which, for this reason, are unlikely to recur.

adjuster. A person who, by profession, examines insurance claims in order to determine their validity and confirm their amount.

adjusting event. An event occurring after the date of a balance sheet, but before it has been signed by the Directors, which provides new or additional information on conditions existing at the date of the balance sheet. The term appears in SSAP 17, Accounting for Post Balance Sheet Events. An adjusting event is required by the Standard to be reflected in the accounts. Examples of adjusting events are:

(a) A valuation of property indicating a permanent diminution of value at the balance sheet date.

(b) The insolvency of a debtor included in the year end figure for debtors.

(c) The announcement of a tax rate applicable to the year ended on the balance sheet date.

(d) The discovery of an error in the accounts.

(e) Decisions taken by the Board of Directors relating to the year concerned, e.g. the amount of a proposed dividend or of a transfer to reserves.

adjustment. An amendment to an accounting figure which is basically correct but which needs to allow for some circumstance not recorded in the book-keeping system. Adjustments in accounting are very common. Good examples are the adjustments made to TRIAL BALANCE (q.v.) figures for ACCRUALS (q.v.) and PREPAYMENTS (q.v.) before they are charged in the PROFIT AND LOSS ACCOUNT (q.v.). Adjustments may also be made to a correctly calculated figure of profit to determine the taxable profit where statutory rules for calculation have to be observed.

administrative costs. An important classification of cost within the profit and loss account. It contains costs which directly relate to administration and might include telephone, office salaries and postage. It will be an objective of management to minimise administrative costs subject to maintenance of the quality of the administrative process.

administrator. A person appointed to deal with the affairs of a deceased person where there is no EXECUTOR (q.v.). This might occur because no executor was named in the WILL (q.v.) or because the named executor is unable or unwilling to act. An administrator is, however, most commonly appointed in an INTESTACY (q.v.), i.e. where no will was left.

administratrix. The feminine form of ADMINISTRATOR (q.v.).

admission charge. An amount charged for the right to enter some sporting or entertainment event.

admission to listing. The action whereby the shares of a company achieve a Stock Exchange quotation and are thus able to be bought and sold through the market.

ad valorem. In proportion to value. Thus an *ad valorem tax* on an article is a tax whose total depends on the value of the article. VALUE ADDED TAX (q.v.) is an example of an *ad valorem* tax.

advance. 1. A loan. Thus a bank manager might make an advance to a business by allowing it an OVERDRAFT (q.v.). The term is used in the PARTNERSHIP ACT 1890 (q.v.) to refer to an amount paid into the business by a partner over and above the agreed capital contribution. In the absence of any agreement to the contrary the Act entitles the partner to interest on such an advance as a first charge against distributable profit.

2. An amount paid as an instalment towards a liability which has already or will shortly mature. For example, a worker might receive an advance on wages to help with unexpected personal expenses. The beneficiary under a trust might receive an advance against income before the precise amount of the entitlement has been determined.

3. An amount required to be paid for a service before the service has been undertaken.

advance corporation tax. An amount of CORPORATION TAX (q.v.) which becomes payable in advance of its otherwise due date as a consequence of the payment by the company of a DIVIDEND (q.v.). Tax legislation requires that this payment is made and it is equal in amount to the TAX CREDIT (q.v.) imputed to the dividend. It should be noted that the payment of advance corporation tax does not ordinarily affect the total tax burden falling on the company but merely the timing of its payment. Any payment for advance corporation tax may be reduced by the amount of tax credits imputed to any FRANKED INVESTMENT INCOME (q.v.) received by the company.

advancement. The action of a TRUSTEE (q.v.) in using funds from a trust for the benefit of a beneficiary in advance of the time when the benefit would normally become available. For example, a trust might be set up whereby the money of a deceased man was to provide an income for his widow for life and then go to his children. The trustee might make advancement of some of the capital to the children during the lifetime of the widow. The power of advancement must be given under the deed constituting the trust.

advance royalty. It is customary for the author of a book to receive an advance ROYALTY (q.v.) at the time the manuscript is delivered. This is then deducted from actual royalties as they accrue. If actual royalties never equal the amount of the advance the shortfall is notionally returnable. Very few publishers would enforce this, however.

adverse variance. A difference between an actual expense or cost and the amount of a budgeted or STANDARD COST (q.v.) such that its effect is to reduce profit below that planned. If, for example, materials are bought at a price higher than standard this will lead to an adverse variance. All adverse variances of MATERIAL (q.v.) amount should be investigated so that the source of any loss or inefficiency can be eliminated as early as possible.

advertising. An important item of business expense appearing in the profit and loss account.

advice note. A document accompanying a delivery of goods which advises as to the kinds, quality and quantity of goods delivered. It does not contain any details of price or total cost. It should be verified that it agrees with the actual goods delivered and with the order that was placed for them.

affinity card. A CREDIT CARD (q.v.) issued on a condition that specified amounts are paid by the issuer to a named charity. The card is usually produced in a distinctive style to indicate this and so also gives publicity to the charity concerned when the card is used.

after hours dealing. Trading in the Stock Exchange which takes place after the official close of business. Such dealing will not be recorded as part of the transactions of the day on which it actually takes place.

after market. The market in a security, usually shares, which develops immediately after their original issue. If, for example, shares in a company were the subject of an OFFER FOR SALE (q.v.) to the public at a price of £1.50 per share but were quoted at £1.90 immediately dealings began on the Stock Exchange it might be said that the after market in the shares had established a useful gain on the issue price.

after tax. Words which signify that the amount to which they relate has already had tax deducted from it so that there is no more to pay.

age admitted. Words used in a policy of LIFE ASSURANCE (q.v.) to signify that the insurer has already seen evidence of the age of the insured, usually a birth certificate, and that no further evidence of this will be required in the event of a claim. Clearly the age of the assured is an important factor in determining the premium in a policy of life assurance.

age allowance. An allowance given against the income of an individual in calculating the amount of income tax due when the taxpayer is over the age of 65. It is given in place of, and is greater than, the PERSONAL ALLOWANCE (q.v.).

agent. One who acts on behalf of another with the authority of that person. The person for whom the agent acts is known as the PRINCIPAL (q.v.). A person wishing to engage in negotiations on matters in which he or she was not particularly skilled might employ an agent with the necessary expertise to negotiate on his or her behalf. Where an agent is concerned with entering into a contract on behalf of a principal, it is the principal who is bound by the terms of the contract and who receives the benefit from it. It should be noted that agency may sometimes be implied rather than expressed. One member of a PARTNERSHIP (q.v.), for example, is deemed to be an agent for all members when conducting business in the name of the firm.

aggregate depreciation. A total amount of deprecation. Where an aggregate is given no analysis is supplied of its components according to assets depreciated or according to periods in which it was charged.

EXAMPLE: The following information appears in the accounts of a company.

	£
Plant and machinery at cost	196,800
Less Aggregate depreciation	84,210
Total	112,590

The aggregate depreciation is all the depreciation charged on currently extant plant and machinery since it was purchased. This may have been at a variety of different dates.

ageing schedule. An analysis of the debtors of a business which shows how old each separate element of debt is. It is useful in assessing the success of CREDIT CONTROL (q.v.) and, since bad debts first show up as late debts, in determining the correct amount for the charge for bad debts in the profit and loss account.

AGM. Abbreviation for ANNUAL GENERAL MEETING (q.v.).

agricultural property relief. A relief given against inheritance tax in respect of property used for agricultural purposes. There are detailed rules determining the conditions under which the relief is available.

AICPA. Abbreviation for AMERICAN INSTITUTE OF CERTIFIED PUBLIC ACCOUNTANTS (q.v.).

airmail. A postal service for letters sent abroad by which the letters are carried by air. The service is more expensive than surface mail. Letters to be sent by airmail are identified by a blue sticker in addition to the postage stamps.

alimony. An amount of money paid regularly by a man under a court order to a former wife from whom he is now divorced.

A list. A list of the holders of partly paid shares in a company at the time of its WINDING UP (q.v.). Persons appearing on the A list are liable to contribute to any deficiency of assets up to the amount remaining unpaid on their shares. In the event of their default recourse may be had to persons appearing on the B LIST (q.v.).

all inclusive concept of profit. The perspective which regards the profit of a business as including all gains whether likely to be repeatable or not. An alternative concept would be to separate profit which is from regular, repeatable activities from that arising from activities which are unusual in size or type.

allocation. The direct association of a particular cost with a specified ACTIVITY (q.v.) or COST CENTRE (q.v.). The process of allocation, in which a cost is dealt with intact, should be contrasted with the process of APPORTIONMENT (q.v.).

allonge. A piece of paper gummed on to a BILL OF EXCHANGE (q.v.) or similar NEGOTIABLE INSTRUMENT (q.v.) to provide more space for ENDORSEMENTS (q.v.) when the space originally available on the back of the document has been used. An allonge is necessary only for a document which is circulated widely during its currency.

allotment. The issue of shares or debentures to a specific person. Shares may be allotted to those who have applied for them in response to an OFFER FOR SALE (q.v.) or a PROSPECTUS (q.v.). In the event of an OVERSUBSCRIPTION (q.v.) the basis of allotment must be determined by the directors of the company. They may allot in full to some applicants and reject others or they may allot to each applicant only a proportion of the number of shares for which they have applied. A PROVISIONAL ALLOTMENT (q.v.) on a RIGHTS ISSUE (q.v.) may also be made and this would be to existing shareholders. BONUS SHARES (q.v.), too, may be allotted to existing shareholders. In these two latter cases the number of shares allotted depends on the level of existing holdings.

allotment letter. The letter sent by a company to a successful applicant for its shares. It confirms the allotment and states the number of shares. An allotment letter is usually transferable to others and can, therefore, be sold.

allowance. An amount permitted to be set off against income or profit in determining the amount liable to tax. An example is the PERSONAL ALLOWANCE (q.v.) which every individual payer of income tax is given. Another example is the CAPITAL ALLOWANCE (q.v.) given to a business in respect of expenditure on designated FIXED ASSETS (q.v.).

alloy. A mixture of metals. Most so-called 'silver' or 'copper' currency is, in fact, made from alloys.

all risks. A type of insurance which covers the insured for any loss or damage to the property insured howsoever caused. The PREMIUM (q.v.) for this type of policy is higher than where the cover is restricted to loss or damage caused by specified risks, e.g fire or theft.

all time high. This refers to a price, or more probably an index of prices, which has reached the highest level ever recorded. Thus share prices may be said to be at an all time high when an index of share prices reaches a higher level than any previously recorded.

all time low. This refers to a price, or more probably an index of prices, which has reached the lowest level ever recorded. Thus share prices may be said to be at an all time low when an index of share prices reaches a lower level than any previously recorded.

almoner. A person responsible for the financial control of an institution providing a humanitarian service, such as a hospital or a home for the aged.

alms. Amounts of money given to a poor person, usually by an institution.

alpha stock. A category of shares traded on the Stock Exchange. It includes the shares of large companies, which are dealt in every day.

alternate director. A director who may act in place of another, e.g. at a meeting of the Board of Directors, when that other director is unable to be present.

amalgamation. The coming together of two or more previously autonomous businesses into a single undertaking.

American Accounting Association. An association of persons in accounting education and research. Most of its members are either practitioners or academics. It is based in the USA but has an international membership. Its quarterly journal ACCOUNTING REVIEW (q.v.) is a respected academic publication. The association was formed in 1916 and adopted its present name in 1936.

American Institute of Certified Public Accountants. The premier body of professionally qualified accountants in the USA. It is often referred to by its initial letters AICPA. A member is entitled to put the designatory letters CPA after his or her name and to be called a certified public accountant. The Institute was founded in 1887.

amnesty. A release from obligations and liabilities arising out of past actions. Thus, in the interests of obtaining full information concerning irregular activities, a company might offer an amnesty to all those co-operating in an investigation. This means that these persons will not be pursued for compensation or retribution arising out of their admitted actions.

amortisation. The process of writing off an asset over a period of years. The term is thus almost synonymous with DEPRECIATION (q.v.), but whereas the term depreciation is applied generally to tangible fixed assets with clearly defined lives, the term amortisation is normally applied to intangible assets with imprecise lives. GOODWILL (q.v.) and DEVELOPMENT COSTS (q.v.) are examples of assets which might be amortised.

analysis. The breakdown of a total figure into its component parts. In accounting, for example, we meet the analysis of VARIANCES (q.v.) or the analysis of SALES (q.v.).
EXAMPLE. Analysis of sales for November:

Region	£
North-east	42,500
North-west	59,260
Midlands	77,640
South-east	63,440
South-west	31,880
Total	274,720

analytical review. Term applied to audit procedures designed to test the fundamental consistency and reasonableness of a set of accounting statements. It will include the calculation of ratios and comparisons with other similar types of business. Analytical review is the subject of an AUDITING GUIDELINE (q.v.).

and reduced. Words which may be required for a period to be added to the name of a company whose capital has been reduced. *See* CAPITAL REDUCTION.

angel. A person who provides finance for theatrical productions. Angels take considerable risks as they may, if the show fails, lose the whole of their investment or, at best, recover a very small part of it. For a big hit show, however, the rewards, which usually consist of a share of the takings, can be enormous.

annual general meeting. A meeting of the members of an organisation which is held in each year to transact routinely occurring business. A company is one type of organisation that is required by law to hold such a meeting. Some others, such as sports or social clubs, may be required to do so by their own rules. The business transacted at a company's annual general meeting includes such matters as consideration of the accounts, appointment of auditors and appointment of directors. Most annual general meetings are largely formal and are not attended by any large number of shareholders.

annual percentage rate. The true rate of interest on money lent. The law now requires that all retail lenders of money state in their quotations an annual percentage rate, usually abbreviated to APR. This is so that all such quotations are on a comparable basis. Previously it was frequently the practice to quote interest as a percentage of the initial sum advanced, when it appeared to be at a much lower rate.

    EXAMPLE. Shylock offers to lend Portia £1,000 at a stated rate of interest of 10 per cent per annum, the total debt to be repaid in equal monthly instalments over 2 years. A bank would charge 12 per cent per annum and thus appears more expensive. Shylock calculates the amount due as follows:

	£
Loan	1,000
Add 2 years' interest at 10% per annum	200
Total	1,200

This is payable as 24 monthly instalments of £50 each.

    £50 per month for 2 years is an annual percentage rate of 18 per cent, nearly double the quoted rate and very unattractive as compared with the bank overdraft. This is because the amount outstanding is reduced progressively but the interest charge in Shylock's calculation was based entirely on the initial sum.

annual report. A document published annually by a company for its shareholders and debenture holders. A copy must also be filed with the REGISTRAR OF COMPANIES (q.v.). The content and form of the annual report is laid down in the Companies Act 1985. It comprises the following main documents:

    (a) balance sheet,
    (b) profit and loss account,
    (c) directors' report,
    (d) auditors' report.

Other documents will be included in compliance with ACCOUNTING STANDARDS (q.v.) or at the discretion of the company.

annual return. A document which must be submitted annually by every company to the REGISTRAR OF COMPANIES (q.v.). It must be submitted within 42 days of the ANNUAL GENERAL MEETING (q.v.) made up to a date 14 days after the meeting. It includes the following particulars:

    (a) address of registered office;
    (b) location of registers of members and of debenture holders;
    (c) details of share and loan capital in issue at the date of the return;
    (d) the indebtedness of the company in respect of charges on its assets;

(e) a list of names, addresses and shareholding of all who have been members since the date of the last return,

(f) particulars of the directors and secretary at the date of the return.

annuitant. A person who receives an ANNUITY (q.v.).

annuity. A fixed annual payment. It may continue indefinitely, but frequently will continue only during the lifetime of a named individual. An annuity may be purchased (from a life assurance company) on terms which depend on current and prospective rates of interest and the actuarial life expectancy of the purchaser. Purchasing an annuity is a useful way in which retirement income can be provided out of capital without the risk that this will become exhausted. An annuity of this kind is taxed in a manner which takes into account that it is notionally partly income and partly a repayment of invested capital. The recipient of an annuity is described as an annuitant.

annuity method of depreciation. A method of providing for depreciation which takes into account the interest forgone by the funds invested in the depreciating assets.

EXAMPLE. A machine is owned having an initial cost of £10,000, a life of 4 years and no SCRAP VALUE (q.v.). Under the STRAIGHT LINE METHOD (q.v.) of depreciation the annual charge is £2,500. Under the annuity method a notional rate of interest has to be applied. Let us say that the rate is 10 per cent per annum. £1 receivable annually for 4 years at 10 per cent is £3.169 (from tables). The depreciation charge is therefore:

$$\frac{£10,000}{3.169} = £3,155$$

This will be partly offset by the credit in the profit and loss account for the notional interest earned:

	£	Profit and loss account Debit £	Credit £	Net £
Opening value of asset	10,000			
Add Notional interest 10%	1,000		1,000	
	11,000			
Less Depreciation	3,155	3,155		2,155
Net book value after 1 year	7,845			
Add Notional interest 10%	785		785	
	8,630			
Less Depreciation	3,155	3,155		2,370
Net book value after 2 years	5,475			
Add Notional interest 10%	548		548	
	6,023			
Less Depreciation	3,155	3,155		2,607
Net book value after 3 years	2,868			
Add Notional interest 10%	287		287	
	3,155			
Less Depreciation	3,155	3,155		2,868
Net book value after 4 years	Nil			

antedate. To give a document a date before that on which it was actually executed. The intention is to give effect to it retrospectively. This may sometimes be illegal as, for example, when a deed of COVENANT (q.v.) is antedated so as to obtain a tax benefit.

ante post. Betting on the outcome of a horse race where the odds are determined at the time the bet is placed, rather than at the time of starting of the race. Ante post betting is available on selected important races only. It has the disadvantage that the stake is lost if the horse does not run. Its advantage is that higher odds may be obtained.

anti-avoidance. A description of measures, usually in the form of legislation, to prevent taxpayers from avoiding the payment of tax by methods which, although technically legal, were not intended in the drafting of the original legislation. Whenever legislation has the effect of burdening people with taxation some will seek a LOOPHOLE (q.v.) in the law which enables them to avoid payment whilst complying with the strict letter of the law. To prevent this anti-avoidance legislation must be enacted which renders these methods themselves illegal for the future.

anti-inflation. Description of a policy adopted by the government with the object of preventing or reducing INFLATION (q.v.).

application. An offer by an investor to subscribe for a specified number of shares in a company. The offer must be made on the prescribed form which is issued only with a PROSPECTUS (q.v.). This means that every applicant can be deemed to have read the prospectus. The application will state the number of shares applied for, the total amount enclosed and the full name and address of the applicant. It must be signed and dated and have a cheque enclosed with it for the amount due on application. Applications are usually subject to the condition that they be for a specified minimum number of shares and that they be for a prescribed round number of shares (e.g. 500, 1,000, 1,500, etc.). An application, once sent, is irrevocable and may be accepted by the company for any number of shares up to the full number applied for.

application and allotment account. An account used when a company makes an offer for sale of its shares. All money received with the applications for shares will be credited to the account. When the basis of ALLOTMENT (q.v.) is determined there will be debited to the account the NOMINAL VALUE (q.v.) of the shares issued, the total of SHARE PREMIUM (q.v.) and any cash returned to unsuccessful applicants or transferred to other accounts in respect of future INSTALMENTS (q.v.). The account will then be closed.

apportionment. The process whereby a single amount is divided according to some formula into portions which are then attributed to some ACTIVITY (q.v.), COST CENTRE (q.v.) or person. The term may arise in one of a number of different connections.

1. *Partnership.* A PARTNERSHIP (q.v.) is a single business whose profit has to be apportioned amongst two or more proprietors. The formula by which this apportionment takes place will be contained in the partnership agreement.

2. *Trusts.* A TRUST (q.v.) may be constituted so that there is one BENEFICIARY (q.v.) or group of beneficiaries who are entitled to all of the income from the trust fund during their lifetime(s) and a residuary beneficiary or group of beneficiaries who will receive the capital value of the fund subsequently. All receipts of the trust must be properly accounted for distinguishing between revenue and capital receipts. Normally this is a straightforward matter of proper identification and presents no difficulty. Apportionment will be required, however, where there is a receipt of money which is partly capital and partly revenue, e.g. the proceeds of sale of shares CUM. DIV. (q.v.).

3. *Taxation.* Where a rate of tax, e.g. corporation tax, changes during the currency of the business's accounting period apportionment of the profit between the time before the change and that after the change will be necessary. This is normally done on a strict time basis not allowing for any seasonal variation in profit.

4. In full or ABSORPTION COSTING (q.v.) apportionment will be required of expenses which are incurred to benefit a number of COST CENTRES (q.v.) but which cannot be identified specifically with any of them. Apportionment of the expenses will be made on some more or less arbitrary basis, e.g. floor area or number of employees.

appraise. To value. Thus an expert might appraise an asset in order to give an authoritative opinion as to its value.

appreciation. An increase in the value of an asset. Appreciation is caused by a change in the market in which the asset is bought and sold. It is most frequently encountered in the case of land and buildings, which commonly increase in value over the long term. Securities dealt in on the Stock Exchange may also appreciate. Appreciation often goes unrecognised in financial accounting. Where it is recognised the surplus so created should not be regarded as a distributable reserve unless and until it has been realised.

appropriation. An amount set aside out of profits for a specific purpose.

appropriation account. An account, normally annexed to the profit and loss account, showing how a business's profit has been deployed in the period to which the account relates. The appropriation account for a PARTNERSHIP (q.v.) will show the profit divided according to the partnership agreement before transfer to the partners' CURRENT ACCOUNTS (q.v.). The appropriation account for a LIMITED COMPANY (q.v.) details taxation, dividends paid and proposed, and transfers to reserves.

APR. Letters standing for ANNUAL PERCENTAGE RATE (q.v.).

arbitrage. A process whereby an investor buys and sells securities and adjusts financing arrangements so as to take advantage of market inequalities in risk and return. It is the main mechanism whereby the market is brought into an equilibrium where the returns on securities are commensurate with the risk attaching to them. Arbitrage may be found in markets other than that for securities, e.g. the commodity market or the foreign currency market.

arbitrageur. One who engages in ARBITRAGE (q.v.).

arbitration. A process sometimes required in a contract whereby a dispute shall be settled by an independently appointed person, the arbitrator. The procedure is binding on the contracting parties and saves the expense and delay involved in taking court action.

arm's length. A term descriptive of negotiation where each party is concerned only to advance his or her own interests and not those of the other party. It may be important to determine whether a transaction was at arm's length in order to ascertain whether a FAIR VALUE (q.v.) was established by the transaction.

EXAMPLE. A man seeks to sell his car to a stranger. The negotiations are at arm's length because he is seeking to get the best price he can without regard to the interests of the stranger. The negotiations break down and the man then sells the car to his son at well below its true value. This is not an arm's length transaction because the man has become concerned to see that his son gets a cheap car.

arrangement. An agreement made by an individual or a company with creditors whereby the latter agree to desist from pressing for immediate settlement in return for a promise of future action which improves their chances of recovering the debt.

arrears. 1. Payment at an interval after the provision of the service to which the payment is related. Electricity bills are commonly paid in arrears, i.e. the electricity is consumed and subsequently is billed and paid.

2. Owing beyond the due date. Thus a tenant who has failed to pay amounts of rent at the time they were due is said to be in arrears with the rent.

Articles of Association. A document setting out the rules governing the internal conduct of a company's affairs. It will deal with such matters as the arrangements for meetings, the appointment and qualifications of directors and the company's power to borrow money and to purchase its own shares. A model set of Articles appears as Table A in the Companies Act 1985 and this may be adopted as its Articles of Association, if the company so wishes. The Articles, a copy of which must be filed with the REGISTRAR OF COMPANIES (q.v.) when a company is registered, may be amended by means of a SPECIAL RESOLUTION (q.v.) of the company.

artificial transaction. A transaction which has of itself no commercial justification but which has been undertaken purely to gain some benefit deriving from the form of the transaction.

EXAMPLE. A person sells some shares and then immediately buys them back again. This has a cost and appears to have no justification as the ownership of the shares is unchanged. Its purpose, however, is to establish a loss so that this can be offset against other gains in order to reduce liability to CAPITAL GAINS TAX (q.v.).

ASC. Letters standing for ACCOUNTING STANDARDS COMMITTEE (q.v.).

A shares. Shares in a company which are in every respect like its ORDINARY SHARES (q.v.) except that they do not carry a vote.

asking price. The amount stated by the vendor of an asset as the price which is required for the asset. It often represents merely a negotiating position and the actual price received may be less than the asking price.

assay. A process by which the purity of a precious metal is determined and certified.

assented stock. A security whose holders have agreed to some course of action so that the agreement is binding on a purchaser of the security. An example would be where a CONVERTIBLE DEBENTURE (q.v.) has been presented for conversion into equity. Assented stock may have a different market value from non-assented stock and may exist side by side with it.

assessment. A statement issued by the Inland Revenue to a company or individual giving the amount of income on which tax is to be charged and the amount of tax which, in consequence, is due. A taxpayer may appeal against an assessment on the grounds that it is incorrect and the appeal must be made within 30 days of its issue.

asset. Some property or legal right owned by an individual or a company to which a money value can be attached.

asset backed. Represented by valuable assets. Thus shares which are asset backed are those of companies which possess real assets such as property and plant and equipment rather than intangible assets of nebulous value such as goodwill or brands.

asset cover. The extent to which a share is represented by valuable assets.

asset stripping. A process whereby a company acquires a controlling interest in another company for the purpose of disposing of its assets. The opportunity arises where the management of the company taken over has underutilised the assets so that the share price is below the market value of the underlying assets. Asset stripping makes a quick profit for the company engaging in it but brings to an end the business of the company taken over.

assignment. The transfer of rights owed by another to some third party. For an assignment to have legal effect it must be absolute, in writing and be communicated to the one owing the right. The most usual example of assignment is when a person who is owed money assigns that debt for payment to another who, perhaps, has greater power or patience to collect it.

associated company. A company in which an investment fulfilling certain conditions is held. These conditions are:

(a) the investing company's interest in the associated company is effectively that of a partner in a joint venture or consortium, or

(b) the investing company's investment in the associated company is for the long term and is substantial (i.e. not less than 20 per cent of the equity carrying voting rights) and, having regard to the disposition of the other shareholdings, the investing company is in a position to exercise a significant influence over the associated company.

In both cases it is essential that the investing company participates in commercial and financial policy decisions of the associated company including the distribution of profits.

This definition of an associated company derives from SSAP 1 which prescribes that, for associated companies, the investing company's share of their profits less losses should be taken into the consolidated profit and loss account (and not merely the dividends received). On the balance sheet the investment in the associated company should be valued at cost less amounts written off plus the investing company's share of post-acquisition retained profit and reserves.

Association of British Insurers. A body representing British insurance companies. It issues codes of practice under which its members operate.

assurance. Indemnity against the financial consequences of some inevitable event such as death. The term INSURANCE (q.v.) is applied to indemnity against the consequences of events which may not occur, e.g. destruction of a property by fire.

assured tenancy. A form of tenancy agreement created by statute which, whilst safeguarding the rights of the tenant, gives the landlord the confidence to let by enabling a fair rent to be charged and limits to be placed on the duration of the tenancy.

ATM. Letters standing for AUTOMATED TELLER MACHINE (q.v.).

attachment of earnings. The consequence of a court order whereby a portion of a person's wages or salary can be deducted before payment and applied in settlement of an obligation to a third person. The process is used only in exceptional circumstances. One such situation might be to oblige a man to give financial support to his estranged or divorced wife.

attainable standard. A particular basis for setting a STANDARD COST (q.v.). Its feature is that standards are set so as to represent a realistic but not impossible challenge to attainment. Thus an attainable standard will normally require a level of efficiency better than has been experienced in the past but less good than that which could be achieved in the most favourable conditions possible. *See also* IDEAL STANDARD; NORMAL STANDARD.

attendance allowance. A social security benefit payable to those who are bound to attend on an invalid.

attendance at stocktaking. This will usually be undertaken as part of an AUDIT (q.v.). An auditor might be thought to have been negligent if there was no attendance at the stocktaking.

attestation. The action of signing a document as the WITNESS (q.v.) to the signature of another. A DEED (q.v.) requires attestation as does a WILL (q.v.). The responsibility of one who attests a document is merely to satisfy him or herself that the signatory was the person they claimed to be and that the document was signed voluntarily. It is not necessary for the witness to understand or approve of the contents of the document itself.

attorney. The power to handle the financial affairs of another with the same authority as they would themselves. It is normally granted where a person becomes, by reason of age or illness, unable to understand the consequences of their own actions and needs their affairs to be dealt with on their behalf.

attributable profit. That part of the total profit currently estimated to arise over the duration of a LONG-TERM CONTRACT (q.v.) which fairly reflects profit arising from the work done to date. The term is used in SSAP 9 which allows credit to be taken in the profit and loss account for attributable profit on unfinished long-term contracts.

EXAMPLE. A civil engineering company is building a bridge which will take 5 years to complete and will yield an ultimate total profit of £1 million. Having regard to the proportion of the work done and the costs incurred and still to be incurred, the company will be able to attribute part of that total profit to each of the 5 years.

auction. An organised method of establishing a fair market price for some property. The potential buyers are assembled and invited to make competitive offers. The property is then sold to the highest bidder. The auction is conducted by an auctioneer who will command the necessary skills to draw the maximum possible price from the gathering and to judge when this has been reached. The completion of the sale is signified by the auctioneer (often by a hammer blow) and there is then an enforceable contract between the successful bidder and the seller. The seller may place a RESERVE PRICE (q.v.) on the property. In that event it will not be sold unless bidding passes that level. An auction is a common device for selling items of a unique or unusual nature such as large houses, works of art and antique furniture.

auctioneer. One who conducts an AUCTION (q.v.).

audit. An examination of accounts and their underlying records in order to be able to express an opinion on their honesty and veracity. Many forms of organisation undergo an audit either voluntarily, under their own rules, or under the requirements of law. An audit may be an INTERNAL AUDIT (q.v.) conducted by employees of the organisation or one conducted by independent persons from outside. The best-known example of an audit is that which, by law, must be undergone annually by every limited company. The auditor must be independent and must be appropriately qualified (in most cases by membership of a professional accountancy body). He or she must produce a report for the members of the company expressing, amongst other things, an opinion on whether the accounts give a TRUE AND FAIR VIEW (q.v.) and on whether they comply with company legislation.

audit brief. A description of the scope and scale of an AUDIT (q.v.). The audit brief for some forms of organisation, e.g. a limited company, is laid down by statute.

auditing guidelines. Statements issued by the professional accountancy bodies which are intended to give persuasive guidance to members on the conduct of an AUDIT (q.v.). Although not prescriptive an auditor should depart from a guideline only where a strong case can be made for doing so.

auditing standards. Statements issued by the professional accountancy bodies which are intended to prescribe the principles and practices which members are expected to follow in their conduct of an AUDIT (q.v.).

auditor. One who conducts an AUDIT (q.v.).

auditors' remuneration. The total amount paid to the auditors of a company for their services in that capacity, including OUT-OF-POCKET EXPENSES (q.v.). The accounting significance of auditors' remuneration is that it is required by law to be disclosed in the published accounts of the company.

auditors' report. An annual report from the auditors of a company to its shareholders that is required by statute to be annexed to its accounts. The auditors are required to state explicitly in the report whether or not it is their opinion that the accounts give a TRUE AND FAIR VIEW (q.v.) and whether or not they comply with the requirements of the Companies Acts. If they are of a contrary opinion they must give details of the matters which have led to this. Where the auditors have no reservations concerning the accounts they will give an unqualified report which is brief and formal. Where reservations do exist these will be set out in full giving what is known as a qualified auditors' report.

audit programme. A plan of work set out by an AUDITOR (q.v.). The establishment of such a programme is an essential safeguard to ensure that no important part of the work is overlooked. The programme will very often be in a standard form with a few additions or deletions necessitated by the particular features of the audit to which it relates. As each piece of work is completed this fact should be recorded on the programme with a note of the date and of the member of staff who actually undertook the work. Apart from its general usefulness, an audit programme could provide valuable evidence in defence against any subsequent charge of NEGLIGENCE (q.v.) on the part of the auditor.

audit risk. The risk that, although an AUDIT (q.v.) has been properly carried out, a matter which materially affects the truth and fairness of the accounts is overlooked. For any but the very smallest enterprises an auditor will be unable to verify every transaction fully. Reliance will have to be placed on verifying the soundness of the system and on test checking a proportion of the items which have been put through it. The possibility that an irregularity will fall through this net will depend on the resources which are applied to the audit. A balance must be struck between keeping the conduct of the audit within reasonable bounds and of keeping audit risk to an acceptable level.

audit trail. That chain of evidence which leads an AUDITOR (q.v.) from an item in the accounts to an underlying document verifying the transaction.

EXAMPLE. A certain company has an expensive piece of machinery represented by a debit balance on the machinery account. The audit trail will lead the auditor to refer to the PURCHASE INVOICE (q.v.) (to verify the price paid for the machine and its date of purchase), the PURCHASE ORDER (q.v.) (to verify that the machine was actually ordered) and the minute book of the relevant meeting of the BOARD OF DIRECTORS (q.v.) (to verify that the purchase was properly authorised according to company procedures).

authorisation. The process of giving authority to a particular course of action. An overdraft given by a bank to a customer must be authorised by the manager. Payment of a company employee's travelling expenses may have to be authorised by the departmental manager.

authorised capital. The amount of capital stated as such in a company's MEMORANDUM OF ASSOCIATION (q.v.). It represents the maximum amount of capital which a company may issue unless the Memorandum is amended. A company's authorised capital must be stated on every published balance sheet.

automatic telling. The provision by means of a computer-linked machine of services normally provided by the counter clerk. In order to use the service a customer has to insert a special plastic card into the machine and key in a PERSONAL IDENTIFICATION NUMBER (q.v.). The machine will then, following further keyed instructions, accept deposits, pay out cash, state the balance on the account or arrange for a new cheque book or a statement to be sent.

AVC. Letters standing for ADDITIONAL VOLUNTARY CONTRIBUTION (q.v.).

average. 1. A single figure representing a group of figures. The arithmetic mean is the measure of average most commonly used by the accountant. Two good examples of the use of average in accounting are the AVERAGE PRICE METHOD (q.v.) of costing stock issues and the WEIGHTED AVERAGE COST OF CAPITAL (q.v.).

2. A term used in insurance to indicate that the insurer will be liable for only part of an insured loss where the premium paid is less than the amount required to cover the full risk.

EXAMPLE. Unwise Company plc has insured its factory for £200,000 although the full rebuilding cost in the event of total destruction would be £400,000. The principle of average means that the company is covered only to the extent of half of any loss actually sustained even though this might fall within the limit of £200,000. Thus if the property sustained damage which cost £100,000 to repair the insurer would meet only £50,000 of this.

average price method. A method of pricing material issues. Its principle is that the average unit price of the stock is recalculated whenever new stocks are purchased at a price different from the average price of the existing stock.

EXAMPLE.

	Quantity (units)	Value £
Existing stock	100	500 (average £5 per unit)
New purchase	200	1,060 (£5.30 per unit)
	300	1,560

Since the stock of 300 units has a total cost of £1,560 the new average price (used for charging issues) is

$$\frac{£1,560}{300} = £5.20$$

An advantage claimed for the average price method is that it smooths out the effects on reported profit of fluctuating raw material costs. It is not widely used in practice largely because it is not permitted as a method of determining cost for UK tax purposes.

average rate of return. An alternative term for ACCOUNTING RATE OF RETURN (q.v.).

averaging. The process whereby a number of transactions of different size are combined so that an average value can be determined. This may be done, for example, in determining the cost which should be attributed to items of stock where there were several purchases at different prices.

avoidable cost. A cost which may be avoided by the discontinuance of a particular activity. All VARIABLE COST (q.v.) is avoidable. FIXED COST (q.v.) specific to an activity is also avoidable. General, non-specific, fixed cost is not avoidable.

avoidance of tax. Escaping from the payment of tax by illegal means, usually by the deliberate concealment of income.

award. An amount receivable by a person following a decision by a person or body in authority. For example, a court may award DAMAGES (q.v.) to a party to a civil action or a company may award a pay increase to its employees.

axe. To cut actual or planned expenditure abruptly. It is usually in response to a situation of emergency.

B

backdate. To give effect to some agreement as though it had been made at a date earlier than its actual date. Pay awards to workers are frequently backdated when the negotiations preceding them overrun the normal deadline.

back duty. Tax relating to a period in the past which was unpaid then because fraudulent or erroneous returns were made. Where fraud is involved the Inland Revenue has power to go back indefinitely into the past in order to recover the tax due. There is also power to impose penalties in proportion to the amounts involved. Where there is no fraud, assessments to tax must be made not later than six years following the end of the chargeable period.

backer. One who supports a venture by providing the finance for it.

backhander. Synonym for BRIBE (q.v.).

backlog depreciation. An adjustment to ACCUMULATED DEPRECIATION (q.v.) to allow for increases in the money value of an asset occurring since the provision arose. It is commonly met in connection with CURRENT COST ACCOUNTING (q.v.).

EXAMPLE. An asset, having an expected life of 5 years, was purchased for £1,000. The first year's depreciation was £200. After 1 year the asset is revalued to a gross cost of £1,200 so that the second year's depreciation is £240. This is charged in the profit and loss account of that year. The provision brought forward from the first year requires an upward adjustment of £40 so that the accumulated depreciation to date is correct at two-fifths of the gross cost of the asset. This additional amount of depreciation is the backlog depreciation. It is correctly charged against the REVALUATION RESERVE (q.v.).

back pay. An amount of wages or salary paid to persons who had received less than their full entitlement at the time of original payment. Back pay commonly arises when a pay award is BACKDATED (q.v.).

backwardation. The amount by which the price of a commodity for immediate delivery differs from its price for delivery at some specified future date.

bad debt. An amount which is legally owed to a business but which it has become impossible to collect. This may occur for a variety of reasons, including the dishonesty or financial collapse of the DEBTOR (q.v.). A debt recoverable in law may still be treated as a bad debt if it is felt that the cost of enforcement would be out of proportion to its amount. The accounting treatment of a bad debt is to credit the debtor's account (thus extinguishing the uncollectable balance) and to debit the profit and loss account (thus showing the bad debt as an expense). CREDIT CONTROL (q.v.) procedures should help a business to minimise the cost of its bad debts.

bail. Money deposited by an arrested suspect as a guarantee that, if released, he or she will appear for trial. The amount of the bail is forfeit if the accused does not appear.

bail bond. A binding promise to pay executed by an accused person or another person which will become enforceable if the accused person fails to turn up for trial. It is an alternative to a cash deposit when a person is granted BAIL (q.v.).

bailiff. An officer of the court whose duty it is to enforce an order whereby a person's property is confiscated in order to settle a debt.

balance. 1. The outstanding amount on any ACCOUNT (q.v.) which is not closed. Balances are designated as DEBIT (q.v.) (signifying ASSETS (q.v.) or EXPENSES (q.v.)) or CREDIT (q.v.) (signifying LIABILITIES (q.v.) or REVENUE (q.v.)).

2. To achieve arithmetical exactitude in a set of accounts. This is usually signified by the extraction and agreement of a TRIAL BALANCE (q.v.).

balance brought forward. A BALANCE (q.v.) which closed an account for the immediately preceding period and which, therefore, commences the current period.

balance carried forward. A BALANCE (q.v.) which closes an account for a period and will, therefore, become the balance which commences the next period.

balance certificate. A share certificate issued by a company to a holder who has sold part of a larger holding. It thus represents the balance of shares held after allowing for those sold.

balance of payments. A value computed for a country as a whole which represents the difference between its payments to other countries and those it receives from other countries. A balance of payments may be either favourable, where there is a net inflow of money, or adverse, where there is a net outflow.

balance sheet. A financial statement of position. It consists of a list of all ASSETS (q.v.) and LIABILITIES (q.v.) including OWNER'S EQUITY (q.v.). A balance sheet is always given a single date (i.e. it does not cover a period of time) emphasising its static nature. The balance sheet is one of the main documents that are legally required to be produced by companies as part of their annual accounts. Like all accounting statements a balance sheet is based on certain principles and conventions (e.g. of valuation at cost and conservatism) and it must be interpreted with caution.

balancing allowance. An amount deducted from a profit subject to tax to allow for the fact that the actual DEPRECIATION (q.v.) incurred in respect of fixed assets has proved to be greater than the total of CAPITAL ALLOWANCES (q.v.) given.

balancing charge. An amount which becomes chargeable to tax when CAPITAL ALLOWANCES (q.v.) given exceed the total DEPRECIATION (q.v.) incurred in respect of fixed assets.

ballot. 1. The drawing of names at random. A ballot may be used to determine the allotment of shares in the case of an OVERSUBSCRIPTION (q.v.).

2. A vote. A ballot may be conducted amongst the shareholders of a company in order to take a decision concerning the company's future.

bands. Stratified ranges of values. Tax rates, for example, are divided into bands so that tax is at one rate on income up to a certain level and a higher rate at income above that level. Directors' remuneration, which must be disclosed in the annual accounts of a company, must be divided into bands. The values of houses are allocated to bands for the purposes of the COUNCIL TAX (q.v.).

bank. A financial institution offering a particular range of services to customers. The main service, for most customers, is the operation of a CURRENT ACCOUNT (q.v.) with a cheque payment facility. Banks will make loans, provide tax advice, executorship and trustee services and undertake investment activities on behalf of customers. Banks will also give safe custody to valuable documents such as life assurance policies and the deeds to property.

bankable. Of great value. A person's agreement may be described as bankable if the person is regarded as very reliable.

25

bank charges. Charges made by a bank to its customers for services rendered to them. The total of bank charges will depend on the number of cheques and other items appearing in the account but may be offset to some extent if a reasonable credit balance is maintained. In the case of personal (as opposed to business) customers some banks offer free banking whilst others will operate an account free of charge provided that its balance does not drop below a stated amount. A bank makes its charges by debiting the customer's current account. This will lead to a discrepancy between the balance shown on a BANK STATEMENT (q.v.) and the amount shown in the CASH BOOK (q.v.) until an appropriate entry is made. For this reason bank charges will frequently appear as an item on a BANK RECONCILIATION STATEMENT (q.v.).

bankers' draft. In effect a cheque drawn by a bank on itself. It is provided to a customer who wishes to settle a debt by a medium which will be as acceptable to his or her creditor as cash, since a bankers' draft will always be met by the bank issuing it.

bankers' order. An instruction by the customer of a bank for a regular fixed amount to be paid to some person or organisation and charged to his or her account.

bank giro. A system whereby transfers of money between accounts held at different banks can readily be made. It was introduced collectively by the major banks as a response to the competition from NATIONAL GIRO (q.v.).

bank holiday. A statutory national holiday. It is so-called because banks are amongst the institutions which are closed on those days.

bankings. Amounts deposited with a bank. For example, a retail business is likely to make daily bankings of its TAKINGS (q.v.).

bank-note. A document issued by a bank authorised to issue such notes promising to pay the bearer on demand a stated sum of money. Bank-notes circulate freely and are the main type of CURRENCY (q.v.). The only note issuing bank in England is the BANK OF ENGLAND (q.v.) and its bank-notes are LEGAL TENDER (q.v.) throughout the UK. Certain Scottish banks also issue notes. These circulate widely in Scotland and are accepted, not always readily, elsewhere in the UK, although they are not strictly legal tender anywhere.

Bank of England. The central bank in the UK. It was founded in 1694 as a normal commercial bank but through the prestige and power it acquired it gained the position of bankers' bank. It was nationalised in 1946. It is now the only note issuing bank in England (there are others in Scotland). In certain areas, e.g. supporting the value of the currency by OPEN MARKET OPERATIONS (q.v.), it acts under the direction and on behalf of the British Government and is an important instrument in the implementation of policy.

Bank of Scotland. The oldest commercial bank in Scotland. It is not a central bank as is the BANK OF ENGLAND (q.v.) but does issue its own bank-notes.

bank rate. The name applied to the official rate of interest set by the Bank of England under government direction up to 1972. This value is now termed the minimum lending rate.

bank reconciliation statement. A statement explaining the difference which occurs between the balance in a bank account shown on the BANK STATEMENT (q.v.) issued by the bank at a particular date and the balance shown at the same date by the CASH BOOK (q.v.). Such differences commonly occur because of the delay in the transmission of information from the customer to the bank and vice versa. The usual elements in a bank reconciliation statement are:

(a) UNPRESENTED CHEQUES (q.v.),
(b) UNCLEARED LODGEMENTS (q.v.),
(c) BANK CHARGES (q.v.).
It is important to prepare bank reconciliation statements on a regular basis in order to detect errors as early as possible.

bankruptcy. A legal condition in which the affairs of a debtor are placed under the control of a RECEIVER (q.v.) appointed to act to the benefit of the creditors. Bankruptcy, which is imposed by a court, is preceded by INSOLVENCY (q.v.). A bankrupt person is subject to a number of restrictions. In particular, the bankrupt may not accept credit without disclosing the fact. A bankrupt may be discharged (and the bankruptcy terminated), again by the court, when all the creditors have been paid or where it is clear that there is no further purpose in maintaining the state of bankruptcy.

bank statement. A statement sent regularly by a bank to its customer setting out details of all transactions on the account since the last statement and a figure for the current balance.

bargain. 1. A legal agreement, or contract, usually involving the payment of money. The term is commonly used in connection with an agreement to buy and sell securities on the Stock Exchange. The number of bargains entered into on a particular day is used as a measure of the level of activity in the market.
2. A purchase at a very favourable price giving exceptional value for money.

barometer stock. Shares of a company which has such wide-ranging interests that its performance can be taken as indicative of the performance of the economy as a whole. The movements of its share price tend to reflect general market trends.

barter. A process of economic exchange not involving the use of money. Goods and services are exchanged directly for other goods and services. It does not normally exist to any great extent in a developed economy but may be used, for example, as a device for avoiding taxation or in cases where a currency suffers from HYPERINFLATION (q.v.) so that there is no wish to hold it.

base date. The starting point for the calculation of an INDEX (q.v.). It is normally set at a value of 100.

base rate. A rate of interest quoted by a bank from which all its other rates are determined. For example, a customer may be charged interest on a loan at '2 per cent above base rate'. Competition amongst banks has the effect that base rates tend to be very much the same for all of them. They are changed from time to time as dictated by changes in the general level of the rate of interest.

base stock. A level of stock regarded as the irreducible minimum with which a business can operate. Where this concept is operated base stock is treated like a permanent asset and is valued at the cost of setting it up in the first place, i.e. that of the initial purchase. All stocks consumed are deemed to be drawn from subsequent purchases and are costed accordingly. The base stock idea has little to commend it and is rarely used in practice. Where rising prices are experienced use of the base stock principle will mean that a substantial proportion of stock will be undervalued in the balance sheet.

basic pension. That pension paid by the State and receivable by all persons of an appropriate age. Many retired people will receive a pension in excess of the basic pension because of additional contributions they have paid.

basic rate of income tax. The lowest rate of income tax and the rate paid by the majority of taxpayers on their marginal income. Certain payments, e.g. interest on bank

27

deposits, must be paid after deduction of tax at the basic rate. The current basic rate of income tax is 25 per cent but this may be changed at any time by a Finance Act. Changes are normally announced as part of the government BUDGET (q.v.). The basic rate of income tax also determines the amount of ADVANCE CORPORATION TAX (q.v.) which a company will pay.

basic wage. The wage received by all workers of a given grade. The actual amount paid will generally exceed the basic rate because of payments for overtime or incentive payments.

basket. A collection of items (for example, shares, goods or currencies) used for the purpose of calculating an INDEX (q.v.).

batch costing. A method of COSTING (q.v.) appropriate where production takes place in a series of batches. It may be contrasted with JOB COSTING (q.v.) and PROCESS COSTING (q.v.).

bear. A stock market term for a person who seeks to make a profit out of a falling market. This is achieved by selling shares that are not actually held with the intention of buying later, at a lower price, just before delivery is required. The bear runs the risk that the market will rise rather than fall, in which case a loss will be incurred. Deriving from the basic definition, a bear market is one where prices are falling, and investors are said to be 'bearish' where there is a widespread expectation of a market fall. The opposite of a bear is a BULL (q.v.).

bearer security. A security where ownership is conclusively evidenced by the possession of a CERTIFICATE (q.v.). It follows that the transfer of ownership of a bearer security is achieved by the handing over of the certificate. Such a security carries a high risk of loss by destruction or theft and the form is not very widely used. Most security certificates are not DOCUMENTS OF TITLE (q.v.) but are evidence of an entry on a register of holders. *See also* REGISTERED SECURITY.

beat down. To persuade the seller to reduce the price by a process of hard negotiation. A buyer with cash who meets a seller with an urgent need for money will often be able to beat down the seller.

bed and breakfast. A stock market term applied to a transaction whereby the holder of a security sells it on one day and buys it back on the next. The object of this transaction is to establish a profit or loss for the purpose of CAPITAL GAINS TAX (q.v.). There can be considerable tax advantages in realising a loss to set off against a profit made on other transactions or in phasing in profits so as to take maximum advantage of exemption limits.

Bedaux system. A particular form of incentive payment scheme. It is named after its inventor Charles Bedaux, an American. The essence of the system is that standard times are determined for the different tasks which labour may be called upon to perform. If a worker is able to achieve the task in less than the standard time a bonus is paid dependent upon the amount of time saved. The advantage to the employer is that more efficient use is made of facilities which are the subject of FIXED COSTS (q.v.).

bellwether stock. A synonym for BAROMETER STOCK (q.v.) that is more commonly used in the USA.

below the line. Appropriations of profit or capital expenditure which have no effect on the reported profits of the current year. The 'line' referred to is that separating the profit and loss account from the APPROPRIATION ACCOUNT (q.v.). Thus revenue items are above and other items are below the line.

benchmarking. The process of establishing guide financial parameters for a business from an examination of a combination of information from similar kinds of business. Thus a business may compare such matters as its liquidity, profitability, efficiency and gearing with an average of those quantities for other businesses of like kind in order to be able to gauge its own health.

beneficial owner. One who, although not the legal owner of a property, nevertheless has a right to all the benefits that would accrue to a legal owner. A bank, for example, may hold shares in a company in its own name but on behalf of a customer. The customer is then the beneficial owner. A parent may hold securities on behalf of a child. The child is then the beneficial owner.

beneficiary. One who obtains benefit under the terms of a WILL (q.v.) or a TRUST (q.v.).

benefit. Value received as of right. Thus a person may receive a benefit from the state arising out of their situation, e.g. low income, ill health or disability.

benefit in kind. A BENEFIT (q.v.) which is given in the form of goods or services rather than in the form of money. An employee receives a benefit in kind if the employment gives the right, for example, to free use of sports facilities or free meals in a canteen.

bequest. An amount left to a person or organisation under a WILL (q.v.).

BES. Letters standing for BUSINESS EXPANSION SCHEME (q.v.).

beta stock. The designation used for the second rank of shares traded in on the stock market. They are less actively traded than those designated ALPHA STOCKS (q.v.).

beta coefficient. A factor used to determine the appropriate HURDLE RATE (q.v.) to use in appraising a risky investment project. The beta coefficient derives from the CAPITAL ASSET PRICING MODEL (q.v.). The underlying theory of this model is that it is not the individual risk of a project which is important in investment decision making but its contribution to the overall portfolio risk. This is a function of the extent to which the risk attaching to the investment under consideration is correlated to the risk attaching to the other investments held.

betterment. The improvement in the value of land by development. Betterment tax or betterment levy is a tax on such increases in value.

betting. Staking a sum of money on the outcome of an event which is not controllable by the person doing so or by the person with whom the bet is placed, and in which there is no financial interest other than that arising from the bet. A person might bet that a certain horse will win a race. If it does so an agreed amount will be won and if not the stake will be lost.

bid. An offer to make a purchase at a stated price. The term is normally used where a person makes such an offer in the course of a sale by AUCTION (q.v.). It is also used to denote the price at which securities can be sold because that price is bid by another person.

bidder. One who makes a BID (q.v.).

bid price. The price offered by one seeking to buy securities. The term is applied to the lower of the two prices quoted by a stock JOBBER (q.v.) or the managers of a UNIT TRUST (q.v.). The higher price is known as the offer price.

big bang. The time on 26 October 1986 when the London Stock Exchange fundamentally changed its form of organisation in a clear break with the past. From that point on member firms could have a dual function acting as both BROKER (q.v.) and JOBBER (q.v.).

Prior to this a firm had, by the rules of the Exchange, to be either one or the other. The date is also significant as it marks the time when face-to-face trading on the floor of the Exchange gave way almost entirely to electronic dealings via a terminal screen.

bill. A request for payment for the supply of goods or services.

bill of exchange. A NEGOTIABLE INSTRUMENT (q.v.) requiring one person to pay a sum of money to another on a certain date to the order of a third person. The bill of exchange was developed as a method of arranging credit facilities between merchants. If A supplied goods worth £100 to B on the agreement that the money should be paid in 3 months' time, A could draw a bill of exchange on B for this amount. B would then accept (i.e. acknowledge by signing) the bill which A could then use to pay a debt to C. Clearly the acceptability or otherwise of a bill of exchange depends on the reputation and financial standing of both the drawer and the acceptor. Legislation governing bills of exchange is contained in the Bills of Exchange Act 1882. The bill of exchange was the precursor of the CHEQUE (q.v.).

bill of lading. A document drawn up in connection with goods carried by sea. It will itemise the goods and state their destination and route.

bills payable. A heading in the balance sheet under CURRENT LIABILITIES (q.v.) which represents BILLS OF EXCHANGE (q.v.) drawn on the business awaiting but not yet due for payment.

bills receivable. A heading in the balance sheet under CURRENT ASSETS (q.v.) which represents BILLS OF EXCHANGE (q.v.) held by the business awaiting collection.

Birmingham Municipal Bank. A savings bank operated by the City of Birmingham. Its distinction is that it is the only bank in the UK operated by a city council.

binary number. A value expressed in a system of counting to base 2. The normal basis of expressing values is the system of counting to base 10. In binary notation the only digits are 0 and 1. Thus 10 in binary means 2 in decimal and 100 in binary means 4 in decimal. The importance of binary numbers is that they used in computers to store and process values.

bingo duty. A tax levied by the government on the game of bingo. This is a game of chance in which money or other prizes may be won.

black. Adjective applied to any day on which a significantly bad event occurred. Thus there might be a 'Black Monday', i.e. a Monday on which a catastrophically sharp fall in the price of shares has occurred, as for example in October 1987.

black economy. That area of economic activity which goes unrecorded and uncontrolled. Persons contributing to the black economy usually do so in order to make an income which escapes taxation or which does not disqualify them from some benefit. Thus a dishonest unemployed person might claim unemployment benefit and then secretly take casual paid work. Another person might do such casual work in addition to a paid job and omit to declare this income for tax purposes. Apart from the fraudulent burden which it places on public funds, the black economy is also of significance in that it is omitted from official measures of national income, which thus tend to understate the true condition of the economy. Where statutory measures exist to protect certain types of employees (e.g. in the matter of safety or conditions of work), members of the black economy are likely to lose the benefit of these.

blackmail. The extortion of money from a person by threatening to reveal facts to their discredit if payment is not made.

black market. An illicit market in goods. The goods are usually those which, because of extreme shortage, are not available through the usual channels. Black market prices are high and often using it involves some illegality.

blank cheque. A cheque which has been signed but where either the amount or the payee's name or both have been omitted. It is highly dangerous to issue a blank cheque as it can, obviously, be used fraudulently. It is sometimes done, however, where the precise amount is not known and delay in issuing the cheque will cause inconvenience. The term is sometimes used colloquially to refer to an open-ended commitment.

blank transfer. A document for the transfer of shares in which the current holder of the shares has signed but the date and transferee's name have been omitted. A person borrowing money on the security of shares may have to complete a blank transfer. This enables the lender to obtain title to the shares by completing and submitting the transfer should the need arise.

blind person's allowance. An allowance against income that is given in computing liability to income tax where a taxpayer is registered as blind.

B list. A list of persons who have ceased to be the holders of partly paid shares in a company within 1 year preceding the WINDING UP (q.v.) of the company. The significance of the list is that those appearing on it may be liable on the winding up to contribute to any deficiency in the event of the inability of the present holders of the partly paid shares to meet it. The liability cannot exceed the amount remaining unpaid on the shares at the time they were held. *See also* A LIST.

blocked funds. Funds which cannot be transmitted from one country to another because of controls on the exchange of foreign currency.

block grant. A sum of money paid by central government to a local authority as a contribution to the total sum required for it to discharge its functions. The rest of its funds will come locally from the COUNCIL TAX (q.v.).

blue chip. A share in a company of established and high reputation and, therefore, a sound investment. It should be noted that even large and famous companies can encounter trading or financial difficulties and that there are risks attaching to investment even in blue chips.

Board of Directors. The collective term applied to the full complement of the DIRECTORS (q.v.) of a company. It is the Board of Directors, rather than individual members of it, which is responsible for directing the activities of the company. Formal meetings of the Board will be held regularly and the approved minutes of the meetings will be conclusive evidence of the decisions which have been taken.

body corporate. An association of individuals regarded in law as a single person with an identity separate from those making up the association. Examples of bodies corporate are limited companies, city councils, universities and professional institutions. The status of body corporate must be conferred by some legal process, e.g. by registration under the Companies Acts or by royal charter. *See also* INCORPORATION.

bona vacantia. Property which has no owner. It could arise when a person dies without leaving a will and where there are no relatives. Another example may arise where a company is wound up but some of its shareholders cannot be traced. *Bona vacantia* becomes the property of the Crown though it will be handed back if a rightful claimant appears.

bond. An interest bearing security. The term is more commonly used in the USA than in the UK for commercial securities. It is, however, quite commonly used here for government securities, e.g. PREMIUM SAVINGS BOND (q.v.).

bonded warehouse. A place for the secure storage of dutiable goods on which duty has not yet been paid. It enables the postponement of the payment and thus reduces the amount of working capital tied up in stocks. Goods may be placed in a bonded warehouse after they have been imported or after they have been produced. Typical content would be spirits, such as whisky, and tobacco.

bond washing. The practice of selling fixed interest securities just before an interest payment is due and then re-buying immediately afterwards. Since the price of such securities includes an amount which reflects the accruing interest, the effect of this is to convert income into capital gains. These may be more lightly taxed.

bonus. An amount paid over and above the regular payment. A worker may be entitled to receive a bonus over and above normal wages in recognition of exceptional effort or output. The holder of a WITH PROFITS POLICY (q.v.) of life assurance will periodically be allocated a bonus which will have the effect of increasing the sum assured and hence the ultimate amount paid out on the policy.

bonus issue. An issue by a company of BONUS SHARES (q.v.).

bonus shares. Shares issued by a company free of charge to its existing shareholders on a *pro rata* basis. Although the number of shares held by an individual investor is increased by a bonus issue, the total value of the company is unaffected, and, other things being equal, there will be an adjustment to the market price of the shares leaving the total value of each holding unchanged. The increase in share capital arising on a bonus issue is achieved by a transfer from RESERVES (q.v.) to share capital. Either capital or revenue reserves may be used for this purpose.

EXAMPLE. Rainfall plc has the following capital structure:

	£
1,000,000 ordinary shares of £1 each	1,000,000
Share premium account	100,000
Profit and loss account	500,000

The ordinary shares have a current market value of £2 each. The directors of the company decided to make a bonus issue on a 1 for 4 basis (i.e. one new share to be added to every four already held) making use of the SHARE PREMIUM ACCOUNT (q.v.) and part of the profit and loss account. After the issue the relevant section of the balance sheet will appear as below:

	£
1,250,000 ordinary shares of £1 each	1,250,000
Profit and loss account	350,000

Other things being equal the market price of the share will fall to £1.60 thus:

$$\frac{1,000,000}{1,250,000} \times £2 = £1.60$$

The purpose of a bonus issue is to bring the nominal capital of the company into line with the actual amount of funds employed in the business on a long-term basis.

booking fee. A charge made by an organisation which makes reservations on behalf of its customers. Thus if theatre or travel tickets are booked through an agency rather than direct a booking fee may be charged.

book-keeper. One who carries out the activity of BOOK-KEEPING (q.v.).

book-keeping. The process of maintaining financial records. The term is generally applied to the DOUBLE ENTRY (q.v.) system. Financial recording may still be termed book-keeping even if the records are maintained in a form other than a conventional book. They may, for example, be on a computer tape.

bookmaker. One who engages in the activity of BOOKMAKING (q.v.).

bookmaking. The activity of accepting bets on a horse race or similar event such that, whatever the outcome, the bookmaker will end up with a profit. This is done by adjusting the odds offered in such a way that losing bets will be sufficient to cover winning bets and leave a margin.

books of account. Any system of records, not necessarily in book form, which records and explains the financial transactions of a business. Some businesses, such as limited companies, are under a legal obligation to maintain books of account. Others, such as sole traders or partnerships, maintain them as a matter of good business practice and for the usefulness of the information which they give.

book value. The debit balance, and hence value, appearing in the BOOKS OF ACCOUNT (q.v.) in respect of an ASSET (q.v.). The book value of an asset, which is the net result of the accounting processes to which the balance has been subject, is not necessarily any guide to the market value of the asset.

EXAMPLES.

	£
Machine:	
Original cost	5,000
Depreciation to date	3,200
Book value	1,800
Debtors:	
Amount outstanding	8,200
Provision for bad debts	250
Book value	7,950

boom. An occasion, or period of time, when economic activity is at its greatest. A boom is characterised by great optimism. Consumers spend freely and businesses make high profits. The dangers inherent in a boom are that reckless business ventures may be commenced, that borrowing becomes excessive and that INFLATION (q.v.) accelerates. A boom is commonly followed by a SLUMP (q.v.) or RECESSION (q.v.).

borrowing. Receiving money from another on the terms that it will be repaid at some future date. It is usually part of the agreement that INTEREST (q.v.) will be paid, relating to the sum borrowed and the time for which it is outstanding. Borrowing is an important source of finance for business. It is not in any sense purely an emergency activity and most businesses will show a measure of borrowing on their balance sheets. One method of borrowing for a company is to issue DEBENTURES (q.v.).

bottomry. The process whereby the master of a ship can borrow money that is required urgently on the security of the ship itself, which, in effect, is thereby subject to a MORTGAGE (q.v.).

bought day book. Synonym for PURCHASE DAY BOOK (q.v.).

bought ledger. Synonym for PURCHASE LEDGER (q.v.).

bounced cheque. A cheque that has been refused payment by the bank on which it is drawn. The usual reason for a bounced cheque is that there are inadequate funds in the account on which it is drawn. It is a criminal offence to offer a cheque knowing that it will bounce.

bounty. A reward offered in the hope that it will persuade someone to perform a desired action.

Bourse. The French Stock Exchange in Paris.

box office. Office where theatre or cinema tickets are purchased. The term has come to mean the total receipts from a theatrical production or a film.

branch. A segment of a business which operates under the tight control of a central part of the organisation. A retail shop, for example, may have branches in many towns. A bank will have branches all over the country. Each branch is likely to have a manager but he or she will typically have very little part to play in making the commercial policy of the organisation.

branch accounts. An accounting process whereby a business controls the activities of its branches and thus of those engaged in managing them. Where a branch manager is given some degree of autonomy, so that he or she may make local purchases of supplies and may decide on the prices to be charged for them, the branch may be accounted for as a separate entity and the manager judged by the overall level of profit achieved by the branch. More usually there is no local decision making and the manager's responsibility is to order supplies through head office and then sell them at prescribed prices. A form of branch accounting may be used which charges these supplies at selling price. This means that the manger who achieves what is expected shows neither profit nor loss. A loss indicates a shortage of either cash or stock, and, if it is unacceptably large, is the subject of an investigation.

brand. A name attaching to a product by which it is recognised by the buying public. Mars Bars, Pears Soap, and PG Tips tea are good examples of brand names attached to products which are held in high esteem by consumers. Brands are acknowledged to have a value. Some argue that this is merely a special case of GOODWILL (q.v.) and should be treated accordingly. Others argue that brands are separable assets and should be shown at a valuation on the balance sheet.

brand leader. A BRAND (q.v.) contributing a very large proportion to the total sales of the product type to which it belongs. It usually sets the standard of quality for that product and it is likely to be very influential in establishing the price.

breach of trust. Some wilful action or omission of action by a TRUSTEE (q.v.) which causes loss to a BENEFICIARY (q.v.). A trustee who carefully and after taking appropriate advice makes an investment which proves to lose money would not be guilty of a breach of trust. One who made reckless investments or sought a private profit out of the administration of the fund would be in breach of trust. A trustee in breach of trust is liable to make full restitution of any loss caused.

breadline. The dividing line between an income which is inadequate to support life and one on which survival is just possible. A person who is struggling on a low income may therefore be said to be on the breadline.

breakeven analysis. An analysis of costs and profits which relates profit to the level of business achieved. It takes its name from the fact that there can be identified some level of activity at which there is neither profit nor loss. This is known as the breakeven point. The value of breakeven analysis is that it enables management to determine an expected level of profit for any level of ACTIVITY (q.v.) and to determine the likely effect of departures from that level. This is of value in the formulation of plans. An important part of breakeven analysis is the categorisation of costs as either FIXED COST (q.v.) or VARIABLE COST (q.v.). *See also* MARGIN OF SAFETY.

breakeven chart. A graphical representation of BREAKEVEN ANALYSIS (q.v.). On the chart will be plotted lines showing total revenue and total cost. The intersection of these is at the breakeven point. Other possible situations can be read off from the chart.

breakeven point. That level of ACTIVITY (q.v.) at which neither a profit nor a loss is made. This will occur when the CONTRIBUTION (q.v.) generated by sales is exactly equal to total FIXED COST (q.v.).

break-up value. The value of a business on the basis that it will be terminated and its assets sold separately. If a business is successful its break-up value is likely to be considerably less than its value as a GOING CONCERN (q.v.). Break-up value is, however, of special significance in the case of a business which is likely to fail, so that its actual break-up is an imminent possibility, and it may also be useful if a very conservative valuation is required.

bribe. A valuable inducement, usually money, to engage in action which is either illegal or of doubtful moral acceptability. For example, an employee of a business might be offered a bribe by a competitor in exchange for providing a mailing list of the business's customers.

bridging loan. A temporary loan given to cover the gap between the purchase of an asset and the sale of another asset, the proceeds of which are required to finance the purchase. Bridging loans are most commonly encountered as advances to private house purchasers pending the sale of their existing residence. Interest is charged and thus the use of a bridging loan can very substantially raise the total cost of moving house.

British Accounting Association. An association of academic accountants and teachers of accounting whose membership is almost entirely resident in the UK. It organises conferences and publishes a quarterly journal, the *British Accounting Review.*

British Accounting Review. The journal of the BRITISH ACCOUNTING ASSOCIATION (q.v.). It is published quarterly.

broker. One who acts professionally as an agent in an organised market. The best-known type of broker is a STOCKBROKER (q.v.) who buys and sells shares on behalf of clients on the Stock Exchange. There are, however, brokers in many types of market. The services of a broker are charged for in the form of a COMMISSION (q.v.) based on the value of the business undertaken.

brokerage. Synonym for the COMMISSION (q.v.) earned by a broker.

brought forward. Transferred from an earlier period of account. The term is applied to a balance which has emerged from the closing off of the records of an accounting period. *See also* CARRIED FORWARD.

bucket shop. Office from which airline tickets can be obtained at reduced prices. Since they are not subject to normal regulatory rules there can be some risks in obtaining tickets from such a supplier. However, many provide a genuine service.

budget. 1. A plan expressed in financial terms. All large organisations prepare such a plan which provides them with an important basis for controlling their activities. Actual results, as they are obtained, are compared regularly with those laid down in the budget. Remedial action can then be taken at an early stage when divergences occur.
2. A major statement on the economic situation and plans for financial legislation given to the House of Commons by the CHANCELLOR OF THE EXCHEQUER (q.v.). Traditionally the Budget is given annually in March and its proposals are embodied shortly afterwards into a FINANCE ACT (q.v.). Sometimes more than one budget may be delivered in a year.

budget holder. One to whom a BUDGET (q.v.) has been allocated and who is responsible for ensuring that expenditure conforms to that budget.

budgeting. The process of preparing a BUDGET (q.v.).

buffer stock. A stock of materials retained for the purpose of maintaining supplies in the event of a shortage.

building society. A financial institution whose main function is to borrow money from savers in order to lend it to persons wishing to purchase a house. It takes several savers to finance one borrower and it is the borrowing activity which is, therefore, most widely promoted. Building societies are non-profit making mutual organisations. The rate of interest they offer is related to the amount they charge and both are influenced by the general market rate for funds. Rates are raised and lowered as required to equate the supply of funds with the demand for them. Building societies are governed by legislation contained in the Building Societies Acts. Amongst other requirements is an obligation imposed on every building society to supply annual accounts to its members. A building society is regarded as a very safe home for savings and they are widely used by small savers. Their loans are all made on the basis of full security through a MORTGAGE (q.v.) on the property whose purchase is financed. Building society interest is paid after deduction of income tax at the basic rate. The borrower receives tax relief on the interest paid through a system known as MIRAS (q.v.).

bulk buying. The practice of buying goods in quantities greatly in excess of current needs in order to gain the benefit of discounted prices. It may be practised by businesses or individuals and requires that there exist facilities for the safe storage of the goods until they can be used.

bull. A stock market term applied to one who expects share prices to rise. A bull will purchase shares in the hope that they may subsequently be sold at a profit. A bull market is one in which the general level of share prices is rising.

bullion. Precious metal, either gold or silver, held in the form of bars as a store of value.

buoyant. A term applied to any market, but especially the stock market, where business is brisk and there is a tendency for prices to rise.

burden. A synonym for OVERHEAD (q.v.). It is commonly used in the USA.

bureau de change. An office where foreign currency can be exchanged into the currency of the country where it is situated. Some are found in banks but they are also quite common at airports and railway stations or in shopping areas in cities, such as London, which are likely to have a substantial number of foreign visitors. The bureau de change makes its profit in setting the rates at which it will exchange money. Although competition ensures that these rates are similar from one bureau to another it may sometimes pay customers to look for the one with the best rate for the currency they wish to exchange.

bursar. The person in charge of the finances of an organisation. The term is most commonly used in connection with such institutions as schools, colleges and hospitals rather than with manufacturing or commercial organisations where such an office is more likely to be called a COMPTROLLER (q.v.) or chief accountant.

business. An organisation which seeks to make a profit by supplying others with some product or service.

business combination. An entity formed by the amalgamation of two or more entities which previously operated independently. It is normally used in connection with the formation of a GROUP (q.v.), which occurs when a company acquires or merges with another by becoming its only or main shareholder.

business cycle. An observed phenomenon that overall business activity varies in a cyclical fashion. The length of the cycle is not completely even and no satisfactory explanation for it has been formulated.

business day. A day on which business is done. It is sometimes included in contracts. For example, if a debt falls due five business days after goods have been supplied, this period would not include Saturdays, Sundays or bank holidays.

Business Expansion Scheme. A scheme established by the Finance Act 1983 which allowed investors in a certain type of company to set off the cost of the investment against their total income for the purposes of income tax. It succeeded the earlier BUSI-NESS START-UP SCHEME (q.v.). In order to qualify the company must not be quoted on the Stock Exchange nor must its shares be dealt with on the UNLISTED SECURITIES MARKET (q.v.). It must also satisfy certain conditions as to the type of trade undertaken and other matters. The effect is to give the investor a subsidy in the form of tax relief against the cost of the investment. The intention is to encourage investment in small businesses which might otherwise seem too risky. This will stimulate innovation in the economy and provide employment opportunities. In order to retain the tax relief the investor must hold the shares for at least five years. The scheme was abolished from 1992/93.

business income. The total income accruing to a business during a particular period of time on the basis that accounting valuations are at CURRENT COST (q.v.). The term was coined by Edwards and Bell for their book *The Theory and Measurement of Business Income*, published in 1961. They saw total business income as being made up of two components, CURRENT OPERATING PROFIT (q.v.) and HOLDING GAINS (q.v.). The separation of these components makes possible the evaluation of management performance in different aspects of its operations. Holding gains will include both realised and unrealised gains.

EXAMPLE. X buys a quantity of stock for £500 and subsequently sells half of it for £400 at a time when it would cost £600 to replace it. Conventional accounting would report this as follows:

	£
Sales	400
Less cost of sale	250
	150

The residual stock would be carried in the balance sheet at historical cost, i.e. £250, even though its replacement would cost £300.

The business income model would report these same facts as follows:

	£
Sales	400
Less Current cost of sales	300
Current operating profit	100
Holding gain*	200
Business income	300

*Of this holding gain £100 is realised and a further £100 is unrealised. The unsold stock would then appear on the balance sheet at its current cost of £300.

business plan. A long-term plan for the policy and operation of a business. It is more comprehensive than a BUDGET (q.v.) and for a longer period. Many businesses prepare such plans for their own purposes. A lender, such as a bank, may require such a plan in order to assess the wisdom of making a loan.

business school. An institution, often a department of a university, where advanced study and research into the processes of business are conducted.

Business Start-up Scheme. A scheme whereby those subscribing for shares in qualifying new companies could obtain relief against income tax for the full amount of the investment. It operated for the tax years 1981/82 and 1982/83 when it was superseded by the BUSINESS EXPANSION SCHEME (q.v.). The intention of both schemes was to strengthen the economy by encouraging investment in enterprises which might otherwise seem to be too risky.

buy and hold. An investment strategy whereby an investor adds to a portfolio of shares as and when this seems appropriate or when funds are available and then retains these investments indefinitely. Its underlying philosophy is that because there is a high correlation between the movements in the prices of different shares there is no point in moving from one to another. Furthermore, the very long-term trend of the market is upward so that there is no point in seeking to take advantage of fluctuations by selling and rebuying.

buy in. The purchase at an AUCTION (q.v.) of the goods by the original seller. This is done in order to prevent the sale to another person at an unrealistically low price. Certain types of horse race carry the condition that the winning horse is immediately auctioned. Buying in is then a mechanism whereby the original owner can retain the horse. Commission is payable to the auctioneer so that the process is not without cost.

buyers' market. A condition of a market such that buyers are in a stronger bargaining position than sellers, e.g. because there is oversupply of the product. Prices tend to fall in a buyers' market.

buy-out. The purchase of a business by some group which is already involved in its operations. A workers' buy-out would occur, for example, if the workforce collectively purchased the business for which they work. A management buy-out occurs when the existing salaried managers buy the business.

by-product. A product which is produced incidentally as a result of a process undertaken for the purpose of making some other product but which, nevertheless, has some value in its own right. A by-product may or may not require further processing before it can be sold. In terms of accounting the net proceeds of sale of a by-product (i.e. sales less further processing costs) are treated as a reduction in the cost of production for the main product. *See also* JOINT PRODUCT.

C

CAAT. Letters standing for COMPUTER-ASSISTED AUDIT TECHNIQUES (q.v.).

cable transfer. The transfer of funds overseas by means of telephone messages. It is done on the instructions of a customer by a bank.

Cadbury Report. The report of the Cadbury Committee on corporate governance published in 1992. The report recommends a code of best practice for corporate governance. Compliance with this code would be voluntary but companies would need to state the extent to which they had failed to comply and their reasons for this. The code has a number of implications for financial reporting. The most important are that interim reports should include balance sheet information and that they should be subject to review by the auditors. Currently such reports are usually unaudited and give only profit and loss account information. Reports are also required from a company's directors and its auditors on the effectiveness of its internal financial control.

cadge. To beg, usually by borrowing small amounts of money with no intention of repaying them.

call. A demand by a limited company to the holders of PARTLY PAID SHARES (q.v.) to pay a further instalment towards the full nominal value. Thus no call can be made on the holders of fully paid shares, nor may any call exceed that part of the capital which is unpaid. Failure to pay a call may result in FORFEITURE OF THE SHARES (q.v.).

called-up capital. That part of the nominal value of the issued share capital of a company which the company has required to be paid up. The holder of a PARTLY PAID SHARE (q.v.) is liable to find the balance of its nominal value if at any time it becomes the subject of a CALL (q.v.).

call option. An OPTION (q.v.) which gives the holder the right to buy securities at a specified future date at a price agreed currently. The option will be taken up if at the specified date the market price of the security is above that embodied in the option. There is a market in options and the price paid for them depends on the view which is taken of the likely course of the price of the underlying security. *See also* PUT OPTION.

cambist. An expert and dealer in foreign exchange.

Canadian Institute of Chartered Accountants. The main body of professionally qualified accountants in Canada.

capacity. The maximum amount which can be produced by a productive resource. Thus one might say that the capacity of a factory was 100,000 units of product per day. Its significance is that this will be the basis for the apportionment of any OVERHEAD (q.v.) relating to the productive resource.

capacity usage variance. A VARIANCE (q.v.) caused by the fact that the volume of production achieved by a particular level of productive capacity has been different from that planned in the BUDGET (q.v.). A capacity usage variance will be adverse if there has been wasted capacity and favourable if the capacity has been used more actively than expected.

EXAMPLE. A factory has a budgeted fixed cost of £500,000 for a forthcoming period and it is planned that it should be used to provide productive facilities to support 50,000 labour hours. The overhead is thus budgeted, using the LABOUR HOUR RATE (q.v.), at £10 per hour. In the event there were 49,000 labour hours worked and thus £490,000 of overhead was absorbed. The remaining £10,000 of expenditure, the cost of the unused capacity, is the adverse capacity usage variance.

capital. The amount invested in a business by its PROPRIETOR (q.v.). In the case of a PARTNERSHIP (q.v.), there will be more than one proprietor. The proprietors of a LIMITED COMPANY (q.v.) are its SHAREHOLDERS (q.v.). To a business its capital is represented on the balance sheet as a liability, i.e. the obligation which it has to the providers of its capital. The capital of a sole trader or of a partnership is variable at will but the capital of a company is, in the short term, fixed and, in the longer term, can be varied only by formal procedures

capital account. That account in a system of accounts which records changes in the indebtedness which a business has to its own proprietor.

capital allowance. The deduction allowed in calculating taxable profits in respect of expenditure on FIXED ASSETS (q.v.). Capital allowances thus take the place of DEPRECIATION (q.v.) in accounts prepared for tax purposes. Capital allowances are a powerful instrument of government policy and can be made to encourage or to discourage investment generally, or differentially to favour particular kinds of investment or investment in particular geographical areas. Capital allowances are given in the form of a FIRST YEAR ALLOWANCE (q.v.) when the asset is first acquired and a WRITING DOWN ALLOWANCE (q.v.) subsequently. However, either may sometimes be at a nil rate.

capital appreciation. An increase in the market value of an asset not caused by any alteration to the asset itself. Thus a PORTFOLIO (q.v.) of shares will be subject to capital appreciation as the stock market price of the shares increases.

capital asset. Synonym for FIXED ASSET (q.v.).

capital asset pricing model. A conceptual model for determining the value of real investment projects, taking into account the effect they will have on overall business risk. The model is based on the idea of RISK AVERSION (q.v.) which is that, for any given rate of return, management will seek to achieve it with the lowest level of risk possible. A project under consideration will be assessed, therefore, not only for its promised rate of return but also for the effect it will have on the overall risk faced by the business. The risk reducing effects of an investment will be at a maximum where the expected variations in its returns are inversely correlated with the collective expected rates of return on the existing investments. The theory might, exceptionally, lead to the paradoxical conclusion that an investment which is expected to show an actual loss is, nevertheless, worth undertaking for its risk reducing properties. The capital asset pricing model derives from PORTFOLIO THEORY (q.v.).

capital budgeting. The process of preparing a plan for the raising of capital funds and for their deployment. For an incorporated business, funds may be obtained from a wide variety of sources. Chief amongst these are issues of ORDINARY SHARES (q.v.) or PREFERENCE SHARES (q.v.) and of LOAN CAPITAL (q.v.). The use of these funds will be to finance some proposed project that is expected to be profitable. The money may be required to purchase fixed assets such as buildings and plant and machinery, and for an additional amount of WORKING CAPITAL (q.v.) associated with their operation. A central concept in capital budgeting is that of the COST OF CAPITAL (q.v.), which is determined by the nature of the finance available and which in turn determines which investment opportunities should be accepted and which rejected. The basic principle of capital budgeting is that all projects should be accepted which promise a rate of return in excess of the cost of capital. This is signified by the emergence of a positive quantity from a calculation of NET PRESENT VALUE (q.v.). A more sophisticated approach to capital budgeting, which includes an analysis of risk, is given in the CAPITAL ASSET PRICING MODEL (q.v.).

capital commitment. An obligation to undertake capital expenditure which has not yet become an actual liability. Capital commitments at the date of a company's balance sheet are required to be disclosed by way of a note together with any other FINANCIAL COMMITMENTS (q.v.).

EXAMPLE. At its balance sheet date X plc has signed a contract with a builder for an extension to its factory. No part of the work has yet been carried out. The company has a capital commitment for the value of the work and should state this as a note to its balance sheet. The value of the extension to the buildings would not, however, appear in the balance sheet and nor would any liability on this account to the builder.

capital cost. The non-recurrent set-up cost of a project. After capital cost has been incurred there will subsequently be recurring RUNNING COSTS (q.v.).

capital equipment. Equipment which has an extended life so that it is properly regarded as a FIXED ASSET (q.v.).

capital expenditure. Expenditure on FIXED ASSETS (q.v.) or other items which will be written off over a period of years by means of DEPRECIATION (q.v.) or AMORTISATION (q.v.).

capital flight. The mass withdrawal by international investors of funds from a country where doubts have arisen about the future course of its economy.

capital gain. A gain made by holding an asset during a period when its market value increases. Securities are often purchased by investors hoping for a capital gain, which may sometimes be more substantial than any income produced by the investment. Capital gains may also be made quite incidentally by those holding an asset for use. Such gains may be liable to CAPITAL GAINS TAX (q.v.).

capital gains tax. A tax on non-recurring profits arising when capital assets are sold. The capital gains tax was introduced into the UK in 1965 and has undergone several changes in form since then. Certain kinds of gain are exempt from the tax, the chief amongst these being the gain on the sale of a property that is the taxpayer's main or only residence. There is also exemption from tax on the first part of the total gain up to an amount revised periodically (in 1992 the amount was £5,800). In determining the cost of an asset which is sold giving rise to a gain changes in the purchasing power of money since March 1982 are taken into account by indexing the purchase price. Capital losses may be set off against capital gains of the same or subsequent periods (but not earlier periods) in computing the chargeable gain. The tax is payable on the disposal of an asset. Disposal may be by sale, gift or destruction.

capital goods. Goods produced by a business which will form the fixed assets of a purchasing business. Thus manufacturing machinery is capital goods.

capital instruments. Securities designed to provide funds for a business. They may be issued on a wide variety of different terms.

capital intensive. Using a great deal of capital relative to other factors of production. Thus a process which is capital intensive will make use of expensive machinery but will have relatively little labour or material input.

capitalisation rate. A rate applied to the annual income produced by an asset in order to determine its capital value. The capitalisation rate will depend on current market rates of interest and on the degree of risk attaching to the income.

EXAMPLE. An investment produces an annual income of £1,000 and this is expected to continue indefinitely. The appropriate capitalisation rate is 15 per cent per annum. Given this information the capital value of the asset is:

$$£1,000 \times \frac{100}{15} \times £6,667$$

capitalise. To treat expenditure as if it were for the purchase of a FIXED ASSET (q.v.). The consequence of this is that it will remain as an asset on the balance sheet until written off by a process of DEPRECIATION (q.v.) or AMORTISATION (q.v.). The term is most commonly applied to expenditure that is treated in this way when there is some element of argument as to whether this is a proper treatment. For example, interest paid is normally regarded as revenue expenditure. If it is paid on funds borrowed to finance the construction of an asset which takes some time to complete, however, it may be capitalised, i.e. treated as part of the cost of acquiring the asset, until such time as the asset comes into productive use.

capitalism. That economic system which is based on the private ownership of property and where its driving force is private profit. Although it can be argued that capitalism is inhuman and leads to the unfeeling imposition of hardship, history has shown that in general it does this to a lesser extent than communism, for instance.

capitalist. A person who derives a living by investing sums of money in enterprises managed by him or herself or by others.

capital loss. A loss occasioned by the sale of an asset at an amount below its cost. Such a loss may be set off against a CAPITAL GAIN (q.v.) in computing any tax due.

capital maintenance. A principle of accounting which states that a profit is the residual revenue of a period after the initial value of the capital of the business has been restored. It is thus necessary to be able to determine the value of that capital in order to calculate profit and this is where the capital maintenance concept is less than completely clear in its practical application. HISTORICAL COST (q.v.) accounting is based on the principle that the money value of capital is to be maintained, for example, while CURRENT COST (q.v.) accounting seeks to maintain the operating capacity of the business, which, if prices have risen, will imply some higher money value for capital.

capital market line. The line on a graph plotting the risk against the return for investment opportunities provided by a market. The market referred to may be the Stock Exchange or the market for real investment projects. The importance of the capital market line is as a datum in PORTFOLIO THEORY (q.v.) or the CAPITAL ASSET PRICING MODEL (q.v.).

capital rationing. A restriction on the investment of capital funds other than that arising from their cost or the availability of investment opportunities. Capital rationing is an artificial constraint on the CAPITAL BUDGETING (q.v.) process and has the consequence that a sub-optimal position will be reached. Capital rationing may exist where, for example, a company restricts growth to that which can be financed by retained profits (rather than by raising extra funds in the market). Another example will occur where a company restricts the issue of extra EQUITY (q.v.) in order to avoid the dissipation of control.

capital redemption reserve. A statutory CAPITAL RESERVE (q.v.) required to be created when share capital of a company is purchased for cancellation or is redeemed out of profits. The reserve is created by transfer from REVENUE RESERVE (q.v.) and has the effect of withholding from distribution those funds absorbed by the reduction of capital. The relevant legislation is contained in the Companies Act 1985. The only purpose for which a capital redemption reserve may be used (and thus disappear from the balance sheet) is in paying up shares which are the subject of a BONUS ISSUE (q.v.)

capital reduction. A process whereby the issued capital of a company is reduced. There are two circumstances in which this might take place. These are:

(1) where future operations of the company are expected to be on a reduced scale so that a smaller level of finance will be required; and

(2) where it has to be accepted that past revenue losses can never be made good and that they amount to a permanent loss of capital.

These circumstances are quite different in their implications. The first involves a return of cash to the shareholders with a consequent diminution in the buffer available for the protection of creditors. The second merely recognises a loss of capital which has already occurred. No cash is paid to the shareholders and no further erosion of the security of the creditors takes place. In order for a reduction in capital legally to be effected a company must pass a SPECIAL RESOLUTION (q.v.) and then apply to the high court for confirmation. Before giving such confirmation the court will take account of any representations from creditors.

capital reorganisation. That process whereby a company amends its capital structure by changing the absolute and relative rights of the providers of its finance. Capital reorganisation might involve conversion of debt into preference shares, amending the nominal value or voting rights of ordinary shares.

capital reserve. A RESERVE (q.v.) in the balance sheet of a company which is not available for distribution to its members. There are several ways in which a capital reserve may arise. If a property is revalued but not realised the surplus should properly be taken to a capital reserve. The SHARE PREMIUM ACCOUNT (q.v.) is a capital reserve arising when the company issues new shares at a price in excess of their NOMINAL VALUE (q.v.). A CAPITAL REDEMPTION RESERVE (q.v.) is a capital reserve arising when the company buys or redeems its OWN SHARES (q.v.). A capital reserve may also arise in a CONSOLIDATED BALANCE SHEET (q.v.) from the processes of consolidation. This occurs when the amount paid by the HOLDING COMPANY (q.v.) for its interest in the SUBSIDIARY COMPANY (q.v.) is less than the underlying NET ASSET VALUE (q.v.).

capital structure. The relative proportions of different types of financing used to make up the total long-term financing of a business. The most important characteristic of a company's capital structure is the relative proportions of EQUITY (q.v.) of all types to DEBT (q.v.).

EXAMPLE. Companies A and B have identical total capital but different capital structures:

Company A	£
100,000 ordinary shares of £1	100,000
	100,000
Company B	
70,000 ordinary shares of £1	70,000
£30,000 10% debentures	30,000
	100,000

The significance of differences in capital structure is that they have an effect on the risk to which equity holders are exposed. The presence of debt, in the case of company B, subjects its shareholders to FINANCIAL RISK (q.v.) to which the shareholders of company A are not exposed.

The effect which capital structure has on the COST OF CAPITAL (q.v.) is an important issue, not fully resolved. *See also* GEARING; MODIGLIANI AND MILLER THEORY.

capital transfer tax. A tax on the transfer of wealth from one person to another either by gift during the donor's lifetime or by inheritance after his or her death. The tax was introduced in 1975 to take the place of ESTATE DUTY (q.v.) and was superseded by INHERITANCE TAX (q.v.) in 1986.

capital turnover. The notional rate at which the capital employed by a business flows through the profit earning cycle. It is calculated as:

$$\frac{\text{TURNOVER (q.v.)}}{\text{CAPITAL EMPLOYED (q.v.)}}$$

capitation. An amount of money paid which depends on a number of people. A school, for example, might receive a capitation based on the number of pupils on the roll.

CAPM. Letters standing for CAPITAL ASSET PRICING MODEL (q.v.).

capping. The process whereby the government seeks to limit the expenditure of a local authority by restricting the grant it makes to that authority.

carat. A measure of weight of precious stones. It is equal to 200 milligrams. The term is also used as a measure of the purity of gold. The pure metal is designated as 24 carat.

carriage inwards. Costs associated with the transport of goods purchased by a business for its own use or for resale.

carriage outwards. Costs associated with the transport of goods sent by a business to its customers.

carried forward. A term applied to a balance which is transferred from the current period to the next period. This occurs whenever a set of records is closed off preparatory to the construction of accounts.

carrying value. A synonym for BOOK VALUE (q.v.).

car tax. A special tax imposed by the government on sales of new cars. It was passed on to the customer in the form of a higher price for the vehicle but was abolished in 1992.

cartel. A small group of people or businesses which seek to influence the markets in which they operate by co-operation on the setting of prices and, possibly, of levels of production.

cash. 1. (noun) The most liquid of all assets and immediately available for the settlement of debts or for making purchases. Strictly the term should apply only to currency, i.e. bank-notes and coin of the realm. In accounting, however, it frequently refers also to favourable bank balances because these are as liquid as cash. In a balance sheet cash is shown as a CURRENT ASSET (q.v.).

2. (adjective) A term describing a transaction where payment is immediate rather than deferred by a period of credit. Thus cash sales are those where the purchaser pays immediately for the goods which have been bought.

3. (verb) To convert an investment or negotiable instrument into cash. Thus a holder of NATIONAL SAVINGS CERTIFICATES (q.v.) may cash them, as may the recipient of a CHEQUE (q.v.).

cash basis. A method of preparing accounts which disregards any non-cash adjustments such as accruals, prepayments and stocks. The cash basis of accounting underlies a RECEIPTS AND PAYMENTS ACCOUNT (q.v.). The basis is often used in accounting for businesses providing professional services. This is because the ultimate receipt of fees cannot always be regarded as certain until payment has actually been made. Small non-profit making organisations such as social clubs frequently use a cash basis, usually because it is easy to operate and adequate for their needs though sometimes because the treasurer is unaware of any alternative method.

cash book. A book containing a record of a business's cash transactions. The cash book, although often included in the category of books of PRIME ENTRY (q.v.), is actually a LEDGER ACCOUNT (q.v.) that is separately kept because of its special importance and its volume. Cash receipts will be recorded on the DEBIT (q.v.) side of the cash book and cash payments on the CREDIT (q.v.) side. Periodically a BALANCE (q.v.) will be struck to determine the amount of cash in hand. This should be verified by means of a count. Bank transactions, as well as those in actual currency, are recorded in a cash book. The basic cash book is sometimes elaborated to provide analysed information by means of a multi-column format.

cash budget. A plan which states in detail the CASH FLOW (q.v.) which is to take place over a specified future period of time. A typical cash budget will show monthly cash flows under a number of headings over a period of 1 year and will indicate the cumulative position so that cash shortages and surpluses can be anticipated and steps taken to deal with them.

cash card. A card which enables the holder to make use of electronic cash dispensing machines. It also allows enquiries as to the state of the account and, sometimes, the facilities of ordering a new cheque book or statement. Cash cards issued by different banks and building societies go under a variety of names such as Cashpoint, Cardcash, Barclaybank, Link, etc.

cash cow. A business or product which produces a large positive cash flow. It does not necessarily mean that it is highly profitable as the cash flow may result in the rundown of fixed assets.

cash crop. An agricultural crop grown for the purpose of sale for cash.

cash discount. An allowance or deduction against an amount owed by a debtor in order to encourage prompt or early payment. The usual way in which it is offered is by means of a note on the INVOICE (q.v.) on the lines of 'Terms 2½ per cent within 7 days, otherwise strictly net.' This would mean that a customer paying within 7 days of the invoice date would be permitted to deduct 2½ per cent from the total bill.

cash dispenser. A machine which will issue cash to the customers of a bank or building society when correctly activated, usually by the insertion of a card and the keying in of a PERSONAL IDENTIFICATION NUMBER (q.v.).

cash equivalent. A short-term, highly liquid investment which can be converted into cash of a known amount without notice. The term is used in FRS 1 in connection with CASH FLOW STATEMENTS (q.v.).

cash flow. The volume of cash moving into and out of a business. The net cash flow is the difference between the inflow and the outflow. If cash flow is not adequately controlled a business may find itself short of cash for paying its immediate liabilities. Wages and creditors for supplies, in particular, must be paid promptly if problems are to be avoided. It should be noted that cash flow is related only loosely to profit. A highly profitable business may have an adverse net cash flow if it invests heavily in new FIXED ASSETS (q.v.) or if large resources are tied up in WORKING CAPITAL (q.v.). Although less common, poor control over cash flow may sometimes result in cash surpluses. If these are held unprofitably in a bank current account this will dilute the overall profitability of the business.

cash flow statement. A statement required by FRS 1 to be produced annually by a company in association with its profit and loss account and balance sheet. The statement will explain how the cash and CASH EQUIVALENTS (q.v.) held by the business have changed between one balance sheet date and the next. The cash flows are required to be shown under specified headings. These are:

Operating activities
Returns on investments and servicing of finance
Taxation
Investing activities
Financing

cashier. A person whose responsibility within an organisation is to receive and issue cash and to maintain records in connection with that activity.

cash in transit. Cash in the process of being transferred from one business to another and not, therefore, appearing in the records of either of them. Cash in transit is of special importance in the preparation of a CONSOLIDATED BALANCE SHEET (q.v.) where the transfer is from one member of the group to another. It must be brought back in as an asset of the group.

cash on delivery. A service offered by the post office whereby, for a charge, the amount payable on purchase of goods will be collected from the recipient on behalf of the seller at the time the goods are delivered.

cash sale. A sale made against the immediate payment of cash, i.e. with no credit given.

cash with order. A term of sale whereby the customer has to pay for the goods at the time they are ordered, i.e. in advance of delivery. This is used in order to prevent a loss occasioned by customers delaying collection of the goods or delaying payment.

casino. A business which earns its profits by offering gambling facilities to its members. It will provide premises in which games such as ROULETTE (q.v.) and chemin de fer can be played.

casual labour. Workers who are employed on a short-term and irregular basis. They are very useful to an employer subject to peaks of demand for labour but, as they are often paid in cash and few records kept, present a particular problem for the collection of the income tax to which they become liable.

caveat emptor. A legal term meaning literally 'Let the buyer beware'. Its implication is that the legal responsibility for ensuring that a purchaser is satisified with goods lies with him or her and not with the seller. There is considerable case and statute law which modifies this general principle.

CCA. Letters standing for CURRENT COST ACCOUNTING (q.v.).

CCAB. Letters standing for CONSULTATIVE COMMITTEE OF ACCOUNTANCY BODIES (q.v.).

cent. A one-hundredth part of a dollar.

centime. A one-hundredth part of a French franc.

central bank. The main bank in each country which acts as an arm of the government more than it does as a bank. It will be responsible for the regulation of the financial system, the establishment of rates of interest and the issue of currency notes. The central bank in the UK is the BANK OF ENGLAND (q.v.).

certainty equivalent. Synonym for EXPECTED VALUE (q.v.).

certificate. A document providing evidence of a stated fact. A share certificate is evidence of the ownership of the shares stated on it. A directors' certificate of a stock valuation provides evidence of the authenticity of that valuation. It should be noted that a certificate cannot be regarded as proof of a fact. It may be forged or the facts may have changed since the certificate was written.

certificate of deposit. A certificate issued by a bank to the effect that a sum of money has been deposited with the bank for a period of time during which it will earn interest. A certificate of deposit may be transferable for value to other persons.

certificate of entitlement to commence business. *See* ENTITLEMENT TO COMMENCE BUSINESS.

certificate of incorporation. A CERTIFICATE (q.v.) issued by the REGISTRAR OF COMPANIES (q.v.) to the effect that, all legal formalities having been complied with, a company has come into being. The document is, in effect, the birth certificate of the company.

certificate of insurance. A document evidencing that a given insurance has been effected. It is usually issued when there is a statutory requirement for such insurance. An important example is the third party insurance required by the drivers of motor vehicles.

certified accountant. A member of the CHARTERED ASSOCIATION OF CERTIFIED ACCOUNTANTS (q.v.).

certified cheque. A cheque which has been certified by the bank on which it has been drawn to the effect that it will be met without question. It is thus as safe as cash so far as the payee is concerned.

certified public accountant. A holder of the main professional accountancy qualification in the USA.

cessation. The discontinuance of a business. The term is of particular significance in the area of taxation. Where a cessation occurs in an unincorporated business, i.e. where the profit is subject to INCOME TAX (q.v.), special rules for the ASSESSMENT (q.v.) of profit for the closing years apply.

CGT. Letters standing for CAPITAL GAINS TAX (q.v.).

chain. A succession of prospective buyers and sellers which occurs in the residential property market where the seller of one property becomes the buyer of another. Chains can become quite lengthy and the whole series of transactions may be held up by the delay caused when one member of it fails to sell a property or has difficulty in arranging finance.

chairman. The director of a company who is chairman of the BOARD OF DIRECTORS (q.v.). The total remuneration paid to the chairman must be separately disclosed in the company's annual published accounts.

chairman's report. A statement on the operations of a businesss over the previous year which appears alongside the annual profit and loss account and balance sheet. This report is not a statutory requirement but it almost always appears. It will generally seek to explain any unusual events which have occurred, express confidence in the future of the business and thank the people employed by the company for their efforts.

Chancellor of the Exchequer. An officer of state second in rank only to the Prime Minister. The Chancellor is responsible for the financial aspects of the government's policy. The best-known activity of the Chancellor is the presentation of the annual BUDGET (q.v.) in which, amongst other things, the government's proposals regarding taxation during the forthcoming year are announced. The Chancellor of the Exchequer is appointed by the Prime Minister.

change of name. An amendment to a company's MEMORANDUM OF ASSOCIATION (q.v.) such that the name of the company is changed. The amendment must be made by a SPECIAL RESOLUTION (q.v.) of the company's members and must be registered with the REGISTRAR OF COMPANIES (q.v.).

Channel Islands. A group of islands under British jurisdiction which lie just off the coast of France. The largest islands are Guernsey and Jersey. The islands have a degree of self-government and taxes are at a lower level there than they are on the mainland.

charge. 1. To debit. An amount might be described as charged to, say, miscellaneous expenses when it is debited to that account.

2. The imposition of a requirement for payment. An accountant sending a bill to a client might be said to have charged for the services provided. A profitable business is subject to a charge for taxation.

3. To give as security for a loan. A MORTGAGE (q.v.), for example, is a charge on the property to which it attaches.

chargeable accounting period. A period of time the profits of which will be assessed for CORPORATION TAX (q.v.). It will often not coincide with a company's financial year as it must begin on 1 April or end on 31 March. The significance of these dates is that the government's financial year for corporation tax ends each 31 March and the rate of tax may change at that date. A company with a year ending on 31 December will have its profits allocated to two chargeable accounting periods. One of these will extend from 1 January to 31 March and the other from 1 April to 31 December. Where a change in the rate of tax has occurred, different rates will apply to the profits of the two chargeable accounting periods. The total profit for the year is divided in a simple *pro rata* basis, i.e. here 1 : 3.

chargeable gain. A capital gain which is chargeable to, CAPITAL GAINS TAX (q.v.). If an investor buys shares and subsequently sells them at a profit there will, subject to certain exemptions, be a chargeable gain. If a person sells his or her main residence at a profit there is not a chargeable gain, because such a transaction has been granted full exemption from capital gains tax.

charge and discharge. An old-fashioned term describing the operation of DOUBLE ENTRY (q.v.) accounting. When value is placed in an account, i.e. debited, the account is said to be charged. It becomes responsible for explaining the use of the funds charged. When value is produced by or taken from the account, i.e. it is credited, the account is said to be discharged. It is, therefore, to that extent, relieved of the responsibility to account.

charge card. A card, possession of which entitles the holder to have amounts payable by him or her, usually for goods supplied, charged to an account maintained by the company issuing the card. There is usually no limit on the total amount which may be charged in this way but the holder is required to settle the account in full when it is presented, usually on a fixed date in each month. An annual subscription is normally charged to the holder for the facility given by a charge card and there is also a charge on a trader accepting the card for payment. The charge card should not be confused with the rather similar CREDIT CARD (q.v.). The best-known examples of charge cards in the UK are American Express and Diners Club.

charitable donation. An amount paid by a company to a charitable organisation. Its accounting significance is that it must be disclosed in the published annual accounts. Unless the charity provides some direct benefit to the company or to its employees a charitable donation may not be an allowable deduction in calculating the profit subject to CORPORATION TAX (q.v.).

charity. An organisation set up to raise and administer funds for some worthy objective. Examples of such objectives are animal welfare, the relief of poverty, the promotion of artistic endeavour, the welfare of orphan children and the protection of the environment. In order to be recognised officially as a charity the organisation must be registered with the CHARITY COMMISSIONERS (q.v.). The status which this confers is of considerable value as the organisation is then exempt from taxation. There are, however, corresponding obligations concerning the use of funds and the production of accounts.

Charity Commissioners. Persons appointed by the state to oversee the operations of charities. It is they who decide whether a particular organisation may be registered as a CHARITY (q.v.). The status of registered charity is important as it confers substantial tax benefits.

chartered accountant. A professional description properly applied in the UK only to persons who are members of one of the following bodies:

The Institute of Chartered Accountants in England and Wales
The Institute of Chartered Accountants of Scotland
The Institute of Chartered Accountants in Ireland

Chartered Association of Certified Accountants. A body of professional accountants in the UK. Membership is granted to persons who have passed the relevant examinations and completed a prescribed period of practical experience as accountants. Members are entitled to use the designation Certified Accountant and to add the letters ACCA (for an associate member) or FCCA (for a fellow) to their names.

Chartered Institute of Management Accountants. A body of qualified accountants in the UK whose members are concerned largely with accounting in support of management in industrial and commercial organisations. Members are entitled to use the designatory letters ACMA (for an associate) or FCMA (for a fellow).

Chartered Institute of Public Finance and Accountancy. A body of qualified accountants in the UK whose members are concerned largely with accounting in public corporations. Many are employed by local authorities. Members of the body are entitled to use the designatory letters CIPFA.

Chartered Institute of Secretaries and Administrators. A body of qualified company secretaries. The curriculum for the examinations contains a considerable amount of accountancy as well as company law and secretarial practice. Members are entitled to use the designatory letters ACIS (for associate members) or FCIS (for fellows).

chartism. The art or science of predicting the future movement of share prices by a careful study of charts or graphs of past performance. Chartism claims to be able to discern both trends and patterns in the charts from which conclusions may be drawn. One of the theories, for example, is that at any one time there exist RESISTANCE LEVELS (q.v.) in the market. These are the levels marking the upper and lower bounds of price outside which investors are unwilling to stray. Thus price movements are contained within them. The resistance levels are not permanent, however, and when one is breached decisively this is taken to mean that it has disappeared and that a completely new level of prices (either higher or lower) will be attained. Considerable controversy surrounds the theories of chartists and much empirical evidence supports the so-called RANDOM WALK THEORY (q.v.) which would imply that movements in the prices of shares are completely unpredictable.

chartist. One who practises CHARTISM (q.v.).

chart of accounts. An index to all the accounts contained in a DOUBLE ENTRY (q.v.) system. It usually allocates to each account a number and arranges accounts in logical subdivisions.

EXAMPLE.

10 Wages control account
11 Office wages
12 Factory wages
13 Transport wages
14 Maintenance wages
15 ....

cheeseparing. Excessively cautious, to the point of meanness, in financial matters.

cheque. A NEGOTIABLE INSTRUMENT (q.v.) ordering a bank with whom the drawer has an account to pay a stated sum to, or to the order of, another person. Since the Cheques Act 1957 a paid cheque has been conclusive evidence of the payment of money thus obviating the necessity of giving a RECEIPT (q.v.) for cheque payments. A cheque may bear a CROSSING (q.v.) or an ENDORSEMENT (q.v.) varying the terms stated on the face.

cheque account. A bank account from which funds may be drawn or transferred to other accounts by means of a cheque. The usual form of a cheque account is the CURRENT ACCOUNT (q.v.).

cheque guarantee card. A card which when presented by the holder at the time of making a payment by cheque will ensure that payment of the cheque is guaranteed by the bank providing the cheque book up to a specified amount, normally either £50 or £100. For the guarantee to operate the recipient of the cheque must verify that the details and signature appearing on the card agree with the corresponding details on the cheque and must then record the number of the cheque guarantee card on the reverse of the cheque. A cheque issued against a cheque guarantee card cannot be stopped by the payer. Banks more commonly now issue multi-purpose cards in which the same card acts as a CREDIT CARD (q.v.) or DEBIT CARD (q.v.) as well as a cheque guarantee card.

child benefit. A social security benefit paid to all families in which there are children.

Chinese walls. Barriers to communication erected within an organisation carrying out both stockbroking and market making activities. There is a potential conflict of interest in these activities and the Chinese walls are intended to avoid any possibility that the firm's interest will be set above that of the client.

churning. The practice, by an adviser managing funds for another person, of buying and selling investments contained in the fund for the sole purpose of creating a dealing commission for him or herself. It is regarded as improper.

CIF. Letters standing for COST, INSURANCE AND FREIGHT (q.v.).

CIMA. Letters standing for CHARTERED INSTITUTE OF MANAGEMENT ACCOUNTANTS (q.v.).

circulating capital. A synonym for WORKING CAPITAL (q.v.).

city. City of London. The term is used to refer collectively to those involved in the financial markets based in London who are often thought of as having a common point of view. Thus it might be said that the city reacted favourably to the Chancellor of the Exchequer's decision to reduce interest rates.

City Code on Takeovers and Mergers. A code of practice to be followed in the event of takeovers and mergers. Its object is to ensure that such activities are carried out in a fair and proper manner and that privileged persons do not gain financial advantage over others by an abuse of influence or inside information. The code was established under the auspices of the Stock Exchange. It does not have the force of law, but the ultimate sanction of the withholding of a Stock Exchange quotation is a powerful force in ensuring compliance.

civil list. The list of those members of the royal family who are entitled to grants from the Exchequer to enable them to discharge their public duties.

claim. A statement by an insured person of an amount due to him or her after suffering loss which has been insured against. The claim should set out the circumstances of the loss and give a statement of the amount believed to be due. It should be supported by any available evidence such as estimates of the cost of repair or of the value of items destroyed or stolen.

claw back. The action of taking back tax reliefs or allowances previously given. Claw back occurs when circumstances change so that entitlement to the relief ceases. An example might occur when an investor under the BUSINESS EXPANSION SCHEME (q.v.) sells the shares before the expiration of 5 years. This is the required period of ownership to qualify for relief. If this requirement is not met, therefore, the tax relief will be clawed back by the Inland Revenue.

clearing. The process of passing a CHEQUE (q.v.) through the banking system so that funds are transferred from the account of the payer to the account of the payee.

clearing account. An account with the bank of the type more commonly described as a CURRENT ACCOUNT (q.v.).

clearing bank. A BANK (q.v.) which is a member of the London Bankers' Clearing House. It therefore has direct access to the facility for clearing cheques drawn on members which that provides. Other banks may use the facility indirectly by an arrangement with a clearing bank.

client account. An account maintained at a bank by a professional person such as a solicitor or an estate agent into which money held on behalf of clients is placed. A solicitor, for example, might deposit the proceeds from the sale of a client's house in the client account. The purpose of the account is to keep money held for clients separate from the firm's own money. It is thus protected from the claims of the firm's own creditors.

close. The time at which the Stock Exchange closes for business for the day. It is the time at which special note is taken of the prices of securities. Thus it might be said that the shares of x plc stood at £1.20 at the close.

close company. A company under the control of five or fewer persons. The category is significant in tax law. A QUOTED COMPANY (q.v.) will escape from being designated as a close company if 35 per cent of its shares are held by the general public. The category was created to prevent a tax abuse whereby persons carrying on a business in the form of a company could escape INCOME TAX (q.v.) on investment income by causing the company to own the investments and then refraining from paying this out as DIVIDENDS (q.v.) to themselves as shareholders or remuneration as directors. The RETAINED PROFIT (q.v.) would build up the value of the business ultimately to be realised as more lightly taxed CAPITAL GAINS (q.v.). For a close company the Inland Revenue may apportion the excess of the RELEVANT INCOME (q.v.) of the company over its distributions in a year amongst its shareholders, taxing them as though this amount had been distributed. This gives rise to what is known as a SHORTFALL ASSESSMENT (q.v.) to tax.

closing entry. An entry made in an account at the close of a financial period and as part of the process of making up the FINAL ACCOUNTS (q.v.). It usually takes the form of a transfer to the profit and loss account.

closing price. The price at which a share or other security had arrived at the close of business of the Stock Exchange on a specified day.

closing rate method. A method of converting, for accounting purposes, amounts expressed in one currency into amounts expressed in a different currency. In the closing rate method, conversion is made at the RATE OF EXCHANGE (q.v.) existing between the two currencies at the date on which the accounting statements are drawn up. The alternative method is the TEMPORAL METHOD (q.v.) under which the rates of exchange applying at the dates of the transactions portrayed are used.

closing stock. The stock of goods held at the end of a specified trading period.

CoCoA. Acronym for CONTINUOUSLY CONTEMPORARY ACCOUNTING (q.v.).

codicil. An addition or appendix to an existing WILL (q.v.). A codicil has the effect of amending the will without the necessity of drawing up a completely new will. The codicil must be signed by the TESTATOR (q.v.) and the signature must be witnessed by two persons in exactly the same way as for the will itself. These need not, however, be the same persons who witnessed the original will.

coin. A unit of currency in the form of a metal token. Coins are made in a variety of shapes and sizes and of a variety of materials. They are highly durable but heavy to carry around. They are, therefore, used for small transactions.

collateral. Secondary or supporting security for a loan. A bank might, for example, make a loan against the main security of a MORTGAGE (q.v.) on property. As collateral they might take a policy of LIFE ASSURANCE (q.v.) on the life of the borrower. When a loan is repaid the collateral is released at the same time as the main security.

collection period. The time taken from the granting of credit to a customer until payment has been received. Such credit is normally given on agreed terms as to the date of payment. Debtors may, however, delay payment so that the actual collection period is longer than that intended. A useful overall measure of the effectiveness of CREDIT CONTROL (q.v.) is to calculate the average collection period from a set of FINAL ACCOUNTS (q.v.). This is given by:

$$\text{Average collection period} = \frac{\text{Debtors}}{\text{Credit sales}} \times 365$$

collective bargaining. The process, usually undertaken by a trade union, whereby the wages of a group of workers are negotiated as a single package. Collective bargaining may lead to national pay scales or to scales applicable only to one employer.

Collector of Taxes. An officer of the INLAND REVENUE (q.v.) whose function it is to collect the taxes assessed by an INSPECTOR OF TAXES (q.v.). The full title of the office is Her Majesty's Collector of Taxes.

collusion. That process whereby more than one person agrees to act together. The term is commonly used where the proposed joint action has a fraudulent intent. Fraud involving collusion is less probable and easier to detect than fraud perpetrated by an individual. It should therefore be an object of INTERNAL CONTROL (q.v.) to make fraud without collusion impossible.

columnar accounts. Accounts making use of multiple columns in order the better to display their information. Where there are several accounts of very similar format, e.g. CURRENT ACCOUNTS (q.v.) in a partnership, they may be in columnar form, using one column for each partner on each side of the account.

combination. A general term applied to the process whereby two or more businesses which were previously independent come under common management. A TAKEOVER (q.v.) is one form of combination and a MERGER (q.v.) is another.

comfort letter. A letter supplied by an accountant to the directors of a company or to sponsors on the occasion of the issue of a PROSPECTUS (q.v.). Unlike the accountant's report this is not required by statute and will not be published. Its object is to re-assure those involved on certain facts in the situation.

commercial. Appertaining to the operation of a business. Thus if an action is justified on commercial grounds this means that it is believed that the taking of the action will be ultimately of benefit to the profitability of the business. Occasionally there may be a conflict between what is ethical behaviour and what is commercial.

commingled fund. A fund in which there are several independent interests but where these interests cannot be identified with specific assets of the fund because these are mixed.

commission. An amount paid to a person or institution carrying out business as agent for another, which is calculated as a percentage of the value of the business. Thus an agent for an insurance company will receive commission calculated on the value of the premiums which are collected. A stockbroker will charge commission proportional to the value of the securities which are bought or sold.

Commissioners of Inland Revenue. Officers of the Inland Revenue appointed to hear appeals by taxpayers. There are the General Commissioners, who are lay people and unpaid, and Special Commissioners, who are full-time civil servants with a specialist knowledge of tax law. Different types of case are presented to each.

commodity. A consumable product in which there is a large organised world wide market. Traders will deal in these markets speculatively with no intention of actually holding or using stocks of the commodity itself. Examples of commodities are cocoa, tobacco, steel and beef.

common costs. Costs which are incurred in the manufacture of a JOINT PRODUCT (q.v.) before the point of separation. For accounting purposes some basis of allocating common costs has to be established.

common stock. Term used in the USA for the EQUITY (q.v.) of a company. It is the equivalent of what in the UK would be termed ORDINARY SHARES (q.v.).

community charge. A local tax introduced to replace the former system of rates. It began in England and Wales in 1990 and in Scotland one year earlier. Its distinguishing feature was that, within a community, every member would pay a fixed amount regardless of income or other circumstances. Some reductions were made for persons of very low income. The tax, popularly called the poll tax, encountered considerable resistance and was abolished after only three years of operation. It was replaced as from 1 April 1993 by the COUNCIL TAX (q.v.).

Companies Acts. The name given to a series of Acts of Parliament concerned with companies. The most recent of these is the Companies Act 1989. This added to the basic law of companies which is contained in the Companies Act 1985. This former Act consolidated and re-enacted legislation contained in a group of Companies Acts extending from 1948 to 1981.

company doctor. A person brought in as a consultant to an ailing company with the object of reviving its fortunes. The term is a colloquial one applied to a person who is, in fact, a management consultant.

company secretary. *See* SECRETARY.

comparability. A characteristic of values which makes it legitimate to draw comparisons between them. Two sets of accounts would have comparability if they had been prepared on the same bases and included similar types of value.

comparative figures. Figures appearing alongside those in a set of FINAL ACCOUNTS (q.v.) to show the corresponding amount for the preceding equivalent period. The provision of comparative figures is a legal requirement in the accounts of limited companies and means, in effect, that two sets of accounts, those for the current year and those for the previous year, are always presented. Where a heading in the accounts has changed its nature, e.g. by more or less detailed analysis or by reclassification, the comparative figures should be adjusted from their actual values to figures drawn on a comparable basis.

compensating error. An error in a DOUBLE ENTRY (q.v.) book-keeping system which, by being equal in amount but on the opposite side, conceals another error. Neither the original error nor the compensating error will thus be detected by a failure to balance.

    EXAMPLE. A cash payment of £100 was recorded by crediting £100 to cash and debiting £10 to a creditor. Normally this error would be revealed when the TRIAL BALANCE (q.v.) failed to agree. However a compensating error was made. Goods valued at £90 were returned to a supplier. This amount was debited to the creditor but no credit entry was made (to purchase returns). It should be noted that there is no connection between an error and its compensating error other than the coincidence that they are equal and opposite in amount.

compensation. An amount of money paid to a person to offset some loss or detriment they have suffered. This loss or detriment may or may not be financial. Thus a person may be compensated by a central fund for money lost when a tour operator fails and is unable to honour its obligation or return money already paid. A person who is injured may be compensated from an insurer for the suffering and deprivation caused by the injury.

compensation for loss of office. An amount paid to the holder of an office to compensate him or her when deprived of that office before the end of its contractual term. Where such compensation is paid to the director of a company it must be disclosed in the published profit and loss account. Compensation for loss of office is normally free of tax to the recipient up to a certain level. Above this level it is taxed as EARNED INCOME (q.v.). A payment in compensation for loss of office is often described as a 'golden handshake'.

competition. That situation where a business has to attract customers by appearing to them to offer a better overall deal than businesses offering similar goods and services. Competition is believed to be in the interests of the consumer as it results in the lowest possible prices for the highest possible quality of goods and services. In practice there are many factors which obstruct the perfect working of competition.

completion. The end of the process whereby the property rights in a piece of land and any building standing on it are transferred from the vendor to the buyer. At this point the full purchase price also becomes payable.

compliance cost. The costs imposed on a business by the need to comply with some legislative obligation. For example, the law requires that a business maintains records concerning VALUE ADDED TAX (q.v.). The cost of doing so is a compliance cost.

complimentary. Free of charge.

composite rate of tax. A rate of tax formerly charged on building societies and banks in respect of interest which they paid to depositors. It was abolished in 1991. It was at a lower rate than the BASIC RATE OF INCOME TAX (q.v.) and was calculated to approximate to the average rate payable by all depositors, some of whom, because of low income, would not be taxpayers. In the hands of the recipient such interest was then regarded as tax-paid at the basic rate. Higher rate taxpayers would suffer an additional charge but non-taxpayers were not able to claim any refund. The system was a convenient way for the Inland Revenue to collect tax from a large number of small investors.

compound interest. A method of calculating INTEREST (q.v.) whereby accumulated interest is periodically added to the PRINCIPAL (q.v.) and then itself commences to bear interest. In contrast SIMPLE INTEREST (q.v.) is calculated on the principal sum only.

EXAMPLE. £5,000 is deposited with a building society in an account bearing interest at the rate of 10 per cent per annum compounded annually. It is withdrawn with accumulated interest at the end of three years. The total amount then due is calculated as follows:

	£
Initial Loan	5,000
Interest at 10%	500
Amount due after 1 year	5,500
Interest at 10%	550
Amount due after 2 years	6,050
Interest at 10%	605
Amount repayable after 3 years	£6,655

comptroller. The officer of a company who is in overall control of all of its financial affairs.

compulsory purchase. A procedure undertaken by government or a local authority to require the owner of land to sell it when it is required for some public purpose such as the construction of a road. The circumstances in which the power can be invoked are carefully prescribed by law.

compulsory winding up. The WINDING UP (q.v.) of a company under a court order. This usually occurs when a company is insolvent. See INSOLVENCY.

computation. Term applied to a calculation, especially of an amount chargeable to tax. Thus the amount of CORPORATION TAX (q.v.) payable by a company will be determined by a computation from its chargeable profits and the tax rate.

computer. An electronic device for handling large amounts of data and for performing mathematical operations very rapidly. A computer has no facility which cannot be performed manually using conventional filing systems and methods of calculation. Its usefulness lies in its enormous capacity for the storage of information and for the speed with which this can be retrieved and processed. The computer has made possible many modern developments such as automatic banking. A computer has no capacity to think and will perform tasks only when these have been formulated into a PROGRAM (q.v.) for it.

computer-assisted audit techniques. The use of a COMPUTER (q.v.) to contribute to the conduct of an AUDIT (q.v.). They are used when the enterprise which is the subject of the audit maintains its records on a computer.

concealment. The action of concealing the fact that assets are owned when there is a legal obligation to declare them. The most common usage of the term is in BANKRUPTCY (q.v.) where the bankrupt person is required to make a full declaration of all assets which may then be available for the satisfaction of the claims of creditors. One who does not do so is guilty of concealment.

concentration of investment. The excessive investment, within a PORTFOLIO (q.v.), of funds in one company or in one industry. This makes the portfolio vulnerable to any special risks affecting that company or that industry.

concept. An idea making up part of a framework within which events are observed and interpreted. Accounting is based on a number of concepts. The ENTITY CONCEPT (q.v.), for example, sees a business as a centre of activity separable from all other centres of activity, including its proprietor and its employees.

conceptual framework. A logical structure which would guide the preparation of accounting statements. There have been several attempts to find a conceptual framework for accounting but none has so far been fully successful.

concert party. An agreement whereby a number of persons acting in concert (i.e. co-operating), purchase shares in a public company. The significance of the situation is that there is a legal obligation on a shareholder to inform a company on becoming the holder of 5 per cent of the issued share capital. This obligation is also imposed on a concert party as a whole so that what are effectively 5 per cent holdings may not be concealed by being registered in a number of separate names.

concession. The giving of a relief or benefit to which the recipient is not, in a literal sense, entitled. The Inland Revenue will sometimes give concessions either to individual taxpayers or generally in the interests of equity or of administrative convenience.

confiscation. The seizing of goods or property in a manner allowed by law. CONTRABAND (q.v.) goods, for example, may be confiscated by officers of Customs and Excise. Stolen property may be confiscated from the hands of the thief.

conglomerate. A group of companies often having nothing in common except their ultimate control. The term is particularly used of large groups with complex structural relationships. Much of big business is conducted through the medium of conglomerates.

connected person. A person deemed in law to be so closely involved with another as to make independent action unlikely. Business partners might be connected persons as would be husband and wife or father and son.

conscience money. Money paid by one person to another, often anonymously, because the payer has a troubled conscience following some improper or illegal failure to pay the money in the past. The Inland Revenue sometimes receives conscience money from people who have in the past made false declarations about their income.

conservatism. A principle of accounting which requires that assets should be stated at the lowest of available valuations and that profits should be reported at the lowest of available figures. The principle has the advantage (which is intentional) that a business should be in at least as favourable a position and should have performed at least as well as its accounts show. Conservatism can be criticised as imparting a consistent downward bias to all accounting statements. A synonymous term often used is that of prudence. This is one of the four fundamental principles singled out for special mention in SSAP 2 and now embodied in the law in the Companies Act 1985.

EXAMPLE. An item of stock was purchased a year ago for £100. It would now cost £120 to replace it but is expected to realise only £80 when sold. The principle of conservatism would require that the stock be valued in a balance sheet at £80 even though legitimate arguments would exist for using valuations of either £100 or £120.

consideration. Some right or benefit accruing to one party to a contract or some loss or detriment occurring to the other. Consideration is a necessary element of any CONTRACT (q.v.) unless the contract be in the form of a DEED (q.v.).

consignment. Goods sent to an agent who is to use his or her best endeavours to sell them but to whom ownership does not pass. Special accounting procedures, known as consignment accounting, have been devised to deal with this type of transaction. Their essential feature is that goods sent out on consignment are not treated as sales, and therefore no profit is reported until they have been sold to a THIRD PARTY (q.v.). Goods still in the hands of the agent are treated as unsold stock and valued (normally) at cost in the balance sheet of the business.

consistency. The principle that similar matters should be treated in a similar way whenever they arise. Clearly, an arbitrary variation in accounting method will produce apparent changes in profit or in balance sheet valuations which are unrelated to any real events. The principle of consistency may, however, sometimes create problems and should not be taken too far. In particular it may sometimes conflict with the principle of CONSERVATISM (q.v.) in which case the latter would normally prevail. If a TRUE AND FAIR VIEW (q.v.) should require a variation in the treatment of an item from that formerly employed then the variation should be made. The principle of consistency, which has long been incorporated into accepted practice, was formalised as fundamental in SSAP 2. It has since been embodied in the Companies Act, 1985.

consolidated accounts. FINAL ACCOUNTS (q.v.) prepared for a group of companies as if they were a single company. A group of companies arises where one company, the holding company, acquires a controlling interest in other companies, its subsidiaries. Because a substantial part of its business is conducted on its behalf by the subsidiaries, the holding company's own accounts will give an incomplete picture of its overall operations. In order that a TRUE AND FAIR VIEW (q.v.) may be presented, consolidated accounts must be prepared.

There are two main methods of consolidation. These are known as the ACQUISITION METHOD (q.v.) and the MERGER METHOD (q.v.). They are not interchangeable and should be used each in its own appropriate circumstances. Broadly the former is correct where the subsidiary was acquired for cash and the latter when it was acquired in exchange for an issue of shares in the holding company to the previous shareholders of the subsidiary.

Although basically consolidated accounts represent an adding together of the accounts of the individual companies, adjustments are commonly required for the following matters: INTERCOMPANY BALANCES (q.v.), INTERCOMPANY PROFIT (q.v.), MINORITY INTEREST (q.v.), PREACQUISITION PROFIT (q.v.).

consolidated balance sheet. A document which shows the position of a GROUP (q.v.) of companies as though that group were a single entity. With the consolidated profit and loss account it makes up a set of CONSOLIDATED ACCOUNTS (q.v.). *See also* ACQUISITION METHOD; MERGER METHOD.

consolidated profit and loss account. A statement which shows the results of a GROUP (q.v.) of companies for a stated period of time on the basis that the group is treated as a single entity. With the consolidated balance sheet it makes up a set of CONSOLIDATED ACCOUNTS (q.v.).

consols. An abbreviation of consolidated stock, an IRREDEEMABLE (q.v.) government security on which a fixed COUPON RATE (q.v.) of interest is paid. The YIELD (q.v.) on consols is often taken to represent the market risk-free rate of interest.

C

consortium. An association of companies formed for the purpose of undertaking a particular activity. There may be no other connection between the companies outside the scope of that activity. A consortium is usually formed when the development costs of a particular undertaking are beyond the resources of any one company or where a particular combination of skills and expertise not usually found within a single company is required.

constant purchasing power. A method of valuation used in accounting for INFLATION (q.v.). Its essence is that accounts are prepared in terms of an artificial currency unit of constant purchasing power. This is related to the real currency in which accounting transactions have been carried out by means of price indices.

constructive total loss. An insurance term used where the cost of recovery or repair of an insured asset will exceed its value after the recovery or repair has taken place. In such cases it is better abandoned and treated as if it had actually been lost.

Consultative Committee of Accountancy Bodies. A committee having representatives from the major professional accountancy bodies in the UK. It concerns itself with matters of common interest to the profession. It is often referred to as CCAB.

consumer goods. Goods which are in a form ready for final consumption as opposed to their being in a form to be used in a manufacturing process by another business.

container accounts. A form of accounting used where goods are supplied in valuable, returnable containers. Its object is to maintain records of the location of the containers and to identify any costs which arise in connection with their loss.

contango. The process of deferring payment due in one Stock Exchange account to a later account. There is an interest charge made for this facility.

contemptuous damages. DAMAGES (q.v.) awarded at such a low level as to indicate the opinion of the court that no significant damage was suffered by the plaintiff, who, although technically in the right, should not have brought the action at all.

contingency. A condition existing at a balance sheet date where the outcome will be confirmed only on the occurrence or non-occurrence of some future event. A contingency may take the form either of a contingent gain or of a contingent loss. The matter is dealt with in SSAP 18. This standard requires that provision should be made for a contingent loss where it is probable that the future event will confirm the loss and where its amount can be ascertained with reasonable accuracy at the date when the accounts are approved. In other cases full disclosure of the known fact should be made. No credit should be taken for any contingent gain. It should, however, be disclosed if it is likely to be confirmed.

contingent liability. A liability whose existence or otherwise will be confirmed by the outcome of some future event. A good example of a contingent liability is the damages which would be payable in the event of a decision against the company in a pending legal action. It is a requirement of company law that contingent liabilities are stated as a note to the balance sheet if not otherwise provided for.

continuing professional education. Education aimed at professionally qualified accountants which has the aim of keeping them up to date with the technicalities of their subject and to enable them to develop new areas of expertise.

continuously contemporary accounting. A form of accounting for inflation which values all assets on the balance sheet at their realisable values. It also involves the creation of an inflation reserve which preserves the real value of the invested capital. In a profit and loss account prepared on the basis of continuously contemporary accounting there will be a number of unusual features. One is that there will be no DEPRECIATION (q.v.). There will appear an item showing the transfer necessary to maintain the purchasing power of the shareholders' equity and another showing the effects of revaluing all assets at their realisable values.

contra. An entry in a double entry account representing the reversal or cancellation of an entry on the other side.

contraband. Goods which are illegally smuggled into a country from another country. The usual reason for doing this is in order to avoid paying import duty or to bypass some prohibition on import.

contract. A legally binding agreement. For a contract to exist a number of elements must be present. These are (with illustrations):

(a) An offer – 'I will paint your house for £100.'
(b) Acceptance – 'I agree to your offer.'
(c) Consideration – The action of painting.

Some contracts must be in writing. These are contracts for the sale of land and contracts of insurance. Other contracts are equally binding if made verbally or even merely implied by a course of action. For example, if you sit in a restaurant and consume a meal there is an implied contract under which you will have to pay for the meal even though you did not actually say that you would. A contract made under SEAL (q.v.) does not require consideration. In other cases the absence of consideration reduces an agreement to the status of a gratuitous promise which is unenforceable at law.

contracting out. The action of signifying that a person does not wish to be part of an agreement where otherwise it will be assumed that he or she does. Employed persons, for example, may contract out of the state earnings related pension scheme, and save its cost, if they are in an occupational scheme giving at least the equivalent in benefit.

contract note. A document evidencing an agreement to buy or sell securities. A stockbroker who buys shares for a client will issue a contract note indicating the name of the security, the amount of it bought and the total amount due, including the broker's COMMISSION (q.v.).

contribution. The surplus of the revenue from an activity over its AVOIDABLE COST (q.v.). The usefulness of the contribution is that it measures how much better off the business is by undertaking the activity as opposed to not undertaking it. The term refers to the contribution made to the overall total of fixed overhead and profit. BREAKEVEN (q.v.) occurs when the total contribution is exactly equal to total FIXED COSTS (q.v.). Contribution is sometimes related to the use of a fixed factor in short supply in assessing the relative profitability of different lines of activity. Thus one might calculate contribution per square metre of factory space or contribution per hour of skilled labour which takes some time to train.

contributory. One who is liable to contribute to a deficiency arising upon the winding up of a company. This can arise either with a company limited by GUARANTEE (q.v.) or a company limited by shares where the shares were not fully paid up. A past holder of partly paid shares may also become a contributory if the company is wound up within 1 year after the shares were disposed of.

contributory pension scheme. A pension scheme to which the beneficiary makes contributions during his or her working life. This is usually done by regular deductions from salary.

control account. An account which holds, in total, the same figures which have been posted in detail to the individual accounts it controls. A debtors' control account, for example, will have debited to it total credit sales and credited total cash received from debtors. The balance on a control account should equal the total of the balances on the individual accounts. Any discrepancy will reveal error and this is the manner in which control is exercised through the mechanism of this account.

controllable cost. A cost which may be controlled by the action of some responsible individual. What is controllable will depend on the extent of the individual's authority. The amount of overtime worked in a department, for example, may be controllable by the manager of that department. The amount charged to the department as an apportionment of the overall cost of general administration will not be. The value of the concept is that it provides a logical and useful way in which a comparison between an actual result and a BUDGET (q.v.) may be analysed.

controlling interest. An investment in a company which is sufficiently large to enable the holder to control the activities of the company. This normally requires possession of more than 50 per cent of the shares carrying voting rights. A HOLDING COMPANY (q.v.) has a controlling interest in its SUBSIDIARY COMPANY (q.v.).

convention. An underlying principle of accounting which is adopted by common usage and can be presumed even if not explicitly stated. It is a convention, for example, that stock will be valued at whichever is the lower, cost or net realisable value.

conversion cost. The cost incurred in manufacturing finished goods. As defined in SSAP 9 it includes all directly attributable costs, such as material and direct labour, production overheads and other overheads which are properly attributable to bringing the product to a state of completion.

convertible currency. A currency which can freely be converted through the market into other currencies. A currency is not convertible if there is no market in it. This may be because legislation in the issuing country forbids conversion or because the currency is regarded as worthless.

convertible debenture. A DEBENTURE (q.v.) which may be converted into equity at the option of the holder. The dates and terms of the conversion are established at the time of the issue of the security. Its advantage for the investor is that entry into the equity may be postponed until the future prospects of the company become more clearly established.

conveyance. The document by which the transfer of the ownership of land and buildings is effected. Each conveyance of such property becomes part of the 'deeds' of the property, which trace its ownership history.

conveyancing. The process of preparing a CONVEYANCE (q.v.) and seeing it through all the necessary formalities. Conveyancing is normally undertaken by a solicitor.

cooking the books. A colloquial term for the falsification of accounting records.

cooling off period. A period of time allowed after an agreement has been reached but before it becomes totally binding. It applies to contracts for the loan of funds or involving other long-term financial commitments so that the borrower or investor may give effect to second thoughts about the agreement if these occur. It acts as a check on the effects of high-pressure sales techniques.

co-operative. A form of business enterprise where the business is operated by and for the benefit of all those involved. This will include workers as well as management.

co-operative movement. A semi-political movement of considerable importance in the UK. Its main outward manifestation is the existence of a chain of co-operative shops. In their traditional form these gave a dividend to members based on the amount they spent there and on the profits. Nowadays this tradition has largely disappeared but some such form of discount is still given to persons who shop there.

copyright. The property right that exists in original works of art, literature, music, etc. Authors automatically own the copyright to anything they produce and this subsists for their lifetime and for 50 years thereafter. Copyright may be sold, in which case it vests in the purchaser. Copyrights may be a valuable asset, e.g. to a publisher, and, as such, may appear on a balance sheet.

core business. That element of the activities of an undertaking which it regards as its chief concern.

corner. To obtain control over the supply and thus the price of some commodity or security by acquiring all, or nearly all, of the available supply.

corporate planning. The process of planning the future activities of a company. The financial dimension to corporate planning is a very important one.

Corporate Report. The title of a discussion paper issued in 1975 under the auspices of the ACCOUNTING STANDARDS COMMITTEE (q.v.). Its purpose was 'to re-examine the scope and aims of published financial reports in the light of modern needs and conditions'. Its main underlying philosophy was that there was 'an implicit responsibility to report incumbent on every economic entity whose size or format renders it significant'. The traditional view had been that a company's primary duty to report lay towards its shareholders. The 'Corporate Report' identified a number of USER GROUPS (q.v.) towards which it saw a company as having an especial duty to report.

corporation tax. A tax on the profits of incorporated bodies. It was first introduced in 1965. The tax is based on the profits of an accounting period and is payable 9 months after the end of that period. For many years different timing arrangements applied to companies which had been in existence at the inception of the tax but these have now been abolished.

corruption. An illegal situation whereby people use a proper authority in an improper way. An example of corruption might be if a planning officer lent support to a planning application because the person submitting the plans had paid money to the officer.

corset. Term applied to controls which are sometimes placed on the banking system over the amount of credit which it may offer to customers. The corset is applied by the Bank of England in times of national difficulty, usually with the object of defeating inflation.

cost. An expenditure required in order to produce some specified output or benefit. The determination of cost may sometimes be a complex matter where expenditures are not directly attributable to identifiable units of output.

cost accounting. That area of accounting concerned with the determination and analysis of costs. It consists of a collection of techniques which are important in guiding the managers of a business when formulating its policy and judging its activities.

cost benefit analysis. A form of analysis used to evaluate projects requiring a substantial investment of funds but which do not yield any return in the form of conventional revenues. Cost benefit analysis is usually applied to public expenditure contracts. Here it requires an evaluation of the benefits to be received by the community as a whole in the event that the expenditure is made. Although benefits must be determined in money quantities this often has to be done on the basis of estimate and judgement.

cost centre. A definable area of activity within a business to which costs can be attributed. Usually a cost centre is a particular department or process with a manager or supervisor who takes responsibility for its operations. All costs are either identified with the cost centre and allocated to it or else, where not identifiable, are apportioned on some reasonable basis.

cost control. The processes whereby management seeks to influence costs so as to keep them within planned limits. There are various techniques of cost control. The preparation of a BUDGET (q.v.) and the use of STANDARD COSTS (q.v.) are the most important.

cost driver. A factor used in ACTIVITY-BASED COSTING (q.v.) to determine the apportionment of costs. Thus the floor space occupied by each of a series of activities might be the cost driver for the apportionment of the rent of the building. Numbers of employees working on each activity might be the cost driver for the services of the personnel department.

costing. The process of determining a cost for some product or some activity. The term is often used as a synonym for COST ACCOUNTING (q.v.).

cost, insurance and freight. A description signifying that the price of the goods concerned includes their safe delivery to the customer.

cost of capital. The amount (expressed as an annual percentage rate) which a business has to pay in order to attract and retain capital funds. The significance to a business of its cost of capital is that it has to ensure that all investments it makes yield a return which is at least equal to the cost of capital. The cost of capital is therefore used as a HURDLE RATE (q.v.) in evaluating capital projects. Capital from different sources will have different costs. Thus the cost of equity is likely to be different from the cost of debt. The overall cost of capital is a weighted average of the costs of the various components in the proportions in which they are used. It is a matter of debate, not fully resolved, as to whether CAPITAL STRUCTURE (q.v.) affects the cost of capital or whether the costs of the various components are mutually interdependent so that the weighted average is a constant. The cost of capital will vary as between one business and another. Higher risk businesses will face a higher cost of capital than lower risk enterprises. The cost of capital is also affected by taxation.

cost of control. The amount paid by a HOLDING COMPANY (q.v.) for shares in its SUBSIDIARY COMPANY (q.v.) over and above the value they would command as an investment, in recognition of the particular benefit which the company gains through control.

cost of goods manufactured. The total amount expended in a period in producing the goods manufactured in that period. The figure is the main product of the MANUFACTURING ACCOUNT (q.v.). It is made up of PRIME COST (q.v.) and FACTORY OVERHEAD (q.v.). In the calculation an allowance is made for any increase or decrease in the value of WORK IN PROGRESS (q.v.).

cost of living. The amount which has to be spent to maintain a stated standard of living. If workers are given a cost of living increase this means that they are given an increase of exactly the amount required to compensate them for an increase in prices which has taken place since the previous increase. Indices are published which purport to measure changes in the cost of living.

cost of sales. The total amount expended in producing or acquiring the goods sold during a period of time. It is an important figure in the TRADING ACCOUNT (q.v.). It should be noted that the cost of sales may differ from the COST OF GOODS MANUFACTURED (q.v.) because of the existence of stocks of goods for sale which may fluctuate in amount.

cost-plus contract. A contract under which the customer agrees to pay the cost of producing the supply with the addition of an agreed percentage as profit. Thus the revenue derived from the contract is not determined finally until the work is complete. It is a useful form of contract in circumstances where it is difficult to estimate costs in advance (e.g. because development work of unknown extent and duration is required) as it guarantees the supplier a fair profit whatever the outcome. It does, however, have the disadvantage that no incentive is given to the supplier to work efficiently as the more costly production is the higher will be the profit. Some agreement is necessary on how costs are to be calculated particularly in respect of allocations of general OVERHEAD (q.v.). Cost-plus contracts are common in connection with work done for the government such as defence contracts. The cost-plus contract should be contrasted with the FIXED PRICE CONTRACT (q.v.).

cost push inflation. Inflation, i.e. rising prices, which seem to be primarily related to increases in the costs of business inputs.

cost reduction. A procedure involving, among other matters, the careful examination of accounting records, having the object of reducing the costs of operating an organisation so as to improve its efficiency. Comparison of accounting figures with those of previous years or with averages known to apply for the industry in which the organisation operates will often reveal sources of wasteful expenditure. Cost reduction will also involve a careful consideration of production methods and administrative procedures and the ways in which these might be made more efficient.

cost-volume-profit. The analysis of the response of cost and profit to changes in volume. It requires, amongst other things, a distinction to be made between FIXED COST (q.v.) and VARIABLE COST (q.v.). The study of cost-volume-profit relationships is well exemplified in the construction of BREAKEVEN CHARTS (q.v.).

coterminous. Having a common end. The term is used of businesses which are members of the same group. It is desirable for the purpose of preparing CONSOLIDATED ACCOUNTS (q.v.) if their year ends are coterminous.

council tax. A local form of taxation based on the value of property.

counsel. A qualified barrister who gives legal opinions. It is often useful before taking some action where the law in the matter is not entirely clear to take counsel's opinion, which will be given for a fee. Although having no formal authority it should represent clear guidance as to the view which would be taken by a court should the matter in question later be challenged in that way.

counterfeit. Fake. Counterfeit bank-notes are a copy of the real thing. They have, of course, no value but it is possible that they may be used and may escape detection for some time.

counterfoil. A tear-off part of a document such as receipt or a cheque which enables the issuer to keep a record of what was shown on the document itself.

coupon rate. A rate of interest stated on the face of a security. Thus a 6 per cent debenture standing in the market at £50 per cent will yield an investor a return of 12 per cent per annum. Its coupon rate, however, remains at 6 per cent.

Court of Auditors. A body charged with the responsibility of regulating and reporting on the financial affairs of the European Community.

covenant. A legally binding undertaking to pay money or to observe obligations. The purchaser of land, for example, may have to covenant that he or she will abstain from using it for specified purposes (e.g. the keeping of livestock). An important type of covenant is that whereby a person undertakes to make a regular payment to another person. Provided that this is made in proper form (i.e. as a DEED (q.v.)) the payee, if not a taxpayer, may reclaim income tax deemed to have been deducted from the payment. This does not affect the liability to tax of the payer. It thus enables, for example, regular donations to charities to be boosted at the expense of the Inland Revenue.

cover note. A document issued by an insurance company accepting a stated risk for a short period pending the issue of a complete policy and the settlement of the premium. Cover notes are commonly issued to car purchasers to enable them to drive legally immediately they have submitted a PROPOSAL (q.v.) to the insurer.

CPA. The designatory letters standing for CERTIFIED PUBLIC ACCOUNTANT (q.v.), a qualification of accountants in the USA.

CPE. Letters standing for CONTINUING PROFESSIONAL EDUCATION (q.v.).

CPP. Letters standing for CURRENT PURCHASING POWER (q.v.).

cr. Abbreviation standing for CREDIT (q.v.).

crash. An abrupt fall in prices. Thus a stock market crash occurs when all security prices are reduced by a substantial amount very quickly. Although much drama is usually made out of the reporting of a crash, they are fairly common in financial markets and recovery always follows.

creative accounting. Accounting which follows the literal rules of legislation and accounting standards but succeeds nevertheless in presenting an unduly favourable picture of a company's position or progress.

credit. 1. A period of time allowed to a purchaser of goods or services before payment for them is required. Credit transactions are very common in business. The advantage to the recipient of credit is that he or she can finance a business with a lower fund than would be required if all supplies had to be paid as soon as they were delivered. The advantage to the giver of credit is that he or she will win customers who are attracted by the facility and might otherwise have gone elsewhere. A further advantage to both is that a number of credit transactions can be settled in one payment and this will economise on administrative costs.

2. The right-hand side of a double entry account. An item recorded on this side is said to be credited to the account and a balance resting on this side is said to be a credit balance. A credit entry signifies that value has flowed from the source indicated by the name of the account, e.g. a payment of cash, a supply of goods, a receipt from a debtor.

credit card. A card (actually made of plastic), possession of which entitles the holder to have amounts payable by him or her charged to an account maintained by the company issuing the card. The holder of the card is given a credit limit which he or she is not permitted to exceed and traders offered the card in payment may be required to obtain telephone authorisation from the credit card company before any sizeable transaction is completed. The cardholder receives a monthly statement and is required to make at least a specified minimum payment (typically 5 per cent of the outstanding balance) towards settlement. Any unpaid amount is carried forward and interest is charged on it. The holders of some credit cards are required to pay an annual fee for the use of the facility but others are free. The income of the credit card company comes from these interest charges and fees and from the discounts required by it from traders taking part in the scheme. Credit cards should be distinguished from DEBIT CARDS (q.v.) and from CHARGE CARDS (q.v.) which in some respects they resemble. Some credit cards issued take the form of AFFINITY CARDS (q.v.) which give some part of the profit derived from their operation to a designated cause. Most credit cards in the UK belong to one of two main groups, Mastercard and Visa.

credit control. The set of procedures which an organisation uses to ensure that it does not give credit to its customers unwisely and that it collects amounts due promptly. Credit control will thus include the establishment of a CREDIT RATING (q.v.) for those to whom it is proposed to give credit and the institution of a follow-up procedure for debts which are not paid by the due date.

credit note. A document evidencing that a credit entry has been made to a debtor's account. If a customer returns goods previously invoiced a credit note may be issued. The effect of this will be to reduce the amount of the customer's indebtedness or, if this has already been settled, to enable the customer to purchase other goods to the value of those returned without further payment.

creditor. One to whom money is owed. Most businesses will buy goods and services on credit and therefore have creditors. On a balance sheet they are normally classified as CURRENT LIABILITIES (q.v.).

credit rating. An assessment of a person's creditworthiness. A high credit rating will imply that the person is considered to be reliable in repaying amounts owed at the due date. Credit ratings range from wholly subjective judgements to a scoring system based on the award of points for such matters as level of income, total domestic commitments, experience with previous credit arrangements, etc.

credit sale. A sale made on the terms that the buyer will pay for the goods after an agreed interval of time, often 1 month.

credit union. An association of persons who agree to make savings and to pool them so that individual members may then be loaned money from this pool at reasonable rates of interest.

creditworthiness. The characteristic of being reliable in the repayment of borrowed money. Before a business lends money or supplies goods on credit it will be wise to check on the creditworthiness of its customer. Creditworthiness is affected both by honesty and by ability to pay.

crosscast. The sum of a number of figures written across the page rather than in vertical columns. The crosscast is of particular significance where amounts in a total column are also analysed into appropriate columns in order to break down the figures into components. The grand total of the analysis columns should equal the total of the main column and this can be verified by means of a crosscast.

crossing. The drawing of two lines across the face of a cheque, usually with the words '& Co' written between them. The effect of a crossing is that the cheque may be paid only by crediting it to a bank account (not in cash). This is a considerable protection against the possibility of fraud should the cheque go astray since payment can be traced to the account holder. A special crossing gives further protection. For example, if the name of a specific bank be written over the crossing then that cheque can be paid only through the specified bank, If the words 'A/c payee only' be included this will nullify the effect of any ENDORSEMENT (q.v.) of the cheque to a THIRD PARTY (q.v.). Most banks now issue blank cheques with a crossing already printed on them.

cross rate. The rate of exchange between two currencies on the assumption that each is exchanged into a third currency. The market should ensure that this is the same as the direct rate of exchange after allowing for transaction costs. If it is not there is an opportunity for speculators to make a profit.

croupier. The person who operates a gambling game such as chemin de fer or roulette.

crown. A pre-decimal coin which did not circulate widely but was issued in the form of coins commemorating special occasions. As such it was held by collectors. The crown was worth five shillings, i.e. a quarter of a pound.

cum cap. A term attached to the quotation of the price of a share meaning that at that price it may be purchased inclusive of the right to receive a recent BONUS ISSUE (q.v.) of shares.

cum div. A term attached to the quotation of the price of a share meaning that at that price it may be purchased inclusive of the right to receive a DIVIDEND (q.v.) currently due. When shares change hands at about the time of a dividend payment the question arises as to whether it is the buyer or the seller who is entitled to the dividend. To settle this question a date is determined on which the share goes EX DIV. (q.v.). Prior to that date the buyer takes the dividend and after that date it remains with the seller. The paying company will always send the dividend to the person whose name appears on the REGISTER OF MEMBERS (q.v.) at the relevant date. Some cash adjustment between buyer and seller may therefore be necessary.

cum rights. A term attached to the quotation of the price of a share meaning that at that price it may be purchased inclusive of the right to receive the benefit of a recent RIGHTS ISSUE (q.v.) of shares.

cumulative preference share. A PREFERENCE SHARE (q.v.) where the dividend right is cumulative. All preference shares have a stated maximum amount of dividend but a company may pay less than this amount giving rise to arrears of dividend. Where the preference shares are cumulative these arrears are carried forward to subsequent years and must be met before any other dividends are paid. Where the preference shares are not cumulative the arrears are lost.

currency. Cash in the form of notes and coin. Currency is the most liquid form of asset. It has the disadvantage of being vulnerable to loss by theft or destruction and of earning no return. Few businesses, therefore, would hold any substantial amount in this form.

current account. 1. An account with a CLEARING BANK (q.v.) on which cheques may be drawn. A current account may not be interest bearing and charges may be made by the bank for its use. For personal customers these are often waived if the account remains in credit. Other services offered to current account holders are those of STANDING ORDER (q.v.) and DIRECT DEBIT (q.v.). A current account holder may be allowed an OVERDRAFT (q.v.) on the account.

2. Any account of regular money exchanges between parties designed to keep an up-to-date record of their positions.

3. An account maintained for each partner in a PARTNERSHIP (q.v.) to record the allocation and subsequent withdrawal of profit.

current asset. An ASSET (q.v.) which is held temporarily as a stage in the profit earning cycle. The usual current assets are stock, debtors and cash.

current cost. A basis of valuation which values an asset at the amount which it would currently cost to obtain. This may be interpreted as being the cost of replacement or the OPPORTUNITY COST (q.v.) of the asset.

current cost accounting. That method of accounting which bases valuations on the current replacement cost of assets. It has been strongly advocated by some as an appropriate form of accounting to use under inflationary conditions although, of itself, it has no necessary relevance to that problem. The operation of current cost accounting requires frequent revaluations of assets. Surpluses and deficits which arise from this process are transferred to a current cost reserve (or revaluation reserve). Legally this may be distributable to the extent that the revaluations have been realised but normally it should be treated as a CAPITAL RESERVE (q.v.). The reserve serves to maintain the productive capacity embodied in the business's invested capital. Current cost accounting was the basis of the infamous ED18 (q.v.) produced by the ACCOUNTING STANDARDS COMMITTEE (q.v.). SSAP 16, now withdrawn, was a standard based on current cost accounting.

current cost reserve. A RESERVE (q.v.) set up to contain the revaluations arising under CURRENT COST ACCOUNTING (q.v.). It may also be called a REVALUATION RESERVE (q.v.). It should be regarded as undistributable and is therefore a CAPITAL RESERVE (q.v.).

current file. A file containing material of immediate and current relevance. The term is used by an AUDITOR (q.v.) to describe the file containing papers relating specifically to the audit in hand. A PERMANENT FILE (q.v.) will also be maintained to contain information of documents of continuing relevance.

current liability. A liability which is to be discharged in the relatively near future. This is usually taken to mean that it will be settled prior to the next balance sheet following the one in which it appears. Examples of typical current liabilities are trade creditors and bank overdrafts.

current operating profit. The profit on the trading activities of the business after charging expenses at current cost. The term is used by Edwards and Bell in *Theory and Measurement of Business Income*. Current operating profit is one constituent of BUSINESS INCOME (q.v.). Another is HOLDING GAIN (q.v.).

current purchasing power. A method of accounting measurement which allows for the effect of inflation on the value of money. It is often abbreviated to CPP and was the method underlying (P)SSAP 7, now withdrawn. Under CPP all HISTORICAL COST (q.v.) values are translated into current equivalents by the use of an index which represents the extent of the inflation which has occurred since the date of the transaction establishing the value.

EXAMPLE. An asset was purchased for £10,000 at a time when an appropriate index of prices stood at 100. The index currently stands at 130 and a balance sheet is to be drawn up. The cost of the asset is:

$$£10,000 \times \frac{130}{100} = £13,000$$

and it is on this figure that the balance sheet value will be based. It should be noted that £13,000 does not necessarily bear any relationship to the current market value of the asset. It is the amount of current purchasing power which historically was sunk in the asset when it was purchased.

current ratio. The ratio between CURRENT ASSETS (q.v.) and CURRENT LIABILITIES (q.v.). It is a useful indicator of the short-term ability of a business to meet its obligations as they fall due. A more stringent test of liquidity is the ACID TEST RATIO (q.v.).

Customs and Excise. That part of the government's administration concerned with the assessment and collection of duties. VALUE ADDED TAX (q.v.) comes within the jurisdiction of the Customs and Excise.

CVP. Letters standing for COST-VOLUME-PROFIT (q.v.).

D

d. Symbol used to represent the penny in the UK in pre-decimalisation currency.

damages. A legal award to a person injured by the tort or breach of contract of another. The amount of damages is assessed by the court at a level intended to compensate the person aggrieved for the loss rather than to punish the defaulter. Thus if A repudiates a contract to purchase a car from B for £1,000 but B is quickly successful in selling the car for that price to someone else, damages, if any, will be limited to the costs involved in making the second sale. A court will sometimes award nominal damages of a very small sum (e.g. one penny). This signifies that although legal right is on the side of the plaintiff, the action has been over a trivial matter.

danger money. An amount paid to a person over and above the normal rate of pay for the work they are undertaking because of special and unusual dangers which attach to it. A diver, for example, might be paid extra when working on a North Sea oil platform because of the particular dangers involved.

dangling debit. A debit balance seeking an account against which it can be written off where such an account does not exist. An example might arise where a business makes a payment for goodwill which it does not want to record as such in the balance sheet. It seeks to write the amount off against reserves but no suitable reserve exists. The balance may therefore be shown as a negative reserve, or deduction from equity.

data. A plural word meaning pieces of information. It is commonly used in connection with information which is supplied to a computer for use, for example, in a DATABASE (q.v.).

database. Although any repository of large amounts of data could be termed a database the term is generally applied to computer software designed for this purpose. The software may consist of a computer file containing large amounts of information already, for example, on companies' financial performance or on share prices, or it may consist of a blank database into which the user can record information as required. This type of database may be used, for example, to maintain up-to-date records of customers or of shareholders.

data processing. The action of recording, analysing or retrieving information. The term is most often applied to computer-based systems for handling very large amounts of information.

Data Protection Act. Legislation relating to information about individuals which is maintained in computer records. Such individuals must be made aware of the existence of the record and be given an opportunity to see a copy of it and, if necessary, correct it.

dated security. A security which has a fixed date for repayment.

day book. A book of PRIME ENTRY (q.v.) in which transactions of a specified type are recorded on a day-by-day basis. Thus there may be a purchase day book (for purchases on credit) and a sales day book (for sales on credit). Totals from day books will be prepared for POSTING (q.v.) periodically to the LEDGER (q.v.). Day books are now regarded as somewhat old-fashioned and may be dispensed with.

days of grace. A period of time following the expiry of an insurance policy in which the insurer will accept the payment of a premium for renewal. Once the days of grace, typically 30 days, have expired the policy is void and the insurer will not be liable under any claim. Cover during the period of the days of grace depends on the ultimate payment of the premium.

deal. A transaction which involves an agreement between two or more parties. The term is sometimes used to refer to the sale of shares from one person to another.

dealer. One who earns a living by buying and selling commodities or securities.

Dearing Report. The report of a committee which in 1990 studied and made recommendations on the future of ACCOUNTING STANDARDS (q.v.).

death benefit. A social security benefit paid to bereaved persons.

death duty. A duty which used to be charged on the estate of a deceased person. It was replaced by ESTATE DUTY (q.v.), by capital transfer tax, and then by INHERITANCE TAX (q.v.).

debenture. A security representing a loan to the company which issues it. Debentures may be bought and sold through the Stock Exchange, as are shares, and their market price is established in the same way. It is, however, likely to be less VOLATILE (q.v.) than the share price. Debenture holders have a right to an agreed fixed rate of interest regardless of the level of profit and, except in the case of irredeemable debentures, the right to a repayment of their PRINCIPAL (q.v.) at an agreed date.

debenture redemption reserve. A RESERVE (q.v.) representing retentions out of profit made for the purpose of redeeming DEBENTURES (q.v.). The reserve is legally a REVENUE RESERVE (q.v.) but, because funds will be used to redeem the debentures, the company may choose to regard it as a CAPITAL RESERVE (q.v.).

debit. To enter an amount on the incoming or left-hand side of an account.

debit balance. A balance such that the debit side of the account contains a greater total value than the credit side. A debit balance signifies either an expense or an asset.

debit card. A card similar in appearance to a CREDIT CARD (q.v.) and which is offered in a similar way in payment for goods and services. The essential difference is that in the case of a debit card such payments are then debited to the holder's bank account in exactly the same way as a cheque. The advantages of a debit card are that it may be used to make larger payments than might be acceptable by cheque (assuming there are sufficient funds in the bank account) and that it can be used to operate automated teller machines with a special PERSONAL IDENTIFICATION NUMBER (q.v.).

debit note. A commercial document notifying a person that a debit has been made to his or her account. Thus if goods previously invoiced were found to have been undercharged a debit note might be issued for the amount of the difference. It should be contrasted with the more common CREDIT NOTE (q.v.).

debt. An amount owed by one person or business to another. The borrowing of money and thus the creation of credit is widespread in modern commerce. Most businesses are partially financed by debt. A useful distinction can be drawn between short-term and long-term debt. A company's CREDITORS (q.v.) represent short-term debt and it will not normally have to pay interest on these amounts. Its DEBENTURES (q.v.) represent long-term debt and will bear interest.

debt collector. One whose function it is to collect money from debtors on behalf of their creditors. A charge will be made for this service. The collector may use stronger tactics than the creditor would be willing personally to use.

debt factoring. A service whereby the factor acquires the right to receive payment from the business's DEBTORS (q.v.) in due course by the making of an immediate cash payment. The advantage of debt factoring from the point of view of the business receiving the service is that it obtains early release of the funds tied up in debts. The factor is rewarded for these services by acquiring debts at a discount against the amount to be collected.

debtor. A debtor is one by whom one is owed money. In most cases the debtors of a business arise when goods are supplied to customers on CREDIT (q.v.) and are to be paid for at an agreed future time. A business's management of its debtors is very important. A complete refusal to give credit is likely to mean that sales which would otherwise be made go to competitors. Nevertheless the giving of excessive credit either in terms of the amount or in terms of the delay before payment is made is also to be avoided. It ties up large amounts of money and runs the risk of BAD DEBTS (q.v.). Debtors form an important component of WORKING CAPITAL (q.v.) and in a balance sheet are classified as CURRENT ASSETS (q.v.). The relative level of debtors will vary from one type of business to another. A food retailing business, for example, will have relatively low debtors because it trades largely on a cash basis. The wholesale supplier, on the other hand, may have very substantial debtors.

debt retirement. The process of removing debt by repaying it.

decimalisation. The process whereby a currency in which the units do not have a decimal relationship one to another is converted to one which does. In the UK decimalisation took place in 1971. Prior to that time the pound sterling was divided into 20 shillings and each shilling was divided into 12 pence. After decimalisation the pound was divided into 100 pence, designated new pence until they had become fully familiar. As another example of decimalisation, Australia, which also used pounds, shillings and pence, decimalised so that its new currency consisted of Australian dollars, of which two equalled 1 old pound, each divided into 100 cents.

declaration of dividend. The publication by a company of a decision taken by its directors that a dividend of a stated amount is to be paid. In making their decision the directors will be constrained by the requirements of company law and by the financial requirements of the business. Once the declaration has taken place the dividend becomes a liability of the company.

declining balance method. A synonym for REDUCING BALANCE METHOD (q.v.).

decommissioning costs. The costs involved in taking a productive unit out of service. Decommissioning costs might be very heavy where special safety or environmental factors are important, as, for example, in the costs involved in decommissioning nuclear power stations.

deduction. An amount by which a sum payable is reduced before the payment takes place. Wages and salaries, for example, are subject to deductions in respect of INCOME TAX (q.v.) and NATIONAL INSURANCE (q.v.). Much investment income is subject to deduction of tax at source.

deed. A legal document which is signed, sealed and delivered by the person making the deed. It is used to contain the most solemn forms of declaration or undertaking. Some forms of contract, e.g. the transfer of the ownership of land, must be in the form of a deed. A promise unsupported by CONSIDERATION (q.v.) will not be enforceable in a court of law unless it be embodied in a deed. A deed of COVENANT (q.v.) is an example of this kind of deed.

deed of covenant. *See* COVENANT.

deep discount bonds. Bonds (i.e. debentures) issued at a price very substantially below their ultimate redemption value. A large part of the overall return to the holder is thus in the form of the difference between what is paid for the bond and the amount at which it is redeemed. There are special tax rules for this kind of bond whereby the gain at the end of the bond's life is taxed as though it had been paid regularly over the life of the bond.

deep gain securities. These are similar to DEEP DISCOUNT BONDS (q.v.) and are taxed in a similar fashion. The difference is that a deep gain security is one which is redeemed at a large premium over its issue price.

defalcation. The stealing of money which has been entrusted to the individual concerned. Defalcation will usually involve the falsification of records in an attempt to conceal what has been done.

default. The failure to meet a financial obligation. A credit customer, for example, who fails to pay an account when it is due is said to default on the debt. Default may have very serious consequences. A company which defaults on interest payments to its DEBENTURE (q.v.) holders may be forced by them into LIQUIDATION (q.v.).

defeasance. The termination of an interest in property according to the terms of some deed.

defensive assets. A synonym for LIQUID ASSETS (q.v.). Since such assets may be realised quickly they are seen as a first line of defence against an emergency. The term is more common in the USA than in the UK.

deferred consideration. CONSIDERATION (q.v.) under a contract, the satisfaction of which will be deferred for an agreed period.

deferred expenditure. Cash which has been paid for goods or services which are to be supplied later or where the benefit is to be felt later. The correct accounting treatment of deferred expenditure is that it should be shown in a balance sheet as a CURRENT ASSET (q.v.) until such time as the goods or services have been consumed.

deferred income. Cash which has been received in payment for the supply of goods or services in advance of the provision of those goods or services. The accounting significance of deferred income is that it should be shown as a liability until the supply is made, at which time it may be shown as revenue.

EXAMPLE. Oak, a tree surgeon, received £1,000 in year 1 in full payment for felling a number of trees. The work was commenced and completed in year 2. The £1,000 should appear in the balance sheet at the end of year 1 as a CURRENT LIABILITY (q.v.). It will then appear as part of TURNOVER (q.v.) in the profit and loss account for year 2.

deferred pension. A pension which is not taken at the normal time for retirement but commenced at some later date. A deferred pension will be at a higher rate than a pension which is not deferred.

deferred shares. Shares whose right to a dividend is postponed until after dividends of a prescribed amount have been paid to other shareholders. In spite of the postponement of dividend rights the amounts ultimately accruing to the holders of deferred shares may, if the company is successful, be very considerable. They are usually held by the original founders of the business.

deferred taxation. Taxation which, owing to the operation of tax legislation, is payable in a year later than that in which the profit to which it relates was recognised. This arises because of so-called TIMING DIFFERENCES (q.v.) between accounts prepared for tax purposes and those prepared for reporting purposes. The subject of deferred taxation is to an extent controversial because it requires a charge for taxation for which there is yet no liability and for which liability, even if it eventually arises, may be very considerably delayed. Deferred taxation is the subject of SSAP 15.

deficiency. A shortfall below what is required. The term is used in INSOLVENCY (q.v.). The deficiency is then the amount by which total assets fall short of total liabilities.

deficit. A shortfall of revenue as against expenditure. A deficit is, in effect, a loss, but the term is often used for non-profit making organisations whose long-term financial aim is to match revenue and expenditure. Thus there is an expectation that the deficit will be offset by surpluses either of the past or of the future.

defined benefit. An amount receivable under a pension scheme which is laid down in advance. The contributions are then calculated so as to lead to this result.

defined contribution. An amount payable by contributors to a pension scheme which is designed so that the benefit ultimately received depends on the amounts and timing of the payments.

deflation. The opposite condition to INFLATION (q.v.), i.e. there is a general fall in the price level.

defray. To reimburse a person for expenses incurred by him or her.

defunct company. A legally registered company which has ceased to trade or to engage in any other activity. It may be relieved of the obligation to submit annual accounts.

***del credere* agent.** An AGENT (q.v.) who agrees to bear the risk of non-payment for the goods by the ultimate customer on behalf of the PRINCIPAL (q.v.).

delivery. A formal process representing the final stage in the execution of a DEED (q.v.). Delivery is by means of a declaration that the deed is signed, sealed and delivered.

delivery note. A document accompanying a delivery of goods which specifies the type and quantity of goods delivered. The delivery note originates from the supplier of the goods. Its accuracy should be verified by a physical check against the goods themselves. It should then be compared with the ORDER (q.v.) to verify that the goods delivered were those actually ordered and with the INVOICE (q.v.) before its payment is authorised.

demand. A request for payment of an amount where the liability arises from a statute. Thus a person will receive a demand for payment of council tax or for the payment of income tax.

demand deposit. An amount deposited with a bank which may be withdrawn on demand, i.e. without having to give any notice.

demerger. The process whereby previously merged businesses are separated so that they resume operations as independent organisations. This may be done because an original merger proved to be unsuccessful or because the combined organisation has grown so large as to be unwieldy. The takeover of a large business may lead to the demerger of some of its parts where the new management has a different business strategy from the old.

de minimis. A legal term implying that a matter is trivial and it is not appropriate to pursue it. If, for example, a debtor sent a cheque for £5,000 in settlement of an account for £5,000.01 1p would strictly still be owed. The principle of *de minimis* would mean that this is unlikely to be pursued.

demonetise. The process whereby a unit of currency is deprived of its status as legal tender. Where, for example, a new style of £20 note is issued the new and the old will circulate side by side for a period of time. At some point the old note will be demonetised so that it can no longer be used. Before that date all such notes should be deposited with a bank.

denomination. The designated value of a unit of currency or a security. Thus common bank-notes have denominations of £5, £10 and £20. Shares might have a denomination of 10p.

departmental accounting. Accounting which allows for the preparation of statements showing the results of the separate departments of a business. This is of value in providing management with information for planning and control purposes.

Department of Trade and Industry. An important government department headed by a Minister and operated by civil servants. It is concerned with the conduct of business in the UK and makes and controls regulations arising from this.

dependant. A person who is dependent on another for subsistence. Thus a child is a dependant of its parents and an elderly person may be a dependant of his or her adult child. The status has tax significance where certain allowances may sometimes be claimed in respect of dependent relatives.

depletion. That process whereby a WASTING ASSET (q.v.) becomes progressively consumed. A quarry, for example, becomes depleted as the material is removed. A charge for depletion, where it occurs, should appear in the profit and loss account.

depooling. The value of plant and machinery acquired by a business is normally placed in a POOL (q.v.) for the purposes of calculating capital allowances. This means that there is no separate treatment of individual items. The taxpayer may, however, elect that short-life plant and machinery is subject to separately calculated capital allowances, i.e. it is not placed in the pool. This is depooling. A consequence of depooling is that on the sale of the asset concerned there may be a BALANCING CHARGE (q.v.) or a BALANCING ALLOWANCE (q.v.)

deposit. An amount of money placed with some person or institution with the intention that it, or its value, should be returned at some future date. Money may, for example, be deposited with a bank in order for it to earn interest or for safekeeping. A deposit may be required from the purchaser of a property pending completion of legal formalities and the payment of the balance of the price when possession is given.

deposit account. An interest bearing account at a bank. It is usual that notice is required before funds may be withdrawn from a deposit account. Cheques may not normally be drawn against the balance in the account.

depositor. One who makes a DEPOSIT (q.v.).

deposit taking company. A company which receives money from investors and pays interest on it. It is subject to legal rules to protect the depositors.

depreciation adjustment. The surplus of current cost depreciation over historical cost depreciation. It is an adjustment which was required by the now withdrawn SSAP 16 (q.v.).

depreciation. The recognition in accounting of the diminution in the value of FIXED AS-SETS (q.v.) which occurs during their use. The calculated amount of depreciation for a period of time is credited to the asset account, thus reducing its BOOK VALUE (q.v.), and debited to the profit and loss account thus showing the cost of using the asset as a charge against revenue. There are many different methods used for calculating depre-ciation, each based on a different concept. The most important methods are the STRAIGHT LINE METHOD (q.v.), the REDUCING BALANCE METHOD (q.v.) and the PRODUCTION UNIT METHOD (q.v.). There is necessarily a considerable degree of arbitrariness in the calculation of depreciation which has the potential to be an important source of distor-tion in accounting statements. There is a standard dealing with depreciation, SSAP 12. In this, depreciation is defined as 'a measure of the wearing out, consumption or other reduction in the useful economic life of a fixed asset whether arising from use, effluxion of time or obsolescence through technological or market changes'. The standard requires that depreciation should be allocated to accounting periods so as to charge a fair proportion to each period during the expected USEFUL ECONOMIC LIFE (q.v.) of the asset. It also requires depreciation to be charged on all fixed assets hav-ing a finite life. This does not include freehold land but does include any building standing on the land.

depression. A condition of the economy whereby activity is at a very low level. Growth in the economy will be low or negative and unemployment will be high during a de-pression.

deprival value. The maximum amount which a business would be prepared to pay rather than lose a specified asset. The deprival value of an asset is thus a measure of its VALUE TO THE BUSINESS (q.v.). The concept appeared in the SANDILANDS REPORT (q.v.) where it was suggested as being the value at which an asset should appear in a busi-ness's balance sheet. It can be shown that deprival value is the lower of two other values. One of these is REPLACEMENT COST (q.v.) and the other is the higher of REALIS-ABLE VALUE (q.v.) and ECONOMIC VALUE (q.v.).

deregulation. The removal of regulations which had previously surrounded some activ-ity. Deregulation of public road transport in the UK, for example, allowed new bus and coach operators to set up in competition with existing operators where regulation had prevented this before.

devaluation. A government action whereby the official rate of exchange between its currency and those of other countries is amended so that the rate of exchange becomes less favourable to the home currency. If the pound is devalued, as has hap-pened more than once, this will, in the short term, make UK exports appear cheap on world markets and give a boost to trade. In the longer term it is likely to contribute to rising prices at home. Devaluation is a step which is usually forced on a government because of the overwhelming pressure of market forces.

development. 1. The process of preparing the way to undertake some activity with a view to making a profit. This may take the form of inventing a new product and bringing it to a stage where it can be produced commercially or it may involve the seeking out of new markets. Expenditure involved in development has the characteristic that the benefits which flow from it are postponed to some future accounting periods. In care-fully defined circumstances it may be carried forward as an asset on the balance sheet and written off against those benefits when they appear in the profit and loss account. The circumstances in which this is permissible are set out in SSAP 13 on RESEARCH AND DEVELOPMENT (q.v.).

2. The action of erecting buildings on a piece of land.

development costs. Costs which have been incurred in the course of DEVELOPMENT (q.v.).

development gains tax. A tax on gains made on the sale of land arising from its DEVELOPMENT (q.v.) potential. The tax was the precursor of DEVELOPMENT LAND TAX (q.v.) and was charged on disposals between 17 December 1973 and 31 July 1976. For a private individual the gain was taxed as if it had been income, i.e. at the individual's marginal rate of income tax, and for a company it was taxed at the corporation tax rate. There was an exemption from the tax in the case of the disposal of a main private residence.

development land tax. The successor to DEVELOPMENT GAINS TAX (q.v.) this was a tax on gains made in holding land which acquired a DEVELOPMENT (q.v.) value. The tax was levied on disposals made after 31 July 1976. It was withdrawn from 19 March 1985.

devise. To leave land or buildings to another person in a will.

difference. There is said to exist a difference where a TRIAL BALANCE (q.v.) extracted from a set of books does not agree. The cause of a difference is always an error in the accounts and this must be located and corrected.

differential accounting. A form of statement which displays the difference between figures arising from two alternative courses of action. Its purpose is to highlight the benefit or otherwise of selecting the one rather than the other. No revenues or costs which are common to both courses of action will appear in a differential cost statement.

dilapidation. Payment made for the restoration to good repair of a building at the end of a lease under conditions imposed by the lease.

dilution. The process whereby the equity holders' interest in a company is reduced by the creation of extra equity in different hands without a commensurate inflow of funds. Dilution may come about when holders of CONVERTIBLE DEBENTURES (q.v.) exercise their conversion rights or when those having an OPTION (q.v.) to acquire shares at a favourable price take up that option.

direct cost. A synonym for MARGINAL COST (q.v.).

direct costing. A synonym for MARGINAL COSTING (q.v.).

direct debit. An instruction given by the customer of a bank to the bank to allow charges to be made periodically to an account at the instance of some THIRD PARTY (q.v.). Direct debits are a very useful way for a customer to make regular payments of an irregular amount, such as in payment of electricity or telephone bills. They are an alternative to the STANDING ORDER (q.v.) which is often used for regular constant payments. A bank will accept direct debit instructions only in respect of approved third parties and it will undertake to indemnify the customer if the facility is improperly used.

direct expenses. Expenses which can directly be associated with some defined segment of activity to the extent that if the segment of activity did not take place the expenses would not be incurred.

direct labour. Labour actually incorporated into a manufactured product. Its cost is a VARIABLE COST (q.v.) and it is an important component of PRIME COST (q.v.) and of DIRECT COST (q.v.).

direct material. Material actually incorporated into a manufactured product. Direct material is a VARIABLE COST (q.v.) and it is one of the important components of PRIME COST (q.v.).

directives. Instructions with an authority which requires them to be obeyed. The European Community has issued many directives which impinge on the preparation of accounts and these have progressively been incorporated into UK legislation.

director. A person appointed by a company to act in the management of the company. A company will normally have several directors who will act together as a Board of Directors. A director stands in the same position as a TRUSTEE (q.v.) with respect to the company. He or she must therefore act at all times in the best interests of the company. There are many legal rules relating to the directors and their duties of which some of the most important are listed below:

    (a)   A register of directors must be maintained by the company.
    (b)   A register of directors' interests must be kept.
    (c)   Directors' remuneration must be disclosed in the annual accounts.
    (d)   The directors must provide, with each year's accounts, a DIRECTORS' REPORT (q.v.).

Directors Disqualification Act. An Act of Parliament which allows persons guilty of dishonest behaviour whilst exercising the responsibilities of a director of a company to be prevented from occupying such a position again.

directors' emoluments. The amounts paid to the directors of a company, whether in their capacity as directors or otherwise. The total amounts must be shown in the published accounts of the company, distinguishing between amounts payable in the different capacities. There must be shown separately the amount paid to the chairman and to the highest paid director (if different). An indication in prescribed form must also be given of the numbers of directors in defined brackets of remuneration.

directors' report. A report required to be attached to a company's annual accounts. Its content is now closely prescribed (Companies Act 1985). The report must include information on all of the following matters:

    (a)   the principal activities of the company during the year;
    (b)   a business review;
    (c)   likely future developments;
    (d)   events which have occurred subsequent to the end of the year which have had an important effect on the company;
    (e)   research and development costs;
    (f)   results and dividends;
    (g)   any arrangements by which a shareholder has agreed to waive a dividend;
    (h)   names of those who have acted as directors at any time during the year;
    (i)   directors' interests;
    (j)   substantial shareholders;
    (k)   purchases by the company of its own shares;
    (l)   whether the company is a CLOSE COMPANY (q.v.);
    (m) fixed assets;
    (n)   charitable and political donations;
    (o)   health and safety at work;
    (p)   disabled employees;
    (q)   employee consultation action.

direct overhead. Overhead which has been incurred in the manufacture of some product such that if the product had not been made the overhead would have been avoided.

direct taxation. Taxation charged upon an individual or corporate taxpayer normally as a proportion of, and variable with, income. Examples of direct taxation are INCOME TAX (q.v.) and CORPORATION TAX (q.v.).

disability pension. A PENSION (q.v.) given to a person who is unable to work because of disability. If this occurred while the person was at work, whether directly caused by the work or not, the payment may come from a private pension scheme. A disability pension may also be due from the state.

disaggregation. The process whereby figures which show the results of a combination of activities are analysed so as to show the results of the separate components of the figures. A business, for example, might disaggregate its results so as to see the portions of its profit which arise from its different products or from different geographical regions.

disbursement. A legitimate payment of money out of some fund. A charity might make disbursements from money it has collected to the causes it was formed to support.

discharge. Release from or termination of some legal condition or obligation. Thus a debt is discharged when it is paid. BANKRUPTCY (q.v.) is terminated by a discharge when the court is satisfied that all the claims of creditors have been met or where it is clear that there is no further purpose in maintaining the state of bankruptcy.

disclaimer. A statement to the effect that no responsibility is accepted for certain matters. A person may, for example, disclaim any financial liability to people who are injured whilst visiting his premises. Not all disclaimers have legal effect. A seller of goods, for example, may not disclaim any responsibility.

disclosure. Giving information about a financial matter which does not appear on the face of the accounts.

discontinued operation. A part of a business which has been discontinued. Its accounting significance is that its contribution should be removed from profit in seeking to form a view about the future profits from continuing operations.

discount. 1. (noun) A reduction from a stated amount. Thus a debtor might be given a discount to encourage prompt payment (a CASH DISCOUNT (q.v.)). Shares are said to stand at a discount if their market price is below the NOMINAL VALUE (q.v.). It is, however, illegal to issue shares at a discount. *See also* TRADE DISCOUNT.

2. (verb) To reduce by some factor. Discounting is the process whereby future cash flows are brought to their PRESENT VALUE (q.v.). It is used in INVESTMENT APPRAISAL (q.v.).

discounted cash flow. A flow of cash over a period reduced to its PRESENT VALUE (q.v.) by the application of DISCOUNT FACTORS (q.v.). The technique is used to evaluate investment proposals. A proposal is *prima facie* worth pursuing if its present value at the business's COST OF CAPITAL (q.v.) exceeds its initial cost.

discount factor. A factor used as a multiplier to convert a future CASH FLOW (q.v.) to its PRESENT VALUE (q.v.). The factor, which is always less than 1, depends on the COST OF CAPITAL (q.v.) and the length of time which is to elapse before the cash flow takes place. The factor is calculated as:

$$\text{Discount factor} = \frac{1}{(1 + r)^n}$$

Where r is the cost of capital

                    n is the number of years due to elapse before the cash flow is received.

Tables of discount factors for a wide range of rates and time periods are available and it is thus normally unnecessary to calculate these values.

discretionary trust. A TRUST (q.v.) under the terms of which the trustees have discretion in distributing its funds.

dishonoured cheque. A CHEQUE (q.v.) which the bank on which it is drawn refuses to pay. This will be because the drawer has insufficient funds in the account or because the payment of the cheque would breach an agreed overdraft limit. It is a criminal offence to issue a cheque which the drawer knows or expects will be dishonoured by the bank.

disinvestment. The opposite to investment. It is thus the realisation of investments.

disposable income. That part of a person's income over which they have genuine discretion because it is not already committed to regular payments such as mortgage repayments and household expenses.

disposal. A critical event in the ownership of an asset chargeable to CAPITAL GAINS TAX (q.v.). The tax is payable in respect of the disposals during the year. Apart from sale, disposal may be by gift or by destruction of the asset.

dissimilar activities. A justification for the exclusion of the results of a SUBSIDIARY COMPANY (q.v.) from CONSOLIDATED ACCOUNTS (q.v.). It means that the subsidiary carries on activities which are so different from those of the rest of the group that consolidation would be misleading.

dissolution. The termination of a PARTNERSHIP (q.v.) business. Dissolution may occur following a voluntary termination of a partnership agreement or involuntarily following the death of a partner.

distress. The action of seizing goods under an order of a court. This is usually because there are amounts of money owed and the goods will be sold in order to raise this.

distress value. A value attaching to the assets of a business on the basis that they have to be sold quickly in order to meet very pressing commitments or to stave off financial collapse. The distress value of assets is likely to be below what could be realised for them in the ordinary course of trade.

distributable investment income. The income after tax derived from investments made by a CLOSE COMPANY (q.v.). Its significance is that it is an element in RELEVANT INCOME (q.v.) which may be calculated in connection with the issue of a SHORTFALL ASSESSMENT (q.v.) to income tax.

distributable profit. Profit which is available for distribution by a company. It will include all profit which has been earned in the course of the trading activity. It will also include REALISED PROFIT (q.v.) on the sale of assets. It will not include any unrealised or purely 'paper' profit.

distribution. A sharing out of an amount of money amongst those entitled to it. A company makes a distribution when it pays a DIVIDEND (q.v.) to its shareholders. In BANKRUPTCY (q.v.) there may be a distribution to CREDITORS (q.v.) of amounts realised by the sale of assets.

distribution costs. Costs associated with transferring goods from a supplier to the customer. Distribution costs would include packing and transport.

distringas. A notice issued by a court preventing a company from registering transfers of shares or other securities.

diversification. The practice of engaging in a wide variety of activities in order to minimise risk. In the case of a business this might involve extending its range of products so that if one or more should run into trading difficulties the success of others should compensate for this. An investor seeking diversification of a PORTFOLIO (q.v.) will buy a range of securities of different kinds. Diversification should be supported by some underlying rationale such as that provided by PORTFOLIO THEORY (q.v.).

divestment. The disposal of sections of a business. This is done usually where a company finds that one of its divisions is carrying out activities not compatible with what it regards as its CORE BUSINESS (q.v.). Divestment often occurs following a takeover as parts of the newly-acquired business are assimilated into the group and other parts are seen as being inappropriate for this purpose.

dividend. An amount received as a share in a specified fund. The term is most commonly met in connection with the payment of an income to the shareholders of a company. Total dividends of a company must not exceed its total profits but are often considerably less than this amount. The dividend will be stated either as a percentage of the NOMINAL VALUE (q.v.) of the capital or as an amount in pence per share. The term dividend is also used to describe the amount paid to a creditor in the BANKRUPTCY (q.v.) of an individual or the WINDING UP (q.v.) of a company. It then represents a share of the available assets and is paid out *pro rata* to the full amounts owed. Winners in a FOOT-BALL POOL (q.v.) or on the TOTALISATOR (q.v.) also receive amounts which are described as dividends.

dividend cover. The number of times over which a company's dividend could have been paid out of the current year's profit. Thus if a company has EARNINGS PER SHARE (q.v.) of 24p and pays a dividend of 12p per share, the dividend cover is 2. Dividend cover is a measure of how secure the current rate of dividend is. Fractional dividend cover is possible where a dividend is paid partly out of an accumulated RESERVE (q.v.).

dividend equalisation reserve. A REVENUE RESERVE (q.v.) which has been formed to provide a buffer between dividends and the profits supporting them. Thus in a good year amounts are transferred to this reserve over and above the dividends paid. In a poor year dividends can be maintained by supplementing profits from the accumulated dividend equalisation reserve.

dividend off. Synonym to *EX DIV* (q.v.). The term is used in the USA.

dividend on. Synonym to *CUM DIV* (q.v.). The term is used in the USA.

dividend yield. The DIVIDEND (q.v.) paid by a company expressed as a percentage of the market value of its shares. It is thus an expression of the actual rate of return in the form of cash which the investor is receiving on the amount currently committed to the investment.

divisional accounting. A technique which allows the measurement of the results of individual divisions within a business. The measurement of divisional performance is a matter of some controversy but two concepts, each enjoying some support, are RESIDUAL INCOME (q.v.) and RETURN ON CAPITAL EMPLOYED (q.v.).

divorce. A legal procedure whereby a marriage is dissolved. It may have important financial implications as one of the former partners, usually the husband, may be required to provide financial support to the other and to any children of the union. This can be in the forms of a division of the assets of the marriage at the time of the divorce, for example the shared home, and of regular payments for an indefinite period of time. Such payments are known as alimony. If an amicable arrangement cannot be made a court will decide on appropriate financial terms for the divorce.

docket. A small piece of paper, often torn from a larger sheet, containing brief details of some transaction.

documentation. Paperwork recording and evidencing an event or transaction. The documentation surrounding the supply of raw materials to a business, for example, will include the ORDER (q.v.), DELIVERY NOTE (q.v.) and INVOICE (q.v.).

documents of title. Documents which provide conclusive evidence of the ownership of some asset. The deeds to a property are documents of title.

dollar. The standard unit of currency in a number of countries, notably the USA. Australia, Malaysia, Singapore and Hong Kong are other countries where the unit is used, though with different values in each case.

dollar premium. An amount which may sometimes be paid over and above the official rate of exchange in order to acquire dollars.

dollar stocks. Shares in companies based in the USA and traded on the New York Stock Exchange.

domicile. The country which a person regards as his or her natural home. It has significance in tax law where it is distinguished from RESIDENCE (q.v.). There are three main categories of domicile. These are domicile of origin (where a person was born), domicile of choice (where the person has chosen to make a permanent home) and domicile of dependency (where domicile is determined by a relationship to another person, e.g. a husband or parent).

dominant influence. An influence which one company has over another such that it is able to dictate the commercial and financial policies of the other without regard to the interests of any other party. This dominant influence might be obtained through a majority shareholding. Its effect is that the two companies form a group and CONSOLIDATED ACCOUNTS (q.v.) are required. The term is used in the Companies Act 1989 and in FRS 2.

donated asset. An asset acquired without cost as a gift from another person. It would be rare for a business to acquire an asset in this way but a charitable organisation may do so. Although the acquisition cost of a donated asset is nil, it should be recorded in the balance sheet at a fair market value at the date of acquisition and then be depreciated in the ordinary way. The surplus resulting from this valuation should be added to capital or ACCUMULATED FUND (q.v.).

donation. An amount of money given by one person or business to another. Donations by a business are not allowable expenses for tax purposes unless given for a reason wholly connected with the trade of the business. Thus political and most charitable donations are not allowable. Donations are a major source of income for most charitable organisations.

donee. The recipient of a DONATION (q.v.).

donor. The maker of a DONATION (q.v.).

dormant company. A company which does not engage in any transactions. Usually a company becomes dormant after a period of normal trading activity. Under the Companies Acts 1985–9 a dormant company need not appoint an AUDITOR (q.v.) if it also qualifies as a SMALL COMPANY (q.v.). A company ceases to be dormant a soon as any transaction takes place.

double account system. A form of published account used in the nineteenth century. It was first introduced by legislation governing the operation of the railways.

double entry. An almost universally used system of financial record keeping. The basic principle of double entry is that every financial transaction is seen as a flow of value from one account to another. The receiving account is debited with the amount and the giving account is credited. An important advantage of double entry is the degree of control which it gives over the accuracy of the records. Because every figure is recorded both on the debit and on the credit side it is possible to extract from time to time a TRIAL BALANCE (q.v.). A failure to balance in this is indicative of an error somewhere in the system.

double taxation relief. Relief given so that a taxpayer is not taxed twice under two separate jurisdictions. Where a UK citizen receives income from property held abroad, this income may already have suffered tax by deduction in its country of origin. Provided that the UK has a double taxation treaty (giving reciprocity) with that country, the taxpayer will receive credit for the overseas tax paid when the UK liability is determined.

doubtful debt. A debt where circumstances have rendered its ultimate recovery uncertain. CONSERVATISM (q.v.) requires that doubtful debts should be treated in the same way as BAD DEBTS (q.v.). They should thus be recorded as an expense in the profit and loss account and be credited to a PROVISION (q.v.) to set off against ultimate default if it occurs. Circumstances which might make a debt appear doubtful are age, knowledge that the debtor is in financial difficulty or a dispute with the debtor over the amount actually owed.

Dow Jones index. An index of share prices calculated for the US Stock Exchange. The index derives its name from those associated with its inauguration. The UK equivalent of the Dow Jones index is the FINANCIAL TIMES STOCK EXCHANGE INDEX (q.v.).

down market. A term describing that part of a market dealing with low price and, often, low quality goods or services.

down payment. A first payment made to secure some article which is to be the subject of a HIRE PURCHASE (q.v.) agreement. Following the down payment there will be an agreed number of further payments to be made over a period of time before ownership in the article passes to the buyer.

dowry. A sum of money given to the husband of a newly married woman by her father. A dowry is rarely paid nowadays in the UK but it was at one time a common practice as a daughter was considered to be a financial burden and it was, therefore, appropriate to make a payment when relieved of this.

dr. Abbreviation for DEBIT (q.v.).

draft. A document requiring one party to make a payment to another from funds which are held by the former.

drawee. A person in whose favour a cheque is made out by some other person, the drawer.

drawer. The person who writes out a cheque in favour of some other person, the drawee.

drawings. Amounts taken from an unincorporated business by its proprietor(s). Drawings thus appear in the accounts of sole traders and partnerships. Drawings are normally made out of profits although they may also be made in the absence of profit.

DTI. Letters standing for DEPARTMENT OF TRADE AND INDUSTRY (q.v.).

duality. That characteristic of accounting transactions which is embodied in DOUBLE ENTRY (q.v.). The duality of a transaction arises from the fact that it is a flow of value from a source to a destination.

dual residence. The state of having RESIDENCE (q.v.) in two places. It has implications for taxation.

due. Payable immediately. A debt which is due has reached the end of the agreed period of credit.

dues. Regular subscription paid for membership of some organisation, e.g a trade union.

dumping. Selling goods in a market, usually overseas, at a price well below cost. The intention is to ruin the indigenous competition and subseqently to benefit from a market freed of that competition.

Dun and Bradstreet. An organisation, based in the USA, which provides information about publicly quoted companies. This is a service chiefly of value to investors through the Stock Exchange.

Du Pont system. A method of analysing financial accounts so as to assess the underlying health of the business. It involves the calculation of certain ratios and their combination in a particular way which, it is claimed, produces a useful single figure measure of performance.

dutch auction. A form of AUCTION (q.v.) in which the price stated at the opening is progressively lowered until a bid is received and a sale concluded. In a conventional auction the bid is progressively raised until all but one buyer have been eliminated.

duty. A form of taxation. Tax, the payment of which is evidenced by affixing or embossing a stamp, is known as stamp duty. Tax on goods entering a country is known as customs duty. Tax on certain goods made in the country is known as excise duty. Some transactions in property are the subject of stamp duty. Alcoholic drinks and tobacco bear excise duty.

duty-free. Not subject to a charge for customs or excise duty. It is usual for duty-free goods to be available to travellers from one country to another. There are, however, limits on the amounts which may be purchased.

E

early leavers. Persons leaving a pension scheme before the normal age for retirement. The usual reason for this is that they have moved to a job with another company. The question arises as to whether their contributions should be repaid to them or whether the benefits of the scheme can be held until they are able to realise them in the form of a pension at retirement. This depends on the rules of the pensions scheme and on the choice of the member.

earned income. Income which arises from some personal remunerative effort. Thus a salary a person receives from an occupation is earned income but interest received from an investment is not. The category is important from a tax point of view because in some circumstances earned income is taxed more lightly than unearned income. Royalties from authorship, even though the book was written many years before, and occupational pensions are classified as earned income.

earned income relief. A tax relief which was, at one time, given against earned, as opposed to unearned, income. This meant that earned income was more lightly taxed.

earnings. The after-tax profits of a company attributable to its ordinary shareholders. It is authoritatively defined in FRS 3 as 'the consolidated profit of the year after tax, minority interests and extraordinary items, and after deducting preference dividends'.

earnings per share. A company's net profit attributable to ordinary shareholders divided by the number of shares in issue. Earnings per share is an important statistic and its inclusion in a company's annual report was made obligatory by SSAP 3. This was first issued in February 1972 and revised in August 1974. It was amended again by FRS 3. Earnings per share is a measure of overall corporate performance.

earnings rule. The rule in the calculation of state retirement pensions the application of which has the effect of reducing pension payments by an amount dependent on any earnings from employment after retirement age.

earnings yield. The EARNINGS PER SHARE (q.v.) of a company expressed as a percentage of its current share price. It thus represents to the investor the amount that is being earned on his or her behalf as a yield on the investment currently embodied in the shares.

earn out. A situation which arises when the consideration for the sale of a business depends wholly or in part on the earnings of the business during the few years following the sale. It is an appropriate form of sale to use where the success of the business depends on the continued involvement of the vendors because of their special knowledge, experience or expertise. It is in the purchaser's interest that this commitment should be wholehearted and this is ensured by the fact that the vendors share in any success they create.

economic income. A concept of business profit, largely of theoretical interest, which relies on asset valuations based on the discounted value of their prospective cash flows. Practical application of the concept is difficult because it requires predictions about the future. A characteristic of economic income is that it incorporates both realised and unrealised elements.

economic indicator. Some national statistic which may be regarded as indicative of the health of the nation's economy. Figures for unemployment, level of retail sales and the value of imports and exports are examples of economic indicators.

economic life. The length of time over which an asset may profitably be used. The physical life of an asset may be considerably longer than its economic life. When the cost of operating an asset rises (because of inefficiency or increased frequency of repairs) above the revenue which it generates it has exceeded its economic life and should not be kept in use.

economic order quantity. That size of regular order for stocks which minimises the total cost of ordering and stocking. There are costs involved in the placing and processing of an order for fresh supplies which will be higher per unit for more frequent small orders than infrequent large ones. Conversely, however, high stocks will cost more to maintain in terms of storage and the risk of deterioration or loss, which will encourage small orders. A balance must be struck at the economic order quantity (often abbreviated to EOQ) between these conflicting pressures. A formula is generally used to determine EOQ. It is:

$$EOQ = \frac{\sqrt{2BN}}{C}$$

Where N is the number of units of stock used in a year
C is the cost per unit per annum of holding stock
B is the cost of processing an order

economic value. The value of an asset computed by discounting its prospective future generation of cash. The economic value of an asset is thus equivalent to its PRESENT VALUE (q.v.). The concept of economic value has not enjoyed much practical attention because of the need, difficult to fulfil, to predict future cash flows. It is, however, one of the quantities to be taken into account in determining VALUE TO THE BUSINESS (q.v.).

economies of scale. The phenomenon, observed in some industries, that large-scale production has a lower unit cost than small-scale production. The potential for economies of scale is often the motive for MERGERS (q.v.).

ECU. Letters standing for European Currency Unit. Sometimes used as a noun, and written ecu, the unit has a value made up of a weighted average of the values of the individual currencies of the member states of the European Community. There is a longer-term proposal that the ecu should replace national currencies as a medium of exchange but it is now an international unit of account.

ED. Letters standing for EXPOSURE DRAFT (q.v.). Each of the Accounting Standards issued up to 1990 under the auspices of the Accounting Standards Committee was preceded by an exposure draft. Its present equivalent, issued by the Accounting Standards Board, is the FINANCIAL REPORTING EXPOSURE DRAFT (FRED) (q.v.).

EDITH. Letters standing for ESTATE DUTIES INVESTMENT TRUST (q.v.).

ED18. An exposure draft on current cost accounting issued in November 1976 as the response of the accountancy profession to the ideas expressed by the SANDILANDS COMMITTEE (q.v.). It was a long and complex document and led to considerable controversy. It was eventually withdrawn following a resolution of a special meeting of the members of the Institute of Chartered Accountants in England and Wales.

EDP. Letters standing for electronic data processing, i.e. the practice of using compu-ters for the storage, retrieval and classification of information.

effective date. The concept of effective date may be an important one. It is the date which is deemed to apply to a particular transaction and is particularly significant where more than one date might appear logically to apply. For example, where one company acquires another by an offer for its shares it will be important for accounting purposes to establish the effective date of the subsequent amalgamation. This might conceivably be (a) the date the offer was made, (b) the date on which it was accepted, or (c) the date on which the payment for the shares occurred. Under SSAP 23 the effective date here would be the earlier of the date on which the offer became unconditional (because sufficient number have accepted it) or the date on which the consideration (i.e. pay-ment) passes.

efficiency. The ratio between a desired output and the necessary input. Measures of the efficiency of various aspects of business operations are numerous and command considerable attention. Maximum profit can be earned only by the highest efficiency of operations.

efficiency audit. An examination of activity and the records associated with it with the intention of forming a judgement on the efficiency with which the activity is carried out. An efficiency audit will usually lead to recommendations as to how efficiency might be improved.

efficiency variance. A VARIANCE (q.v.) arising when the level of efficiency of operations is either greater or less than that envisaged in the BUDGET (q.v.). An efficiency variance may be encountered in connection with LABOUR (q.v.) costs or VARIABLE OVERHEADS (q.v.).

EXAMPLE. A certain product is planned to require 3 labour hours at a cost of £10 per hour. Its standard labour cost is thus £30 per unit. In a certain period 100 units of pro-duct were completed and the number of labour hours expended was 320 at a total cost of £3,200. Labour has worked longer than planned for this level of production by 20 hours and this is a measure of the shortfall of efficiency. There is an adverse efficiency variance of £200 (i.e. 20 hours × £10).

efficient market. A market in which prices respond immediately to available informa-tion. There is considerable evidence that the STOCK EXCHANGE (q.v.) acts as an efficient market. This carries the implication, important to FUNDAMENTAL ANALYSIS (q.v.), that in-vestors cannot, by careful study of company accounts, buy shares at advantageous prices. This is because the price would already have moved to take into account the in-formation before the investors could assimilate it and act.

efficient market theory. The theory that the stock market is an EFFICIENT MARKET (q.v.). There is considerable empirical evidence in support of the theory which carries the im-plication that knowledge about individual companies will not allow an investor consist-ently to make above average returns from stock market activities. There are three forms of the efficient market theory. These are:

(1) the 'weak' form which states that the market responds only to information arising within itself, i.e. past prices and their trends but not to information from outside, i.e. company reports;

(2) the 'semi-strong' form which states that the market responds fully to all publicly available information; and

(3) the 'strong form' which considers that the market responds to all information, even that which is known only by insiders.

efficient portfolio. A PORTFOLIO (q.v.) of investments, which, for a given level of risk, maximises the rate of return or, for a given return, minimises the risk. It is a concept used in PORTFOLIO THEORY (q.v.). Any portfolio actually selected by an investor must logically satisfy the criteria for an efficient portfolio. If this were not the case the investor could achieve a better combination of risk and return and ought to do so.

elastic demand. A condition of the demand for a product such that it is very responsive to changes in price. An increase in the price of a product in elastic demand will reduce the total revenue from sales.

elastic supply. A condition of the supply of a product such that an increase in the market price will bring forth a more than commensurate increase in the amount of the available supply.

election. A choice between alternatives. A shareholder, for example, may be given the opportunity to make an election to receive a dividend in the form of new shares rather than cash.

electronic transfer of funds. The movement of money effected not by physical means but by means of information sent electronically. An account could, for example, be debited in the computer records of one bank and the information sent by telephone line to the computer of another bank where a different account could be credited.

elimination. Removal of information from a set of accounts usually because of the existence of offsetting balances. An example is the elimination of intercompany balances in a consolidated balance sheet where one company in a group owes money to another. The items in question would appear as creditors and debtors respectively in the company's own balance sheets but would disappear in the consolidation into the group balance sheet.

embezzlement. The crime committed by an employee who cheats his or her employer of money. It is no longer recognised as being a different crime from theft.

emergency code. An income tax code number issued by an Inspector of Taxes to an employer for PAYE purposes for an employee whose tax allowances have not yet been determined. Such a code would give effect to the personal allowance for a single person but to no other allowance. It would be operated until the proper code could be issued.

emoluments. Remuneration received in connection with the holding of some office. The term is frequently used concerning payments to the DIRECTORS (q.v.) of a company. It is a requirement of the law that information in respect of directors' remuneration should be disclosed in the company's annual report.

employee. A person who has entered into a contract to work for another person or for a company. The status of employee confers certain rights, for example with respect to working conditions and security of employment, and carries certain obligations, for example to serve the employer faithfully.

employee reporting. Reporting financial and other information to employees. A company's legal obligation is to report to shareholders but it may also report to its employees voluntarily. Ideally the information given to employees should be especially relevant to their needs and enable them to make judgements concerning the security and prospects of their employment.

employee share ownership scheme. A scheme operated by a company whereby its employees can acquire shares in the company for which they work. These may be issued free of charge in proportion to salary and length of service or they may be purchased by the employee at a favourable price.

employer. One who has entered into a contract with another person whereby work is provided on a regular basis and is paid for in the form of an agreed wage or salary. An employer has responsibilities towards his or her employees, e.g. in the matter of their health and safety whilst at work. It is also the employer's responsibility to administer the employee's national insurance and income tax payments.

employers' association. An association to which an EMPLOYER (q.v.) may belong. It deals with matters affecting the relationship between employers and their workforce. It is the counterpart of the TRADE UNION (q.v.) to which the employees may belong. It is authoritatively defined in the Trade Union and Labour Relations Act 1974.

employment report. A report, issued with the annual accounts of a company, giving details of its record as an employer during the period under review. It is not currently compulsory for a company to produce this report but it was strongly advocated in 'CORPORATE REPORT' (q.v.). It was there suggested that it should include, amongst other things, statistics on numbers employed, age distribution of workforce, hours worked and information on education and training.

EMS. Letters standing for EUROPEAN MONETARY SYSTEM (q.v.).

encashment. The process of exchanging a CHEQUE (q.v.) or POSTAL ORDER (q.v.) for cash.

encumbrance. Some liability which attaches to a property and thus imposes a burden on its owner. The obligation to pay GROUND RENT (q.v.) on a leasehold property is an example of an encumbrance.

endorsement. A form of words written on the back of a legal document whose effect is to vary the terms of the document. Endorsements are commonly used on cheques. Such an endorsement will have the effect of making the cheque payable to bearer if the endorsement consists simply of the signature of the payee, or payable to a specified third person if that person's name is included. The drawer of a cheque can prevent effective endorsement by means of a special CROSSING (q.v.). An endorsement on an insurance policy, which must be made by the company issuing the policy and not by the policy holder, will have the effect of curtailing or extending the cover otherwise given under the policy.

endowment method. A method of providing for DEPRECIATION (q.v.) whereby an annual instalment is invested in an endowment policy (q.v.) which will mature at the time the asset falls due to be replaced. Although described in some textbooks this method is virtually never used in practice.

endowment policy. A form of life assurance policy under which the sum assured is paid either on death or on survival until a specified date. Endowment policies usually run for a maximum of between 20 and 30 years. They are a useful way of saving for a specified purpose such as retirement or the payment of school fees. A policy may be described as a 'with profits' policy. In that case the original sum assured is enhanced periodically by bonuses declared out of profits made by the issuing company. Until 1984 a measure of tax relief was given against premiums paid on any policy of life assurance on the life of a taxpayer or his or her spouse. This made the endowment policy a particularly attractive form of saving. Although that relief has now disappeared for new policies, the proceeds of the policy when it matures are still tax-free in the hands of the beneficiary.

engagement letter. A letter addressed by an accountant to his or her client setting out the exact terms of the agreement between them at the time the services of the accountant are first engaged. Its significance is that it will define clearly the scope of the work undertaken and thus protect the accountant from any subsequent charge of NEGLIGENCE (q.v.) if work outside that scope is not undertaken but should, in the opinion of the client, have been undertaken.

enterprise. An organisation undertaking an activity which involves risk and promises a reward commensurate with that risk.

enterprise zone. An area designated by the government as being one where it wishes to encourage new business to establish itself. The reason is usually that the area is one of high unemployment, perhaps because older industries there are declining. Positive financial inducements are available to persuade business people to operate in enterprise zones.

entertainment expenses. Amounts paid by a business in providing food, drink and hospitality to its customers and others. Its significance is that such amounts are not an allowable expense in determining the liability of the business to corporation tax (or, if not incorporated, income tax).

entertainment tax. A tax which used to be levied on the sales of tickets to theatrical performances and entertainments of a similar kind. Although entertainment tax has now been abolished VALUE ADDED TAX (q.v.) is levied on such ticket sales.

entitlement. A right to some benefit often, but not necessarily, monetary. A creditor, for example, is entitled to receive payment. A shareholder is entitled to receive a copy of the company's annual report.

entitlement to commence business. The right, given by means of a certificate issued by the Registrar of Companies, for a public company to commence business. The entitlement will not be granted until the company has complied with legal formalities and has raised a minimum amount of capital. A private company does not require this certificate and is entitled to commence business as soon as it has been issued with its CERTIFICATE OF INCORPORATION (q.v.).

entity concept. A concept of accounting which sees a business as an entity in its own right separate from its managers or its proprietors. The accounting concept sometimes coincides with legal fact. This is true in the case of a limited company which is a separate legal person from its shareholders. In the case of a sole trader, however, the legal entity is the proprietor and the business is merely one of his or her activities.

entrepreneur. A person operating an ENTERPRISE (q.v.).

entry. An amount recorded in the financial records of a business.

entry value. The value at which an asset would enter the business, i.e. its replacement cost.

EPOS. Letters standing for electronic point of sale. It refers to the system whereby a customer in a shop can pay for goods by having a CREDIT CARD (q.v.) or DEBIT CARD (q.v.) 'swiped' through a machine which communicates directly to their charge or bank account.

EPS. Letters standing for EARNINGS PER SHARE (q.v.).

equal pay. The principle that men and women doing identical work should be paid identically. Although this is now enshrined in the law, until comparatively recently it was common for female workers to be paid less than men merely on account of their gender.

equitable apportionment. An apportionment of income received by a trust between the beneficiary entitled to income and the one entitled to capital according to principles laid down in EQUITY (q.v.) law.

D

equity. 1. A branch of law based on the principle of justice even where this is in conflict with the strict application of the letter of the law.

2. The risk capital of a business. In the case of a company it is made up of share capital and reserves.

equity accounting. The method of accounting for an ASSOCIATED COMPANY (q.v.) required by SSAP 1. The main feature of the method is that the investment in the subsidiary is recorded in the balance sheet of the holding company at a valuation which takes into account the profits or losses accrued by it and attributable to the holding company since the acquisition of the investment.

equity linked. Having a value depending on the level of the stock market. Some policies of LIFE ASSURANCE (q.v.) are equity linked so that the amount realised when the policy matures depends on the level reached by share prices at that time.

equity of redemption. A principle of law which gives one who has a MORTGAGE (q.v.) against a property the right to redeem this by paying all sums owed to the creditor secured by the mortgage.

ERM. Letters standing for EXCHANGE RATE MECHANISM (q.v.).

error or mistake. An error in calculation or mistake of fact which leads to an incorrect assessment to income tax. If such an error or mistake is discovered within 6 years of the end of the tax year to which it applies, an amendment can be made whether this is to the advantage of the taxpayer or not. Where this would bear harshly on a low-income taxpayer who had acted honestly and where the error was made by the Inland Revenue there may be some remission of the amount due. In the absence of fraud, tax matters cannot be reopened after the expiration of 6 years.

escalation clause. A clause contained in a contract, usually for major construction work, which permits the overall price payable to be increased above that originally agreed to allow for the increased costs of labour and material. Because inflation makes it very difficult to predict the level of cost throughout the duration of construction, escalation clauses are quite common.

escrow. A legal document held in abeyance until some conditions have been satisfied or some time period has elapsed.

estate. The term used to describe the totality of the assets left by a deceased person.

estate agent. One who acts professionally in the negotiations of sales and purchases of property. An estate agent is normally engaged by the seller of the property and therefore acts in the interests of the seller. The agent is responsible for advertising and such other activity as is necessary to locate a suitable buyer and for advising on an appropriate price. The agent's income is derived from COMMISSION (q.v.) charged to sellers, based on the value of the property sold. An estate agent, by virtue of the experience gained in dealing with properties, may be called upon to provide a professional valuation of a property for balance sheet purposes even where no sale is contemplated. Estate agents often hold money on behalf of clients (e.g. deposits paid by the purchasers of a property). Under the Estate Agents (Accounts) Regulations 1981 this money is required to be held in a special clients' bank account. The AUDIT (q.v.) of an estate agent's accounts must verify that this has been properly done and that adequate records have been kept.

Estate Duties Investment Trust. An investment trust formed by a consortium of banks to take an equity interest in businesses which might otherwise be required to close in order to settle the duties payable on the death of the owner.

estate duty. A tax on wealth left by a deceased person. It was abolished in 1975 and replaced by a more comprehensive CAPITAL TRANSFER TAX (q.v.) now replaced by INHERITANCE TAX (q.v.).

estimate. 1. A forecast of the total cost of specified work given before the work is undertaken by the person who may be called upon to undertake it. Thus one might obtain an estimate from a builder before asking for an extension to a property. Although the purpose of an estimate is to give some idea of the obligation which may be incurred, the party giving the estimate is bound only to take reasonable care in preparing it. He or she cannot be held to it in the event that unforeseen circumstances cause the cost to be higher than expected. It should be contrasted with a QUOTATION (q.v.).
2. A judgement of the value of a quantity which cannot accurately be determined. Many estimates are used in accounting. DEPRECIATION (q.v.), for example, depends on an estimate of the useful life of the asset. Some ACCRUALS (q.v.) or PREPAYMENTS (q.v.) may have to be based on estimates. Estimates are frequently used as a basis for figures in a BUDGET (q.v.).

ETF. Letters standing for ELECTRONIC TRANSFER OF FUNDS (q.v.).

ethical investment. Investment which has regard to the morality of the activity carried out by the companies which are the subject of the investment. An ethical investment policy may, for example, decline to invest in companies whose activities were damaging the environment or who carried out a discriminatory employment policy. Some UNIT TRUSTS (q.v.) and INVESTMENT TRUSTS (q.v.) have been set up with the object of conducting only ethical investment.

Eurocheque. A special form of cheque issued by a bank to its customers on request which permits the account holder to draw cheques in European currencies. There is a charge for this service.

Eurodollars. Funds in USA currency held in accounts in Europe.

European currency unit. An artificial currency unit having a value determined by the weighted average of the values of the currencies of members of the European Community. Some expect that it will eventually form the day-to-day medium of exchange for transactions within Europe and that national currencies will be abolished.

European Economic Community. A group of European countries committed to economic co-operation. It was established by the Treaty of Rome in 1957. Britain became a member in 1972. A considerable amount of legislation affecting accountants is enacted in the interests of European harmonisation. This includes many of the accounting requirements of the Companies Acts 1985–9.

European Monetary System. A mechanism established by treaty amongst the members of the European Community whereby the fluctuations of exchange rates between European currencies is held within narrow bands. Realignment (i.e. revaluation) is possible in extreme cases but normally a government is expected to take appropriate action (e.g. active market intervention or variation in rates of interest) to hold its currency within the agreed band.

evaluation. The action of placing a value on some asset or project. The use of the term would normally imply that no value had previously been ascribed to the asset or project.

evasion of tax. *See* TAX EVASION.

ex ante. Looked at from before the event. A profit calculated *ex ante* would be one calculated on the basis of the facts known or projected at the beginning of the financial period to which it relates. It is a largely theoretical idea as in real life profits are generally determined *EX POST* (q.v.).

ex cap. Without capitalisation rights. This term is attached to the price of a share quoted on the Stock Exchange to signify that a buyer will acquire the shares without the benefit of a recent rights or bonus issue.

exceptional item. An item in the annual accounts of a company which, whilst lying within the ordinary scope of the business of the company, is exceptional by virtue of its size. Where it has made a MATERIAL (q.v.) difference to the level of profit which would otherwise have been reported it should be disclosed. An exceptional item should be distinguished from an EXTRAORDINARY ITEM (q.v.). Both terms are defined in FRS 3.

excess. The amount which an insured person will have to pay out of his or her own resources in the event of a claim under the policy. It will be deducted from the total amount of the loss in determining the amount paid by the insurer. An excess may be voluntary, i.e. accepted by the insured person in return for a reduced premium, or imposed as a condition of the policy. Its purpose is to reduce the number of very small claims, which are administratively expensive to process, and also to give the insured person an incentive for minimising the risks covered by the policy.

excess profits tax. A tax that was levied in the UK during the World Wars, which sought to tax most heavily profits which could be deemed to arise due to the special circumstances of wartime conditions. Excess profits were determined by what had been established as normal profit during peacetime.

exchange control. Restrictions imposed by government on transfers of money into or out of the country. Exchange controls in the UK have now been abolished but at one time they limited the amount of money which a person going on holiday abroad could take and imposed restrictions on the purchase of goods from overseas.

exchange rate. The rate at which one currency can be exchanged for another. This is governed by the market in the currencies and will fluctuate over time, sometimes quite widely. A government may influence the rate at which the domestic currency is exchanged for other currencies by entering the market itself to buy or sell its own currency. Such action, however, is used to meet short-term crises as it would be ruinously expensive to operate it over a long period. The exchange rate and its fluctuations may be a critical matter for businesses which either import raw material or export their finished product so that the settlement of accounts requires either the purchase or sale of foreign currency. Such a business may protect itself from the risk which this creates by HEDGING (q.v.).

Exchange Rate Mechanism. That process which limits fluctuations in exchange rates between European currencies to movements within a narrow band. The participating governments are committed to taking action, by intervening in the currency market or by domestic economic policy, to prevent fluctuations outside the agreed range.

exchequer. The finances of the government. Thus a reduction of taxation is said to bring a loss to the exchequer.

excise duties. Duties on goods produced inside the country imposing the duty. Taxes on beers brewed or spirits distilled in the UK are examples of excise duties.

ex div. A note attached to the quotation of the price of a share indicating that it is purchased without the right to receive a recent dividend. This right remains with the seller. When shares change hands at about the date of the payment of a dividend the question may arise as to whether it is the buyer or the seller who is entitled to the dividend. In order to avoid this a date is determined on which the share goes *ex div*. *See also* CUM. DIV.

execution only. A cut-price service offered by some stockbrokers whereby they will carry out instructions to buy and sell shares but will not offer any investment advice.

executor. One who is appointed under the terms of a WILL (q.v.) to carry out its directions. An executor becomes legally the owner of all the property of the deceased but must deal with it and dispose of it as directed by the will. An executor may benefit under a will if the TESTATOR (q.v.) so directs but may not be a WITNESS (q.v.) to the signing of the will.

executrix. The feminine equivalent of EXECUTOR (q.v.).

exemplary damages. Damages (q.v.) of such an amount that they exceed that required to compensate the plaintiff for loss and contain an element of punishment for the defendant. Their award is comparatively rare.

exemption. A relief from a rule which generally applies. Thus persons on a very low income are given an exemption from taxation. A main private residence carries the benefit of an exemption from capital gains tax if it is sold.

exempt private company. A type of company which was given statutory exemption from the need to file an ANNUAL RETURN (q.v.) with the REGISTRAR OF COMPANIES (q.v.). The category was abolished by the Companies Act 1967.

exempt supply. Goods or services supplied which are exempt from VALUE ADDED TAX (q.v.). Examples are insurance, education and postal services.

ex gratia. Some action, normally the payment of money, taken where there is no legal necessity to do so but where some moral obligation is recognised. An insurance company, for example, might indemnify a policyholder from a loss which lies outside a very strict interpretation of the policy because the company prefers not to be seen to avoid liability on a technicality. Such an indemnity might then be described as being an *ex gratia* payment. It may be necessary to stress the *ex gratia* nature of any payment to preclude the payment from being interpreted as an admission of liability. In that case it might be considered inadequate and an attempt to enforce a higher payment be sought through the court.

existing use. A basis of valuation which supposes that the asset concerned will continue to be used in the same way in the future as it is currently. This may not always be the most appropriate basis of valuation. If, for example, existing farmland is likely to become available for development its valuation as agricultural land may seriously understate its true value.

exit value. A value placed on an asset by reference to what could be obtained if it were realised. Realisation might be by immediate sale or by its progressive use in a revenue creating activity.

expected value. The anticipated average value of future cash flows taking into account their probability of occurrence.

EXAMPLE. A certain activity is predicted to produce a cash flow of uncertain value in one year's time. Possible values and their probabilities of occurrence are as shown in the first two columns of the table below:

Value	Probability	Value × probability
£		£
1,000	0.3	300
2,000	0.5	1,000
3,000	0.2	600
		1,900

The third column shows the calculation of the expected value of the cash flow, which is £1,900. Expected values might be calculated for a number of years into the future in connection with a calculation of expected NET PRESENT VALUE (q.v.).

expenditure. Amount of cash disbursement. Expenditure may be categorised as revenue expenditure or capital expenditure. Revenue expenditure is that incurred in current activities to purchase goods and services which are consumed immediately. It is written off as incurred in the profit and loss account. Capital expenditure is that incurred in purchasing assets which give a benefit extending over a number of accounting periods. Such expenditure is normally subject to a charge for DEPRECIATION (q.v.) or AMORTISATION (q.v.).

expenditure tax. A form of taxation sometimes advocated but never put into practice in the UK in which people are taxed on the basis of what they spend rather than what they earn. It is thus an alternative form of tax to INCOME TAX (q.v.). One argument for expenditure tax is that taxation should be charged according to a person's ability to pay. Expenditure reflects better the taxpayer's own idea of ability to pay than does income. A practical objection to an expenditure tax is that it would be very difficult to assess and administer. In particular, a changeover from income tax to expenditure tax would cause considerable disruption.

expenditure variance. A VARIANCE (q.v.) arising when the total expenditure on OVERHEAD (q.v.) is different from that envisaged in the BUDGET (q.v.). It is thus a reflection of the variation in the prices of items making up the total of overhead.

EXAMPLE. In a budget the planned level of fixed overhead expenditure was £250,000. Although the items making up the budget were all as anticipated, the amounts payable in respect of them totalled only £240,000. There has thus been a favourable expenditure variance of £10,000.

expense. A value which has expired during the current accounting period. An expense may be represented by a cash payment, such as wages. Alternatively it may be calculated as a portion of the value of a fixed asset, i.e. DEPRECIATION (q.v.), or as an amount written off a current asset, e.g. BAD DEBTS (q.v.). An expense will be charged in the profit and loss account.

experience deficit. That part of the deficit recognised by a pension fund on an actuarial valuation which occurs because events have differed from the expectations which formed the basis of the previous actuarial valuation.

experience surplus. That part of the surplus recognised by a pension fund on an actuarial valuation which occurs because events have differed from the expectations which formed the basis of the previous actuarial valuation.

exploration cost. Cost incurred in exploration which had the hope of leading to exploitable deposits of oil or minerals. The accounting significance of such cost is that it will be recovered through production if successful but will be completely lost if not. Prudent accounting treatment will be to write it off to the profit and loss account in the period in which it is incurred.

export credit guarantee. A form of insurance against loss occasioned by the default of overseas debtors. It is offered, against the payment of a premium, by a government department set up for the purpose. Its object is to encourage overseas businesss by minimising one of the risks of engaging in it.

ex post. Looked at from after the event. A profit calculated *ex post* would be one calculated on the basis of the facts known or projected at the end of the financial period to which it relates. This is the normal manner of calculating profit in practice but the term *ex post* is most often used in academic discussion on methods of measuring profit. The alternative point of view is EX ANTE (q.v.).

exposure draft. A document issued for comment before its contents are finalised. The term is commonly applied to the exposure drafts issued by the ACCOUNTING STANDARDS COMMITTEE (q.v.) or ACCOUNTING STANDARDS BOARD (q.v.). These are draft Accounting Standards.

ex rights. Designation attached to the price of a quoted security indicating that the price is for the shares without the right to participate in a recent RIGHTS ISSUE (q.v.) which remain with the seller.

EXTEL. Abbreviation for Exchange Telegraph Company, an organisation which supplies financial and commercial information.

extended credit. Credit for goods supplied granted on terms which allow a longer period of credit than is usual. Extended credit may be payable by instalments with or without interest, Typically, it will be for a period not exceeding 1 year. Extended credit is often offered to the purchasers of consumable durable goods such as furniture and household appliances.

external funds. Funds raised by a business from persons outside the business, i.e. shareholders or lenders. Internal funds would be obtained by a retention of profits.

externalities. Costs and benefits arising from business activities which are not directly felt by the business itself. Pollution caused by some manufacturing process imposes a cost on the community at large which is not met by the manufacturer causing the pollution. Improved employment given by the setting up of a business in an area confers benefits on traders with whom the new incomes are spent. Externalities are not conventionally taken into account in determining the overall result of business activities. A particular branch of accounting theory, known as SOCIAL RESPONSIBILITY ACCOUNTING (q.v.) would support the idea that they should be considered.

extraordinary items. Items appearing in a profit and loss account which arise from abnormal or unusual events lying outside the ordinary range of the business's activities and which are not expected to recur. They were the subject of SSAP 6 (first issued in 1974) which required them to be shown separately. This standard has now been superseded by FRS 3 which amends the format of the profit and loss account but maintains the special category of extraordinary item. Under the standard, extraordinary items should be shown separately in the profit and loss account after the profit or loss on ordinary activities. The tax attributable to them should also be shown separately and there should be an adequate explanation of the nature of the items.

extra-statutory concession. A concession of some kind offered by the Inland Revenue to taxpayers which is justified by equity or administrative convenience but which does not have any explicit statutory force.

extrinsic. Determined by outside factors. Assets have an extrinsic (as opposed to INTRINSIC (q.v.)) value in that it is determined by the state of a market which lies outside any inherent characteristics the asset might itself possess.

ex works. At the point of leaving the factory. If production is valued on an ex works basis it means that its value excludes any additional cost required to put it into a saleable condition or position, e.g. subsequent transport costs.

F

face value. A value evident from an examination of the object itself. Currency has a face value, as do stamps and postal orders.

factor. One who sells goods in order to make a profit. *See also* DEBT FACTOR.

factory cost. The total cost of manufacturing a product not including the subsequent costs of selling and distributing it. Factory cost is the main figure emerging from the MANUFACTURING ACCOUNT (q.v.).

factory overhead. An OVERHEAD (q.v.) which specifically relates to the operation of a factory. Total overhead would also include administrative overhead. The accounting significance of factory overhead is that it is included in the MANUFACTURING ACCOUNT (q.v.) and is a component of the manufacturing cost of the product. Examples of items which might form part of factory overhead are factory rent and rates, heating and lighting, depreciation of machinery, labour supervisory wages and maintenance costs.

fair value. The value of an asset which would be established by an ARM'S LENGTH (q.v.) transaction in an open market.

EXAMPLE. X sells to his son some shares in a company for £1,000. Their value to the son at cost is, therefore, £1,000. Had they been bought on the Stock Exchange the shares would have cost £1,500. The fair value is, therefore, £1,500.

Where a company acquires an asset which it pays for by an issue of its own shares rather than by cash, the asset should be brought into the balance sheet at its fair value which is not necessarily the NOMINAL VALUE (q.v.) of the shares issued. Where fair value exceeds the nominal value of the shares this would necessitate a transfer to the SHARE PREMIUM ACCOUNT (q.v.).

false accounting. The process of preparing accounts which are known to be misleading and untrue for dishonest purposes.

false market. A market which is not at a level determined by the genuine interplay of supply and demand. A false market is either made so deliberately or it is caused by special circumstances. For example, the price of shares could be depressed by selling enough to start unfounded rumours. A false market could be created if news emerges that a company is affected by fraud but there is no information as to its type or extent.

falsification. The process of making deliberately incorrect entries in the BOOKS OF ACCOUNT (q.v.). The purpose of falsification is either to conceal that a fraud has taken place or to present figures which show an unfairly optimistic or pessimistic view of the business's operations. A person might, for example, falsify accounts in order to reduce the liability to tax. Another might falsify them to make a business look more attractive to a potential buyer.

family income supplement. A social security benefit given to families on very low incomes.

fare. An amount charged for the provision of passenger transport, e.g. on buses, trains, ferries, etc.

farm accounts. Accounts giving the results of farming activities. They are of interest because of the special problems concerned with the valuation of marketable produce, growing crops and livestock. Marketable produce may be valued at its realisable value rather than cost so that the profit on it is included in the accounts for the year in which it is produced. This is justified by the certainty attaching to many market selling prices. Livestock may be valued on the HERD BASIS (q.v.) which allows for developing value as animals mature and new ones are born.

farthing. A coin representing an amount of one-quarter of a pre-1971 penny. It was demonetised in 1960.

FASB. Letters standing for FINANCIAL ACCOUNTING STANDARDS BOARD (q.v.).

favourable variance. A cost or revenue variation of actual from budget or standard which has the effect that the profit is better than that planned. Thus the purchase of materials at a price below the standard price will lead to a favourable variance as will the more efficient use of labour than expected.

FCA. The designatory letters of a fellow of the INSTITUTE OF CHARTERED ACCOUNTANTS IN ENGLAND AND WALES (q.v.).

FCCA. The designatory letters of a fellow of the CHARTERED ASSOCIATION OF CERTIFIED ACCOUNTANTS (q.v.).

FCMA. The designatory letters of a fellow of the CHARTERED INSTITUTE OF MANAGEMENT ACCOUNTANTS (q.v.).

feasibility criterion. A criterion which all accounting techniques must meet if they are to have practical application. However desirable a particular type or form of accounting information may be, it may not be feasible to provide it and, in that case, it will not be provided. Provision of the information may be unfeasible on grounds of impossibility, high cost or the time taken to obtain it.

federal reserve bank. A bank in the USA which acts as central bank for the area in which it is situated. There is a network of federal reserve banks which act broadly together to fulfil the central banking function for the whole country.

fee. An amount charged for the provision of a professional service. An accountant will charge a fee for advising a client on financial matters. A solicitor charges a fee for giving legal advice.

fictitious asset. A debit balance representing past expenditure not giving rise to any real asset. The term is applied to such items as PRELIMINARY EXPENSES (q.v.) or discounts on the issue of debentures. Thus a fictitious asset arises from a genuine transaction and is not, therefore, wholly a fiction. At one time it was the practice to write off fictitious assets as and when convenient. Under recent legislation (Companies Act 1985) it is no longer legal for a company to carry a fictitious asset in its balance sheet.

fidelity insurance. An insurance which may be taken out by an employer in order to protect the business from the wrongdoing of an employee.

fiduciary. Imposing the obligations of a trust. An accountant stands in a fiduciary relationship to a client who trusts him or her to handle the client's affairs competently and confidentially. A fiduciary relationship imposes legal as well as moral obligations. Thus an accountant could be sued for NEGLIGENCE (q.v.) or a trustee for BREACH OF TRUST (q.v.).

FIFO. Letters standing for FIRST IN FIRST OUT (q.v.).

filing of accounts. The action of submitting a company's accounts to the REGISTRAR OF COMPANIES (q.v.) where they become publicly available. Every company is required to file accounts every year.

film rights. The rights attaching to a work of literature for it to be made into a film. In the absence of any contrary agreement (e.g. with a publisher) these belong to the author. In the case of a successful novel these rights might have great value.

filter. A device whereby price movements on the Stock Exchange are categorised as indicative of the emergence of a new trend. It is usually applied by supposing that a movement of some significant percentage (e.g. 10 per cent) in one direction or another is likely to be continued into a trend whilst a move of less than this is not. Such an indication is clearly of use in the timing of the buying and selling of investments. There is no theoretical justification for the application of a filter and empirical work seems to confirm that its use does not guarantee success.

FIMBRA. Letters standing for FINANCIAL INTERMEDIARIES, MANAGERS AND BROKERS REGULATORY ASSOCIATION (q.v.).

final accounts. The set of accounting statements produced by a business at the end of its financial year. The final accounts always include a profit and loss account and a balance sheet.

final dividend. The last dividend to be paid in respect of a given financial period. A final dividend may follow the payment of one or more INTERIM DIVIDENDS (q.v.). A final dividend of a given amount is proposed by the directors of a company but has to be approved by the members in general meeting before it is paid.

finance. Money which has to be committed to a project or a business enterprise to enable it to operate. Finance is needed to enable the purchase of FIXED ASSETS (q.v.) and to provide WORKING CAPITAL (q.v.). The intention is that the amount used to finance an enterprise should be conserved intact and that it should earn sufficient to provide an adequate rate of return on the investment.

Finance Act. An annual Act of Parliament which embodies the proposals contained in the BUDGET (q.v.) and other matters relating to taxation. Sometimes more than one Finance Act is passed in the same year so that one may see references to the Finance Act 1979 and the Finance (No. 2) Act 1979.

finance lease. A lease of an asset having the characteristic that substantially all of the risks and benefits of owning the asset pass to the lessee. The accounting significance of this is that, under SSAP 21, such a transaction should, despite its legal form, be treated as if the price of the asset had been borrowed and had then been expended in the purchase of the asset. It follows from this that there will appear in the profit and loss account amounts representing the interest payments on the notional loan and also depreciation on the asset. In the balance sheet there will appear the written down value of the asset and a corresponding liability for the unpaid portion of the debt. This treatment has implications for the profitability of the business and for the GEARING (q.v.) revealed by the balance sheet.

financial accounting. That branch of accounting concerned with the production of information for persons not concerned with the day-to-day running of the business. The main products of the financial accounting process are the annual profit and loss account and balance sheets. The term is usually taken, however, to include all the records underlying these statements and thus to be concerned with all administrative financial record keeping.

Financial Accounting Standards Board. The standard-setting body in the USA. It is often abbreviated to FASB. It was established in 1972 as the successor to the ACCOUNT-ING PRINCIPLES BOARD (q.v.). Its members are salaried and full-time unlike those of the APB who were unpaid volunteers. The FASB issues STATEMENTS OF FINANCIAL ACCOUNT-ING STANDARDS (q.v.) and Interpretations.

financial commitment. An obligation to undertake substantial expenditure entered into at the date of a balance sheet but not yet having been incurred or become a liability. Companies are required to disclose their financial commitments in the annual report.

financial futures. Currencies exchanged on the basis that they are to be delivered in the future, e.g. in 3 months' time. The rate of exchange for a financial future will depend on whether it is expected that rates will fall or rise and will incorporate an amount to compensate for the risk that this expectation will prove false. The value of such futures is that they enable businesses or persons dealing in currencies to protect themselves against some of the risks of rate fluctuations.

financial instrument. A document evidencing a contract under which some form of finance is raised by the issuer of the instrument. Their terms can vary considerably and accounting for them may, therefore, raise important issues.

Financial Intermediaries, Managers and Brokers Regulatory Association (FIM-BRA). An association having codes of practice which govern the proper conduct of its members in their dealings with the public.

financial management. The efficient raising and deployment of capital funds. Finance is a resource used by a business in the same way as its physical resources and efficiency in handling it is important to overall profitability.

financial modelling. A technique, usually involving computer spreadsheets, whereby the behaviour of a business under different prospective sets of circumstances can be predicted. It can be a useful tool to management in forecasting the financial implications of their decisions.

financial planning. The process of preparing forecasts and budgets so that requirement for finance can be foreseen.

financial reporting. The process of reporting the financial position and progress of a business to persons outside that business. The publication of a company's annual profit and loss account and balance sheet is the main component of financial reporting.

Financial Reporting Council The body having overriding jurisdiction over the production of FINANCIAL REPORTING STANDARDS (q.v.). It provides guidance to the ACCOUNTING STANDARDS BOARD (q.v.) which undertakes the actual work.

Financial Reporting Exposure Draft (FRED). A draft FINANCIAL REPORTING STANDARD (q.v.) issued for constructive comment as part of the process of moving towards a definitive standard.

Financial Reporting Review Panel. A body operating under the auspices of the FINANCIAL REPORTING COUNCIL (q.v.). Its function is to enquire into cases where there has been failure by a company to conform to accounting standards so that its accounts do not give a true and fair view.

Financial Reporting Standard (FRS). A statement of prescribed accounting treatment of specified matters issued by the ACCOUNTING STANDARDS BOARD (q.v.). It is intended to be applied to all statements intended to give a true and fair view. The failure to observe a Standard would be *prima facie* evidence that a true and fair view had not been given.

financial risk. A risk imposed on the proprietors of a business by the use of debt finance. Debt has a prior claim against trading returns in the form of interest. Because this is fixed in amount the variations in profit are magnified in proportion to the amount of debt. This magnification of variation is the financial risk.

Financial Services Act. A statute controlling the retail provision of financial services.

Financial Times. A daily newspaper published in London and concerned mainly with financial news and general news with financial implications. It is unusual in being printed on pink newsprint. It carries a more extensive list of stock market prices than any other newspaper and it publishes indices of share prices. The oldest and most well-known of these is the FINANCIAL TIMES ORDINARY SHARE INDEX (q.v.).

Financial Times Ordinary Share Index. An index of share prices based on the values of thirty quoted shares. It has now been largely superseded by more widely based indices but is of particular interest as it has been calculated daily for 50 years. It therefore provides the longest continuous record available of the movements of share prices.

Financial Times–Stock Exchange Index. An index of share prices. It is more broadly based than the older FINANCIAL TIMES ORDINARY SHARE INDEX (q.v.) and can therefore be regarded as more representative. Both do however move broadly in line with one another.

financial year. The year for which a business draws up its accounts. It may terminate on any convenient day, but commonly selected dates are 31 March, 30 June, 30 September and 31 December. Sometimes a financial year may be rounded to exactly 52 weeks so that it does not coincide exactly with a calendar year. The government's financial year for corporation tax runs from 1 April to the following 31 March.

fine. A money penalty for wrongdoing. It is usually imposed by a court of law but professional associations may sometimes fine their members.

finished goods. Goods held by a business which are ready for sale to its customers. Pending such sale finished goods are normally valued at their cost of production.

first class. The best that is obtainable. Extra prices can be charged for first-class goods or services.

first in first out. A method of pricing materials drawn from stock based on the presumption that the materials are used in the order in which they were acquired. In times of rising prices the application of first in first out, commonly abbreviated to FIFO, results in a lower charge to profit and loss account and a higher valuation for stock in the balance sheet than other methods.

First Lord of the Treasury. An office of state held by the Prime Minister, who is thus Prime Minister and First Lord of the Treasury.

first time buyer. A person buying a house who has never owned one before. Their significance is that they are frequently people with good expectations but having currently low incomes and accumulated savings. Many lenders will give special consideration to such people in the form of low deposits and sometimes low fixed rates of interest in order to attract their custom.

first year allowance. A CAPITAL ALLOWANCE (q.v.) given against an asset in the first year of its use and used in computing a liability to tax. A first year allowance is a rate established by legislation. Currently, for many classes of asset, it is nil. In subsequent years a WRITING DOWN ALLOWANCE (q.v.) will be given.

fiscal. Relating to the raising and use of money by government.

fiscal drag. The delay which occurs following the implementation of tax or public spending plans and the observation of their effects within the economy.

fiscal neutrality. A desirable characteristic of governmental spending and taxation policy which leaves the decisions of individuals unaffected by the tax implications and governed by the same considerations as would have guided them in the absence of the policy. For example a tax on Cheddar cheese but not on Red Leicester cheese does not have fiscal neutrality because it would cause consumers, regardless of their preferences to move consumption from Red Leicester to Cheddar cheese in order to save money.

fiscal year. The year designated by the government for tax purposes. In the UK the fiscal year runs from 6 April to the following 5 April. This applies to both INCOME TAX (q.v.) and CAPITAL GAINS TAX (q.v.). For CORPORATION TAX (q.v.) the term used is financial year and this ends on 31 March.

fixed asset. An asset held for the purpose of providing a service for the business which owns it. It is usually held, therefore, for a relatively long period, hence the term fixed. Examples of fixed assets are land, buildings, machinery, furniture and equipment. Companies are required by the Companies Act 1985 to show fixed assets under appropriate headings on their balance sheets. Fixed assets are normally subject to a charge for DEPRECIATION (q.v.).

fixed benefit pension. A pension in which the benefit to be received is fixed independently of the contribution made to the fund. It usually then depends on a combination of terminal salary and length of service.

fixed charge. A component of the total price charged which is independent of the quantity purchased. Electricity, gas and telephone bills all contain a fixed charge in addition to a unit charge applied to usage.

fixed contribution pension. A pension where the contribution is fixed and the ultimate benefit is then determined by the amount which has been contributed.

fixed cost. A cost which does not vary with the level of output. An example of a fixed cost is the rent of a factory. A fixed cost is usually fixed only up to a certain level of production. Beyond that a higher fixed cost is likely to be incurred as bigger capacity has to be engaged.

fixed exchange rate. A rate of exchange between two currencies which is kept at a fixed level. A fixed exchange rate is, in practice, very difficult to maintain.

fixed interest. A rate of interest determined at the outset of a contract and unchanging from that point on. Commercial debentures and government stocks are issued on a fixed interest basis. Bank overdrafts, on the other hand, normally bear interest which fluctuates with market rates.

fixed overhead. OVERHEAD (q.v.) which does not vary with the level of activity. In practice fixed overhead is usually fixed over only a certain range of the level of activity. If this increases beyond that level the fixed overhead will step up to a new level as extra capacity has be opened.

fixed price contract. A contract where the price to be paid is fixed before the work is commenced. The term normally applies to a contract for the construction of a major capital item such as a building, a bridge or a ship. A fixed price contract should be contrasted with a COST-PLUS CONTRACT (q.v.).

fixture. An object which is attached to the inside of a building so that it is not readily movable but which does not form part of the structure. It is normally the case that fixtures are regarded as being included in a contract for the sale of a building unless they are explicitly excluded. It is thus not permissible for the seller to remove them before vacating the property. Fireplaces, shelves and built-in cupboards are examples of fixtures.

flat rate. A rate which applies to all. Thus if a solicitor makes a flat rate charge for preparing a will this means that the rate will apply for the most complicated and time consuming wills as much as to the simple straightforward ones.

flexible budget. A BUDGET (q.v.) which varies with the actual experienced level of activity. Such a budget takes account of the fact that if activity is either greater or less than expected a fixed budget for variable items of expense is inappropriate.

flexitime. A characteristic of some contracts of employment whereby the employee has some flexibility concerning hours of work within a prescribed framework. Usually this dictates the number of hours to be worked in a week and stipulates that the employee must be present during 'core time', say from 10.00 a.m. until 3.00 p.m. An employee may thus leave early or start late on some days and make up this time by early starts or staying late on others.

float. A small amount of cash maintained to facilitate day-to-day transactions. A petty cashier, for example, will be given a float so that small cash expenses can be met as they arise. When the contents of a till are removed for banking a small float of coin may be left so that change can be given to customers. As the existence of a float is a temptation to dishonest persons it should be kept to a minimum amount and its continued existence should be verified from time to time.

floating charge. A legal charge, as security for a loan, on the assets generally of a business. It is an alternative to a charge on an identified major asset. The advantage to a business of giving a floating charge is that it enables it to continue to deal with its assets in the ordinary course of business whilst using them as security.

floating exchange rate. A rate of exchange between foreign currencies which is allowed to move freely according to market forces. Most exchange rates are, in reality, to an extent managed by government intervention in the market.

floor. 1. The lowest level which a price reaches.
2. The trading area of the Stock Exchange. Since BIG BANG (q.v.) very little trading has been done on the actual floor.

florin. A coin predating the decimalisation of the currency and then valued at two shillings. It was so named because of the image of a rose which appeared on its reverse. On decimalisation the florin became the 10p piece. Subsequent issues of coins of that value retained the same size and weight as the florin until they were replaced in September 1992 by a smaller coin.

flotation. The action whereby a company becomes quoted on the Stock Exchange so that its shares may freely be bought and sold by members of the public. The flotation is usually achieved by either a PLACING (q.v.) or a public offer for sale of the shares.

FOB Letters standing for FREE ON BOARD (q.v.).

football pools. A form of gambling, very popular in the UK, in which participants stake small amounts on their forecasts of the results of a number of football matches. Usually the object is to forecast eight games which will result in a drawn result. The total amounts staked, after deduction of taxes, expenses and the pools promoter's profits are divided amongst the winners. The prizes may be very substantial (up to £2 million) but depend upon the number of winners in a particular week.

FOOTSIE. Popular name for the FINANCIAL TIMES–STOCK EXCHANGE INDEX (q.v.).

forecast. A prediction of future events. A business BUDGET (q.v.) will be based to an extent on forecasts of general business conditions and of their effect on costs and selling prices. A SALES FORECAST (q.v.) is an important foundation to any business plan.

foreclosure. The action taken by a lender of money against a MORTGAGE (q.v.) when, on the default of the debtor, the property is sold in order to obtain payment of the amounts due. After foreclosure the lender is entitled only to payment of what is owed. Any surplus is payable to the original owner of the property. If the amount realised is insufficient to settle the debt, on the other hand, the balance still remains payable.

foreign currency translation. The process whereby accounting quantities expressed in a foreign currency are converted into the equivalent quantities in UK currency. This is the subject of SSAP 20. There are two main methods of translating foreign currency, and they are considered appropriate in different circumstances. These are the temporal method, in which conversions are done at the rate of exchange which applied at the time of the transaction giving rise to the item, and the closing rate method, in which conversions are carried out at the rate of exchange applying at the date when they are done.

forensic accounting. Accounting concerned with the detection and punishment of crime. An accountant tracing the effects of a fraud in order to determine the amounts involved and the persons responsible would be engaging in forensic accounting.

forestry. The activity of cultivating trees with a view to profit. Forestry presents special accounting problems because of the very long time span during which the crop is growing in which no cash revenue will be earned. In these circumstances some appropriate method of valuing the partly mature trees is required before profit can be determined.

forfaiting. A service provided by a specialist bank whereby the bank will purchase foreign currency obligations at a discount on a WITHOUT RECOURSE (q.v.) basis. The effect is to remove the risk of non-payment from transactions with persons overseas.

EXAMPLE. John, a UK trader, sells goods to Francois, a French customer. Francois promises to pay 10,000FF for the goods in one month's time. John sells his right to receive 10,000FF from Francois to a forfaiter at a discount (to give the forfaiter an income). The forfaiter then assumes the responsibility for collecting the debt from Francois and the risk that Francois will not pay.

forfeiture of shares. Action taken by a company as a final sanction against a shareholder in default in respect of an amount owed on the shares. Where shares are partly paid a company may at any time call up the unpaid amount. In the event that a shareholder fails to pay the amount due the company may, if all else fails, declare the shares forfeit, i.e. cancelled. The former shareholder then has no further claim on the company. Such shares may be re-issued at a price which is at least equal to the amount of the default.

forgery. The action of creating a false document or of illicitly amending an existing one. A person would, for example, commit forgery who writes out a cheque and signs it with a copy of another person's signature so as to obtain funds fraudulently. Forged banknotes are quite commonly made and put into circulation.

form. A literal interpretation of a situation. In accounting the substance, rather than the form, of a transaction is most important. For example, a lease may sometimes be in form a contract whereby the lessee hires an asset for a specified period of time and pays a specified rent for it. In substance it may, however, be a contract whereby a sum of money is borrowed and then spent on acquiring ownership of the asset.

format. A style imposed on certain accounting statements. The Companies Act 1985 prescribes formats for published accounts. There are four alternative formats for the profit and loss account and two alternatives for the balance sheet. The law requires that one of these be adopted in each case.

Fortune. A famous business periodical published in the USA.

forward market. A market which enables the purchaser to buy commodities or foreign currency for future delivery at a price which is determined currently. Its use is a protection against an adverse movement of prices although it also means forgoing the benefit of any favourable movement.

forward rate. The amount which has to be paid currently for the purchase of a commodity or currency for delivery at some future date. The forward rate will depend on expectations of how rates will change in the future tempered by an assessment of how confidently that expectation is held.

founders' shares. Shares occasionally issued by companies to those involved in the initial promotion of the business. They do not carry any dividend until dividends payable on ORDINARY SHARES (q.v.) reach a certain level. They are then entitled to the residue of profits. Rewards to the holders of founders' shares may be very substantial if the company does well.

fractional share. A portion of a share to which a person becomes entitled, perhaps as a consequence of a BONUS ISSUE (q.v.). Since fractional shares cannot be registered it is usual for all of them to be amalgamated and sold so that the cash proceeds can be distributed to those entitled to them.

franchise. A licence to carry on operations under a name or trademark owned by somebody else. Franchise holders are often also given substantial support and national advertising. For this they will make a payment, usually based on turnover. Many organisations which seem to have a large number of branches are, in fact, operating on a franchise basis so that the branches are independent businesses.

franked investment income. Dividends received by a company subject to CORPORATION TAX (q.v.) from another company also subject to corporation tax. Their significance is that they are regarded as tax paid and no further tax is payable in the hands of the recipient. In the accounts of a company, franked investment income should be shown at the net amount received plus the amount of the TAX CREDIT (q.v.) associated with it. The tax credit should then be added to the tax charge further on in the profit and loss account. This is the treatment prescribed in SSAP 8.

franked statements of recommended practice. Statements of recommended accounting practice in particular industries which have been developed by persons in those industries and then franked, i.e. approved, by the Accounting Standards Committee (now Accounting Standards Board).

fraud. Obtaining some benefit from another person by dishonest deception. Financial fraud includes the issue of a fraudulent PROSPECTUS (q.v.) so as to induce investors to support a doubtful enterprise and the making of fraudulent entries in books of account so as to conceal MISAPPROPRIATION (q.v.) of funds. Fraud, if detected, may be punishable by a fine or a term of imprisonment or both.

fraudulent preference. A payment made to a creditor by an insolvent person or company with the intention that the creditor should be given an advantage over other creditors of equal rank. Such payments are illegal and may be recovered.

FRED. Letters standing for FINANCIAL REPORTING EXPOSURE DRAFT (q.v.).

freehold. A form of ownership of land in which the holder has absolute possession of the land for all time. A freehold may be subject to the rights of others, e.g. rights of way or covenants to the benefit of the owners of adjoining property. No provision for DEPRECIATION (q.v.) need be made in respect of freehold land although the buildings standing on the land should be depreciated over their useful life.

freelance. One who provides services to all comers and is not employed by one employer. Thus a freelance journalist will contribute to whichever magazines and newspapers will accept their work. Freelance earnings are taxed under Schedule D in income tax law.

free of tax. An amount not subject to taxation in the hands of the recipient. The term is used in each of two distinct situations. An amount may be stated to be free of tax because, although taxable, tax has been deducted before the payment was made. Thus to basic rate taxpayers dividends from companies and bank interest are free of tax. Alternatively, the term may refer to sums which are not subject to taxation because of special legislative privilege. Genuinely tax free receipts are interest on NATIONAL SAVINGS CERTIFICATES (q.v.) and LUMP SUM (q.v.) receipts from approved pension schemes on retirement.

free on board. Term signifying that a price quoted by the seller of goods includes all costs, including transport and other charges, incurred up to the time that the goods are loaded on to a ship for transport abroad.

free port. A port into which goods may be received without payment of import duty provided that they are in transit to another country.

freepost. A service offered by the post office whereby people may write to certain specified addresses without paying postage by writing the word 'FREEPOST' on the envelope. Postage is actually paid by the recipient.

free reserve. A REVENUE RESERVE (q.v.) which has not been allocated to any defined purpose.

freeze. The prevention of increases in prices or wage rates.

freight. An amount charged for the transport of goods.

friendly society. A form of organisation, recognised by law, which exists for its members to give mutual assistance. Friendly societies have certain tax privileges, recently curtailed but not extinguished, which enable them to invest members' funds very profitably. Legal recognition involves certain obligations placed on societies in terms of their range of permitted activities and their reporting requirements.

fringe benefit. A benefit, usually received in KIND (q.v.), given to an employee in addition to a salary. The usual range of fringe benefits includes the provision of free or subsidised meals, private health insurance, cars, etc. Some fringe benefits are taken into account in assessing an individual's liability to INCOME TAX (q.v.).

frozen fund. A sum of money, usually in a bank account, which has been prevented from being used. Money deposited by a foreign country on which we have subsequently declared war might be frozen by government decree. The funds of a deceased person are frozen until an EXECUTOR (q.v.) under the WILL (q.v.) has been ascertained.

FRS. Letters standing for FINANCIAL REPORTING STANDARD (q.v.).

FTSE. Letters standing for FINANCIAL TIMES–STOCK EXCHANGE INDEX (q.v.). Pronounced 'footsie'.

full cost. A cost which includes an element for fixed overhead. It contrasts with direct or MARGINAL COST (q.v.).

full-time working director. A DIRECTOR (q.v.) who works in a company on a full-time basis. The status has tax implications.

fully diluted earnings per share. EARNINGS PER SHARE (q.v.) calculated on the basis of the number of shares potentially, as well as actually, in issue. Shares taken into account, apart from those already issued, include those for which an option to acquire is outstanding and those which might be issued on conversion of a CONVERTIBLE DEBENTURE (q.v.).

fully insured scheme. A pension scheme in which all of the benefits are guaranteed by an independent insurance company.

fully paid shares. Shares in respect of which the full nominal value has been paid to the company. No further CALL (q.v.) may be made on the shareholders in respect of fully paid shares.

fund. A sum of money held for a specified purpose. The fund is normally held in the form of cash or of highly marketable securities. One example of a fund is a SINKING FUND (q.v.).

fundamental analysis. The analysis of financial statements with a view to determining the investment potential of a company's shares. The theory underlying fundamental analysis is that a study of accounting information will reveal the intrinsic value of a company's shares. If the market value lies below this intrinsic value then they are a good investment and if it lies above they are not. The theory relies on there being such a thing as intrinsic value and on the idea that the market price will eventually revert to it. The empirical evidence seems to be against this.

funded pension scheme. A pension scheme where the contributions are actuarially determined to provide a fund adequate to meet the obligations involved in paying the benefit.

funds flow statement. A statement summarising the main changes in liquid funds held by a business over a period of time. Companies were required by SSAP 10 (now withdrawn) to produce such a statement from 1976 to 1991. This has now been superseded by FRS 1 which requires the production of a CASH FLOW STATEMENT (q.v.).

funeral expenses. The costs associated with holding a funeral for a deceased person. They are a first charge on the estate and will be paid out of the estate by the executor.

fungible assets. Assets which, although they may have been acquired at different times, are not distinguishable one from another. A company may hold several parcels of shares in another company bought at different times and at different prices. As one share has exactly the same rights and value as another share, however, these cannot sensibly be seen as separate and distinguishable investments. The shares are fungible assets.

future prospects. Reasonable anticipations of the opportunities which will become available. A PROSPECTUS (q.v.) issued in respect of the proposed issue of shares in a company will contain a section referring to future prospects to help readers to decide whether or not to invest in the shares. The DIRECTORS' REPORT (q.v.) issued annually in connection with a company's accounts will make reference to the company's future prospects.

futures. Commodities or currencies priced on the basis that they are to be delivered in the future, e.g. in 3 months' time. The price for a future will depend on whether it is expected that prices will fall or rise and will incorporate an amount to compensate for the risk that this expectation will prove false. The value of futures is that they enable businesses or persons dealing in commodities or currencies to protect themselves against some of the risks of price fluctuations.

G

GAAP. Letters standing for GENERALLY ACCEPTED ACCOUNTING PRINCIPLES (q.v.).

gains. A term used to describe profits of an irregular or non-recurrent nature, e.g. CAPITAL GAINS (q.v.), HOLDING GAINS (q.v.).

gambling. Staking money on the outcome of a chance event. Gains from gambling are not subject to income tax unless they are of such a regular nature as to constitute a trade or profession. Gambling debts are not enforceable in a court of law.

gaming. Synonym for GAMBLING (q.v.).

gamma. A term applied officially to some stock market securities which are traded in rarely and in which there is a thin market.

***Garner* v. *Murray*.** A famous case, heard in 1904, establishing the rule that in PARTNERSHIP (q.v.) losses due to the default of an insolvent partner fall on the remaining partners in proportion to their capitals rather than in the proportion in which they share trading losses. The rule is now known as the rule in *Garner* v. *Murray*.

EXAMPLE: The partnership of A, B and C is dissolved after a period of unsuccessful trading and after substantial losses have been accumulated. The partnership agreement provides that profits and losses are to be shared equally. After the realisation of the assets and settlement of liabilities there is a deficiency to be set off against the partners' capital accounts of £44,991. The calculation of the amounts due to the partners is:

	A £	B £	C £
Original capital	24,000	48,000	12,000
Less Deficiency (equally)	14,997	14,997	14,997
Due to/from partners	9,003	33,003	(2,997)

C should now pay into the business the sum of £2,997, which, when added to the residue from the realisation of assets, will give exactly the amount required to pay to A and B the balances shown as due to them. If C is insolvent and unable to pay, the rule in *Garner* v. *Murray* will apply as shown:

	A £	B £
Amount shown above	9,003	33,003
Less C's deficiency in proportion to original capitals	999	1,998
Amount finally due	8,004	31,005

garnishee order. A court order to a debtor that the debt is to be discharged to some person other than the original creditor.

gate money. The total amount of takings at a sporting event. These are usually collected at a gate as the spectators enter.

GATT. Letters standing for GENERAL AGREEMENT ON TARIFFS AND TRADE (q.v.).

gazumping. The practice whereby the vendor of a property increases its price after an informal agreement but before formal contracts have been exchanged. Although clearly unfair the buyer has no redress because no contract for the sale of land is binding until it is in writing.

GDP. Letters standing for GROSS DOMESTIC PRODUCT (q.v.).

geared buyout. The purchase of a business, usually by the existing management, financed to a substantial extent by borrowed money.

gearing. The ratio between DEBT (q.v.) finance and EQUITY (q.v.) finance. Its significance is that the presence of debt, which imposes a fixed interest charge on the profit and loss account, increases the sensitivity of the amounts available to equity holders to variation in profit. Investment in a geared company carries more risk of low returns but also more possibility of higher than average returns. Gearing is given by the formula:

$$G = \frac{D}{D + E}$$

Where G is the level of gearing
D is the market value of the debt
E is the market value of the equity

gearing adjustment. An adjustment which may be made in accounts prepared on a current cost basis. It was required under the now withdrawn SSAP 16. It allows for the proportion of a company's funds which have been borrowed and to that extent abates the transfer otherwise indicated to the CURRENT COST RESERVE (q.v.).

General Agreement on Tariffs and Trade. An international treaty whereby tariffs which limit free trade are limited in extent by agreement amongst the countries which are signatories to the agreement.

General Commissioners of Income Tax. A lay body of persons authorised to hear taxation appeals. Their responsibility is to determine the facts of the case so that the law can then be properly applied.

general ledger. A section of the LEDGER (q.v.) containing the non-personal accounts. The general ledger contains the capital account, fixed asset accounts, profit and loss account, etc., but not the accounts of individual debtors and creditors. The general ledger is sometimes called the nominal ledger.

generally accepted accounting principles. Principles so widely used and accepted that they may be presumed to underlie all accounting statements. The term, often abbreviated to GAAP, was coined in the USA by the FINANCIAL ACCOUNTING STANDARDS BOARD (q.v.). The GOING CONCERN CONCEPT (q.v.) and CONSERVATISM (q.v.) are good examples of GAAP.

general partner. A partner in a LIMITED PARTNERSHIP (q.v.) who has unlimited liability for the debts of the business. Every limited partnership must have at least one general partner.

general reserve. A REVENUE RESERVE (q.v.) created for unspecified purposes. It represents a decision to retain some part of the profit of a company from distribution. Some commentators feel that it serves no real function and would prefer to leave all retained profit in the profit and loss account.

gift. An amount of money or other valuable item transferred from one person to another without the expectation or requirement of any payment. If shares are transferred as a gift the transfer is not subject to STAMP DUTY (q.v.). Gifts during a person's lifetime may have to be taken into account in assessing liability to INHERITANCE TAX (q.v.).

gift tax. A tax on amounts of money or other valuables transferred by way of gift from one person to another. There is no gifts tax, as such, in the UK but some aspects of INHERITANCE TAX (q.v.) operate like a gifts tax.

gift token. Vouchers issued by some chain stores against a cash payment equal to their face value. The vouchers may be exchanged for goods to their face value at any store in the chain.

gilt-edged security. A security which is guaranteed by the government. It is so called because default is out of the question. As an investment a gilt-edged security is very safe but this may be reflected in a rather unexciting performance.

giro. A system of banking for dealing with simple transactions involving the transfer of funds from one person to another. The term was introduced into the UK when the Post Office set up the National Giro. It has since been adopted by the clearing banks for their own operations in this field.

glamour stock. A share in a company which appears to have a dazzling future, often in some new field which is as yet untried. It is a characteristic of a glamour stock that its price will rise well above what is justified by any realistic expectations. This is likely to be followed ultimately by the disappointment of a collapse.

GND. Letters standing for GROSS NATIONAL PRODUCT (q.v.).

Gnomes of Zurich. The powerful banking interests in Zurich, Switzerland. The term became current during financial difficulties in the UK during the 1960s.

GNP. Letters standing for GROSS NATIONAL PRODUCT (q.v.).

going concern. A business which has become established and has thus achieved a momentum of activity tending to favour its long-term survival. The significance of the concept is that a going concern is likely to have a greater value than the BREAK-UP VALUE (q.v.) of its assets. This superiority of value is termed GOODWILL (q.v.). If a person wishes to dispose of a business it will usually be better to sell it as a going concern than it will be to cease operations and realise the assets piecemeal.

going concern concept. The concept which states that a business for which accounts are prepared is to be regarded as having an indefinite life extending into the future. If accounts were not prepared on this basis, stock and fixed assets would have to be valued on the basis of their immediately realisable value in a balance sheet. There could be no justification, either, for placing a value on DEFERRED EXPENDITURE (q.v.) or WORK IN PROGRESS (q.v.). The going concern concept is, therefore, an important determinant of many of the figures appearing in a set of final accounts. It would not be applied in the few cases where it is known that a business has ceased, or is about to cease, trading.

going rate. The current price or charge for some object or service. Thus one might speak of the going rate for motor servicing or for hotel accommodation.

gold. A precious metal which is of significance because of its widespread use as money. In Victorian times it circulated as coin in the form of sovereigns. Nowadays its monetary use is limited to payments between countries.

golden credit card. A special CREDIT CARD (q.v.) issued to selected customers and made distinctive in appearance from the normal credit card. Its holders are entitled to special privileges such as unsecured bank loans and high credit limits. Possession of the card is regarded as a status symbol as they are issued only to persons with a high income.

golden handcuff. A term built into a person's contract of service such that there would be substantial financial penalties in leaving that employment. The payment of a large bonus at the expiry of 5 years subject to continuous employment up to that date would be an example of a golden handcuff.

golden handshake. A colloquial expression for COMPENSATION FOR LOSS OF OFFICE (q.v.).

golden hello. A colloquial term referring to a situation where a person was induced to leave a previous employment in order to take up the present one by the payment of a large sum of money.

gold reserves. Amounts held by a country in the form of gold. These are used for settling international transactions and thus fluctuate with the balance of payments.

golden share. A single share in a company having special voting rights and held by the government following privatisation of a previously publicly owned business. The purpose of the golden share is that it enables the government to veto any change of ownership in the company which it considers undesirable (such as its acquisition by a foreign company) without the necessity for maintaining a majority shareholding.

gold standard. A system whereby a country's currency is either in the form of gold or of notes against which gold is held by the central bank. The value of the currency then depends on the price of the metal. The UK abandoned the gold standard between the First and Second World Wars.

goods. Physical items of trade. It is a general term which applies to all the items making up the sales or purchases of a business.

goods in transit. Goods which are in the process of being transported from one business to another. For a business goods in transit from it must be included either in sales or in stock but not both. Goods in transit to it must be included in purchases and stock or in neither.

goods received note. A document raised internally by a business stating the quantities and types of goods which have been received from a supplier. It is used as confirmation that the goods appearing on an INVOICE (q.v.) have actually been received as specified before payment is made for them.

goodwill. The value which a business possesses over and above the realisable value of its SEPARABLE ASSETS (q.v.). Goodwill is attributable to the momentum and reputation which is acquired by an established business operating successfully. One element of it is the probability that the customers will return to a supplier who has satisfied them rather than go to a new one.

Internally generated goodwill is rarely valued in a business's balance sheet even though it is a vital contributor to the earning of profit. Where a business is acquired as a GOING CONCERN (q.v.), the purchaser will normally pay explicitly for goodwill as an a element in the total purchase price. Such purchased goodwill may appear in the balance sheet at cost but good practice requires that it be subject to AMORTISATION (q.v.) over a fair period. Under the Companies Act 1985 companies are forbidden to include internally generated goodwill in the balance sheet and must write off purchased goodwill, where it appears, over the period of its effective life. SSAP 22 allows this treatment but prefers that normally goodwill is written off to reserves immediately it arises. This treatment is, however, controversial and may be amended in a new standard. Goodwill may also arise when preparing CONSOLIDATED ACCOUNTS (q.v.) representing a surplus of the purchase price of the shares in a SUBSIDIARY COMPANY (q.v.) over their underlying net asset value.

government grants. Money given by the government for specified purposes. A business may receive a government grant to encourage it to set up in a particular area, e.g. where there is high unemployment. The accounting treatment of government grants is prescribed in SSAP 4. This states that revenue grants should be set off against the items of expenditure to which they relate. Capital grants should be released to profit and loss account over the same period as that over which the asset is depreciated.

Governor of the Bank of England. A high-ranking official who is the chief executive of the Bank. The activities of the Bank are carried out, in name, by the Governor.

grace. See DAYS OF GRACE.

granny bond. A colloquialism for an index-linked NATIONAL SAVINGS CERTIFICATE (q.v.). The term derives from the fact that, when first issued, these certificates were available only to persons of retirement age. They are now available to all. The real value of the certificates is maintained by linking it to the INDEX OF RETAIL PRICES (q.v.). Bonuses are added regularly so that a small real income is provided.

grants. See GOVERNMENT GRANTS.

gratis. Free of charge.

gratuity. Synonym for TIP (q.v.).

green. Environmentally conscious. Thus a business is said to be green if it conducts its processes so as to minimise any adverse impact on the environment, e.g pollution, or if it designs its products with a similar objective in mind. There is a current public awareness of the importance of the environment and many businesses are discovering that it is to their commercial advantage to be 'green'.

green card. A document issued by a motor insurer to an insured person to evidence that cover under the policy has been extended to travel abroad. Many insurance companies will issue such a card without charge provided that they are informed of the intended foreign travel before it takes place. Sometimes, however, an extra premium will be charged.

green pound. The value of the pound sterling as established for the purposes of the European Common Agricultural Policy.

grey market. Term applied to semi-official dealings in shares conducted outside the normal trading hours of the Stock Exchange. Grey market dealings in newly issued securities may take place before the official date on which dealings commence. They are eagerly studied as a source of information as to the likely price to be achieved by the shares when dealings commence officially.

groat. A now long obsolete English coin which had the value of fourpence.

gross domestic product. The total value of all the goods and services produced by a country for use within its own borders during a period of time. It is thus less than the GROSS NATIONAL PRODUCT (q.v.) which includes goods and services sent overseas.

gross estate. The total value of the assets left by a deceased person before deducting inheritance tax or any of the expenses of administering the estate.

gross income. Income before any deductions (e.g. of income tax) have been made. Thus a person's gross income will include the salary paid by an employer, income from other activities and income from investments all at their before tax amounts. In the case of income received net of tax it will be necessary to GROSS UP (q.v.) the amount in order to determine the gross income.

gross national product. The total value of all the goods and services produced in a country during a specified period of time, usually 1 year. It is a measure of the wealth producing capacity of a country. In a healthy economy gross national product will generally rise every year.

gross profit. The difference between sales revenue and the direct cost of the goods sold. It is a measure of the basic profit earning potential of the business. It is the main figure arising from the TRADING ACCOUNT (q.v.).

gross profit rate. The percentage which GROSS PROFIT (q.v.) bears to SALES (q.v.). The gross profit rate may be regarded as an indicator of the effectiveness of the basic profit earning process of the business. The gross profit figure which might reasonably be expected will vary from one type of business to another.

EXAMPLE. A certain business has achieved sales of £1 million in the year just completed. There was a gross profit of £250,000. The gross profit rate is thus:

$$\frac{£250,000}{£1,000,000} \times 100\% = 25\%$$

gross up. The process whereby a payment net of tax can be restated at its untaxed equivalent. If a taxpayer receives a payment of £75 after deduction of income tax at the rate of 25 per cent this should be grossed up, as follows;

$$£75 \times \frac{100}{75} = £100$$

Bank and building society interest is paid after deduction of tax. In order to assess a taxpayer's total liability to tax this must be grossed up at the standard rate of income tax.

gross wages. A person's WAGES (q.v.) before deducting income tax, national insurance contributions and other deductions.

gross yield. The annual income deriving from a security expressed as a percentage of the capital sum invested and before making any deduction for taxation.

EXAMPLE. A purchases some shares at a total cost of £1,000. During the ensuing year dividends are received totalling £75. The related TAX CREDITS (q.v.) totalled £25. The gross yield is:

$$\frac{£75 + £25}{£1,000} \times 100 = 10\% \text{ per annum}$$

ground rent. An annual payment by the owner of a LEASEHOLD (q.v.) during the life of the lease. Notionally it is a rent for the land occupied during that period but it often bears no relationship to what a market level of rent would be. A ground rent may be fixed at the commencement of the lease or may be subject to periodic review.

113

group. Two or more companies where one controls the activities of the other(s). A group usually arises where a company acquires a controlling fraction (i.e. over 50 per cent) of the shares of another company. The existence of a group gives rise to the need for CONSOLIDATED ACCOUNTS (q.v.).

group accounts. Accounts which reflect the activities of a GROUP (q.v.) of companies as opposed to merely one member of the group. Group accounts were first required by the Companies Act 1948. Although a variety of forms used to be allowed for group accounts the form now prescribed, other than in exceptional circumstances, is that of CONSOLIDATED ACCOUNTS (q.v.).

group insurance. Insurance which is made available to a person at favourable premium rates because of membership of a particular group. A member of a specified motoring organisation, for example, might be offered favourable terms for motor insurance. The commercial justification for group insurance is that the members of the group concerned are collectively seen as a lower risk than the population at large. Although this may often be the case there is also an element of pure promotion in the offer.

growth. That process whereby a business becomes larger. The success of many types of businesses depends on continual growth and this is more often achieved by acquiring other established business than it is by increasing the size of the existing activity.

growth stock. Shares in a company which is expected to expand over a long period of time. The price of its shares should also, therefore, rise steadily over the long term.

guarantee. 1. A legally binding assurance that an obligation will be met. If a financially insubstantial person wishes to raise a loan a guarantee from another, more substantial person may be required. The person giving the guarantee, the guarantor, would be legally bound to meet the amount of the debt together with accrued interest if the debtor were to default.

2. A promise given by the manufacturer of a consumer durable product to its purchaser that repair or replacement will be carried out free of charge if faults develop within a specified period following the date of purchase. This promise is popularly termed a guarantee but is more correctly termed a warranty. Although valued by the customer and thus useful in marketing the product, the protection given by a guarantee is usually less than that available under consumer protection legislation. *See also* WARRANTY SERVICES.

guaranteed minimum pension. An amount guaranteed to be paid under a pension scheme. There may in the event be a higher pension than this but this amount can be relied on totally.

guarantor. One who gives a GUARANTEE (q.v.).

guinea. An archaic unit of currency finally swept away on decimalisation in 1971. Until that time it was common for professional fees, e.g. those of accountants, and some prices, to be quoted in guineas even though there was no guinea note or coin. A guinea was one pound, one shilling (£1 1s 0d) or, in decimal terms, £1.05.

H

half-crown. A coin which was abolished in 1971 when the currency was decimalised. It had a value of two shillings and sixpence, i.e. 12½p.

halfpenny. Up to decimalisation in 1971 this had a value of half of an old penny and enjoyed a wide circulation. A new halfpenny was issued in 1971 (worth a little more than one old penny). It was never popular owing to its very small size and was eventually abolished when inflation reduced its value to negligible proportions.

hallmark. A mark engraved on an article made of precious metal to signify that it has been assayed and found to be of the metal and purity specified. The hallmark also symbolically signifies the date and location of the production of the article.

hammered. Term applied to a member of the Stock Exchange, i.e. a broker or a market maker, who has become unable to meet his or her obligations because of insolvency.

Hang Seng Index. An index reflecting movements of share prices on the Hong Kong Stock Exchange.

Hansard. The official transcript of proceedings in the House of Commons. It is the ultimate authority on what was said in the House.

hard currency. A currency, like sterling, which is acceptable throughout the world. For a currency to be hard the economy of the country from which it emanates must be stable and managed in such a way as to inspire confidence.

hardware. Computer equipment. The term is applied not only to the computer itself but also to peripheral equipment such as disc drives, visual display units and printers. Programs for the computer are termed SOFTWARE (q.v.).

harmonisation. The process whereby UK laws are made compatible with those of other members of the European Community. This has had considerable implications for financial reporting where many features of recent company legislation arise directly from the need for harmonisation.

head lease. The main lease where there are in existence subleases.

hedging. Engaging in financial operations with the intention of reducing risk. For example, a person who had a forthcoming obligation which had to be met in a foreign currency may purchase it in advance as a hedge against an adverse variation in the rate of exchange. A person buying shares might engage in hedging by simultaneously buying a PUT OPTION (q.v.) for the shares lest their value should fall.

herd basis. A basis of accounting for the profit of a farmer arising from the management of LIVESTOCK (q.v.). It has special significance in determining the farmer's liability to income tax. Use of the herd basis allows the farmer to treat a collection of animals of the same type as a FIXED ASSET (q.v.). The alternative would be to treat each animal separately and thus to determine a profit or loss on the occasion of each disposal.

hereditament. A property which is subject to local taxation.

Her Majesty's Collector of Taxes. Full formal title of the COLLECTOR OF TAXES (q.v.).

Her Majesty's Inspector of Taxes. Full formal title of the INSPECTOR OF TAXES (q.v.).

HIBA. Letters standing for HIGH INTEREST BANK ACCOUNT (q.v.).

hidden reserve. Synonym for SECRET RESERVE (q.v.).

high. The maximum value reached by the price of a security during a defined period of time. It is an expression used in the Stock Exchange. If the shares of a certain company reach a high for the year this means that this is the maximum price reached during the year so far. An all-time high would be the maximum price ever reached to date. The term is also applied to movements of an index of share prices.

high interest bank account. These are offered by a number of banks. The banks often require the observance of conditions concerning the minimum balance and the size of transactions in exchange for favourable rates of interest on the balance.

high street bank. Term used to denote one of the banks which can be seen in any shopping centre, e.g. Lloyds and Barclays.

hire of plant and machinery. Amounts paid by a business for the use of plant and machinery which it does not itself own and which does not, therefore, appear as a FIXED ASSET (q.v.) in its balance sheet. The accounting significance of this amount is that company law requires that a company should disclose amounts paid under this heading.

hire-purchase. A form of credit given to a consumer to enable the purchase of durable goods. Technically, hire-purchase is an agreement whereby the customer hires the goods for a specified period for an agreed regular payment. At the end of the period there is then the option to buy the goods for a nominal amount (often £1). The hire charge is set at a rate which pays the price of the goods plus an appropriate amount of interest for the period of the agreement. Hire-purchase differs from an EXTENDED CREDIT (q.v.) sale in that, during the period of the payments, the seller retains the property in the goods and can repossess them if the buyer defaults. This right is subject to certain legal restrictions so that a buyer in difficulty will not lose the goods when they have been substantially paid for.

In accounting for hire-purchase the question arises as to when the profit is realised and should be included in the profit and loss account. The normal practice is to apportion the total profit *pro rata* over the hire payments and to recognise it progressively as those payments are made. Thus if half of the payments have been paid then half of the profit will have been recognised. Instalments still to come (effectively a debtor as far as the seller is concerned) should be valued at their cost element (i.e. with a provision to offset profit and interest still to be earned) and shown separately on the balance sheet.

It is rare for a business to purchase assets on hire-purchase but, where it does so, the transaction should be treated in exactly the same way as a FINANCE LEASE (q.v.).

historical cost. The money figure at which an asset was originally acquired. Historical cost forms the basis of many accounting valuations. Stock is normally valued at cost less amounts written off by way of DEPRECIATION (q.v.). Although having the great merit of objectivity, historical cost has some weaknesses as a measure of value, particularly during a period of inflation.

hoard. A store without any obvious use and without any reward. It may be applied to cash held by a person who neither uses it nor places it at interest.

holder in due course. The holder of a BILL OF EXCHANGE (q.v.) who has received it in the ordinary course of business for value without any notice of any irregularities or defect of title of its previous holders. A holder in due course obtains a good title to the value embodied in the bill.

holding company. A company which controls the activities of one or more other companies (known as its subsidiaries). Control is usually achieved by acquiring a majority, i.e. over 50 per cent, of the shares. It is possible for a holding company to own most of its assets and to earn most of its profits through the medium of other companies which it controls. For this reason a holding company is required to present GROUP ACCOUNTS (q.v.). These will usually be in the form of CONSOLIDATED ACCOUNTS (q.v.).

holding gain. A gain made when the market value of an asset rises after it has been acquired. For example, if stock is bought for £5 per unit and its purchase price subsequently rises to £6 per unit there has been a holding gain of £1 per unit. Conventional accounting does not report holding gains separately. They emerge as an unidentifiable component of trading profit when they are realised. Proponents of CURRENT COST ACCOUNTING (q.v.) argue that holding gains should be separately calculated and shown. They argue that they arise from a different activity from trading so that they may be the result of wise buying or may be merely accidental. It has also been suggested that holding gains are a manifestation of inflation and are not, therefore, gains in any real sense at all.

holiday home. A residential property owned for the purposes of occupation during holidays. It is thus a second home. As such any gains made on its disposal are the subject of CAPITAL GAINS TAX (q.v.). It will also be subject to the COUNCIL TAX (q.v.).

holiday pay. An amount to which a person terminating a contract of employment is entitled to receive in lieu of holiday not yet taken.

honorarium. A token payment made to a person who has voluntarily undertaken a service which would normally command a fee. It is thus an expression of gratitude rather than a payment for the work done.

horizontal integration. An amalgamation of two businesses or divisions of a business engaged in the same stage of manufacture or distribution. The combination of two iron smelters or of two retailers would each be an example of horizontal integration. *See also* VERTICAL INTEGRATION.

hotchpot. A rule whereby property disposed of by a deceased person during his or her lifetime must be taken into account in determining the entitlement of his or her heirs under the will.

HOTGAS. Letters standing for Head of the Government Audit Service.

hot money. Money which it is undesirable to hold for more than a very short period. The term is applied to money which is shifted rapidly around international markets in order to take advantage of short-term fluctuations in interest rates. It may also be applied to money which has been dishonestly acquired so that its possession carries a risk of detection.

housekeeper allowance. An allowance given against income in calculating liability to income tax where the taxpayer, being a widower or widow, has some other person living with him or her acting as a housekeeper. The allowance was withdrawn for years after 1988–89.

housing association. An association formed for the purpose of owning residential property and letting it at low rents to those needing it. It is a non-profit making organisation.

housing benefit. A social service benefit given in appropriate circumstances to assist people on low incomes in paying for the cost of housing.

human resource accounting. A financial representation of the value of the team of employees which a business possesses. Conventional accounting disregards human resources entirely, recording only the cash costs of employment, i.e. wages and salaries, benefits, national insurance, training and recreation. It has, however, long been recognised that human resources are a very important factor in the earning and maintaining of profit. As one example of this, short-term profits might be boosted at the expense of the unrecorded human resources by cutting down on training and welfare expenditure. In the long run, however, employees would become dissatisfied and leave or be poorly trained and inefficient and the costs associated with these factors would rise. No technique of human resource accounting is universally accepted but two approaches have been suggested. One is that the actual cost of recruiting and training a new employee should be CAPITALISED (q.v.) and then AMORTISED (q.v.) over the term of a person's employment. The other is that the workforce should be valued in the balance sheet at the PRESENT VALUE (q.v.) of its prospective contribution to future revenues.

hurdle rate. A rate of return which a proposed investment must be expected to achieve if it is to be accepted. The hurdle rate is a useful device in the appraisal of proposed capital projects. It is set by reference to a company's COST OF CAPITAL (q.v.) but may also allow for the different riskiness of different projects.

hush money. Money paid to a person to induce him or her to keep silent about some matter which it is desired should not be made public. It has connotations of dishonesty. Hush money might for example be paid to an employee of a company who has uncovered some wrongdoing by the company to prevent him or her from divulging this to the appropriate authority.

hybrid finance. A type of finance which has some of the attributes of equity and some of the attributes of a loan. A CONVERTIBLE DEBENTURE (q.v.) is an example of hybrid finance.

Hyde Guidelines. A set of guidelines on CURRENT COST ACCOUNTING (q.v.) which were issued for use from the time of the abandonment of ED18 (q.v.) and the issue of SSAP16 (q.v.).

hyperinflation. INFLATION (q.v.) at a pace so rapid as completely to undermine the value of a currency as a medium of exchange. When hyperinflation occurs price rises amounting to several thousand-fold over a year are experienced. No one wishes to hold money and trade is either conducted in the form of BARTER (q.v.) or by the use of a convenient foreign currency. Hyperinflation occurred in Germany between the wars and, more recently, in Yugoslavia before the break-up of that country.

hypothecation. The setting aside of a sum of money or identified goods for a specified purpose.

I

IAS. Letters standing for INTERNATIONAL ACCOUNTING STANDARD (q.v.).

IATA. Letters standing for INTERNATIONAL AIR TRANSPORT ASSOCIATION (q.v.).

ideal standard. A particular basis for setting a STANDARD COST (q.v.). It is based on the assumption that ideal conditions will prevail during the period for which the standard is to apply and that production will thus be at the most efficient level possible. The advantage claimed for an ideal standard is that it motivates management to the best possible achievement. On the other hand, it may be said that, since perfection is impossible to reach, it may be so unrealistic a target that no effort will be made to reach it. *See also* ATTAINABLE STANDARD; NORMAL STANDARD.

idle capacity. Productive facilities, such as factory space or plant and machinery, which are not used. Idle capacity may occur because of bad management or because of a shortage of productive opportunities. In a seasonal business the capacity which must be made available to meet peak demand may inevitably be partly idle in times of low demand. Unplanned idle capacity may manifest itself in the form of UNDERABSORBED OVERHEAD (q.v.).

idle time. Time during which a worker is paid but is not doing any productive work. There is no implication of indolence in the term idle time. It may occur because a general shortage of work makes it impossible to use the worker's time productively or because a hold-up in another process forces a period of waiting. The cost of idle time should be treated as OVERHEAD (q.v.) rather than LABOUR (q.v.).

illiquid assets. Assets which are not readily converted into cash. Good examples of illiquid assets are buildings and plant and machinery. There are degrees of illiquidity and an asset may be either very or only moderately illiquid.

IMF. Letters standing for INTERNATIONAL MONETARY FUND (q.v.).

immovable property. Property which, by its nature is fixed in terms of situation, i.e. land and buildings.

imperial measures. Weights and other measures still used in the UK but which are gradually being replaced by the metric system. Yards, feet and inches are imperial measures of length and pounds and ounces are imperial measures of weight.

impersonal account. An account other than with a person. Thus an account with a debtor is a personal account. A cash account is an impersonal account.

impersonal ledger. Synonym for NOMINAL LEDGER (q.v.).

import duty. A tax imposed by a government on goods of specified types entering the country. In the UK import duty is administered by HM Customs and Excise. The object of imposing an import duty may be to raise money or it may be to protect the markets of domestically produced goods by making foreign imports more expensive.

imposed budget. A BUDGET (q.v.) laid down, without consultation, by a higher authority than those working to the budget. An imposed budget might, for example, be applied by the Board of Directors of a company to the manager of a particular department. A disadvantage of an imposed budget is that it is formed without the benefit of the experience and advice of those who have to operate it. It may also result in a less co-operative attitude towards compliance.

imprest system. A method of controlling PETTY CASH (q.v.). A FLOAT (q.v.) of known amount is issued to the petty cashier who uses it to make payments supported by proper VOUCHERS (q.v.). Periodically, the float is reimbursed to the extent of the payments made since the last reimbursement. The petty cashier should, therefore, always be able to account for the full amount of the float either in cash or in paid vouchers.

imputation system. The system whereby, currently in the UK, income tax on dividends is accounted for. The system was introduced in 1973. A company may pay dividends to its shareholders out of its taxed profit without having to bear any further amount of tax. The dividend in the hands of the shareholders, however, is deemed to have already borne tax at the prevailing rate of income tax. This so-called imputed tax is termed a TAX CREDIT (q.v.) and is taken into account in determining the shareholder's own tax position.

inactive stock. Shares or other securities in which there is very little trading.

incentive scheme. A method of calculating wages designed to induce workers to operate more efficiently. Any form of PIECEWORK (q.v.) payment is an incentive scheme but many are more complex than this. A typical scheme sets a target for production for a particular period and pays bonus rates for any production above this level. Although an incentive scheme may lead to higher levels of wages this should be more than compensated for by the more effective use of capital resources.

income. The inflow of wealth accruing to an individual or a business over a period of time. Income has come to be very significant for a number of reasons. It is taken to be a measure of the success of an activity, and is the criterion of taxable capacity and a measure of what may prudently be consumed. The concept of income, particularly of business enterprises, and its measurement is central to accounting. A useful definition, attributable to the writings of the economist Hicks, is that income is that amount which may be distributed in a particular period of time and leave an entity as well off at the end of the period as it was at the beginning. This definition, whilst a useful idea, still leaves many practical problems of income measurement to be resolved. It is, however, the basis of the CAPITAL MAINTENANCE (q.v.) concept for the measurement of business income.

income and expenditure account. An account drawn up to show the results over a period of time of the activities of a non-profit making organisation. The principles for drawing up an income and expenditure account are identical to those underlying a profit and loss account. In the long run it would be expected that income would be approximately equal to expenditure. In any single period, however, there may be a surplus (profit) or deficit (loss).

income statement. An accounting statement showing the calculation of the INCOME (q.v.) of an entity for a period of time. It is a general term that covers both the PROFIT AND LOSS ACCOUNT (q.v.) and the INCOME AND EXPENDITURE ACCOUNT (q.v.).

income stock. Shares which are held for the income they will provide, i.e. there is no expectation that their capital value will grow.

income support. A social security benefit given to persons whose incomes are inadequate to support them.

income tax. A tax on income. Individuals and PARTNERSHIPS (q.v.) are subject to this tax. Income is reduced by a number of ALLOWANCES (q.v.) depending on the circumstances of the taxpayer, before the taxable income is determined. Tax is then levied at a variety of rates. These currently stand at 20 per cent for the lowest slice of income, 25 per cent for the next band and 40 per cent for all income beyond that band. Bands and rates are changed from time to time. The main rate, applying to the major part of most incomes, is known as the basic rate and is currently 25 per cent. Rates of income tax and allowances are announced and then incorporated into legislation annually.

incomplete records. A set of accounting records which do not comprise a full double entry system. Incomplete records are commonly met with in the case of very small businesses where the proprietor does not have the time or the knowledge to maintain proper books. There are special methods used to prepare final accounts from such records. Typically, a set of incomplete records will comprise a detailed statement of bank transactions provided by the bank and supported by counterfoil paying-in slips and cheques, together with rough records on cash expenditure, year end stocks, debtors and creditors, Incomplete records is a favourite topic in examination questions as it tests a candidate's knowledge of accounting principles.

incorporation. The process of creating a corporation or legal person. It is used where a group of people brought together for a common activity wish to have a corporate existence separate from that of the individual members. An incorporated body can enter into contracts and can sue and be sued in its own name. Its membership may vary without affecting its own status. The process of incorporation in the UK is undertaken in one of three ways. These are (a) by royal charter, (b) by special Act of Parliament and (c) by registration under general legislation, such as the Companies Acts 1985–9. Most trading companies are incorporated by registration. Many prestigious non-profit making organisations, e.g. universities and professional bodies, are incorporated by royal charter.

incremental cost. The increase in total expenditure caused by the addition of one small element to the level of activity. If the production of a factory is increased by one unit the full cost of that unit will involve an element for the fixed overhead. The incremental cost will be limited to the extra material and direct labour used in its production.

indebtedness. The extent to which a company or an individual owes money to another. The total indebtedness of a business is a component in the calculation of its level of GEARING (q.v.). The greater its indebtedness the more a business is subject to influence or compulsion by its creditors.

indemnity. A contractual obligation to compensate some other person in the event that a loss is suffered from some prescribed cause. The most commonly encountered example of an indemnity is a contract of insurance in which the insurance company agrees, in return for the payment of a premium, to indemnify the insured against a defined type of loss if it occurs. Other examples arise, however. If a SHARE CERTIFICATE (q.v.) is lost a company may nevertheless agree to register a transfer of the ownership of the shares if it is given an indemnity by the transferor against any loss which might occur in the event that the missing certificate is subsequently found and improperly used.

indenture. A written agreement in the form of a deed. The term is commonly used for an agreement between a master and apprentice. The name dates from the ancient practice, not now usual, of writing two identical copies of the deed on one sheet of paper. They were then divided by a wavy freehand cut. The precise matching of these cuts would verify the authenticity of the deed should this ever be disputed.

121

E

independence. The condition of being able to advise or to act in the sole interest of a client. An auditor requires independence so that an honest opinion on accounts can be expressed without fear of the consequences. A financial adviser needs independence if the advice given is to be wholly unbiased. Independence may be compromised if the adviser has a financial interest in giving certain advice whether or not it is the best advice to give. This might happen if an auditor relies for a substantial part of his or her fee income on maintaining the goodwill of the Board of Directors of a particular company or if the commission of a financial adviser depends on selling the products of one company.

independent taxation. A form of taxation whereby married women are taxed separately from their husbands. An election to independent taxation for earned income has been available for some time. It was, however, a valuable option only where both the husband and the wife had substantial incomes. Independent taxation has now become the basic principle for all.

index. A pure number which represents the movement of some quantity which is an amalgam of many component movements, e.g. prices of shares on the Stock Exchange. The index is actually an average, sometimes appropriately weighted, standardised by relating it to a prescribed base date at which it is set at 100.

indexation. The process of linking a price or a value to an index.

index linking. The practice of varying recorded money values so as to preserve their real values in times of changing price levels. Index linking always in practice refers to raising figures in line with inflation. It is commonly used in connection with valuations contained in insurance policies. Thus the insured value of buildings which are the subject of a policy of fire insurance may be raised annually in line with an index of rebuilding costs so as to prevent the building from becoming underinsured. Index-linked NATIONAL SAVINGS CERTIFICATES (q.v.) and certain other index-linked government securities are available to investors.

index of retail prices. An index which measures the general level of retail prices and changes in that level. The index is produced monthly under government auspices and is widely regarded as a reliable measure of INFLATION (q.v.).

index tracking. An objective of the management of a portfolio of investments that its value moves precisely in line with the index of share prices. Unit trusts which offer index tracking appeal to certain types of investor. Index tracking is not always easy to achieve as the purchase or sale of the shares making up the index in sufficient quantities may, of itself, influence prices.

indicator. Some measurable quantity which is used as a guide to some characteristic or quality which cannot be directly measured. Figures for the level of unemployment in the country, for example, may be an indicator of the state of the economy. The movement of share prices may be an indicator of investor confidence in the future.

indirect cost. A cost not directly attributable to an identifiable unit of production. Examples of indirect costs are supervisory wages, maintenance and administrative costs.

indirect labour. Labour employed on work other than that directly incorporated into a product. It should thus be contrasted with DIRECT LABOUR (q.v.). Examples of indirect labour are labour employed on maintenance and that employed on supervision. Indirect labour should be classified as OVERHEAD (q.v.) and treated accordingly.

indirect material. Inputs to a productive process having the physical characteristics of MATERIAL (q.v.) but which do not become part of the actual composition of the product. Materials used to clean and polish a product would be examples of indirect materials.

indirect overhead. OVERHEAD (q.v.) which is not incurred specifically for the manufacture of an identifiable product but which benefits a number of products to unidentifiable extents.

indirect tax. A tax on goods or services such that it is paid only by the consumers of those goods or services. It should be distinguished from DIRECT TAXATION (q.v.). VALUE ADDED TAX (q.v.) and CAR TAX (q.v.) are examples of indirect taxes.

individual voluntary arrangement. A proposal made by a debtor in financial difficulty with his or her creditors. The object of the arrangement is that the debtor be permitted to manage his or her affairs with a view to the best advantage of all concerned.

Industrial and Commercial Finance Corporation. A body set up to provide finance for industry. The finance comes from the BANK OF ENGLAND (q.v.) and the commercial banks.

industrial buildings. Buildings used for industrial purposes, e.g. factories and warehouses. Special rules relate to industrial buildings in calculating CAPITAL ALLOWANCES (q.v.). Currently the rate is 4 per cent. This is calculated on the initial cost unlike most capital allowances which are calculated on the reducing balance of expenditure.

industrials. A category of ordinary shares listed on the Stock Exchange. In practice it contains the shares of those companies not fitting into any other specialised category (e.g. stores, food manufacturing, engineering, etc.) and might, therefore, be accurately named 'miscellaneous'.

industrial society. A mutual society having the objective of giving support to members of a particular industry. It must be formally registered at the Registry of Friendly Societies and its accounts must be subjected to AUDIT (q.v.).

industrial tribunal. A body formed to examine cases involving contract of employment. It may make awards, such as compensation in the case of the wrongful dismissal of an employee.

inefficiency. The condition existing where some activity is capable of being achieved by a lesser consumption of resources than currently experienced. Much accounting information has the object of indicating to managers the source of inefficiencies in the operation of their businesses. The elimination of these is a method of improving profit without the exertion of any extra effort.

inefficient market. A market in which new information is absorbed slowly so that prices take some time to react to it. It is a characteristic of an inefficient market that a knowledgeable participator who can act quickly will be able to make profits at the expense of other participants. Commodity markets and the Stock Exchange are efficient markets. The markets in second-hand cars and in residential property tends to be inefficient. This is a function of how quickly information can permeate the whole market.

inelastic demand. Demand (for goods and services) which is relatively unresponsive to price changes. Its relevance for businesses is that the supplier of goods in inelastic demand may increase prices quite substantially and will experience a less than proportionate reduction in sales. TURNOVER (q.v.) will therefore rise.

inelastic supply. Supply (for goods and services) which is relatively unresponsive to price changes. A shortage will, therefore, lead to disproportionately higher prices which will not result in sufficient extra supplies to relieve the shortage.

inertia selling. The process of seeking to sell goods by requiring that the prospective purchaser acts only if he or she does not wish to purchase. Mail-order offers are sometimes made of a series of publications of which the first is free and on approval. Others will be sent and charged for automatically if the recipient does not positively signify that this should not occur.

inflation. The steady decline in the value of the currency unit evidenced by generally increasing prices. Inflation causes considerable problems in accounting where money is the basis of measurement. The HISTORICAL COST (q.v.) basis is particularly vulnerable to inflationary distortion.

inflation accounting. Methods of accounting which seek to avoid the distortions existing with conventional accounting during periods of inflation. They include CURRENT PURCHASING POWER (q.v.) and CURRENT COST ACCOUNTING (q.v.).

ingot. A block of precious metal, such as silver, gold or platinum, made to a standardised weight. It is a convenient form in which to store BULLION (q.v.).

inherit. To acquire money or other property under the terms of a WILL (q.v.).

inheritance tax. A tax on the property left by a deceased person based on the value of the ESTATE (q.v.). The proportion which is payable depends on the total value of the estate. Small estates are not taxed and large ones bear tax at a rate of up to 40 per cent. The rates and exemption limits are changed by the government from time to time.

initial allowance. A form of CAPITAL ALLOWANCE (q.v.) given for tax purposes in the year in which an asset is acquired. It will be at a rate determined by tax legislation (and may be nil) and is calculated as a percentage of the cost of the asset.

Inland Revenue. That department of the civil service concerned with the assessment and collection of taxes. The chief work of the Inland Revenue is in connection with INCOME TAX (q.v.) and CORPORATION TAX (q.v.).

input. Resources which are consumed by a profit earning activity.

inscribed stock. A form of security where ownership is evidenced by entry in a register and no certificate of ownership is issued.

insider dealing. Dealing on the stock market in shares by those wishing to take advantage of their inside knowledge of a company's affairs. This might be done where there is advance knowledge of exceptional trading results or of a takeover offer. The rules of the Stock Exchange do not permit insider trading. It has now also been made a criminal offence under the Companies Act 1985.

insolvency. A state where the total assets of an entity are insufficient in value to meet its total liabilities. An individual who is insolvent may be made bankrupt (*see* BANKRUPTCY). It is illegal for an insolvent company to continue trading.

Inspector of Taxes. An officer of the INLAND REVENUE (q.v.) concerned with the assessment of liability to INCOME TAX (q.v.), CORPORATION TAX (q.v.) and CAPITAL GAINS TAX (q.v.). It is to the Inspector of Taxes that an individual will address his or her annual TAX RETURN (q.v.). All tax is assessed according to the rules laid down in legislation but the Inspector has some power of discretion in unclear cases. A taxpayer may appeal against an Inspector's decision if dissatisfied with it. The full title of the officer is Her Majesty's Inspector of Taxes.

instalment. One of a series of payments making up a total sum. The issue price of shares, for example, may be payable by instalments. A creditor may be allowed to pay what is owed in instalments.

instant access. A type of interest bearing account offered by a BUILDING SOCIETY (q.v.) or bank in which the depositor may withdraw the money without notice. The penalty for doing so is that interest is usually paid at a lower rate than on accounts for which notice of withdrawal is required.

Institute of Chartered Accountants in England and Wales. The largest body of professionally qualified accountants in the UK. It was founded in 1880 by the grant of a ROYAL CHARTER (q.v.). Its members are entitled to be called chartered accountants and to use the designatory letters ACA (for an associate member) or FCA (for a fellow) after their names.

Institute of Chartered Accountants in Ireland. The main professional body of accountants in Ireland. It has members working in both Northern Ireland and in the Republic.

Institute of Chartered Accountants of Scotland. The main professional body of accountants operating in Scotland. The majority of its members are Scottish but this is not a requirement for membership.

Institute of Taxation. A body of persons especially knowledgeable and experienced in taxation. Before admission members are required to pass examinations and submit evidence of professional experience in the field. They are entitled to the designatory letters ATII (for associate members) or FTII (for fellows) after their names.

institutional investor. A corporate investor such as a bank, insurance company or pension fund. The activities of institutional investors have a very profound effect on the levels of stock market prices. This is because they have a very substantial amount of money to invest and buy and sell relatively large holdings of shares.

instrument. A security which provides a mechanism whereby a company can borrow money. Instruments are issued with a variety of different terms relating to rates of interest payable, redemption and convertibility.

insurable interest. That element necessary in any contract of insurance to distinguish it from a wager or bet and to render it legally enforceable. An insurable interest is an interest in the outcome of a contingency other than that arising under the contract of insurance. Thus people may insure their houses against fire because that event would cause them substantial financial loss if they were not insured. They could not, however, insure against the possibility that a certain horse might win a race because they would suffer no loss if that should occur. A betting contract is not enforceable through a court of law.

insurable risk. A risk against which it is possible to insure. Ultimately the decision as to what is an insurable risk must be taken by the company offering cover but it must contain certain definable elements. The risk must be of such a nature that its probability can be determined with reasonable accuracy so that a premium may be established. It must also be of such a nature that the company can spread its exposure to the risk. War risks are not usually insurable for this reason. Any person seeking to insure a risk must also have an INSURABLE INTEREST (q.v.) in it.

insurance. The business of assuming risk of financial loss in return for the receipt of a premium. The essential difference between a contract of insurance and a gambling agreement (where also a payment may be made on the happening of some chance event) is that there must exist in the former an INSURABLE INTEREST (q.v.).

insurance broker. One who acts for clients in their dealings with insurance companies. An insurance broker should be able to advise clients on the best policy available in any particular field bearing in mind the cover given, the cost and the circumstances of the client. The broker should also assist in processing claims under a policy. The income of the insurance broker is derived from COMMISSION (q.v.) paid by the insurance company and the client is not usually charged directly for the service.

insurance policy. A formal document issued by an insurer setting out the terms of an insurance contract. It will contain details of the cover given and of any restrictions on that cover.

insured. A person or company who holds a policy of insurance indemnifying them against specified risks.

insurer. One who undertakes to indemnify another against specified risks in consideration for the payment of a premium. Insurers are normally insurance companies specialising in such business.

intangible asset. An asset which has no physical or documentary form. Intangible assets include GOODWILL (q.v.), patents and trademarks. Other examples are RESEARCH AND DEVELOPMENT EXPENDITURE (q.v.) and DEFERRED EXPENDITURE (q.v.).

integrated accounting. A form of accounting in which FINANCIAL ACCOUNTING (q.v.) and COST ACCOUNTING (q.v.) records are maintained in the same set of books. It involves the keeping of double entry cost ledgers and ensuring that the balances on these are included in the TRIAL BALANCE (q.v.). The advantage of integrated accounting is that the cost records are readily reconcilable with the financial records.

intellectual property. A valuable, though intangible, asset created by the exercise of human intelligence and imagination. The manuscript of a book is an example of intellectual property. Another is a computer program.

intercompany balance. An amount of indebtedness existing between one member of a GROUP (q.v.) of companies and another. It may arise where one company makes a LOAN (q.v.) to another or where there is trading between the companies. The significance of intercompany balances is that they must be eliminated by set-off when CONSOLIDATED ACCOUNTS (q.v.) are prepared.

intercompany profit. A profit made by one member of a GROUP (q.v.) of companies as a result of trading with another. This arises quite commonly. It has accounting significance in the preparation of CONSOLIDATED ACCOUNTS (q.v.). All intercompany profit must be eliminated from the consolidated profit and loss account. Any intercompany profit reflected in a stock valuation, i.e. on goods which have not yet passed to customers outside the group, must also be eliminated from the consolidated balance sheet.

intercompany transaction. A TRANSACTION (q.v.) taking place between members of the same GROUP (q.v.). The significance of intercompany transactions is that they need to be eliminated in the preparation of CONSOLIDATED ACCOUNTS (q.v.). Sales from one company to another, for example, do not contribute to the overall TURNOVER (q.v.) of the group. Similarly profits earned by one company from another must not be allowed to form part of the total stock valuation.

interest. 1. The payment made in exchange for the facility of borrowing money. The total amount payable is a function of the sum borrowed and the length of time for which it is outstanding. Interest is generally, therefore, stated as a percentage rate per annum. *See also* COMPOUND INTEREST; SIMPLE INTEREST.

2. A financial concern for the outcome of an enterprise. A shareholder has an interest in the company in which he or she holds shares. There may be a conflict between an interest and a contractual obligation. For example, if a company purchases land

from one of its own directors, the director has a private interest in obtaining as high a price as possible for the land and an obligation, as a director, to buy it on the most favourable possible terms for the company. Such a conflict of interest should be declared by the director at the meeting of the Board where the matter is discussed. Where directors of a company hold interests in the company in the form of shares, debentures or options in respect of these, these must be recorded in a REGISTER OF DIRECTORS' INTERESTS (q.v.) and disclosed in the DIRECTORS' REPORT (q.v.).

interest in expectancy. An interest which will crystallise on the happening of some event such as the expiration of a lease.

interfirm comparison. A comparison of results between businesses engaging in a similar line of activity. Its value is that those taking part in the comparison may see how their attainments match up to those of others. In order to preserve confidentiality and protect a competitive position, interfirm comparisons are usually done through a trade association which issues average figures with which members can compare their own results.

interim audit. An AUDIT (q.v.) conducted part way through an accounting period. It has as its object either the greater effectiveness of the audit effort by a more immediate examination of transactions or the spreading of the total workload of the audit over a period. It does not lead to a formal report. The audit of a large company will almost always include one or more interim audits.

interim dividend. A DIVIDEND (q.v.) paid by a company during the course of its financial year. Normal practice is for a company to pay one interim dividend about halfway through the year and one FINAL DIVIDEND (q.v.) after its end. Practice varies considerably, however, and a company may pay several interim dividends (perhaps with no final dividend) or no interim dividend at all.

interim report. A report on progress prepared part way through a financial year. There is no legal obligation on a company to produce interim reports. Rules imposed by the Stock Exchange, however, require all quoted companies to produce an unaudited interim report giving turnover and profit halfway through each financial year.

internal audit. An AUDIT (q.v.) of a business carried out by employees of that business as opposed to independent outsiders. Most large companies have an internal audit department. An internal audit does not have the same independence or credibility of one conducted by independent outside auditors and in no sense replaces it. Where, however, the internal auditor reports directly to senior management and so remains independent of departmental managers the internal audit can be a valuable part of INTERNAL CONTROL (q.v.).

internal check. Some device built into a system of records which, by its operation, will reveal error. DOUBLE ENTRY (q.v.) is an important form of internal check, as is a CONTROL ACCOUNT (q.v.).

internal control. The set of accounting and other procedures which seek to ensure that financial dealings are honestly undertaken and properly recorded. It will be an important part of internal control, for example, that separate parts of the system are under separate control so that fraud without collusion is impossible. Another part will be that all actions are properly authorised and fully documented so that a complete AUDIT TRAIL (q.v.) is left behind.

internal rate of return. The rate of return generated by a project on the capital invested in it. By definition, if the prospective returns yielded by a project are discounted at the internal rate of return they will equal the initial investment required, i.e. the NET PRESENT

VALUE (q.v.) will be nil. Internal rate of return is difficult to calculate by manual methods and is less popular as a means of investment appraisal than is net present value. In some circumstances a projected set of cash flows will lead to two different values for the internal rate of return. This may occur where there are large cash outflows (e.g. for the restoration of a site) at the end of the project's life. Where the internal rate of return is to be used as a method of investment appraisal, a project, to be acceptable, needs to show an internal rate of return in excess of a HURDLE RATE (q.v.).

International Accounting Standard. An accounting standard promulgated by the International Accounting Standards Board and intended to apply to all financial statements irrespective of their country of origin. Compliance with the UK STATEMENTS OF STANDARD ACCOUNTING PRACTICE (q.v.) and FINANCIAL REPORTING STANDARDS (q.v.) automatically ensures compliance with any related international standard as they are made to be compatible. The International Accounting Standards Board was set up in 1973.

International Air Transport Association. An association of the main air carriers of the world. It issues codes of conduct for dealing with customers and has a compensation scheme for travellers who are let down.

international camping carnet. A document issued to campers and caravanners who are members of an accredited club (e.g. the Caravan Club or the Camping and Caravanning Club). It gives third party liability insurance and may be produced to the proprietor of a camping site as evidence of the existence of this cover.

International Monetary Fund. A fund set up in 1944 to facilitate financial transactions and trade between nations. Contributions are made to it by member countries which have the right to borrow against the fund in defined circumstances.

international money order. A document used for transferring small amounts of money from one country to another. An international money order may be purchased at the counter of a bank. They are normally available designated either in sterling or in American dollars.

inter vivos. During life. Gifts made *inter vivos* may be taxed on the same basis as if they had passed at death where this occurs within a prescribed period after the gift.

intestacy. The state of death in the absence of a WILL (q.v.). Under the laws of intestacy the estate of the deceased is dealt with by an ADMINISTRATOR (q.v.) (there being no will to name an EXECUTOR (q.v.)) and must be disposed of in accordance with very precise statutory rules.

intra vires. Within the power of. The powers of the directors of a company are defined in the company's ARTICLES OF ASSOCIATION (q.v.) and they must act within these. The term should be contrasted with its opposite, *ULTRA VIRES* (q.v.).

intrinsic value. A value inherently part of the object to which it relates. The intrinsic value of a business is a concept central to the practice of FUNDAMENTAL ANALYSIS (q.v.). Most informed commentators hold the view, however, that there can be no such thing as an intrinsic value. Value depends on a market and derives from the balance struck between an owner's reluctance to sell and a buyer's eagerness to buy.

invalid care allowance. A social security benefit paid to invalids who require constant care. Unlike some benefits it is subject to income tax.

inventory. 1. A synonym for STOCK (q.v.). The term is most commonly used in the USA.
2. A detailed list of items, e.g a list of the contents of a property which require to be insured.

investigation. A detailed independent examination of accounts set up for a specific purpose. Many of the procedures for the investigation are similar to those used in an AUDIT (q.v.). Some, however, will be determined by the nature of the purpose of the investigation. An investigation may be conducted where fraud is suspected or where a company gets into severe difficulties, although its accounts seem to show a strong position.

investing activities. The activities of a company which relate to investing funds either in shares or interest bearing securities or in productive fixed assets. The term is one of the headings to be used in CASH FLOW STATEMENTS (q.v.) as required by FRS 1.

investment. The action of deploying funds with the intention and expectation that they will earn a return for their owner. A distinction may usefully be made between real investment and financial investment. A real investment is made where resources are used to purchase fixed and current assets for use in a productive activity. An example would be where a company sets up and equips a new factory to manufacture a product. A financial investment is made where a person uses money to purchase a legal right or receive an income in the form of INTEREST (q.v.) or a DIVIDEND (q.v.). The loan of money to a bank or the purchase of shares on the Stock Exchange are examples of financial investments. Financial investment may precede real investment, where money lent to a bank is then lent to a business, but may also be independent of it as when existing shares in a company are bought by one person from another.

investment allowance. A form of CAPITAL ALLOWANCE (q.v.) which was at one time given over and above other allowances totalling the cost of the asset. Total capital allowances would thus exceed total cost. Investment allowances were given in respect of new equipment only, i.e. not second hand, and their function was to encourage investment in such equipment.

investment appraisal. The process of evaluating an investment opportunity. It is an essential part of the process of CAPITAL BUDGETING (q.v.). There are several widely used methods of investment appraisal. The most important are PAY-BACK (q.v.), AVERAGE RATE OF RETURN (q.v.), NET PRESENT VALUE (q.v.) and INTERNAL RATE OF RETURN (q.v.).

investment club. An association of private individuals who invest their funds on a joint basis. It is usual for each club member to make a regular payment into the club's funds and for its decisions on which investments to buy and sell to be made by a committee. Like any other club an investment club is likely to a have a social purpose, but its underlying rationale is that the members can obtain enjoyment from making investment decisions and possible financial benefit from those decisions with funds which are greater than they could command individually.

investment grant. A grant given by the government to encourage a specified type of capital expenditure. Investment grants are given in furtherance of some government policy such as encouraging the development of new industry in an area of heavy unemployment. The accounting treatment of investment grants is dealt with in SSAP 4 which requires them to be released to the profit and loss account over the period of the useful life of the asset acquired.

investment income surcharge. An additional levy of INCOME TAX (q.v.) on income derived from investments. It was introduced in 1971 and abolished in 1984. At that time it was charged at the rate of 15 per cent on investment income exceeding £7,100 per annum.

investment property. A property which is held for the rental income it will produce or for the potential for capital appreciation rather than for occupation or use. SSAP 19 deals with investment properties. Under this standard there is no requirement to provide depreciation and such properties should be valued in the balance sheet at market value.

investment strategy. A plan for investment based on some defined objectives. Thus an investor may have a strategy believed to lead to the maximum capital growth in a PORTFOLIO (q.v.) with the minimum risk.

investment trust. A company whose business it is to hold investments. Shareholders in an investment trust are thus indirectly participants in a wide range of investments. An investment trust fulfils some of the functions of a UNIT TRUST (q.v.) but differs in that it is closed and applies its investment policy to a fixed fund. Shares in investment trusts often stand in the market at below their NET ASSET VALUE (q.v.). They are, therefore, an inexpensive method of investing money.

investor. One who invests money in shares or other securities with the intention of making a gain. Financial information will be important to an investor in making decisions about which investments to hold and how long to retain them.

invisible earnings. A component of the amount which the UK earns from its dealings with other countries. It arises from the export of services, such as insurance and financial services, as opposed to earnings from the sale of manufactured goods.

invoice. A routine document evidencing the despatch of goods and giving details of quality, quantity and price. A trading business will produce sales invoices to send to its customers and will receive purchase invoices from its suppliers. The invoice is the basis on which payments for the goods will be made.

IOU. A written acknowledgement of a debt. It is usually regarded as an informal document providing a memorandum of the debt rather than intended as being available as evidence in a court. The letters are an abbreviation of the expression 'I owe you'.

IRR. Letters standing for INTERNAL RATE OF RETURN (q.v.).

irrecoverable. An amount theoretically owed or available to an individual person or company but which for some reason cannot be realised. A BAD DEBT (q.v.) is an example of an item which is irrecoverable. ADVANCE CORPORATION TAX (q.v.), normally recoverable by deduction from the overall liability to corporation tax may be irrecoverable if there is no liability against which it can be offset.

irredeemable stock. An interest bearing security which will never be repaid. An industrial company may occasionally issue an irredeemable DEBENTURE (q.v.) stock, but most irredeemable stock is issued by the government. A feature of irredeemable stock is that its market value is determined solely by the prevailing rate of interest.

Isle of Man. Although part of the UK the Isle of Man has its own legislative body and its residents have certain tax privileges.

issued capital. The nominal value of the amount of capital so far issued by a company. This cannot exceed the company's AUTHORISED CAPITAL (q.v.). It is no reliable indicator of a company's actual market value.

issuing house. An institution concerned with the handling of share issues.

Issuing Houses Association. An association protecting the interests of ISSUING HOUSES (q.v.).

J

jobber. Synonym for MARKET MAKER (q.v.). The term jobber is now regarded as old-fashioned.

job centre. An office, with many branches, operated by the government, which assists persons who are seeking jobs to find them.

job costing. A method of cost determination applied in a business whose activity is made up of a number of distinct jobs. A good example is that of a car repairer. Job costing requires careful record keeping so that DIRECT MATERIAL (q.v.) and DIRECT LABOUR (q.v.) can be correctly allocated to the appropriate job. A calculated amount for OVERHEAD (q.v.) is also added. This is commonly determined as a percentage of labour costs.

job sharing. A system of employment whereby a job which would normally be held by one person is held by two or more who each work on a part-time basis. It is in the nature of job sharing, however, that they will work at different times so that full-time cover is given.

joint account. A bank account held in the names of two or more persons whereby either can make deposits or draw cheques on the same account. Many married couples operate joint bank accounts.

joint and several liability. A legal liability which is both a JOINT LIABILITY (q.v.) and a SEVERAL LIABILITY (q.v.).

joint liability. Legal liability for debts falling on a group of people jointly. It is in contrast to the alternative of SEVERAL LIABILITY (q.v.) although both may exist at the same time. If a group of people are indebted to another person and have joint liability, the creditor may sue the group but may not sue an individual member of the group.

joint owner. One who shares the rights and responsibilities of the ownership of an asset with one or more other persons. Shares in a company may, for example, be held in joint ownership, e.g. of husband and wife.

joint product. A product which is necessarily produced at the same time and in the same process as another. Petrol and lubricating oils are joint products of the process of refining crude oil. The costing of joint products up to the point of separation is impossible by any direct method and needs to be done on some arbitrary basis. One basis is to split the joint cost in proportion to the weights of the products at the point of separation. Another, often more satisfactory, is to split costs on the basis of market value at that stage.

joint stock company. A company whose capital is subscribed by applicants for shares. It will often be a LIMITED COMPANY (q.v.) but may, rarely, be an unlimited company. A joint stock company is an example of an incorporated body.

joint tenancy. A form of the joint ownership of property whereby in the event of the death of one of the joint owners the property passes automatically to the survivor. A husband and wife may own their home on the basis of a joint tenancy.

joint venture. A single transaction or group of transactions carried out by more than one person who, however, intend no permanent business association. If A and B, each of whom is in business as a sole trader, together make a purchase of bankrupt stock and then sell it at a profit to the general public before again going their separate ways, this will be a joint venture. Accounting for joint ventures requires that expenditures and revenues made and received on behalf of the joint venture are identified and recorded and that the overall profit is calculated and divided amongst the participants in some agreed proportion. Where a business relationship is continuing indefinitely this is regarded not as a joint venture but as a PARTNERSHIP (q.v.).

journal. A chronological record of all transactions in which a business has engaged. From the journal the items are posted to the LEDGER (q.v.) wherein are maintained the DOUBLE ENTRY (q.v.) records. The journal is thus one of the books of PRIME ENTRY (q.v.). In earlier times it was normal practice to record all items in a journal. This was done in a form which facilitated the posting process and at the same time, by means of a narrative, gave a full explanation of the transaction. More recently the journal was used only for less commonplace transactions, i.e. those which needed special explanation. Many businesses nowadays omit to keep a journal.

Journal of Accounting Research. An academic journal reporting research in the discipline of accounting. It commenced publication in 1963 under the joint auspices of the Institute of Professional Accounting, the Graduate School of Business, the University of Chicago and the London School of Economics and Political Science, University of London. The latter institution is no longer associated with its publication. There are two editions of the journal each year and an annual supplement is also produced.

Journal of Business Finance and Accounting. An academic journal containing articles on financial and accounting topics. It commenced publication under that name in 1974 and appears four times in each year.

judgment. A ruling of a court of law. A judgment may impose the obligation on one person to make a payment to another. Failure to make the payment then becomes a very serious matter.

junk bonds. Securities evidencing a loan which are worthless because of the poor credit status of the borrower.

just in time. A method of STOCK CONTROL (q.v.) such that the aim is to purchase stocks so that they will be delivered at exactly the point in time at which they are required. The benefit of the method is that stock holding is kept to a minimum and little capital is tied up in it. The risk is that supplies will be delivered late with consequential interruptions to production. A just in time policy must, therefore, be operated under very tight contracts with the suppliers.

K

key money. An amount payable by the lessee of a residential property to induce the landlord to accept him or her as a tenant. It is usually payable outside the formal contract between the parties.

key person. A person who is of vital importance to a business. This will usually be because of that person's special knowledge of the business. It is possible to insure against the possibility that such a person will be lost to the business if he or she dies or is disabled.

kind. The basis of a payment made in the form of goods rather than money. If a person remunerates a gardener by allowing him or her to take some of the produce of the garden this would be a payment in kind.

kitty. A pool of money contributed by a number of people for the purpose of making payments for their joint benefit.

knock-down. Description of a price which has been substantially reduced usually because of adverse trading conditions. A trader faced with high stocks and short of funds may have to sell goods at knock-down prices in order to realise them.

knock for knock. Term given to an agreement amongst motor insurers that, in the event of an accident involving parties having different insurers, each insurance company will meet the cost of the damage to its own client's vehicle. In strict law one company should pay for all the damage caused by the party at fault. The knock for knock agreement avoids the effort involved in establishing fault on the occasion of each accident.

know-how. Skill and knowledge acquired from research and/or experience. Know-how is a valuable asset, particularly of businesses involved in highly technical activities, but does not normally have an identifiable cost and does not therefore figure in the balance sheet. Where one business is purchased by another the know-how it possesses may be very important in fixing its price.

krugerrand. A South African coin containing exactly 1 ounce of pure gold. It is not LEGAL TENDER (q.v.) and does not circulate as CURRENCY (q.v.). Its function is to provide a convenient medium whereby investors can hold gold. Its value fluctuates directly with the price of gold.

L

labour. The work of human employees and, by extension, the cost of that work. When used without qualification it may be taken to mean DIRECT LABOUR (q.v.) and it is treated as part of the PRIME COST (q.v.) of the product. Indirect labour which is not incorporated into the product, e.g. maintenance labour, supervisory labour or clerical labour would be categorised as part of OVERHEAD (q.v.). Labour may be remunerated in a variety of ways and this may have an important bearing on the accounting treatment of the item. Particular attention needs to be given to IDLE TIME (q.v.) for labour paid at a standard rate for the day, BONUS (q.v.) and other INCENTIVE SCHEME (q.v.) payments and OVERTIME (q.v.).

labour hour rate. A device for enabling OVERHEAD (q.v.) to be charged equitably to production. The technique requires that, in advance of a period of account, a forecast is made of total overhead and of the number of hours which will be worked by labour. This may be done globally (i.e. for the business as a whole) or it may be done separately for each department. A labour hour rate is then computed as the total overhead divided by the total number of hours for which labour will work. This is then applied to production as it occurs by multiplying the number of hours worked on a given portion of production by the labour hour rate. Any discrepancy between the forecast figures and what actually occurs will lead to either UNDERABSORBED OVERHEAD (q.v.) or OVERABSORPTION (q.v.) of overhead.

EXAMPLE.

Expected overhead for Department E in
forthcoming year: £200,000
Estimated number of labour hours expected to be
worked in the department: 5,000

The labour hour rate is $\dfrac{£200,000}{5,000} = £40$

If a particular piece of production is subsequently subjected to 5 hours of work in the department it will be charged with 5 × £40 = £200 of overhead.

It should be noted that the labour hour rate relates entirely to overhead and that the amounts of pay given to labour are not relevant to its calculation.

labour intensive. The characteristic of production methods which require large applications of LABOUR (q.v.) and uses relatively little capital equipment.

labour turnover. A measure of the number of people who leave an organisation and thus have to be replaced. High labour turnover is costly in terms of recruitment and training of new people and it may also be an indication of a bad relationship between management and workers.

lame duck. An enterprise which cannot survive without outside assistance.

land. The most enduring form of asset. It is distinguished in accounting terms by requiring no charge for DEPRECIATION (q.v.).

land certificate. A certificate issued by the LAND REGISTRY (q.v.) to the effect that the land specified has been registered with the registry.

landlord. The owner of property which is rented out to another person. The landlord is entitled to receive an agreed amount of RENT (q.v.) and has the responsibility of maintaining the property in a good state of repair.

Land Registry. A government office which has the function of registering the ownership of land. Not all land is registered but when it is it makes easier its transfer on sale.

last in first out. A method of pricing stock issues which works on the basis that an issue is deemed to be drawn from the latest available delivery. It is often abbreviated to LIFO. Theoretically, the method should be applied to stocks which are issued in this fashion. Coal is a good example. It is non-perishable and therefore no attempt is made to use older stocks before newer. Issues are drawn from the top of the pile. In practice little attention is paid to the actual physical handling of the stock in the selection of a pricing method and its accounting consequence is more influential. LIFO may be used because, in times of rising prices, it values COST OF SALES (q.v.) at a recent, and therefore near current, price.

EXAMPLE. The following table shows deliveries and issues of stock costed on the LIFO basis.

	Units	Total cost
		£
Delivery A	100	200
Delivery B	100	250
	200	450
Issue 1 – 80 units (deemed to be from delivery B)	80	200
	120	250
Issue 2 – 50 units (20 from B and 30 from A)	50	110
Stock at end	70	140*

* All valued as being part of delivery A.

Last in first out is not accepted as a method of pricing stock issues for use in the calculation of profit for tax purposes.

laundering. The process of passing funds through a number of transactions in order to conceal their origin. It is used for money acquired illegally. For example, bank robbers might use the cash stolen to place large bets on a racecourse. Some of these would win giving them money, the origin of which could be safely acknowledged.

learning curve. An expression used to denote that any new activity takes time to become established and is likely to become more efficient after that time. The underlying idea is that knowledge of a new activity is gained by experience over time and could be plotted as a graph. When the learning curve reaches its peak (where it should stay) maximum efficiency has been achieved. One would expect a learning curve to rise rapidly at first and then more slowly as the peak is approached. A higher cost of production during the early stages of a new activity would be the expected practical manifestation of the existence of a learning curve.

leaseback. The process of taking a lease on property which was previously sold by the LESSEE (q.v.) to the LESSOR (q.v.). The object of this process is to release funds which were previously tied up in fixed assets.

leasehold. A form of tenure of land whereby the holder has possession for a defined period of years. A lease is typically for a period of 99 years after which time the land reverts to the freeholder. During the term of the lease an annual GROUND RENT (q.v.) will be paid by the leaseholder.

lease or buy. Term applied to a type of decision, i.e. whether to rent an asset or to buy it, which is often faced by a business. It can be resolved by means of DISCOUNTED CASH FLOW (q.v.) calculations.

leasing. A process of hiring rather than buying fixed assets. Its advantage is that the acquisition of assets can be achieved without a large initial outlay of funds. A genuine leasing arrangement, an OPERATING LEASE (q.v.), is one where the user hires the asset for part of its life and it then reverts to the owner, who may lease it to another party for the remainder of its life. A FINANCE LEASE (q.v.) is one where the LESSEE (q.v.) uses the asset for substantially the whole of its useful life and the lease payments are calculated to cover the full cost together with interest charges. It is thus a disguised way of purchasing the asset with the help of a loan. SSAP 23 required that assets held under a finance lease be treated on the balance sheet in the same way as if they had been purchased and a loan had been taken out to enable this. There will thus be charged in the profit and loss account interest on the loan and depreciation on the asset rather than the actual amounts of the lease payments as would be the case for an operating lease.

ledger. The collection of accounts making up a DOUBLE ENTRY (q.v.) system. Where records have been kept accurately a complete list of all balances in the ledger, in the form of a TRIAL BALANCE (q.v.) will balance. The ledger is often subdivided into CASH BOOK (q.v.), SALES LEDGER (q.v.), PURCHASE LEDGER (q.v.) and NOMINAL LEDGER (q.v.). These divisions are purely a matter of administrative convenience and do not affect the underlying principle. The ledger can then be usefully thought of in terms of running to several volumes.

ledger account. An account contained in the LEDGER (q.v.) and therefore forming part of the DOUBLE ENTRY (q.v.) system.

legacy. An amount of money or other item of value received from a deceased person under the terms of a WILL (q.v.). The recipient of a legacy, known as a legatee, may be liable for INHERITANCE TAX (q.v.) if the estate is sufficiently large.

legal aid. A service whereby persons on low incomes may obtain aid from the state towards paying for their costs when involved in legal action.

legal tender. The maximum amount which a creditor is bound by law to accept in settlement of a debt in a particular type of currency. Thus copper coins are legal tender up to 20p, 5p and 10p pieces up to £5 and 50p pieces up to £10. The intention of the law of legal tender is to prevent an unwilling debtor from inconveniencing a creditor by paying large amounts in the form of small change. A creditor is not, however, prohibited from accepting amounts above that which is legal tender and the rule is rarely invoked.

legatee. One who is in receipt of a LEGACY (q.v.).

lender of last resort. The Bank of England is the lender of last resort in the UK. If needed, it will always lend money to a commercial bank, at a rate of interest.

lessee. One who leases property from another.

lessor. One who leases property to another.

letter of allotment. A formal letter sent by a company to an applicant for shares or other security informing the applicant that an allotment has been made and of the amount allotted. A letter of allotment will normally be renounceable. If so, entitlement to the shares represented by the document may be transferred to another person by signing the appropriate form of renunciation and delivering the document. If no such action is taken then the shares embodied in a letter of allotment will be registered in the name of the allottee and a SHARE CERTIFICATE (q.v.) will be issued. The letter of allotment then ceases to be of any value.

letter of credit. A letter from a trader in one country authorising a trader in another country to draw on credit provided by a bank. It is thus a method of settling debt between parties in different countries. Its provision requires the co-operation of banks in both countries.

letter of regret. A letter which informs the applicant for shares in a company that the application has been unsuccessful.

letter of weakness. A letter drawn up by an accountant for a client whose accounting procedures have been reviewed. It sets out areas in which the system is weak or insecure and generally makes recommendations as to how matters might be improved. A letter of weakness is commonly provided following the AUDIT (q.v.) of a business's records at which time such weaknesses as there are become apparent.

level funding. A situation arising where a public service is allowed funds equal to the amount received in the previous period. This means that it will not be able to expand or improve its activities.

level of activity. The amount of ACTIVITY (q.v.) engaged in by a business. The level of activity can vary considerably according to market conditions and it has a very considerable effect on the amount of profit which can be earned.

level playing field. A term used to describe fair trading conditions. If a manufacturer in one country has to pay a heavy tax on some important input and this tax is not payable by manufacturers in another country then they are not operating on a level playing field as the one has a competitive handicap.

leverage. Synonym for GEARING (q.v.) commonly used in the USA.

leveraged buyout. Synonym for GEARED BUYOUT (q.v.).

levy. To place some financial burden on people or businesses. A government, for example, may levy taxation. The owner of a trademark may make a levy on those licensed to use the trademark.

liability. A legal obligation expressed in terms of money. Liabilities may be payable in the short term, e.g. CREDITORS (q.v.), in the long term, e.g. redeemable DEBENTURES (q.v.) or may exist for the lifetime of the business, e.g. irredeemable debentures.

LIBOR. Letters standing for LONDON INTERBANK OFFICE RATE (q.v.).

licence. Authorisation to engage in some activity. The licence is usually evidenced by some document and may be issued automatically following payment and/or the observance of certain conditions. The user of a television set, for example, must purchase a television licence and the driver of a car must hold a driving licence. Some licences are for the purpose of raising revenue and some are to enable the exercise of control over an activity. One business may issue a licence to another to enable it to manufacture a product to an agreed specification and attach a recognised trademark to it.

licensed dealer in securities. One who is permitted under the terms of the Prevention of Fraud (Investments) Act 1958 to deal in securities. Dealing will include buying them and then reselling them to clients.

licensed deposit taker. One who is permitted to accept deposits.

lien. A legal right to retain possession of another person's property until a contractual obligation (usually payment) has been fulfilled. Thus an accountant has a lien over a client's books in respect of an unpaid fee arising from professional, accountancy services. A lien applies only to property which is an element of the contract which it is sought to enforce. The accountant, for example, would not have a lien over the client's car.

life assurance. An insurance against a person's death. A policy of life assurance may be in one of a number of forms. A term assurance covers the life for a stated period of time. If death occurs during that time a claim may be made but if it does not there will be no claim. ENDOWMENT POLICIES (q.v.) become payable on the expiration of a stated period or on earlier death. Whole life policies are payable on death whenever it occurs. Rates of PREMIUM (q.v.) take into account the actuarial probabilities associated with each type of policy.

life assurance premium relief. A relief given against income tax to persons paying premiums on policies of life assurance on either their own life or on that of a spouse. The relief was terminated for new policies from 14 March 1984 but continues to be available on existing policies taken out before that date. The relief is given by a reduction in the amount of premium paid by a percentage related to the standard rate of income tax. The life assurance company then reclaims this amount from the Inland Revenue.

life expectancy. The average life remaining to persons of a specified age. Life expectancy statistics are used by life assurance companies to assess the premiums they charge. It is important to note that life expectancy does not apply to an individual but to the population as a whole.

life tenant. A person who has the use of, or income from, some property owned by a trust for the duration of his or her lifetime. After that it will pass to some other person.

LIFO. Letters standing for LAST IN FIRST OUT (q.v.).

limited. A word which must form part of the name of a company to indicate that its members have LIMITED LIABILITY (q.v.).

limited company. A company the members of which have LIMITED LIABILITY (q.v.).

limited liability. A legal privilege granted to the members of some incorporated bodies. By far the most numerous and important of these are limited companies carrying on a business. The effect of limited liability is that, although a member may lose the whole of his or her investment in a business, he or she may not be called upon to pay in any more. The introduction of limited liability (by the Companies Act 1855) was a prerequisite to large-scale public involvement in corporate investment. Limited liability is also granted in the case of certain types of partnership which are then known as LIMITED PARTNERSHIPS (q.v.).

limited partnership. A form of PARTNERSHIP (q.v.) in which one or more, but not all, of the partners have LIMITED LIABILITY (q.v.). Limited partnerships are rare as their function is usually best served by a PRIVATE COMPANY (q.v.). The legislation under which limited partnerships are permissible is the Limited Partnership Act 1907. It requires that the partnership should also have one or more general partners (i.e. with unlimited liability).

limiting factor. That factor in a business situation which places a limit on expansion. The limiting factor may be the availability of material, skilled labour or factory capacity. Its importance is that it places a limit on a BUDGET (q.v.) and that it should be a concern of management to use its limiting factor in as profitable way as possible. This is important in deciding whether, for example, factory space is to be devoted to one product or to another.

linear programming. A mathematical technique with some application in the field of multi-period CAPITAL RATIONING (q.v.). The technique enables a choice of the optimum to be made from a wide range of complex options.

line of credit. A facility, such as a bank overdraft, which allows the holder to draw credit up to a certain agreed amount.

liquid assets. Assets which are either in the form of cash or in a form which can readily be converted into cash. Thus cash itself, bank balances, debtors and marketable securities would all be classified as liquid assets. The converse of liquid assets is ILLIQUID ASSETS (q.v.).

liquidated damages. An amount incorporated into a contract as a penalty for non-performance which represents a genuine pre-estimate of the amount of the damage which would be caused by the breach.

liquidation. The process of turning assets into cash. The term is usually applied when a business has been terminated so that all its assets have to be sold. This enables it to pay its obligations and make a return of the residual capital to its PROPRIETOR (q.v.).

liquidator. One charged with the responsibility of realising the assets of a business which has ceased trading.

liquidity. The characteristic of convertibility into cash. Assets have varying degrees of liquidity. Cash and bank balances are highly liquid. Buildings and machinery are largely illiquid.

liquidity ratio. Synonym for ACID TEST RATIO (q.v.).

lira. The unit of currency in Italy.

list price. The price for an article which appears in the manufacturer's catalogue. Many retailers will be subject to competitive pressures to sell goods at below the list price.

listed security. A security which is dealt in on the STOCK EXCHANGE (q.v.). Many trading companies have their shares listed. Other listed securities are government and corporation loans.

livelihood. The activity whereby a person earns an income supportive of their life.

livestock. An asset consisting of fish, animals or birds. It is usually applied to an agricultural business to refer to cattle, pigs, sheep, etc.

living. A post occupied by a vicar in the Church of England.

Lloyd's. An association of people offering insurance. It is organised in such a way that the risks and the premium income associated with them are spread over a large number of participators.

loan. A sum of money advanced by one person to another with the intention that the amount concerned should ultimately be repaid. Usually INTEREST (q.v.) is payable in respect of a loan. Loans are very common in business. They should be accounted for, in the accounts of the borrower, by showing them as liabilities on the balance sheet and showing any interest paid as an expense in the profit and loss account. In the records of the lender the loan appears as an asset and the interest as income.

loan capital. Capital provided on the basis that a stated rate of interest is paid on it and its holders have no other claim on the outcome of business operations. The principal sum loaned is frequently repayable at a stated date but examples of irredeemable loans may also be found. The fixed rate of interest regardless of profit is the distinguishing feature of loan capital.

loan shark. A person who makes loans to people on very harsh terms. This usually includes a high rate of interest and may also include very onerous penalties for default. People having very low incomes, who cannot borrow money elsewhere, sometimes fall into the hands of loan sharks.

loans to directors. Money lent by a company to its own directors. Because such transactions could be open to abuse company legislation requires full disclosure of the terms and amounts of such loans in the published accounts.

local taxation. A tax which applies only to persons living in a certain area. The COUNCIL TAX (q.v.) is the main example of local taxation in the UK.

London Interbank Office Rate. A rate of interest used by banks amongst themselves. It is, however, related to general interest rates and underlies rates charged by the banks to customers.

long-dated stock. Fixed interest security which is not redeemable for many years. The price of such stocks is influenced much more by the rate of interest paid on them than it is by the amount at which they will ultimately be redeemed.

long-term contract. A contract entered into for the supply of a single item or service such that the activity of meeting the contract extends over more than one accounting period. The term is used in SSAP 9 on stock and long-term contracts. The significance of a long-term contract is that the profit earned under it may be taken into the profit and loss account progressively over the period of the contract where certain criteria are met. It follows that the balance sheet value of WORK IN PROGRESS (q.v.) on such a contract will be valued at cost plus ATTRIBUTABLE PROFIT (q.v.).

long-term debt. Debt which need not be repaid in the near future. *See also* LOAN CAPITAL.

loophole. Some defect in a set of rules which allows a practice not envisaged by those drafting the rules but which would not have been approved by them. It has often been very profitable to search for loopholes in tax legislation where tax can be avoided by entering into artificially constructed transactions which manage to defeat the precise wording of the statutes. Substantial parts of tax legislation (ANTI-AVOIDANCE (q.v.)) have been enacted specifically to close loopholes but new ones are frequently discovered.

loss. An excess of expenses over revenues. A loss is prima facie evidence that the business activity is being conducted unsuccessfully. Business may, however, be conducted at a loss deliberately during a period when a market is being established or as a service to customers who bring highly profitable business to other divisions of the company. Tax legislation allows losses to be set off against profits in determining an individual's or company's tax liability.

loss adjuster. An expert employed by an insurance company to assess the amount of its liability when a claim has been made. The loss adjuster will be required not only to determine the total value of the damage concerned but also to determine the extent to which it is to be indemnified under the policy. This will depend in part on whether the event causing the damage is properly an event insured against and in part on whether the value insured was adequate.

loss leader. A product which is sold knowingly at a loss or uneconomically low profit with the object of attracting the attention of customers to more profitable lines. A supermarket, for example, might sell very cheap bread in the hope that, when in the shop, customers will do the rest of their shopping at its normal prices.

loss of profits insurance. A form of INSURANCE (q.v.) which indemnifies the insured against the effects of loss of business following the occurrence of an event insured against. If the factory premises of a company are damaged by fire, the cost of repairs will normally be covered by a fire insurance policy. As important to the company, however, may be the reduction in profit which results from the disruption to its normal business activities. It is this secondary loss which loss of profits insurance would make up.

loss relief. A relief against taxation given where a business incurs a loss. The relief is always given as a set-off against earlier or later profits so that no relief can be obtained unless the business is at some time profitable.

lot. An item in an AUCTION (q.v.) sale. A lot may consist of a single object or a collection of objects which have been grouped together for the sale.

lottery. A form of gambling whereby the participators purchase numbered tickets in the hope of winning a large cash prize. The winner is selected by drawing a number at random. In some countries state-operated lotteries are an important source of finance. A state lottery is shortly to be introduced in the UK.

low. The lowest level reached by the price of a security during a specified period of time. Thus a share might be at a low for the year or at an all-time low.

lower of cost or net realisable value. A generally accepted prudent basis for the valuation of STOCK (q.v.). It involves determining the cost and the net realisable value (i.e. prospective sales proceeds less direct costs of selling) for each different category of stock and applying the lower of the two figures item by item. The total stock valuation may thus contain some items at cost and others at net realisable value. It is this basis of valuation which is required by SSAP 9.

ltd. A recognised abbreviation of the word limited. A PRIVATE COMPANY (q.v.) must have this word or its abbreviation as part of its name.

lump sum. A substantial amount of money paid at a single point in time. The term is commonly encountered in particular situations. A member of an occupational pension scheme, for example, will normally receive, in addition to a regular pension, a lump sum at the date of retirement. The holder of an ENDOWMENT POLICY (q.v.) will receive a lump sum at its maturity. Under some contracts a beneficiary may be able to choose between receiving a lump sum and an ANNUITY (q.v.).

Lutine bell. A bell once belonging to a ship named the *Lutine* kept at Lloyd's, the insurers. It is traditionally sounded when news of a disaster is about to be announced.

M

machine hour rate. A technique for apportioning OVERHEAD (q.v.) to particular elements of production. It is a useful method to use in the case of highly mechanised production where a LABOUR HOUR RATE (q.v.) would be too sensitive to minor and incidental variations in the time spent by labour. The calculation of a machine hour rate requires that all overheads are allocated (*see* ALLOCATION) or apportioned (*see* APPORTIONMENT) to individual machines or groups of machines. The total overhead imputed to a machine in this way is then divided by its actual or estimated running hours to give a machine hour rate. Segments of production will then be required to ABSORB (q.v.) overhead at the machine hour rate applied to the length of time which each spends on the machine. It should be noted that the direct costs involved in operating a machine (e.g. the raw material it uses) are not included in the machine hour rate as they can be charged directly to the product as part of its PRIME COST (q.v.).

magnate. A wealthy and influential business person.

mail order. A method of retail selling whereby the customer submits an order by post or by telephone having made a selection of goods from an advertisement or a catalogue. Payment is usually made at the time of the order by cheque or by credit card. The goods are then sent to the customer by post. There are significant cost savings to the supplier in not having to maintain a chain of retail premises and some part of this can be passed to the customer in the form of lower prices or, more probably, better service. Typically the buyer has the right to a full refund for any reason whether specified or not if not satisfied with the goods on receipt.

main residence. A private house where a person lives for most of the time or which is regarded by the person as his or her main residence. Its significance is that any gain made by a person in disposing of the main residence is free from CAPITAL GAINS TAX (q.v.). Where a person owns more than one property he or she has the right to nominate any one of them as the main residence within two years of its acquisition. If this is not done the Inspector of Taxes will decide on the facts which appears to be the main residence.

mainstream corporation tax. The main sum paid or payable in respect of CORPORATION TAX (q.v.). Under the IMPUTATION SYSTEM (q.v.) tax may become payable in advance of its normal due date in the form of ADVANCE CORPORATION TAX (q.v.). The total liability to tax is reduced by the amounts of these payments leaving the mainstream corporation tax outstanding.

maintenance. 1. The process of keeping fixed assets, such as buildings and machinery, in a good working order. It gives rise to an important item of OVERHEAD (q.v.) expenditure.

2. Payment made by one person towards the cost of living of another towards whom there is either a legal or moral obligation. Thus a divorced man might pay maintenance to his ex-wife under an order of a court.

majority shareholder. A shareholder in a company who holds more than 50 per cent of the shares. Such a shareholder can outvote the others on any matter.

managed fund. A collection of securities which is subject to active supervision in order to achieve defined objectives, e.g. maximum income or maximum capital growth. A UNIT TRUST (q.v.) is an example of a managed fund.

management accounting. That area of accounting concerned with the provision of information for the use of management. It may be contrasted with FINANCIAL ACCOUNTING (q.v.) which is concerned largely with the provision of information to interests outside the business such as lenders and shareholders. Included in management accounting are matters such as COSTING (q.v.), BUDGETING (q.v.) and INVESTMENT APPRAISAL (q.v.). In its nature it is often concerned with small segments of business activity where financial accounting is more usually concerned with the overall picture. Management accounting statements are often less formalised than those of financial accounting and may be prepared on an *ad hoc* basis to meet a particular informational need. The distinction between the two, however, is not a rigid one and fully integrated systems may exist. Both rely on the same basic sources of information.

management buyout. The purchase by managerial employees of the business for which they work from their employing company. A management buyout most commonly occurs when the business is under threat of closure and the existing management team believe that they can save it. It carries high risks but, if successful, the rewards can be very great.

management consultant. One who offers the professional service of advice on problems connected with the management of a business. Management consultancy services are frequently offered by the same large firms of accountants who offer audit and taxation services. There are also many specialist consultants.

management fee. The fee charged to a unit trust by its managers for their services. It is ultimately paid by the unit holders.

mandate. An authority given to take some action. A Board of Directors may, for example, be given a mandate to carry out some controversial proposal by putting the proposal to a general meeting of shareholders and receiving the approval of the meeting.

manufacturing account. A statement designed to determine and report overall manufacturing cost. Its main components will be MATERIAL (q.v.), LABOUR (q.v.) and FACTORY OVERHEAD (q.v.) costs. An adjustment must be made for any change in WORK IN PROGRESS (q.v.). The total manufacturing cost will be transferred to the TRADING ACCOUNT (q.v.).

margin. The difference between the selling price and the basic cost of a product. It equates to the GROSS PROFIT (q.v.).

marginal cost. A cost directly attributable to a specified segment of production. Marginal cost usually includes MATERIAL (q.v.), LABOUR (q.v.) and VARIABLE OVERHEAD (q.v.).

marginal costing. A form of costing in which only directly variable costs are taken into consideration. The special value of marginal costing is in decision making. If the revenue arising from the implementation of a decision exceeds the marginal cost, then the overall profit of the business will be increased. The excess of revenue over marginal cost is termed the CONTRIBUTION (q.v.).

marginal rate of income tax. That rate of tax which a taxpayer pays on the highest portion of income. For many taxpayers the marginal rate will be the same as the standard rate. It will, however, be higher for a higher rate taxpayer. The significance of the marginal rate is that this is the rate which should be used in calculating the effect on net earnings of any changes such as the earning of additional income or the claiming of any reliefs.

marginal relief. Relief given to a taxpayer where a step up in the rate of tax would otherwise penalise him or her unduly. It smooths out the transition from one band to another.

marginal revenue. The increase in revenue occasioned by a small increment in the volume of trade. It may not be the same as the current price because an overall reduction in price might need to be made in order to sell the increment.

margin of safety. The level of TURNOVER (q.v.) which could be lost by a business before it arrived at its BREAKEVEN POINT (q.v.). The concept of the margin of safety is used in BREAKEVEN ANALYSIS (q.v.) and is a measure of how vulnerable profit is to unexpected fluctuations in the level of activity.

mark. The unit of currency in Germany.

mark down. To reduce prices below a previously stated level. A retailer might mark down goods for the purposes of the annual sale.

market. A mechanism by which buyers and sellers are brought into contact. Sometimes this may require their physical presence, as in the case of retail market but very often it will not do so. The Stock Exchange is a market and there are also very large markets in foreign exchange and in commodities where the business is carried out by specialised dealers rather than by the ultimate buyers and sellers.

marketable. Readily saleable. Marketable securities, for example, are those which are quoted on a stock exchange. Marketable assets are those for which buyers can readily be found.

market analysis. The study of stock market trends with a view to predicting the future course of security prices. A particular type of market analysis is practised by CHARTISTS (q.v.) who graph market movements and purport to observe and interpret developing patterns in the graphs. The EFFICIENT MARKET THEORY (q.v.) predicts that the stock market follows a RANDOM WALK (q.v.) and that its movements cannot therefore be predicted.

market capitalisation. The total value of a company determined by multiplying the stock market price of its shares by the total number of shares in issue. Although frequently calculated and stated as a measure of the size of a company it is not necessarily a realistic estimate of the value of the business as an entity. It may fluctuate widely from day to day and, because it is based on trading in a small proportion of the company's shares, does not necessarily represent what a purchaser of the entire company would have to pay for it.

market maker. A member of an organised market, such as the Stock Exchange, whose function it is to buy what is offered and sell what is required at prices determined by the market maker. It is these prices, different for buying and selling in order to create a TURN (q.v.), which keep buyers and sellers in equilibrium.

market price. The price of goods or services established by the interplay of supply and demand in a market.

market share. The proportion of the whole market for specified goods which is supplied by one supplier. There are many goods where there cannot be any realistic expectation of an increase in total demand. A supplier may still grow, however, by increasing its market share at the expense of its competitors.

market value. The value of an asset based on the amount which it is believed it would command if sold. Some assets, such as securities, are traded regularly on an organised market and their value is relatively simple to establish. The market value of, for example, specialised plant and machinery may, however, be more difficult to establish.

Markowitz. Person responsible for the initial formulation of PORTFOLIO THEORY (q.v.).

mark-up. The amount which a retailer adds to the cost of goods in order to establish the price to be charged to customers. The mark-up determines the level of GROSS PROFIT (q.v.).

marriage. The process whereby a man and a woman enter a contract, avowedly for life, which recognises them as a married couple. There are very important financial implications arising from marriage. The most important is that what is legally the property of only one party to the marriage, e.g. the home in which they live, may be regarded by a court as being joint property in the event of any dispute. A man is under an obligation enforceable under law to give financial support to his wife and, if there are any, to the children of the marriage. If a person dies INTESTATE (q.v.) a proportion of the estate will go absolutely to the surviving husband or wife by operation of law.

married couple's allowance. An allowance against income given for the purposes of calculating income tax to a married couple. They are thus treated more favourably from a taxation point of view than if they were two single people.

massage. To process accounting figures in such a way as to give a misleading impression short of actual FALSE ACCOUNTING (q.v.). This may be done by the style of the presentation or by the adoption of discretionary accounting practices which give the desired result.

master budget. The overall plan for a business's financial activities to which its sectional plans must relate. The master budget would normally be prepared in the form of a summarised projected profit and loss account and summarised projected balance sheet. These would then be amplified by detailed subsidiary budgets.

Mastercard. The name of one of the main world-wide organisations supporting a CREDIT CARD (q.v.).

matched bargain. A type of share transfer in which the person wishing to sell shares is matched directly against a person wishing to buy them through the offices of an intermediary. The intermediary does not, therefore, agree to buy and hold the shares as occurs in normal stock exchange transactions. Matched bargains are used where the number of transactions taking place in a particular company's shares is very small.

matching. A fundamental accounting principle, whereby, in computing profit, all costs are set off (or matched) against the revenues to which they relate. Thus profit is not the revenue of a period less the expense of the period. It is the revenues of a period less the expenditure, whenever incurred, involved in producing those revenues. There are many practical difficulties in the way of achieving perfect matching. The main types of matching which are encountered in practice may be classified as:

(a) Matching by direct association. For example, materials and labour appear on the profit and loss account of the period in which their product is sold.

(b) Matching by time. For example, electricity and telephone costs cannot be associated directly with production and are therefore charged against the revenues of the period which benefits from this expenditure.

(c) Matching by arbitrary apportionment. For example, depreciation. A more or less arbitrary form of matching must be used when other methods are unavailable.

material. 1. The cost of the physical substance incorporated into a product during a manufacturing process. Its importance is that it is one of the main classifications of cost. The recording of material costs is an important function of STOCK CONTROL (q.v.) methods. Material is one component of PRIME COST (q.v.), the other being LABOUR (q.v.).

2. Significant. In accounting, a distinction is made between material items or adjustments (i.e. those large enough to make a real difference) and those which are immaterial (i.e. unimportant). Normal practice is to reserve meticulous attention to accuracy only for material items. Accounting standards and company legislation make numerous references to material items. What should be regarded as material is a matter of judgement and guidance is rarely given. Any matter which will affect a reported figure by over 5 per cent would probably be deemed material, however.

materiality. The characteristic of being MATERIAL (q.v.).

material requisition. A document requiring and authorising the issue of material to production. The material requisition is an important part of the documentation of a system of STOCK CONTROL (q.v.) and serves to prevent the wasteful or illicit use of materials.

maternity allowance. A social security benefit given to women on the birth of a child.

matrix. An organised way of displaying financial or other data so as to display the interdependence of the figures.

maturity. The date at which a long-term financial obligation falls due. Thus a policy of life assurance reaches maturity at death or at the end of a prescribed period of time. A government security reaches maturity at the date it is due to be repaid.

Maundy money. Specially minted coins presented annually by the Queen to selected elderly people on Maundy Thursday which is the Thursday immediately before Easter. In origin the custom was a means of giving assistance to the poor. Its function is now largely ceremonial although the Maundy coins have some value as collectors' pieces.

means testing. The use of information about a person's income and other resources to determine their entitlement to some benefit. Its purpose is to enable the benefit to go only to those who genuinely require it.

medium of exchange. That which serves to facilitate exchange of valuable goods and services for other goods and services but has no other intrinsic value of its own. Cash is the only important medium of exchange.

medium-sized company. A company of a size defined in the Companies Act 1985 and thereby permitted to publish modified annual accounts. The criteria for this size given in the Act are: turnover in the range £1.4–5.75 million; balance sheet total in the range £0.7–2.8 million; average number of employees 50–250. Although the accounts filed with the Registrar may be modified, full statutory accounts must still be sent to shareholders.

member. A member of a company is synonymous with a SHAREHOLDER (q.v.).

members' voluntary liquidation. The WINDING UP (q.v.) of a company following a decision of the shareholders in circumstances where the company is not INSOLVENT (q.v.) and, therefore, the creditors can be satisfied in full.

memorandum account. A statement taking the form of an account but which forms no part of the DOUBLE ENTRY (q.v.) system. Usually a memorandum account duplicates and explains further the information given in a ledger account.

Memorandum of Association. A formal document with which a limited company is registered. It sets out the following matters:
    (a) The name of the company.
    (b) The fact, if this is the case, that it is to be a public company.
    (c) The country (i.e. England, Wales or Scotland) where the registered office is to be situated.

(d) The objects of the company. (This is the OBJECTS CLAUSE (q.v.).)

(e) A statement that the liability of the members is limited.

(f) The amount of share capital with which the company is to be registered. (This is the AUTHORISED CAPITAL (q.v.).)

(g) A statement that named subscribers, who each undertake to take a specified number of shares, wish to form the company.

merchant bank. An institution concerned with giving a financial service to business. This includes advising on and arranging share and loan issues and mergers and takeovers.

merger. The amalgamation of two or more businesses which were previously separate. The term is properly applied where the parties to the amalgamation are of comparable size and influence and where the combination is effected by an exchange of shares so that shareholders in the original companies become shareholders in the group. Where there is a cash purchase of one company's shares by another to effect the combination, this is more correctly termed a TAKEOVER (q.v.).

merger method. A method of preparing CONSOLIDATED ACCOUNTS (q.v.) which may be appropriate when the HOLDING COMPANY (q.v.) acquires its interest in the SUBSIDIARY COMPANY (q.v.) by means of an issue of its own shares. The distinguishing feature of the merger method is that the investment in the subsidiary is valued in the books of the holding company at the nominal value of the shares issued in order to acquire it. In the consolidation all figures appear as if the companies had always been amalgamated. One consequence is that fixed assets continue to be valued at their existing book values and that no account is taken of the PREACQUISITION PROFIT (q.v.) of the subsidiary. The definition of a merger is currently contained in SSAP 23.

merger relief. The relief, given under s.131 of the Companies Act 1985, given to a company from the obligation to create a share premium account when shares are issued of a value greater than their nominal value in furtherance of a business combination. The availability of merger relief is a prerequisite to the use of the MERGER METHOD (q.v.) in consolidated accounts.

merger reserve. A CAPITAL RESERVE (q.v.) appearing in the consolidated balance sheet for a group of companies arising where the value of the underlying assets acquired exceeds the value of the consideration given for them.

merit award. An increase in wages or salary given to a person because of the quality of the work which they have performed.

mezzanine finance. Finance which is neither purely equity, i.e. shares, or loan finance but has some of the characteristics of each. CONVERTIBLE DEBENTURES (q.v.) are an example of mezzanine finance.

middle market value. A value placed on a stock market security by striking an average between its OFFER PRICE (q.v.) and its BID PRICE (q.v.) both of which are quoted in the OFFICIAL LIST (q.v.). It is a common way of valuing investments for the purposes of PROBATE (q.v.) and for a note to a company's final accounts in respect of investments which are held by the company.

milk. To take full advantage of a profitable situation often without regard to the interests of others. A retailer selling an inferior product for an apparently attractive price may, for example, be said to be milking the customers.

minimum lending rate. The minimum rate of interest charged by the BANK OF ENGLAND (q.v.) for discounting first-class bills of exchange. No longer announced in public except in times of crisis when the Bank reserves the right to give a clear signal to the money markets.

minimum subscription. The amount stated in a PROSPECTUS (q.v.) relating to an issue of shares which is the minimum amount to be applied for before ALLOTMENT (q.v.) may take place. Unless a certain minimum amount of finance is raised the viability of the project set out in the prospectus would be in jeopardy. It is therefore illegal to allot shares if the minimum subscription is not reached.

mint. A factory where coins are made. In the UK, coins are made at the Royal Mint.

minority interest. The equity of shareholders in a SUBSIDIARY COMPANY (q.v.) as shown in the consolidated balance sheet. The minority interest represents the nominal capital and reserves attributable to the minority shareholders.

minority shareholder. A person who holds less than 50 per cent of the shares of a company. Such a person can be outvoted on any issue by a combination of other shareholders.

minute. A record in writing of a decision taken at a meeting. The minutes of meetings of a Board of Directors may be important in the verification by an AUDITOR (q.v.) of the authority for transactions undertaken by a company.

MIRAS. Letters standing for MORTGAGE INTEREST RELIEF AT SOURCE (q.v.).

misappropriation. The diversion of funds for an improper or dishonest purpose. If, for example, an employee of a business causes that business to pay his or her private bills that will be misappropriation.

miser. One who takes pleasure in the mere possession of cash but has no intention of putting it to any use.

mix variance. A difference between actual cost and budgeted cost explainable from the fact that a different mix of raw materials has been used from that envisaged in the budget.

mobility allowance. A social security benefit given to disabled persons to enable them to run appropriate personal transport.

modified accounts. Less detailed accounts which SMALL COMPANIES (q.v.) and MEDIUM-SIZED COMPANIES (q.v.) are permitted under the Companies Act 1985 to file with the Registrar of Companies. Such companies must still present full accounts to their shareholders.

Modigliani and Miller theory. A theory that CAPITAL STRUCTURE (q.v.) is not a factor in determining the COST OF CAPITAL (q.v.). The theory argues that the total value of a business is the same whatever its method of financing. The theory depends on the validity of a fairly rigid set of assumptions and is not fully accepted as a description of the real world.

moiety. One half. It might be applied to the division of a trust fund equally between two people.

monetary assets and liabilities. Assets and liabilities which have a value fixed in money terms. Their significance is that neither market price changes nor changes in the general level of prices will alter their money value. In time of inflation the holding of monetary assets is a source of loss in real terms and of monetary liabilities a source of gain. Examples of monetary assets are cash, bank balances and debtors. Examples of monetary liabilities are creditors, bank overdrafts and debentures.

monetary working capital adjustment. An adjustment which was required under SSAP 16 to show the net loss or gain caused by inflation and attributable to the holding of MONETARY ASSETS AND LIABILITIES (q.v.) by a company.

money. That which is used as a medium of exchange. At various times in the past money has been a substance, such as a precious metal, which had uses other than its use as currency. Modern money is purely a token and much of it exists only as balances recorded in accounting records.

moneylender. One who lends money. The term is usually applied to those who lend cash in relatively small amounts to people who are not creditworthy enough to borrow from a bank. Interest charged is thus quite high and repayment terms rigorously enforced.

money market. The market operated by financial institutions for money to borrow and to lend. Its operations are a determinant of the rate of INTEREST (q.v.).

money measurement. The accounting concept which refers to the use of money as the scale against which accounting measurements are made. It has the advantage of reducing all quantities to a common factor and thus making them directly comparable. It has, however, certain disadvantages. One is that matters which cannot be measured in terms of money, e.g. the general well-being of the workforce or the reputation of the business, are generally omitted from accounting statements however relevant they might otherwise be. Another is that money measurement is vulnerable to distortion brought about by changes in the general price level.

money purchase scheme. A pension scheme whereby the pension ultimately paid depends on the amount of money which has been saved by the member. This money is used to purchase a lifetime ANNUITY (q.v.).

money supply A measure of the total amount of money circulating in the economy at a specified point in time. Its relationship to the volume of goods available at the same time is one factor governing the degree of INFLATION (q.v.) in the economy.

Monopolies and Mergers Commission. A governmental body responsible for investigating monopolies and mergers. It has the power to intervene where situations exist or proposals are made which are regarded as limiting competition to an extent incompatible with the public interest.

month one basis. A basis of deducting PAYE taxation from an employee to be used pending receipt of the P45 form giving details of income and tax deducted from a previous employer. It works on the basis that the current employment is the first job the employee has held.

moonlighting. The practice of earning money by doing work outside a person's normal employment. A person who was a shop assistant during the day and then visited people in their homes to sell life assurance in the evening for the extra income this would bring might be said to be moonlighting.

mortgage. A legal charge on property which holds it as security for a loan. The owner of a property who requires to borrow money (sometimes for the purchase of the same property) executes a deed of mortgage in favour of the lender and deposits the deeds to the property with it. The effect of the mortgage is that no dealings in the property can take place without the permission of the lender (the mortgagee). In the event of DEFAULT (q.v.) by the borrower (the mortgagor) from the agreed terms of payment of interest and repayment of principal, the lender may sell the property and make up the default out of the proceeds. The process is known as FORECLOSURE (q.v.).

mortgagee. One who lends money to another on the security of a MORTGAGE (q.v.).

mortgage interest relief at source. The method whereby payments of mortgage interest by a taxpayer are given immediate relief from income tax. This is usually shortened to MIRAS. Under the system mortgagors deduct income tax at the basic rate from the interest component of their total repayments.

mortgagor. One who borrows money from another and gives a MORTGAGE (q.v.) as security.

multi-currency capital. The capital of a businesss which is designated in more than one currency.

multinational company. A company whose business interests extend across national boundaries. This gives rise to many financial and accounting problems. One important problem is the effect on the business of fluctuating exchange rates between currencies. Another is the incidence of taxation under different jurisdictions.

multiple applications. Numerous applications for shares in a company all from the same applicant. This practice was at one time allowed and indeed welcomed as it contributed to the success of an issue. It is now commonly made a condition of a share offer that each applicant submits only one application. To submit more than one would then be fraudulent.

multiple shop. A retail organisation which has many branches in different locations. It is a characteristic of multiple shops that they are very similar in style and in the goods which they stock. They will often have goods manufactured for them which can be sold under the brand name of the shop. W. H. Smith and Sainsbury's are good examples of multiple shops.

mutual fund. The American equivalent of the UNIT TRUST (q.v.).

mutual organisation. An organisation owned by those who are its customers. A BUILDING SOCIETY (q.v.) is a mutual organisation as are many LIFE ASSURANCE (q.v.) companies. Such an organisation exists for the benefit of its members to whom all profits are returned.

mutually exclusive projects. Projects such that engagement in one automatically excludes engagement in another. In appraising the investment potential of mutually exclusive projects they should be ranked according to NET PRESENT VALUE (q.v.) to determine which are the better alternatives.

N

naked debenture. A DEBENTURE (q.v.) which is not supported by SECURITY (q.v.).

name. 1. The name by which a limited company is known. The name of a company is contained in its MEMORANDUM OF ASSOCIATION (q.v.) and can be changed only by SPECIAL RESOLUTION (q.v.). For a limited company the name must contain the words 'Limited' or 'Public Limited Company' or some acceptable abbreviation. Which term is used depends on whether the company is a PRIVATE COMPANY (q.v.) or PUBLIC COMPANY (q.v.).
2. A member of Lloyd's, the insurers. To be a name a person must be elected to that position and must put up a substantial cash deposit. The name will join a syndicate with other names and insurance business will be transacted on behalf of the syndicate by an underwriter. A name may profit considerably from membership of Lloyd's but there is also the risk of substantial loss.

narration. That part of the entry in a JOURNAL (q.v.) which explains the transaction which is recorded there. The narration is particularly important for non-routine transactions where their nature is, otherwise, not apparent.

narrower range investments. Investments defined as such in the Trustee Investments Act 1961. Their significance is that a TRUSTEE (q.v.) may freely invest the funds of the trust in such investments, taking financial advice in cases where the Act requires this. The characteristic of these investments is that they are risk-free interest bearing government-backed securities.

narrow market. A market in the shares of a particular company, or some other security, characterised by little activity. In a narrow market any unusual increases in activity can cause a disproportionate effect on price.

national assistance. Financial aid given by the state to persons who have an inadequate income. In the UK the right to national assistance is determined by legal rules.

national debt. The amount which the government of the country owes arising out of its issue in the past of government securities. The interest payable on the national debt is a charge against the funds raised by taxation.

National Giro. A personal banking service offered through post offices. In addition to normal bank facilities such as a cheque book, National Giro provides a simple method of paying bills by direct charge to an account.

national income. A measure of the total wealth producing capacity of a nation. It is the total of the incomes of all its residents.

national insurance. A form of taxation raised explicitly to meet the cost of the welfare state. Every working person has deducted from wages or salary an amount, determined by statute and amended from time to time, for national insurance. A further contribution is required from the employer. Benefits derived from national insurance include health care, sickness benefit and pensions.

nationalisation. The process whereby a government takes into state ownership designated businesses or industries. This may be done without the compensation of the existing owners, but compensation, on a government-determined formula, has always been a feature of nationalisation in the UK. The immediate post-war Labour government embarked on an extensive programme of nationalisation which brought the railway, steel and coal industries into public ownership amongst others. Much of what was then done has since been reversed under a policy of PRIVATISATION (q.v.).

National Savings Certificates. A form of investment offered to savers by the government and available for purchase personally at post offices or by post. Each issue of certificates has its own terms and rates of interest. A fixed sum is invested and interest is credited periodically. The amounts are graduated so as to give maximum benefit when the certificate is held for its full term, normally 5 years. The interest on National Savings Certificates is completely free of all taxation. There is a limit to the amount which an individual may invest in any one issue. Index-linked National Savings Certificates are a particular form of this investment in which the increase in value is not predetermined but depends on movements in the retail price index.

National Savings Stock Register. A register of holdings of certain designated government securities offering the facility that they may be bought and sold by small investors over the counter of a post office.

negative cash flow. An outflow of cash.

negative equity. A situation where a mortgaged asset becomes worth less than the loan secured on it so the proceeds of its sale would be insufficient to redeem the loan. The term is usually applied in the case of the ownership of mortgaged residential property. It has serious financial consequences for those in the situation as it means that, on moving house, a substantial extra amount has to be found to clear the old mortgage before funds become available to place a deposit on the new.

negative goodwill. This exists when the price paid for the purchase of a GOING CONCERN (q.v.) is less than the combined value of the separable assets. The financial logic of such a situation would be that the going concern would be closed and the assets sold separately but this might not happen if the purchaser felt that better management could rectify the situation.

negative growth. A term meaning a contraction. A company which experienced a lower turnover in one year than in the previous year might prefer to say that sales were subject to negative growth rather than that they had contracted.

negligence. Carelessness where a duty of care exists. An accountant may be guilty of negligence, and therefore liable to be sued by an aggrieved client, if he or she fails to apply to his or her work the standard of care reasonably to be expected from a person of his or her qualifications. Whether or not an adequate fee was paid for the work is irrelevant in a case of negligence.

negotiability. That characteristic of certain valuable documents which enables entitlement to the benefits they represent to be passed from person to person by ENDORSEMENT (q.v.) and delivery. Cheques and bills of exchange are examples of negotiable instruments.

negotiable instrument. A valuable document in which property may be passed by simple delivery. Examples of negotiable instruments are CHEQUES (q.v.) and BILLS OF EXCHANGE (q.v.).

negotiation. The process of arriving at an agreement. A person selling a business might enter into a negotiation with the person wishing to buy it as to the price. The outcome of negotiation will depend, amongst other things, on the negotiating skills of the parties.

nest egg. Personal savings which have no explicit purpose except to add to the owner's financial security. A person who has accumulated an amount of cash over a period of time might be said to have put together a nest egg.

net. An amount remaining after deducting charges which diminish it. A net profit is the final profit after all expenses have been deducted. A net price is the amount payable by a customer after deducting any DISCOUNT (q.v.).

net assets. That part of the total value of the assets of a business which remains after allowing for every LIABILITY (q.v.) which would fall to be met out of the assets.

net asset value. A value attached to a share in a company based on the assets of the business attributable to the shareholders divided by the number of shares in issue. The balance sheet value of assets attributable to shareholders can be most simply determined by adding share capital and reserves. Net asset value is usually substantially below the market price of a share (because of the existence of GOODWILL (q.v.) not valued in the balance sheet). It is not, therefore, a particularly useful measure; nevertheless it is frequently quoted when shares are the subject of comment.

EXAMPLE. The following figures are taken from the balance sheet of a certain company.

Share capital	£
1,000,000 shares of £1	1,000,000
Share premium account	100,000
Profit and loss account	850,000
Shareholders' funds	1,950,000

$$\text{Net asset value} = \frac{\text{Shareholders' funds}}{\text{Number of shares}}$$

$$= \frac{£1,950,000}{1,000,000}$$

$$= £1.95 \text{ per share}$$

net basis. A basis for calculating EARNINGS PER SHARE (q.v.) which includes in the tax charge against earnings any irrecoverable ADVANCE CORPORATION TAX (q.v.) and any foreign taxation arising out of the distribution of dividends. The term is used in SSAP 3 and should be contrasted with NIL BASIS (q.v.).

net book agreement. An agreement whereby retailers of books will sell at prices which are uniform and which are determined by the publisher. This is the last remaining example of RESALE PRICE MAINTENANCE (q.v.) in the UK.

net book value. *See* BOOK VALUE.

net current assets. CURRENT ASSETS (q.v.) less CURRENT LIABILITIES (q.v.). It thus represents the uncommitted portion of a business's liquid resources. It would be regarded as a very unhealthy position if a business were found to have a negative value for net current assets, i.e. that current liabilities exceeded current assets.

net present value. The aggregate of all cash flows to and from a project, discounted appropriately to give their present values. In most cases a project will require an immediate initial outlay and this will result in a series of future cash inflows. The net present value is then the sum of the discounted cash inflows less the undiscounted (because immediate) outlay. Net present value is a measure of the extent to which a project earns more or less than the required rate of return or COST OF CAPITAL (q.v.).

153

F

EXAMPLE. A certain project which requires an immediate outlay of £25,000 promises future annual cash flows of the amounts appearing in the table below. The cost of capital is 10 per cent per annum and the project will have no TERMINAL VALUE (q.v.).

Year	Projected cash flow £	Discount factor	Present value £
1	8,000	0.909	7,272
2	10,000	0.826	8,260
3	8,000	0.751	6,008
4	6,000	0.621	4,098
5	4,000	0.631	2,484
			28,122
Less Initial outlay			25,000
Net present value			+£3,122

The fact that the net present value is positive implies that the project is expected to earn more than the cost of capital. Prima facie, the proposal should be adopted.

net profit. The profit made by a business after allowing for all expenses, direct and indirect.

net realisable value. The value of an asset based on the amount which would be received if it were sold, after allowing for all costs of realisation. The Companies Act 1985 requires that, in the published accounts of limited companies, CURRENT ASSETS (q.v.) are valued, item by item, at the lower of cost or net realisable value. This is particularly relevant to the valuation of stock.

net worth. The total value of the assets of a business less the total value of its outside liabilities. For a company, net worth thus equates with the total of SHARE CAPITAL (q.v.) and RESERVES (q.v.).

neutrality. A desirable characteristic of taxation whereby its existence does not change decisions concerning the economic activity of the taxpayers. A neutral tax, whilst raising money for the government, will not change the balance of a business's investment activities nor influence its choice of sales mix.

new entity. A concept which may be used in preparing CONSOLIDATED ACCOUNTS (q.v.) whereby the group arising from the combination is regarded as a a new entity and FAIR VALUES (q.v.) are attributed to all the assets of the combining businesses. The principle is rarely used in practice it being much more common to revalue only the assets of the company which has been taken over.

new issue. An issue of securities which adds to the stock of securities available as opposed to merely transferring a security from one person to another. A company which is floated on the Stock Exchange may make a new issue of shares.

new money. An element in an offer in wage bargaining negotiations which represents an increase in the cost of wages to the employer. It is to be distinguished from a situation where a rise is offered subject to improvements in efficiency or to restructuring which leaves the cost to the employer unaltered even though individuals may be paid more.

new penny. The name given to the smallest denomination of the British currency on decimalisation in 1971. There were 100 new pence in the pound. The name distinguished this from the old penny of which there were 240 in one pound. The term new penny has now largely fallen into disuse as memories of the old currency have faded.

New York Stock Exchange. The main market in America for securities. It is situated in Wall Street, New York. It is often, for this reason, referred to colloquially as Wall Street.

night safe. A facility provided by a bank whereby a trader can deposit cash in a safe accessible from the street after the bank's trading hours. The trader will attend the branch the following day for the money deposited in the night safe to be retrieved, counted and credited to a bank account.

Nikkei average. An index of share prices representing their movement on the Japanese Stock Exchange in Tokyo.

nil basis. A basis for determining EARNINGS PER SHARE (q.v.) which supposes that distributions (which may affect the tax position) were nil. It is to be contrasted with the NET BASIS (q.v.). Normally the nil basis and the net basis will give identical results. The two situations in which they are not identical are:
(1) where there is irrecoverable ADVANCE CORPORATION TAX (q.v.); and
(2) where overseas tax is unrelieved because the dividend payments have restricted the amount of DOUBLE TAXATION RELIEF (q.v.) available.

noble. A now obsolete British coin which was worth one-third of a pound.

no claims bonus. A reduction in premium given to an insured person by an insurance company on condition that there have been no claims on the insurance in the previous period of cover. They are generally restricted to policies of motor insurance and reflect the fact that claims experience is a useful measure of the risk to which the insurer is actually exposed.

no claims discount. Another name for NO CLAIMS BONUS (q.v.).

no credit interval. The period of time for which a company's surplus of LIQUID ASSETS (q.v.) over CURRENT LIABILITIES (q.v.) could pay for current outgoings on operations. It is thus a measure of the business's dependence on credit in order to continue. The higher the no credit interval the longer the company could survive if credit were curtailed or withdrawn.

nominal account. An account other than one with a person. Examples of nominal accounts are those relating to buildings or stock.

nominal capital. The share capital of a company at its nominal amount, i.e. the number of shares multiplied by the nominal amount of each. The actual capital of the company will often also include reserves.

nominal damages. DAMAGES (q.v.) awarded by a court of a very small amount. They represent the view of the court that the plaintiff in a civil action is technically in the right but has not suffered any significant loss from the matter which is the subject of the complaint.

nominal ledger. That portion of the double entry system containing accounts other than personal accounts. A nominal ledger will typically contain accounts for such items as capital, fixed assets of various kinds, long-term loans, sales, purchases and expenses of various kinds.

nominal value. The face value of a security. It is not necessarily the value at which it was first issued which may have been at a PREMIUM (q.v.). Ordinary shares may be issued with a nominal value of, say, 10p each. These shares will continue to be referred to as 10p shares even though the price at which they are bought and sold on the stock market may differ substantially from this. Shares without a nominal value, or shares of NO PAR VALUE (q.v.) have for some years been advocated but their issue in the UK would be illegal under current legislation.

nominee. One who holds shares in a company on behalf of another. Thus a bank might act as a nominee on behalf of a customer. The original purpose of nominee holdings was to conceal the existence of large blocks of shares in common beneficial owner-ship. There is now a legal obligation for a person holding in excess of 5 per cent of the shares in a company, whether in his or her own name or through nominees, to declare that fact.

nominee shareholding. A holding of shares by a person or institution on behalf of someone else.

non-adjusting event. A term appearing in SSAP 17 to refer to an event occurring after the date of a balance sheet but before it had been signed which has no bearing on conditions existing at the date of the balance sheet. Unlike an ADJUSTING EVENT (q.v.), a non-adjusting event does not require any amendment to the accounts. It must be dis-closed (i.e. by a note) if:

(a) it is so MATERIAL (q.v.) that knowledge of it is required by those using the accounts to obtain a proper understanding of the financial position of the company; or

(b) its effect is to complete or reverse a transaction entered into before the year end, the main intention of which was to present a particular position in the balance sheet. Such an activity is known as WINDOW DRESSING (q.v.).

Disclosure must be made of the nature of the non-adjusting event and an estimate given of its financial effect. Where no estimate can be made there should be a state-ment to that effect.

Examples of non-adjusting events are:

(a) Losses of fixed assets or stocks arising from unpredictable catastrophe.

(b) Issues of shares or debentures.

(c) Mergers and acquisitions.

(d) Proposals for capital reconstruction.

non-compliance. Taking action or omitting to take action such that a regulation has been breached. Failure to prepare annual accounts by a company would be a non-compliance with the requirements of company law.

non-coterminous periods. Accounting periods of subsidiary companies within a GROUP (q.v.) which do not end on the same date as that of the holding company. This makes the consolidation of their results difficult and should generally be avoided. Where it can-not be avoided FRS 2 requires that there should be given for each subsidiary to which this applies its name, its accounting date and the reason for using a different account-ing date from the rest of the group. It also requires that adjustment be made for any ab-normal transactions where otherwise the accounts would be distorted.

non-executive director. A DIRECTOR (q.v.) of a company who has no day-to-day re-sponsibilities within the company. His or her responsibilities would be discharged by at-tendance at meetings of the Board and contributions towards the formulation of policy.

non-monetary items. Items in a balance sheet which are not money or having a value established in money terms. The term thus includes stocks and all fixed assets.

non-profit making organisation. An organisation existing for a purpose (e.g. charit-able or social) other than that of making a commercial profit. The accounts prepared for the organisation should reflect the purpose for which it was formed. The revenue ac-count of a non-profit making organisation is normally referred to as an INCOME AND EX-PENDITURE ACCOUNT (q.v.). A difference between total income and total expenditure is referred to as a surplus (if favourable) or deficit (if adverse). There should also be pre-pared a balance sheet which will feature an ACCUMULATED FUND (q.v.) in place of the capital account of a commercial organisation.

non-resident. A person whose natural home is in the UK but who lives abroad. The status has tax implications.

non-statutory organisation. A body which is not set up under the provisions of an Act of Parliament. As such its powers may be limited.

no par value shares. Shares which have no NOMINAL VALUE (q.v.). Although changes in the law to allow the issue of shares of no par value have been advocated in some quarters their issue is not currently legal in the UK. An advantage of shares of no par value is that the proceeds of any issue of shares are credited in full to the share capital account and no SHARE PREMIUM ACCOUNT (q.v.) is required. Each share represents a unit of ownership of the company which is meaningful as a proportion of the whole but not as having any stated value.

normal level of activity. That level of activity in a business which is normally experienced. Its significance is that it should be used to calculate that element of FIXED OVERHEAD (q.v.) which may properly be included in stock valuations.

normal profit. A term used by economists to signify that level of profit which is just sufficient to induce an ENTREPRENEUR (q.v.) to remain in business.

normal standard. A particular basis for setting a STANDARD COST (q.v.). It is based on the assumption that conditions during the period will be the average of those experienced in the past and that the efficiency of production will therefore be at whatever experience shows to be the normal level. A criticism which may be aimed at this basis of standard setting is that it does not encourage any improvement over past achievement. *See also* ATTAINABLE STANDARD; IDEAL STANDARD.

normal volume. That volume of production which was anticipated in the preparation of a BUDGET (q.v.). The level of normal volume is important in determining the amount of FIXED OVERHEAD (q.v.) to be charged to a unit of production.

normal wastage. That level of wastage of materials in production which is regarded as inherent in the process used. The cost of normal wastage should be treated as part of the cost of production and not separately analysed. Any wastage over and above normal wastage is termed ABNORMAL WASTAGE (q.v.).

notes. Securities issued by a company and evidencing a debt. The term is more commonly used in the USA than in the UK and generally refers to short-term loans.

notice of assessment. A document issued by the INSPECTOR OF TAXES (q.v.) to a taxpayer informing him or her of the amount on which he or she is to be charged income tax and of the amount so charged.

notice of coding. A formal notice issued by an INSPECTOR OF TAXES (q.v.) to an income taxpayer receiving remuneration from employment. The notice states the individual's TAX CODE (q.v.) and the manner in which it has been calculated. The code depends upon the ALLOWANCES (q.v.) against income which apply to the individual. The employer will also be notified of the code and this will be applied to TAX TABLES (q.v.) in order to determine the amount to be deducted from remuneration as it is paid. Coding is an integral part of the PAY AS YOU EARN (q.v.) method of collecting income tax.

notional rent. An amount included in the profit and loss account in respect of rent where none is, in fact, paid because the business owns its own premises. The amount will be shown as both income and expense so that it does not affect net profit. The object is to demonstrate clearly the benefit to the business of owning its own building and the cost to it of consuming that benefit rather than realising it by letting the building to another party.

not negotiable. Words written on the CROSSING (q.v.) of a cheque. Strictly they limit rather than prevent the negotiation of the cheque, i.e. passing the benefit of it to another person by ENDORSEMENT (q.v.). The effect is that the recipient receives no better title to the cheque than the previous holder.

novation. The substitution in a contract of one debtor for another with the agreement of the creditor.

NPV. Letters standing for NET PRESENT VALUE (q.v.).

numismatics. The activity of collecting coins.

O

objectivity. The essential characteristic of that which may be measured and independently verified. It is to be contrasted with subjectivity which is the characteristic of opinions and judgements. Objectivity is regarded as a desirable characteristic of accounting statements as it most closely equates them to statements of fact. There are also implications for the AUDITOR (q.v.), who can vouch only for objective information. Complete objectivity in accounting statements cannot be achieved as some judgements must be used. Examples of judgements which are commonly made are those concerning the recoverability of debts, the prospective realisable value of stocks and the useful lives of fixed assets.

objects clause. That clause in the MEMORANDUM OF ASSOCIATION (q.v.) of a company which sets out the objects for which the company has been formed. The importance of the objects clause is that a company may not carry out any activities not authorised therein. To do so would be to act ULTRA VIRES (q.v.) and thus illegally. Objects clauses are usually drafted so as not to be too restrictive. An objects clause may be changed by the passing of a SPECIAL RESOLUTION (q.v.).

obsolescence. The process of becoming obsolete. Its accounting significance is that it is one of the factors leading to a reduction in the useful economic life of a FIXED ASSET (q.v.) and therefore requiring the provision of DEPRECIATION (q.v.).

occupational pension. A PENSION (q.v.) which a person receives by virtue of having retired following the completion of a career in a certain occupation. Normally the pensioner will have made a substantial contribution towards the cost of the pension during his or her working life although occasionally such a pension may be paid for entirely by the employer.

odd lot. A small number of shares in an unusual quantity, for example, 23 shares. The sale of such an odd lot of shares may involve a higher COMMISSION (q.v.) than usual from a STOCKBROKER (q.v.).

odds. The relationship between the amount offered on a successful bet and the amount staked. The less it is probable that the bet will succeed the higher the odds that will be offered.

off balance sheet financing. Indirect finance which does not appear on the balance sheet. Plant may be hired rather than purchased, for example. Another example is the use of a DEBT FACTORING (q.v.) service.

offer for sale. A document whereby a party other than the company itself offers the company's shares for sale to the general public. An offer for sale, made usually by an ISSUING HOUSE (q.v.) or MERCHANT BANK (q.v.) is similar in form to a PROSPECTUS (q.v.) issued by the company itself. In spite of its name, an offer for sale is not legally an offer which would imply that a binding contract could be made by its acceptance. It is an invitation to make an offer (by an application for shares) which may be accepted (by an ALLOTMENT (q.v.)) or not.

offer price. The price at which a security is offered for sale. It should be contrasted with the lower BID PRICE (q.v.).

Office of Fair Trading. An office operating under government auspices to which persons aggrieved by unfair practices in the retail trade may complain.

officer. One who holds office. Officers of a company include its directors and its secretary. No officer of a company may act as AUDITOR (q.v.).

Official List. A list of security prices published daily by the Stock Exchange. It is regarded as an authoritative statement of security prices and is used whenever an accurate valuation of an investment is required. This might be needed, for example, when a person dies to determine the value of his or her ESTATE (q.v.).

Official Receiver. A government official responsible for handling the affairs in BANKRUPTCY (q.v.) of individuals or the WINDING UP (q.v.) of companies. The official receiver's responsibility is to ensure an orderly realisation of assets and their proper application in meeting the claims of creditors and others.

offshore funds. Funds maintained outside the UK mainland, i.e. in the Isle of Man or the Channel Isles. Before 1984 the interest on such funds could be accumulated free of taxation. When the fund was then realised the total gain would be subject to CAPITAL GAINS TAX (q.v.) and not to INCOME TAX (q.v.). This tax loophole has now been closed. Offshore funds still maintain the right to pay interest gross. Bank deposit accounts on the mainland bear interest from which tax has to be deducted before payment.

OFTEL. A body which exists to protect the interests of telephone users against British Telecom, the main provider of the service.

OHMS. Letters standing for ON HER MAJESTY'S SERVICE (q.v.).

Old Lady of Threadneedle Street. Affectionate term for the Bank of England. It refers to the street in London in which the bank's head office is situated.

ombudsman. A person who is appointed to see fair play and adjudicate in any dispute. A number of industries supplying consumers now have an ombudsman whose view is usually treated as binding even though it may not have legal force.

on account. Description applied to a payment which is a part, but not the whole, of a total amount owed. The payment by a debtor of small amounts 'on account' may signify that the debtor has difficulty in paying and that, ultimately, some part of the debt will prove to be bad.

on approval. Goods supplied on the basis that the prospective purchaser may accept or reject them after a reasonable period of inspection. Goods supplied on approval should not be accounted for as sales until accepted by the prospective purchaser or until the approval period has expired.

oncost. A synonym for OVERHEAD (q.v.). It is used most commonly in the USA.

one parent benefit. A social security benefit which is paid to a person who is single-handedly bringing up a child.

On Her Majesty's Service. When imprinted on an envelope this designation allows the communication to go post free. It is used on correspondence of an official government nature, such as letters from an Inspector of Taxes. It is often abbreviated to OHMS.

ono. Letters standing for OR NEAR OFFER (q.v.).

open cheque. A cheque which does bear any form of CROSSING (q.v.). Such a cheque may be cashed by anyone into whose possession it comes whether honestly or not.

opening stock. The STOCK (q.v.) as it stood at the beginning of a financial period.

open market operations. Activity by the Bank of England in the currency market when it wishes to influence the rate of exchange. An example would be the purchase of sterling in order to support its rate of exchange against a foreign currency.

open market value. A value determined by a market on which no restrictions have been placed.

operating activities. Those activities entered into by a business as part of its normal trade. The term is used in a CASH FLOW STATEMENT (q.v.) prepared as required in FRS 1. This standard distinguishes operating activities from returns on investments and servicing of finance, taxation payments, investing activities and financing.

operating lease. Any lease other than a FINANCE LEASE (q.v.). This is the definition in SSAP 21. It is a lease where the substance as well as the form of the transaction is that an asset is hired by a business for a limited period of time in return for the leasing payments. At the end of that time the asset will be returned to its owner who may then lease it to some other business.

operating profit. The profit deriving from the operation of the basic business process. This profit is then reduced by charging against it business expenses such as the costs of administration.

operating ratios. Ratios calculated from a set of accounts which throw light on the profit making activities for a period of time. Examples are the GROSS PROFIT RATE (q.v.) and the rate of administrative costs to sales.

opportunity cost. The cost of an action in terms of the value of the best alternative opportunity thereby forgone. It is a term borrowed from economics, but the concept has important relevance for financial decision making.

EXAMPLE. Material bought for £1,000 some time ago had proved surplus to requirements. It could be sold for £250. A possibility occurs of using the material in another product. In determining the true cost of making this other product the correct cost to impute to the material is not £1,000, its original cost, but £250, the value of the opportunity of realisation forgone.

optimum. The best course of action available in the existing circumstances. Many management accounting techniques are directed towards finding the optimum amongst the range of available alternatives. Thus management might seek the optimum use of financial resources through CAPITAL BUDGETING (q.v.) and the optimum product mix through CONTRIBUTION (q.v.) analysis.

option. The right to decide whether or not to enter into a transaction on agreed terms within an agreed period of time. A person wishing to buy a house for £150,000 if the finance can be raised might take an option on it for, say, 1 month (for which a payment will be made). This gives time for the finance to be sought. At the end of the month the option holder can then decide whether to go ahead with the deal or not. There is a market in options on stock market securities. This is used as a HEDGE (q.v.) against wide price fluctuations. A put option gives the right to sell securities in the future at a price agreed now and a call option gives a similar right to buy.

order. A document originating the process whereby a company makes a purchase by requesting the supply of specified goods from another company. Its significance is that it authorises the purchase of the goods concerned and forms part of the AUDIT TRAIL (q.v.).

ordinary activities. Those activities of a business which form part of its normal trading and thus of a kind which can be expected to recur regularly.

ordinary resolution. A resolution which may be carried by a simple majority of those voting. It should be contrasted with a SPECIAL RESOLUTION (q.v.) which requires a three-quarters majority of those voting. The terms are normally used in connection with meetings of the shareholders of a company when the law determines those matters which may be decided by an ordinary resolution.

ordinary shares. The basic risk capital of a LIMITED COMPANY (q.v.). Ordinary shares must have a stated NOMINAL VALUE (q.v.) but their market value is determined primarily by general expectations about the company's prospects. Every company must have some ordinary shares. On a WINDING UP (q.v.) of a company ordinary shareholders will receive the surplus, if any, after all other obligations have been met.

or near offer. Words attached to the price of an article offered for sale which imply that the vendor is willing to consider an offer below the stipulated price provided it is not too far below it. The term is normally used in the case of second-hand household goods, used vehicles and previously occupied residential property.

OTC. Letters standing for OVER THE COUNTER MARKET (q.v.).

out-of-pocket expenses. Expenses incurred by a professional person in carrying out duties on behalf of a client and requiring to be reimbursed by the client in addition to any fee payable. Travelling and postage might be included in this category.

output. The product of a manufacturing process.

outwork. Work done as part of a process of production by persons in their own homes. They are not usually employees of the business for which they work and are paid, often at very low rates, only for what they do.

overabsorption. The charging to costs of more OVERHEAD (q.v.) than the actual amount incurred. This will occur where actual production is at a higher level than that envisaged in the BUDGET (q.v.). The effect of overabsorption is that profits are actually higher than they appear to be from the cost accounts. The difference could be regarded as the benefit arising from the more efficient use of fixed resources.

overcapitalised. Having more funds than can profitably be employed in the business. An overcapitalised company should take steps to return its surplus funds to its shareholders. Unless these are represented by REVENUE RESERVES (q.v.) this may require a REDUCTION OF CAPITAL (q.v.).

overcharging. The practice of charging prices which are higher than are justified by costs or by market conditions.

overdraft. The drawing out from a bank account of more than has been deposited in it. An overdraft is, in effect, a loan by the banker to the customer and interest will be charged on the outstanding balance. It is normal for a customer requiring an overdraft to agree with the bank on an overdraft limit, i.e. a maximum level to which the overdraft will be permitted to rise. An overdraft is a very useful form of short-term finance as interest is calculated on the fluctuating balance on a day-to-day basis. Thus interest savings can be made by the temporary deposit of surplus cash without formally terminating the loan arrangement. Where a customer creates an overdraft without prior agreement the bank may refuse to honour the cheques. If it does so it will normally charge a much higher rate of interest than would be the case for a formally authorised overdraft.

overdue. Remaining unpaid beyond the date when payment had been agreed. An overdue payment may be the first sign that the debt is about to become bad.

overextended. The condition of having taken on greater financial commitments than can comfortably be managed.

overfunded. Having greater resources available than are required for the activity in hand.

overhead. The cost of the facilities surrounding production which do not, however, directly become part of the product. Overhead is one of the main classifications of cost. Typical items of overhead are depreciation of machinery, lighting and heating, maintenance and supervisory salaries. Direct overhead is that which can immediately and directly be associated with particular segments of production. Its cost can thus be allocated to that production. A bigger costing problem is presented by indirect overhead, i.e. overhead from which many segments of production benefit. This has to be attributed to individual segments by some method of APPORTIONMENT (q.v.). Such a method is bound to be to an extent arbitrary. Overhead may be usefully classified for some purposes as FIXED OVERHEAD (q.v.) or VARIABLE OVERHEAD (q.v.).

overnight position. A POSITION (q.v.) which is allowed to persist from one day to the next.

oversubscription. The situation which exists, in a public offer of shares, when applications are received for more shares than are on offer. An oversubscription means that a decision has to be made on how the shares are going to be allotted. There may be some scaling down of all applications or a BALLOT (q.v.) may be used.

over the counter market. A market in the shares of a specific company operated by a LICENSED DEALER IN SECURITIES (q.v.). Although now it has largely disappeared it is used where the shares are quoted neither on the Stock Exchange nor on the UNLISTED SECURITIES MARKET (q.v.). Dealings on an over the counter market may be very few in number and usually concern quite small companies.

overtime. Time worked by labour in excess of the normal contracted amount. Thus if a worker is engaged on the basis of a 44-hour week and actually works 52 hours in a certain week there will be 8 hours of overtime. It is usual to pay for overtime at higher than the normal rate of pay, e.g. time and a quarter or time and a half. This is a necessary inducement to enable the work to be done but can also be justified in that it allows capital equipment to be used more intensively and therefore more profitably. The excess of pay over the rate which would normally be paid (known as the overtime premium) should be treated for accounting purposes as OVERHEAD (q.v.) rather than as LABOUR (q.v.). This is on the basis that it is the totality of production which requires the overtime to be worked rather than that small part of production which happens to be undertaken during that time.

overtrading. An amount of trading activity which exceeds that for which the business is financed. The consequence will be a shortage of liquidity which will prejudice the business's activities and, in extreme cases, end them.

owners' equity. That part of the overall value of a business which is attributable to its proprietors. It is thus the total value of the assets less the claims of creditors and lenders to the business.

own shares. Shares of the company being referred to. Prior to the Companies Act 1981 it was illegal for a company to purchase its own shares. It may now do so under stringent conditions designed to ensure that this does not have the effect of a reduction in capital. Briefly, the shares must be purchased out of profits otherwise available for distribution or out of the proceeds of a fresh issue of shares made for the purpose.

Once purchased the company's own shares must be cancelled. The rules are now embodied in the Companies Act 1985. A company may not purchase its own shares unless there is a general authority in the ARTICLES OF ASSOCIATION (q.v.) and the specific purchase is also authorised by the members by ORDINARY RESOLUTION (q.v.).

P

p. Symbol standing for penny in the post-decimalisation currency of the UK.

P11D. A form sent by an employer to the Inland Revenue at the end of the income tax year giving details of the taxable benefits in kind and expense payments made to the employee during the year.

P45. A form given by an employer to an employee who leaves. It details pay and taxation to date and is handed to the new employer so that the PAYE tax deductions can be applied correctly to the employee.

P60. A form issued by an employer to an employee at the end of a tax year. It states the amount of taxable pay during the year and the amount of tax deducted.

Pacioli. A fifteenth-century Italian monk, teacher and writer on mathematics. Luca Pacioli is regarded as the father of DOUBLE ENTRY (q.v.) book-keeping. An explanation of its basic principles appeared in his *Summa de Arithmetica, Geometrica, Proportioni et Proportionala* published in 1494.

package deal. A proposal offered with a number of components which have to be taken or rejected as a whole.

paid-up capital. That part of the nominal issued share capital of a company which has been paid up by the shareholders. In most cases the paid-up capital is the same as the issued capital because the shares are FULLY PAID (q.v.).

paid-up policy. A policy of endowment or whole life insurance on which no more premiums have to be paid. Sometimes where a policyholder wishes to cease paying the premiums but not to cancel the policy this may be converted to a paid-up policy at an agreed valuation.

Panel on Takeovers and Mergers. A body working under the auspices of the Stock Exchange to supervise takeovers and mergers. The rules under which the panel operates are many and complicated but their intention is to ensure that takeovers and mergers are conducted so that all parties to them are treated fairly.

paper profit. A profit arising from the change in market value of an asset which has yet to be realised. A person who buys shares for £1,000 and later finds that they are worth £1,500 but does not sell them is said to have made a paper profit of £500.

par. Synonym for PAR VALUE (q.v.).

parent company. Synonym for HOLDING COMPANY (q.v.).

pari passu. Equally in every respect. If a new issue of shares is made which is to rank *pari passu* with an existing issue this means that the rights of the two sets of shareholders will be indistinguishable in every way.

part exchange. A transaction involving the purchase of goods by one person from another where part of the purchase consideration is satisfied by the handing over of different goods and part by means of a cash payment. Part exchange is usually found where second-hand goods are exchanged between individuals with a cash adjustment to allow for their difference in value.

participating preference share. A PREFERENCE SHARE (q.v.) which carries a right over and above its preferential right to share further in profits once the DIVIDEND (q.v.) payable to the holders of ORDINARY SHARES (q.v.) exceeds a stated level.

partly paid shares. Shares in a company on which an amount less than the full nominal value has been paid by their holders. The unpaid part of the capital may be called up by the company at any time and remains a liability of the shareholders in the event that the company is wound up.

partnership. The relationship which exists between two or more persons carrying on a business in common with a view to profit. There will be an agreement between the partners, either expressed formally or implied by conduct, as to the contributions which each will make towards the capital of the business and of the share of the profit or loss each will take or bear.

Partnership Act 1890. Legislation which defines PARTNERSHIP (q.v.) and governs its conduct.

part-time. A description of a contract of employment under which the employee works for less than the number of hours normally required of an employee and receives commensurately smaller remuneration. There are many jobs which can be done on a part-time basis. Part-time workers generally, however, have less job security than do full-time workers.

par value. Equal to NOMINAL VALUE (q.v.). Thus a share stands at its par value if its market price happens to equal its nominal value.

pass a dividend. The action by a company of failing to pay a DIVIDEND (q.v.) at a time in the financial year when a dividend is usually paid. When the directors decide to pass a dividend it is usually taken to mean that the company is in difficulty. Either its profit is very low or it is making an actual loss.

pass book. A book issued by a bank or building society in which are entered details of an account with a customer. It has to be presented on the occasion of each transaction in order to be made up to date. The traditional pass book is being phased out by most institutions in favour of computer-produced statements.

passive fund management. An inactive custody of a fund of investments.

patent. The legal right given to a person to the exclusive use of the idea embodied in an invention for a period of years. In order to be effective a patent has to be registered. A patent is a valuable right which may be bought and sold. It may legitimately appear in a balance sheet, when it would be classified as an INTANGIBLE ASSET (q.v.), where a cost can be imputed to it. It should be subject to AMORTISATION (q.v.) over the period of its life.

pawn. To pledge an asset with a PAWNBROKER (q.v.) as security for a cash loan.

pawnbroker. One who lends cash on the security of some personal possession of value, usually jewellery. The borrower may redeem the item within a stated period of time by repaying the amount of the loan with interest. In the event of the default of the borrower the pawnbroker is entitled to sell the subject of the pledge.

pay and file. A system of dealing with taxation, used in the USA, whereby the taxpayer submits payment of the amount of tax due at the same time as submitting the statement of income on which the calculation is based.

pay as you earn. The method of charging INCOME TAX (q.v.) to wage and salary earners. An employer is required by law to deduct the appropriate amount of tax from payments of wages and salaries before they are made. The amount deducted is then accounted for by the employer to the Inland Revenue. The great merit of the system, usually referred to as PAYE, is that it obviates the making of detailed tax ASSESSMENTS (q.v.) for large numbers of employees with uncomplicated tax affairs. It is designed to collect over the tax year precisely the amount due for that year. Each employee is issued with a TAX CODE (q.v.) based on the ALLOWANCES (q.v.) to which he or she is entitled. By reference to this code and to the cumulative gross pay, the cumulative tax to be deducted can be determined from TAX TABLES (q.v.) provided by the Inland Revenue. For a person on a constant wage or salary the PAYE system makes an even, regular charge for tax. It can, however, operate in an anomalous fashion. If, for example, a person ceases employment during the tax year he or she will have overpaid tax and will receive rebates for a period after that date.

pay as you go. A form of pension arrangement where the employer makes no advance provision for the payment of its pensioners but charges the amounts actually paid to its profit and loss account at the time they occur. Clearly in such a system the security of the pension depends on the continuance of the business which pays them.

pay-back. A method of capital investment appraisal which considers the time taken for a project to repay the capital sum invested in it. Thus if a project requiring a capital investment of £10,000 will then yield net returns of £5,000 per annum, its pay-back period is 2 years. In using this method it is usual to specify a required pay-back period (say, 3 years) and then to accept projects which pay back more quickly than this and reject those which take longer. A fundamental disadvantage of the pay-back method is that it takes no account of profit.

pay-day. The day on which workers are paid. It is normally the same day in each week or in each month.

PAYE. Letters standing for PAY AS YOU EARN (q.v.).

payee. One to whom a payment is addressed. The person to whom a cheque is made out, for example, is the payee.

payer. One who makes a payment.

pay freeze. A situation in which wages and salaries are held at existing levels. It might be imposed by a government as a policy to reduce inflation or by a company wishing to contain its costs. A pay freeze is very difficult to maintain for more than a short period of time.

paying in book. A bound book of PAYING IN SLIPS (q.v.) issued by a bank to customers who frequently pay in cheques or cash. Each slip has a COUNTERFOIL (q.v.) which provides a record of the deposits made with the bank.

paying in slip. A blank form which must be completed by a customer wishing to make payments of cheques or cash into his or her bank account. On it must be written details of the deposit. After checking the bank will use the paying in slip to update its own records.

paymaster. One who controls the payment of cash. Although the term can be used as the title of an office it is often used colloquially to indicate the ultimate source of funding and, therefore, the one with financial power. The government, for example, is the paymaster for public sector salaries.

payment. The voluntary transfer of cash from one person to another.

payment in advance. Payment made before the end of an accounting period in respect of benefits to be received in a subsequent period. Insurance premiums and payments of RATES (q.v.) are common examples of payments in advance. They are treated in the balance sheet as current assets. Where they are relatively small in total amount they are frequently amalgamated with debtors.

payment in kind. A payment not in money but in valuable goods or services. A domestic servant, for example, who receives board and lodging as part of the contract of service is, to that extent, receiving a payment in kind.

payment on account. A payment made by a debtor of part only of an amount owed. Where a debtor makes frequent payments on account this is often regarded as a sign that he or she is in financial difficulty and it may signal an imminent BAD DEBT (q.v.).

pay-off. A final payment intended to terminate a contractual relationship. It is often applied to the final payment made to an employee who is leaving.

payroll. Literally a list of names of all employees of a business but often used to mean the total amount paid to them. Thus a business might say that it had 500 people on its payroll or it might say that it had a payroll of £4 million.

payroll giving. A system whereby a person in receipt of wages or a salary can agree to regular deductions which are then given to charity.

payroll tax. A tax charged on employers and depending on the number of people they employ. Although the idea has been discussed there is currently no explicit payroll tax imposed in the UK. It could be argued that the employer's contribution to NATIONAL INSURANCE (q.v.) payments is a form of payroll tax.

payslip. A document given to an employee to explain how his or her net payment of wages or salary is calculated. It will show the gross amount and the amounts of any deductions such as income tax and national insurance.

peace dividend. That amount by which the population at large is expected to benefit from a reduction in governmental defence expenditure consequent on a more peaceful world. It is likely to be felt in the form of reduced taxation.

pecuniary. Involving money. If a person is said to have gained a pecuniary advantage from some situation this means that they have acquired some money out of it.

peer review. A review of some person's activity by some other person involved in the same activity. A peer review of the work of an AUDITOR (q.v.) would require an examination of that work by another auditor.

pegged exchange rate. A rate of exchange between two currencies which is never permitted to fluctuate. It may, in practice, be very difficult to achieve.

pegged price. A price which is held constant.

penalty. A payment made by a person in restitution for some wrong or default which has been committed. A builder who has agreed to construct an office block by a certain date may be subject to a penalty if this deadline is not met. A law breaker may suffer a penalty in the form of a FINE (q.v.).

penalty clause. A clause contained in a contract whereby one party agrees to pay a stated PENALTY (q.v.) to the other in the event of a delay in the completion of the contract.

penny. The smallest unit of currency in the UK.

penny pinching. Acting so as to cut costs to the minimum at every opportunity. The use of the term often implies that the amounts saved are small relative to the inconveniences suffered.

penny share. A share in a company which is quoted on the Stock Exchange at a very low amount. It usually arises where the company, whilst maintaining its existence, has no commercial success and pays no dividend. Some investors choose to hold a proportion of penny shares in the hope that there will, at some time in the future, be a revival in the fortunes of the company. This does occasionally happen, sometimes when a new management takes over. When it does the rise in value can be spectacular. Many penny shares languish for many years and then become valueless.

pension. Income provided for a retired person. Pension schemes present a difficult accounting problem since uncertain future benefits have to be provided out of investments made currently. There are two possibilities. One is that pensions may be funded. This means that enough is invested currently to meet an actuarial calculation of the amounts due when the employee retires. The other is that pensions paid currently are treated as current expenses. Pensions are normally contributory. This means that the employee pays part of the cost whilst at work. A pension is subject to tax as EARNED INCOME (q.v.) when it is paid. Contributions made by employees are an allowable deduction in calculating their income tax liability and the income and capital gains earned by an approved pension fund are tax free.

pension cost. The cost to a company of providing a pension for its employees. The amount borne by the company is likely to be part only of the total cost, the rest being borne by the employees themselves.

pensioner. One who is in receipt of a PENSION (q.v.).

pension fund. A fund built up over a period of time by contributors in order to provide subscribers with a pension on retirement. The purpose of the fund is to keep money belonging to the prospective pensioners separate from that of the employing company. The actuarial value of the fund's liabilities can be determined from time to time so as to ensure that its size is adequate to meet them.

PEP. Letters standing for PERSONAL EQUITY PLAN (q.v.).

peppercorn rent. A rent which consists of a trivial payment, for example 1 penny per annum. A peppercorn rent enables the legal status of a TENANT (q.v.) to be created whilst in effect allowing him or her to occupy the property rent free.

P/E ratio. Letters standing for PRICE-EARNINGS RATIO (q.v.).

per capita. Expressed as an average per head of a population. Thus if the cost of providing a certain service is described as £10 *per capita*, the total cost is £10 multiplied by the number of people receiving the service.

performance bonds. An amount deposited by a contractor against the possibility that the contract will not be completed. In that event the sum deposited will be used in meeting compensation.

period cost. A cost related to a period of time as opposed to being related to a level of activity. The term is more common in the USA than in the UK where such a cost would normally be referred to as a FIXED COST (q.v.).

permanent difference. A difference between accounting profit and taxable profit which persists in the long run. It is to be contrasted with a TIMING DIFFERENCE (q.v.). Both terms arise in connection with DEFERRED TAXATION (q.v.) and are used in SSAP 15. Examples of permanent differences are those caused by expenses not allowable for tax, i.e. those not incurred wholly for the purposes of the business.

permanent file. A file kept by the AUDITOR (q.v.) of a company to record information of permanent significance about the client. The permanent file might contain copies of the company's Memorandum and Articles of Association and of the names and addresses of its directors.

permanent health insurance. An insurance enabling the insured person to make claims in the event of ill health. It is a term of such a policy that the acceptability of the risk and the amount of the premium are fixed at its inception. These cannot be changed if there is a subsequent deterioration in the health of the insured.

permanent interest bearing shares. Securities issued by a building society which are traded on the Stock Exchange. The holders are not, as are ordinary depositors with the building society, able to withdraw the funds from an account.

permission to deal. The permission granted by the Council of the Stock Exchange to a company allowing its shares to be bought and sold through the Stock Exchange. Many conditions regarding the number of shares available, the past history of the company and the information which it undertakes in future to supply have to be met before the permission is granted.

perpetual inventory. A method of keeping stock records such that the quantity in hand of any item can be determined immediately. Perpetual inventory requires that records are updated by an entry every time a purchase or an issue of an item of stock takes place. Quantities recorded by a perpetual inventory should not be relied upon absolutely and should be verified periodically by a STOCK TAKING (q.v.).

perpetuity. A matter which continues for ever. The law does not favour perpetuities and there is a rule against them in trust law. No trust can be set up to last longer than 21 years after the expiry of all lives then in being.

perquisite. Some benefit which attaches to an employment over and above the wages or salary paid. The right to a company car or to first-class rail or air travel might be perquisites of certain jobs. Colloquially known as 'perk'.

personal account. An account with a real person and distinguished from a NOMINAL ACCOUNT (q.v.). Accounts with debtors and creditors are examples of personal accounts.

personal allowance. An amount allowed to be deducted from a person's income in determining the amount subject to INCOME TAX (q.v.). A married couple is given a higher total personal allowance than two single persons.

personal equity plan. An investment plan undertaken by an individual with an approved plan manager such as a bank. This type of plan was created by statute and has the characteristic that, provided the rules are observed, all income and capital gains accruing to the plan are free from taxation.

personal finance. That area of financial matters which concerns individual people. It will include the provision of mortgages, loans, insurance and savings opportunities. Personal finance has become a large industry.

personal identification number. A secret number issued to the holder of a CREDIT CARD (q.v.) or DEBIT CARD (q.v.) which is used when cash withdrawals are made from automatic dispensing machines. It is envisaged that eventually the personal identification number may take the place of a signature in authorising transactions entered into with these cards.

personal ledger. A section of the whole LEDGER (q.v.) containing accounts with real persons. Thus the SALES LEDGER (q.v.) and the PURCHASE LEDGER (q.v.) are examples of personal ledgers.

personal pension plan. A scheme whereby an individual can save money to purchase a pension on retirement. It is normally operated by an insurance company and would be used by a person whose occupation does not automatically provide a pension.

personal representative. The person who deals with the affairs of a deceased person. It is a general term which applies equally to an EXECUTOR (q.v.) or an ADMINISTRATOR (q.v.).

personalty. Property consisting of cash, goods, furniture and other movable property. It is to be contrasted with REALTY (q.v.). The term is often applied in describing such property forming part of the ESTATE (q.v.) of a deceased person.

petition in bankruptcy. A formal application to the court asking that a named person be judged BANKRUPT (q.v.). It is usually presented by a creditor who has not been paid but may be presented by the insolvent person him or herself.

petroleum revenue tax. A tax levied in respect of profits from the exploitation of oil deposits in the North Sea.

petty cash. Small amounts of currency maintained to cover trivial day-to-day expenses. Expenditure in this form should be recorded in a special book, the petty cash book. Control over petty cash is often maintained by use of the IMPREST SYSTEM (q.v.).

petty cashier. A person who is responsible for the custody and accounting for PETTY CASH (q.v.).

piecemeal distribution. A process whereby the assets of a business in LIQUIDATION (q.v.) are distributed to the proprietors as and when they are realised. Piecemeal distribution is usually encountered in the case of PARTNERSHIP (q.v.). In making piecemeal distributions care must be taken that all liabilities are first settled in order of priority and that, thereafter, no partner is paid any amount which subsequent events might show not to be due. The technique used to achieve this is to calculate at each stage the correct distribution on the assumption that no more will become available. The calculation is performed on a cumulative basis as the liquidation continues.

piece rate. The rate of pay attributable to a unit of production in PIECEWORK (q.v.).

piecework. A form of contract of employment where the worker is paid according to the amount of work achieved as opposed to the number of hours worked.

pilferage. That part of stock which is lost because items have been stolen. The term usually applies to small but repeated acts of theft often by employees. The perpetrators often do not see their action as reprehensible as the stock is usually small in amount and taken for personal use, e.g. in jobs around the house rather than for profit.

PIN. Letters standing for PERSONAL IDENTIFICATION NUMBER (q.v.).

pink form. An application form for shares in a company, printed on pink paper and giving the person using it a right to preferential treatment when allotments are made. A company issuing shares may give pink forms to employees or to others having an existing connection with the company.

pin money. Small amounts of money earned casually by a person to supplement his or her main income.

piracy. Strictly the term means the seizing of goods from ships on the high sea, i.e. outside any jurisdiction. The term is now, however, applied to certain infringements of rights, e.g. the use of computer software which has been illegally copied rather than purchased.

pittance. A very small, and thus inadequate, wage.

placing. A method of obtaining a subscription for shares in a company. The shares are not offered publicly but are issued to persons or institutions who have previously agreed to take them. A placing is a relatively inexpensive method of raising equity finance and there is no uncertainty about whether the shares will be taken up.

planning. The process of deciding on a proposed future course of action. The impact of planning on financial matters is reflected in a BUDGET (q.v.).

planning permission. The right which attaches to a piece of land to use it in a specified way, usually by erecting a building on it, and which is given by a local authority following an application to it. The granting of planning permission may increase the value of a piece of land many times over.

plant and machinery. Equipment used in a productive industrial process. Plant and machinery is shown in a balance sheet as a FIXED ASSET (q.v.). It is subject to DEPRECIATION (q.v.) so that its cost is spread over the period of its useful life. For tax purposes CAPITAL ALLOWANCES (q.v.) may be claimed in respect of expenditure on plant and machinery.

plant replacement reserve. A RESERVE (q.v.) created by retentions of profit for the purpose of meeting the costs of replacing plant. As the DEPRECIATION (q.v.) charge causes retentions equalling the original cost of the plant, the additional plant replacement reserve is required only when replacement costs are rising. It is, therefore, in essence a form of inflation accounting. The plant replacement reserve is legally a REVENUE RESERVE (q.v.) but will probably be treated as a CAPITAL RESERVE (q.v.).

plastic money. Term applied to any form of CREDIT CARD (q.v.), CHARGE CARD (q.v.) or DEBIT CARD (q.v.).

PLC. Letters standing for public limited company. A PUBLIC COMPANY (q.v.) must have this abbreviation (or the words in full) as part of its name.

pledge. To offer as security for a loan.

plough back. To allow profits to accumulate in a business rather than to be withdrawn by the proprietors so that the extra resources thus made available can be used in financing the expansion of the business.

pluvius policy. A type of insurance taken out by the organisers of an event to protect themselves from the risk that its financial success will be affected by adverse weather conditions.

pocket money. A small amount of money given to a person regularly for small amounts of personal expenditure. The term is often applied to an allowance given by a parent to a child.

poison pill. An onerous contract with a collaborator entered into by a company to deter an unwelcome takeover. The contract will not be enforced against the existing management but would be enforced if the takeover were successful.

policy. A contract of insurance.

political contributions. Amounts paid by a company to a political party. The accounting significance of such amounts is that they must be disclosed in the annual accounts. They are also a disallowable expense in computing the liability to CORPORATION TAX (q.v.).

poll tax. A tax the main characteristic of which is that every member of the population pays the same absolute amount regardless of circumstances. Such taxes are generally very unpopular. The COMMUNITY CHARGE (q.v.) was a form of poll tax and was so unpopular that the government was forced to withdraw it after only 3 years of operation.

pool. Expenditure on fixed assets not yet relieved against tax through the medium of CAPITAL ALLOWANCES (q.v.). When an asset is acquired it will qualify for an INITIAL ALLOWANCE (q.v.) at a prescribed rate (which may be nil). The residue of the expenditure will then be added to the pool of all similar residues when its total will qualify for annual WRITING DOWN ALLOWANCES (q.v.). The proceeds of sale of an asset will be credited to (i.e. reduce) the pool.

pooling of interests. A synonym for MERGER (q.v.).

portfolio. A collection of investments. The term usually refers to a collection of investments of a similar type. Thus an investor may hold a portfolio of stock market securities. A company may invest in a portfolio of real capital projects. A property company may hold a portfolio of properties for rent. The term is sometimes extended by analogy. Thus an accountant may have a portfolio of clients and an insurance company a portfolio of risks.

portfolio theory. A theory of DIVERSIFICATION (q.v.) carried out in order to reduce RISK (q.v.). Originally applied to stock market investments, the theory may now be applied to any risky PORTFOLIO (q.v.). The essence of portfolio theory is that diversification will succeed in reducing overall risk only if the risks of the individual components of the portfolio are not positively correlated. The portfolio effect of an individual investment is the effect which it will have on the overall riskiness of the portfolio to which it is added. This is as important to a rational investor as any characteristic possessed by it as an individual investment.

position. A dealer's relationship with a particular security. He or she might hold the security and thus have it available for sale or might have oversold it and thus be in a position where subsequent buying is required to cover the position.

position statement. Synonym for BALANCE SHEET (q.v.).

postal order. A document purchased at a post office which enables the purchaser to send small amounts of money through the post with little risk. The recipient's name is entered on the postal order before despatch and, as an additional protection, it may be crossed so that it is payable only through a bank. A charge is made for the service in the form of a poundage added to the purchase price.

post balance sheet event. An event occurring after the date of the balance sheet but before it has been finalised by its being approved by the Board of Directors. There is a standard dealing with Accounting for Post Balance Sheet Events (SSAP 17). This standard classifies such events as either ADJUSTING EVENTS (q.v.) or NON-ADJUSTING EVENTS (q.v.). The former require an amendment to the balance sheet while the latter do not.

post-cessation receipts. Amounts received by a business after it has permanently finished trading. Their significance is that they will be subject to income tax either as received or as an addition to the profit of the business in its last year of trading.

post-dated cheque. A cheque on which is given a date later than that on which it is actually issued. The effect of post-dating a cheque is that the payee cannot present it for payment until the lapse of a period of time. This may be to allow for an agreed period of credit or to enable the drawer to assemble the funds for payment of the cheque.

posting. The action of recording a financial transaction by means of an entry in the LEDGER (q.v.). Posting is usually done from a book of PRIME ENTRY (q.v.).

Post Office. The Post Office has a primary responsibility for providing postal services in the UK. Because, however, it has a public office in a very widespread network of locations it is also the point at which people deal with the government for many purposes, e.g. savings and collection of social security benefits.

pound. The unit of currency in the UK.

poundage. The fee charged by the Post Office when it issues a POSTAL ORDER (q.v.). It is paid in the form of an addition to the price of the postal order.

pound cost averaging. An advantage claimed for the system of investing in shares (usually through a UNIT TRUST (q.v.) or shares in an INVESTMENT TRUST (q.v.)) by means of regular equal amounts. The effect is that when prices are low more units and when they are high fewer units are purchased. The average price paid is then lower than the a strict arithmetical mean of the prices experienced.

poverty. The state of having an inadequate income to support a proper standard of living. The perceived definition of poverty varies over time and persons who may be regarded as in this condition today would probably not have been so regarded a hundred years ago. It is thus, to an extent, a relative state.

poverty trap. The situation where an unemployed person in receipt of social security benefits cannot take up employment without finding his or her net income reduced because of the consequent loss in benefits.

power of attorney. A legal authority given by one person to another to allow the latter to deal with the former's money and other assets as though they were his or her own. The power may be given when the person giving it has become, through age or infirmity, unable to conduct his or her own affairs, or where a long absence abroad is contemplated.

preacquisition profit. A revenue reserve of a SUBSIDIARY COMPANY (q.v.) which came into being before the HOLDING COMPANY (q.v.) acquired control. Under the ACQUISITION METHOD (q.v.) of constructing a consolidated balance sheet a preacquisition reserve is unavailable for distribution to the members of the holding company.

predator. A company seeking to take over another company whose existing management does not support the takeover.

predecease. To die before another person. The provisions of a WILL (q.v.) may be affected if one of the persons named in it as a beneficiary predeceases the TESTATOR (q.v.).

preference share. A type of share in a company with carefully prescribed preferential rights over ORDINARY SHARES (q.v.). Preference shareholders are entitled to the first part of the available profit as DIVIDEND (q.v.) up to a stated maximum and to a first distribution up to their nominal value in WINDING UP (q.v.).

preferential creditor. A creditor in a BANKRUPTCY (q.v.) or a WINDING UP (q.v.) who is entitled by law to priority of payment over other creditors. Preferential creditors include creditors for wages, salaries, rates and tax.

preliminary announcement. An announcement by the directors of a company concerning the results achieved during a year after the end of the year but before full, audited accounts are published.

preliminary expenses. The expenses involved in setting up a company. At one time these might be regarded as CAPITAL EXPENDITURE (q.v.) and recorded as an asset on the balance sheet. Never regarded as good practice, this has now been made illegal by the Companies Act 1985 and preliminary expenses must be written off. This may be done against profit or, if there is one, against the SHARE PREMIUM ACCOUNT (q.v.).

premium. 1. The sum paid, usually annually in advance, to an insurer under a contract of insurance. The premium, which provides the funds out of which claims can be met and the income of the insurer, is calculated from a consideration of the risks involved.

2. An amount in excess of the nominal value of a security. For example, if a company's shares of a nominal value of £1 stand in the market at a price of £1.20 they are said to be at a premium of 20p. A company may issue shares at a premium in which case the total amount of that premium must be credited to a SHARE PREMIUM ACCOUNT (q.v.). If a person becoming a new partner in an established partnership is required to pay a surplus over and above a capital contribution in recognition of the existence of GOODWILL (q.v.), that surplus payment may also be termed a premium.

premium savings bond. A form of investment offered by the government to private savers and available for purchase at post offices. No regular interest is paid on the bond but an equivalent amount is made available for a range of cash prizes. These are awarded to those holders who are successful in the regular draw. The prizes awarded on premium savings bonds are completely free of tax.

prepaid expenses. Amounts already paid which will fall to be treated as expenses in a forthcoming period. An example of a prepaid expense is an insurance PREMIUM (q.v.) where the benefit of the cover provided, or some part of it, relates to a subsequent accounting period. A prepaid expense should appear on the balance sheet and be classified as a CURRENT ASSET (q.v.).

prepayment. Synonym for PREPAID EXPENSES (q.v.).

present value. The value at the present time of the prospect of receiving a sum of money at some future time after allowing for the time value of money. Present value is a concept vital to the appraisal of capital projects. It is calculated by applying a DISCOUNT FACTOR (q.v.) to the amount actually to be received.

Prestel. A network of computers accessed by telephone and operated by British Telecom. Subscribers obtain access to a large amount of regularly updated information on financial and other matters. Transactions, such as the payment of bills, the ordering of goods and dealings in investments, may also be undertaken through Prestel. It was established in the mid 1970s and is the first such service in the world.

pre-tax. Before allowing for taxation. Thus the pre-tax profit of a company is the amount it has earned before allowing for CORPORATION TAX (q.v.).

price. The amount charged for a unit of a product or service by its supplier. It may be used to refer to the value at which a security is changing hands in the market.

price/earnings ratio. The relationship between the market price of a company's shares and the EARNINGS PER SHARE (q.v.). It is often referred to as the P/E ratio. It is calculated as:

$$P/E \text{ ratio} = \frac{\text{Price of share}}{\text{Earnings per share}}$$

It is a measure of how expensive a share is. Other things being equal, the lower the P/E ratio the better the investment.

price index. A mathematical quantity derived for the purpose of measuring movements in the general level of prices. A price index is essentially a form of average, weighted according to the relative importance of its components, and expressed as a percentage of its value at some defined base date. The best-known price index is the RETAIL PRICE INDEX (q.v.) published monthly under government auspices.

price level adjustments. Adjustments made to accounting quantities to compensate for the distorting effects of INFLATION (q.v.). The adjustments may be made by applying a PRICE INDEX (q.v.) to the original figures.

price variance. A VARIANCE (q.v.) caused by the fact that the price paid for some input costs more or less than that which was anticipated in the BUDGET (q.v.). The term is usually applied to the case of a price variance relating to MATERIAL (q.v.).

EXAMPLE. A budget allows for each unit of a certain product to make use of 5 kg of material at a price of £2 per kg. Actual production of 1,000 units took 5,000 kg of material but this cost £2.10 per kg. The total expenditure was thus £10,500. There was an adverse price variance of £500 (10p × 5,000).

price war. A situation where businesses seek to defeat competitors by cutting the prices of their goods to lower levels. A price war may be very expensive as prices may eventually be cut to the extent that losses are incurred. The surviving participants in a price war may improve their profitability by then increasing prices in the knowledge that competitors no longer exist. The danger of a price war is that all participants will be ruined.

pricing. The process of determining the price at which goods or services will be sold. This may be based strictly on cost or it may be conditioned by the competitive position in which the business finds itself.

prime cost. The total cost of the factors of production directly and visibly incorporated into a product. The prime cost thus consists of the total of the cost of LABOUR (q.v.) and MATERIAL (q.v.). Prime cost does not include any element of overhead.

prime entry. The original record of a financial transaction made in a JOURNAL (q.v.), DAY BOOK (q.v.) or CASH BOOK (q.v.). A book of prime entry is not part of the DOUBLE ENTRY (q.v.) system but provides a source from which POSTING (q.v.) to the ledger can be done.

primogeniture. An ancient legal principle which gave priority of inheritance to an eldest (i.e. earliest born) son. The principle was abolished in 1925.

principal. 1. A sum of money lent on which interest is being paid.

2. The ultimate party to a contract. The principal need not necessarily be the one who negotiated the contract as this may be done by an AGENT (q.v.). The principal is, however. the one who is bound under the terms of the contract.

prior charge. A charge on an asset as security for a debt which takes priority, usually because it was given earlier, than another charge on the same asset.

prior year adjustment. An adjustment contained in a set of accounts which relates wholly to a matter which occurred in a previous period. It will normally arise because some error in an earlier year's accounts has been discovered, or because there has been a change in accounting policy to which it is desired to give retrospective effect. SSAP 6 on accounting for EXTRAORDINARY ITEMS (q.v.) and prior year adjustments requires that the latter be dealt with by amending the opening balance of RETAINED PROFIT (q.v.). The effect of the change would be separately noted.

private company. A company which, by its ARTICLES OF ASSOCIATION (q.v.), restricts the transfer of its shares to those approved by the directors. A private company is designated by the term 'limited' (often abbreviated to ltd) in its name. Its shares may not be quoted on the Stock Exchange as the shares of such companies must be transferable without restriction.

private investor. An individual person who holds investments for his or her own private benefit. Recent government policy has been to encourage an increase in the number of private investors.

private ledger. A section of the NOMINAL LEDGER (q.v.) containing accounts confidential to the proprietor and therefore kept separately. Typically, the private ledger will contain accounts relating to capital, profits and DRAWINGS (q.v.). It is most likely to be encountered in very small businesses where such matters are the concern only of a sole proprietor who may wish to keep information about his or her personal income and wealth from employees.

private sector. That part of the economy which is under private, as opposed to government, control. It has been recent government policy to increase the relative size of the private sector by a process of PRIVATISATION (q.v.).

privatisation. The process of selling to private investors businesses which were previously under public ownership. It is the reverse of the process of NATIONALISATION (q.v.).

prize. A sum of money or a valuable object awarded to a person in recognition of some achievement or following success in a draw. Prizes are not normally subject to taxation.

probate. The authority given to a person to deal with the estate of a deceased person according to a WILL (q.v.). Probate is not granted until certain declarations have been made and duties have been paid.

proceeds. The amount of money arising from a transaction or series of transactions. Thus the proceeds of a sale of fixed assets will be the total amount received from them. The proceeds of a share issue will be the amount of money raised by it. The terms usually imply that all costs associated with the transaction have been deducted.

process costing. A technique for determining the unit cost of the output of a continuous industrial process. The special problem connected with process costing is that of the valuation of WORK IN PROGRESS (q.v.).

production unit method. A method of calculating depreciation in which the amount charged to the profit and loss account in the year is proportionate to the amount of product turned out by the asset. The method is based on the idea that the productive life of an asset will expire according to the extent to which it is used.

EXAMPLE. A machine is produced for £180,000 and it is expected that it will turn out 1 million units of product during its life. At the end of that time it will be valueless. The depreciation charge, using the production unit method would be:

$$\frac{£180,000}{1,000,000} = 18\text{p per unit}$$

Thus in a year in which 200,000 units were produced the depreciation charge would be:

$$18\text{p} \times 200,000 = £36,000$$

professional indemnity insurance. A form of insurance which can be taken out by persons offering a professional service, such as accountants. The policy idemnifies the insured against the direct financial consequences of an error in their work.

profit. A surplus of the revenues of a trading concern over its costs. Profit is regarded as the ultimate test of business effectiveness. No business can survive for long if it does not make a profit.

profit after tax. The profit of a company after allowing for the corporation tax due on the profit. The figure must be shown in the company's published profit and loss account. It is the fund out of which dividends may be paid.

profit and loss account. 1. A financial statement in which is computed the profit or loss made by a business during a defined period of time. Its fundamental concepts are RECOGNITION OF REVENUE (q.v.) and the MATCHING (q.v.) of costs against that revenue. DEPRECIATION (q.v.), ACCRUALS (q.v.) and PREPAYMENTS (q.v.) are the important adjustments made to CASH FLOW (q.v.) in determining profit. For a company a profit and loss account is a legal document which must be produced annually in the form required by the Companies Act 1985.
2. A description frequently applied to the item on a company's balance sheet referring to the RETAINED PROFIT (q.v.). It is the cumulative residue of a series of individual profit and loss accounts after taking into account distributions.

profit before tax. The profit of a company before any deduction has been made in respect of corporation tax. The amount must be shown in the published profit and loss account.

profit centre. A segment of the activity of an organisation to which income and costs are attributed so as to determine its profit. If a business is divided into profit centres it can be seen whether each sector is making a worthwhile contribution to the whole. Poorly performing segments can be closed or action taken to improve them.

profiteering. The making of an unfair or disproportionately large profit by exploiting a situation. Profiteering might occur, for example, if traders put up prices excessively for a product which is in short supply but has not, in fact, cost them any more to buy than usual.

profit forecast. A forecast by the management of a business of the profit expected to be made in a forthcoming period. Managements are not obliged to make profit forecasts but they may do so if, for example, they are seeking to raise extra finance or wish to fight off a takeover bid.

profit planning. The formulation of plans leading to a realistic level of profit and the implementation of those plans.

profit-related pay. An element of the pay of an employee which depends on the profit of the business. Since 1987 such pay has been more lightly taxed than other income.

profit sharing. A scheme whereby the employees of a business are entitled to some share in its profits as well as to the wages and salaries which they earn. The advocates of profit sharing see it as a useful contributor to the general morale of the workforce and as an incentive to efficient working.

profit taking. The action of investors following a rise in the value of shares whereby they sell shares in order to realise their profit. Such action by a sufficient number of investors may halt or reverse the rise in price and helps to explain why long uninterrupted price rises are rarely observed in the stock market.

pro forma. In the form of. A *pro forma* balance sheet is a statement showing what the position would be if certain proposed steps were taken rather than one showing an actual position.

program. A set of instructions in a language comprehensible to a COMPUTER (q.v.) which enable it to perform some required task. Thus a certain computer may have one program to enable it to calculate wages and another to enable it to analyse sales. Collectively computer programs are known as SOFTWARE (q.v.). The American spelling of program has become universally accepted for this application of the word.

programme trading. Trading in securities which is not subject to immediate decisions but follows from decisions made in the past as to the timing of investment. For example, an investor might give instructions that shares in a certain company are to be bought if they fall to £1.20 per share.

progressive tax. A tax which increases more than proportionately in relation to that which is being taxed. Income tax is an example of a progressive tax. Persons on the highest incomes pay tax at a higher rate than those on low incomes. This means that not only a greater absolute amount but also a greater amount as a proportion of income is paid.

progress payment. A payment made by a customer towards the total payment due under a contract which has not been completed. Where, for example, a builder undertakes to construct factory premises over a lengthy period of time it will be usual for the contract to provide that progress payments will be made at defined stages of completion. The recipient of progress payments should deduct them from the value of WORK IN PROGRESS (q.v.).

promissory note. A document in which a person promises to pay a certain sum to another person on an agreed date or on demand. It will normally be given in exchange for a loan or for credit.

promoter. One who initiates and undertakes the processes necessary to bring into being a LIMITED COMPANY (q.v.).

promotion costs. Costs incurred by a business in bringing its products to the attention of potential customers. It would include the cost of advertising and the costs of campaigns such as free samples, reduced price offers and competitions.

proof coin. A coin produced to exceptionally high standards of workmanship with the intention that it should be held by a collector rather than be put into circulation.

proof in bankruptcy. The formal establishment of the right of a creditor to participate in payments out of the estate of a bankrupt person. It will be achieved by the presentation of documents to the court.

proper accounting records. Records of financial transactions in a form sufficient to explain them fully. A limited company is legally bound to maintain proper accounting records and the AUDITOR (q.v.) is required to satisfy him or herself that this has been done, or to report accordingly if not.

property. An asset in the form of land or buildings.

proposal. A form completed by a person wishing to be issued with an insurance policy. Because a contract of insurance is *UBERRIMAE FIDEI* (q.v.) it is important that this proposal is complete and accurate. This means that it is not sufficient merely to answer the questions appearing on the form if there is other important information which they do not elicit. If a proposal conveys inaccurate or incomplete information the insurer may avoid liability in the event of a CLAIM (q.v.).

proposed dividend. A dividend proposed for payment by the directors of a company subject to the approval of the company in general meeting. Conventional practice is to show a proposed dividend as a current liability in a balance sheet even though, at the date of the balance sheet, it is not actually due.

proprietor. One who owns or has a share in the ownership of a business. Thus the shareholders of a company are its proprietors as are the partners in a partnership business.

pro rata. In proportion to. Thus an offer of shares by a company to its existing shareholders, a RIGHTS ISSUE (q.v.), will be made *pro rata* with the size of their existing holdings.

prospectus. A document inviting an application for shares or other securities. A prospectus relating to shares in a company must contain information prescribed by law. This includes financial particulars for the previous 5 years, if applicable, and a statement of future prospects.

protectionism. A policy of government which has the effect of giving competitive advantage to home industry by imposing duties on goods imported into the country.

protection money. Money illegally demanded from an individual or business under the threat that some violence will otherwise be committed. The payment of the money 'protects' the payer from that violence.

provident society. A mutual organisation which uses the savings of some members to finance loans to other members at reasonable rates of interest and with reasonable terms of repayment.

provision. An amount set aside, by charging it in the profit and loss account, to provide for depreciation or for any known liability the amount of which cannot be determined with complete accuracy. A provision is thus to be distinguished from an ACCRUAL (q.v.) which is to provide for a known liability of known amount. Any amount set aside for an unspecified purpose is properly known as a RESERVE (q.v.).

provisional allotment. An allotment of shares to be confirmed if and when the shares are paid for. Such an allotment is made to existing shareholders in the case of a RIGHTS ISSUE (q.v.). Letters of provisional allotment are negotiable and can thus be sold in the market by shareholders unwilling to make further investment in the company.

proxy. One who acts on behalf of another. It is very common for shareholders either unwilling or unable to attend a meeting of shareholders to appoint a proxy who may then attend the meeting and record a vote in accordance with their wishes. The proxy may be a company officer such as the chairman of the meeting.

prudence. A principle of accounting to the effect that accounting statements should be prepared on a cautious basis, avoiding undue optimism. It has been said that the purpose of a balance sheet is to 'show that the financial condition of the company is at least as good as that stated and not to show that it is not or may not be better'. Prudence was one of the four fundamental ACCOUNTING CONCEPTS (q.v.) given in SSAP 2. It is now embodied as a basic principle in the Companies Act 1985. An alternative term for prudence is conservatism. Its application must mean that accounts are always biased towards giving a pessimistic view of profits and valuations.

publication of accounts. The accounts of a company are published when they are made publicly available. This is done by filing a copy with the REGISTRAR OF COMPANIES (q.v.).

publication standard. Financial statements prepared and audited with the same attention and care as statements intended for publication as part of the annual accounts. It follows from this that publication standard statements should show a true and fair view of their subject.

public company. A company having no restriction on ownership or transfer of its shares. It is distinguished by the use of the letters PLC as part of its name. They stand for public limited company. A company must be a public company before it can be quoted on the Stock Exchange. Not all public companies are quoted, however.

public ownership. Ownership by the government on behalf of the people.

public sector. That part of the economy which is under government control. It has been recent government policy to reduce the relative size of the public sector by a process of PRIVATISATION (q.v.).

punitive damages. DAMAGES (q.v.) awarded of an amount exceeding any actual damage suffered by the plaintiff with the intention that the defendant should suffer some element of punishment for the conduct which is complained of.

purchase day book. A book of prime entry in which is recorded the purchases made by a business on a day-to-day basis. The entries are subsequently posted to the creditors' accounts in the PURCHASE LEDGER (q.v.) and the purchases account.

purchase invoice. An INVOICE (q.v.) which has been received from the supplier of goods purchased. It will specify the nature and quantity of the goods supplied, their price and the total amount payable. The purchase invoice is a source document for the preparation of postings to the PURCHASE LEDGER (q.v.).

purchase journal. Synonym for PURCHASE DAY BOOK (q.v.).

purchase ledger. A section of the ledger containing the accounts of those persons from whom the business buys goods on credit. The purchase ledger will thus be the source of the amount of TRADE CREDITORS (q.v.).

purchase order. An order issued by a business to a supplier in respect of goods which are required. The issue of a properly authorised purchase order before goods may be supplied is an important safeguard against purchases being made improperly and charged to the business. A business whose practice it is to issue purchase orders will decline to pay for any goods supplied in the absence of such an order.

purchase requisition. A document requiring and authorising a purchase by a business. It is an important part of STOCK CONTROL (q.v.). It ensures that goods are not bought which are not required for some proper purpose.

purchase returns. Goods, previously treated as purchases, which have been returned to a supplier for refund or credit. In the accounts, purchase returns should be treated as reducing the value of PURCHASES (q.v.).

purchases. The value of goods bought for resale or for use in a manufacturing process. The total of purchases is an important element in the calculation of COST OF SALES (q.v.).

purchasing power. The ability to buy things. Its most familiar use is in reference to the purchasing power of the currency unit. When there is inflation this purchasing power is said to decline.

pushdown. An amount written off the value of the investment in a SUBSIDIARY COMPANY (q.v.) in the books of the HOLDING COMPANY (q.v.) logically required when goodwill arising on consolidation is written off against reserves in the consolidated balance sheet. The acknowledgement of the loss in value of goodwill 'pushes down' the value of the investment by the amount of the goodwill which is therein embodied.

put option. An OPTION (q.v.) giving the holder the right to sell a security at some future date at a price agreed at the present. A put option may be used by an investor wishing to limit the possibility of loss through investing in a risky security. There is a market in options and the prices are regularly quoted.

pyramid selling. A type of selling based on the principle of the chain letter. There may be no actual goods involved but merely literature. Each participant is offered the attraction that large sums of money will accrue for very little effort. In practice this does not occur.

Q

qualification shares. A number of shares which a director of a company is required, by its ARTICLES OF ASSOCIATION (q.v.), to hold before he or she is entitled to take office. Not all companies require directors to hold qualification shares and, where they do, the number is usually quite small.

qualified audit report. An AUDITORS' REPORT (q.v.) which expresses reservations on certain matters of concern to the auditor. This may be in terms that indicate that the accounts to which the report refers are inaccurate or misleading and fail to give a TRUE AND FAIR VIEW (q.v.). Alternatively the reservation may be on the grounds that evidence was not available to the auditor to enable an opinion to be formed one way or the other.

quality control. The subject of an AUDITING GUIDELINE (q.v.) to the effect that auditors should take active steps to plan and monitor their work so as to ensure its quality.

quarter. A period of time equal to 3 calendar months, i.e. one-quarter of a year. It is a conventional billing and accounting period.

quarter day. The quarter days are 25 March (Lady Day), 24 June (Midsummer Day), 29 September (Michaelmas Day) and 25 December (Christmas Day). They are traditionally written into contracts requiring regular payments (e.g. of rent) as the dates on which payments are to be made.

quasi-loan. The consequence of a transaction where one party, the lender, makes a payment on behalf of another, the borrower, with the agreement that the borrower will ultimately repay the lender. Quasi-loans by a company to its directors are subject to disclosure provisions set out in the Companies Act 1985.

quasi-subsidiary company. A company which does not fulfil the legal definition of a subsidiary company as set out in the Companies Act 1985 but which nevertheless is effectively controlled indirectly by another company.

quick assets. Assets which are highly LIQUID (q.v.). Cash and bank balances are good examples.

quick succession relief. A relief given against INHERITANCE TAX (q.v.) where a person inheriting money then dies within 5 years so that the same sum becomes liable to tax for a second time.

quid pro quo. Something done in exchange for another thing done or given. Thus an employee might agree to work late, the quid pro quo being that he or she is allowed to leave early on another occasion.

quotation. 1. A firm statement of the total cost for which specified work will be undertaken. Thus a business wishing to have built an extension to its factory may ask a builder to give a quotation. Once a quotation is accepted the one giving it is contractually bound to complete the work for that figure. A quotation should thus be contrasted with an ESTIMATE (q.v.).

2. Inclusion in the list of securities traded in a recognised market. Thus before the shares of a company may be bought and sold on the Stock Exchange application must be made for a quotation on that market.

quoted company. A company whose shares are quoted on the Stock Exchange. Most large companies are quoted companies. Their shares are, as a consequence, readily realisable.

quoted investments. Investments which are listed on the Stock Exchange.

R

R & D. Letters standing for RESEARCH AND DEVELOPMENT (q.v.).

racket. Some activity in which money is unfairly or even dishonestly taken from members of the public. This is usually done by charging an exorbitantly high price for goods or services.

rack rent. The rent which a property would command in a free market.

raffle. A draw for prizes usually organised to raise funds for some charitable purpose. Very often the prizes are donated and the money paid for the tickets is then wholly profit for the cause.

rake-off. A proportion of the proceeds of some activity received by one who has contributed to it in some way. The term is used colloquially to mean a payment in the form of a COMMISSION (q.v.).

random sample. A sample drawn in such a way that every member of the population has an equal chance of being selected. Sampling is used in the field of auditing where a random sample of transactions may be examined in order to form a view as to the accuracy of the bulk. Clearly, if the sample is not random, e.g. if it selected to include only items of known accuracy, it will not allow a valid conclusion to be reached.

random walk theory. The theory that stock market prices follow a random path and that, therefore, their future course is not predictable. The random walk theory arises from the EFFICIENT MARKET THEORY (q.v.) of stock market behaviour.

ranking. Placing items in an order of merit or of size. Items on a balance sheet may be ranked in order of LIQUIDITY (q.v.). Holders of PREFERENCE SHARES (q.v.) rank before holders of ORDINARY SHARES (q.v.) in the payment of a DIVIDEND (q.v.). The ranking of investment projects, done by calculating for each a NET PRESENT VALUE (q.v.), is important in cases of MUTUALLY EXCLUSIVE PROJECTS (q.v.), or of CAPITAL RATIONING (q.v.).

ransom. An amount demanded illegally for the return of a kidnapped person or a stolen object of value. The threat is usually made that the person will be killed or the object destroyed if the ransom is not paid.

rateable value. A notional annual rental value attributed to property in the UK which formed the basis of charging the form of local property tax known as rates. Rates on domestic property have now been abolished and replaced by the COUNCIL TAX (q.v.).

rate of exchange. The rate at which the currency of one country can be exchanged for the currency of another. A different rate of exchange exists between any two currencies and in each case is established by market forces. The rate of exchange has an accounting significance when accounts prepared in one currency have to be translated into statements in another currency. It also has a practical significance for those either buying raw materials or selling finished products abroad. Rates of exchange fluctuate frequently. Governments may sometimes intervene to influence them. For example, the BANK OF ENGLAND (q.v.) may either buy or sell pounds in order to smooth out fluctuations in the value of STERLING (q.v.).

G

rate of interest. The percentage which annual INTEREST (q.v.) bears to the capital sum on which it is paid. Thus a rate of interest of 10 per cent means that £1,000 invested for 1 year would earn £100. There will be a number of rates of interest in force at any one time so that a borrower is likely to find that he or she will pay a higher rate of interest than would be received if he or she were an investor. High rates of interest generally prevail during times of economic difficulty.

rate of pay variance. A VARIANCE (q.v.) caused by a difference between the rate of pay of labour envisaged in establishing a BUDGET (q.v.) and that actually experienced.

EXAMPLE. A budget was based on the plan that labour would be employed for a total of 5,000 hours at a rate of pay of £10 per hour. This gives a total budgeted expenditure of £10,000. Although 5,000 hours were actually worked, labour's rate of pay was £11 per hour. The difference between the actual cost of £55,000 and the budgeted cost, i.e. £5,000, is an adverse rate of pay variance.

rates. A form of local taxation paid by property owners. At one time it was paid by domestic as well as business property occupiers. Now domestic property occupiers pay a COUNCIL TAX (q.v.) and rates are restricted to business occupiers.

rating. An assessment of quality. A company is said to have a high rating if analysts believe that its shares are a good investment.

ratio. The relationship between one value and another. The calculation of ratios is an important technique for analysing and understanding balance sheets and profit and loss accounts.

raw materials. Materials acquired for incorporation into a manufactured product. Raw materials are normally valued at cost for accounting purposes.

ready money. Synonym for cash and hence meaning immediately liquid funds.

real estate. Land and buildings.

real income. Income measured in such a manner as to eliminate the distortion due to inflation.

real investment. Investment in physically productive assets such as plant and machinery as opposed to investment in securities.

realisable income. The profit of a business calculated on the basis of valuing all its assets at realisable values. It is one of the concepts employed by Edwards and Bell in their book *Theory and Measurement of Business Income.*

realisable value. The amount which would be received if an asset were sold. It is argued that this basis of valuation, not commonly used in practice, would show more clearly the alternative uses forgone of the resources employed in the present business.

realisation concept. A fundamental accounting concept which states that profits should be recognised only when they have been realised or when realisation is assured.

realised profit. A profit which has become available in the form of cash, usually following the sale of the asset in which it is embodied.

EXAMPLE. An investor purchased some shares for £10,000 1 year ago. These shares now have a market value of £15,000 and thus a profit has been made of £5,000. This profit becomes a realised profit when the shares are sold.

real terms profit. A profit calculated after taking into account the effects on the figures of INFLATION (q.v.).

realty. Property consisting of the ownership of land or of an interest in land. The term is often used in describing property forming part of the ESTATE (q.v.) of a deceased person. It should be contrasted with PERSONALTY (q.v.).

real value. A value expressed in terms which make it independent of the value of money. Real value is thus of special significance in times of inflation.

EXAMPLE. A property had a value in year 1 of £100,000 and in year 10 of £200,000. Thus its money value had doubled. An index of prices which stood at 100 in year 1 had increased to 300 in year 10, so that money had declined to one-third of its earlier value. The real value of the property has, therefore, declined (by one-third).

rebate. A return of part of the amount paid for goods or services or a reduction in the amount charged for them given in specified circumstances. For example, a small user of the telephone may be entitled to a rebate against its rental.

receipt. A document evidencing that money has been received. Payments made by cheque no longer require a receipt as the paid cheque is legally acceptable evidence of the payment. When a payment is made in cash, however, proof of payment in the event of a dispute may be difficult if no receipt has been obtained.

receipts and payments account. An account of the activities of an organisation for a period of time in terms of the amounts of cash received and paid under a number of headings. It takes no account of ACCRUALS (q.v.) or PREPAYMENTS (q.v.). A receipts and payments account would not generally be regarded as adequate to describe the activities of a trading organisation but it is commonly encountered in statements prepared by clubs and social organisations. Even in this area an INCOME AND EXPENDITURE ACCOUNT (q.v.) would usually be more informative.

receiver. One who manages a company with a view to orderly LIQUIDATION (q.v.). When a receiver is appointed, normal trading is suspended except to the extent that it assists in the process of liquidation, e.g. by allowing the sale of a GOING CONCERN (q.v.).

recession. A condition of the economy of a country under which business is conducted at a reduced level. It is also characterised by unemployment and falling prices.

recognition of revenue. The inclusion of revenue in the profit and loss account. Revenue may be recognised when a contract of sale is made or, alternatively, when the cash has actually been received. It is regarded as bad practice to recognise revenue before either it has been received in cash or its ultimate receipt has become certain (i.e. there is a legally enforceable debt).

reconciliation. An explanation of the difference between two figures which purport to express the same quantity. A reconciliation may be needed, for example, between the amount of cash shown in a business's balance sheet and that shown on its bank statements due to such items as UNPRESENTED CHEQUES (q.v.).

reconstruction. A process of amending the financing arrangements of a limited company. It may include the writing off of accumulated losses by the REDUCTION OF CAPITAL (q.v.) or the amendment of the rights of particular classes of shareholders. Reconstructions are normally undertaken to place a company on a sound financial footing for a fresh start after a period of difficulty.

recorded delivery. A service operated by the Post Office whereby a signature is obtained on the delivery of a letter. It is thus possible to verify its arrival. It is a useful service for the transmission of documents which are important but of little intrinsic monetary value.

recourse. The right to require payment from a person other than the one having a primary liability. If, for example, the drawee of a bill of exchange fails to honour it on maturity the holder may have recourse to other persons who have endorsed the bill since it was first drawn.

recoverable. Capable of being realised. The recoverable value of an asset is that amount which can be converted into cash, either by immediate sale or by a process of realisation in normal use.

recovery stock. The shares of a company which are currently at a depressed price because of temporary factors having an adverse effect on the company but from which it is believed that it will recover. An investor will buy recovery stocks in the belief that they represent an investment with a good prospect of substantial gains.

red. The colour in which negative figures are traditionally recorded. Thus to be 'in the red' at the bank is to have a bank overdraft. For a business to 'go into the red' is for it to make a loss.

redeemable shares. Shares issued on the terms that the holders will at some future date be repaid the amount which they invested in the company. Redeemable preference shares were first permitted under the Companies Act 1948. Redeemable ordinary shares are now permissible under the Companies Act 1985. In the case of a PUBLIC COMPANY (q.v.) the redemption must be achieved in a manner which prevents there being any reduction in capital. This is done either by making a new issue of shares in replacement for those redeemed or by making the redemption out of profits which would otherwise be available for distribution. In the latter event a further distribution of those profits must be prevented by making a transfer from the profit and loss account to a CAPITAL REDEMPTION RESERVE (q.v.).

redemption. The process of repaying an obligation. The term is used when a limited company pays off its DEBENTURES (q.v.) or where a MORTGAGOR (q.v.) pays off the debt secured by the MORTGAGE (q.v.).

reducing balance. One of the methods available for calculating the amount to be charged as DEPRECIATION (q.v.). The amount is calculated by applying a fixed percentage each year to the net BOOK VALUE (q.v.) of the asset. Since this steadily declines, application of the reducing balance method means that a greater part of the asset's value is charged in the early part of its life than is charged in the later part. It is sometimes argued that this realistically represents the fact that new assets provide a better (and therefore more valuable) service than old. A characteristic of the reducing balance method is that the asset value is never completely extinguished so long as the asset is in existence. In practice, however, its value will quickly decline to negligible proportions.

EXAMPLE. An asset purchased for £10,000 is to be depreciated by the reducing balance method at the rate of 30 per cent per annum. This will lead to the following values:

Year	Book value of asset at start £	Depreciation for year at 30% reducing balance £
1	10,000	3,000
2	7,000	2,100
3	4,900	1,470
4	3,430	1,029 and so on

reduction of capital. A process whereby the share capital of a limited company is diminished either by repayment or by writing down its value. In either case there are safeguards to ensure that the interests of creditors are not prejudiced. There are two circumstances in which a reduction of capital might be sought. The first is where a company finds itself with excessive funds for which no profitable use can be found. This might occur if there has been a permanent diminution in the level of business available. In this case the company might repay part of the capital rateably to its shareholders. The second is where a company has large accumulated losses where there are no prospects of recovery. The debit balance on the profit and loss account may then be extinguished by writing an appropriate amount from the nominal value of the shares so that, for example, £1 shares are reduced to 50p shares. Under provisions contained in the Companies Act 1985 a company is now permitted to purchase or redeem its OWN SHARES (q.v.). Thus is not strictly a reduction of capital as, in that case, the capital must be replaced by a fresh issue of shares or by a CAPITAL REDEMPTION RESERVE (q.v.).

redundancy payment. A payment made to an employee who has been dismissed by reason of redundancy. There is a statutory entitlement to redundancy pay for all employees, the amount depending on length of service and level of pay. Many employers pay more than the statutory minimum.

refer to drawer. A form of words written by a bank on a cheque drawn on it. Although it literally invites the payee to consult the drawer of the cheque it amounts to a refusal to pay the cheque, usually because funds are not available in the account on which it is drawn.

refund. To pay back an amount previously paid. Thus the purchaser of goods which prove to be unsatisfactory may be refunded the purchase price by the seller.

regional development grant. A grant given by the government to encourage companies to establish businesses in regions of the country which are economically depressed. The accounting treatment of such grants is prescribed in SSAP 4.

registered office. An address to which official notifications to a limited company can be sent and thus its address for legal purposes. Every company must have a registered office. This is very often not its business address but that of a bank, an accountant or a solicitor.

registered post. A service offered by the Post Office whereby the material is handled in a secure way and a signature obtained on delivery. It is thus possible to verify safe delivery. Where the material is lost or damaged in transit compensation may be claimed.

registered security. A security, ownership of which is recorded in a register maintained by the organisation issuing the security. It is to be contrasted with a BEARER SECURITY (q.v.). Most company shares and government stocks are registered securities. Transfer of ownership is achieved by means of the execution of a transfer document which acts as an authority for the appropriate amendment to the register to be made. The main advantage of registered securities is that they cannot be lost by theft or physical damage.

register of charges. A register to be kept by a company recording all charges against any of its assets. These charges arise in connection with the use of assets as security against a loan. The register of charges is one of the statutory books of a company.

register of debenture holders. A record required to be kept by a company. It lists the debenture holders of the company by name and address and records the amount of debentures which each holds. An entry in the register of debenture holders is conclusive evidence of the ownership of the debentures.

register of directors and secretary. A record required to be kept by a company. It gives for each person his or her name, any former names, and addresses. For directors it must also give nationality, business occupation and particulars of any other directorships held. In the case of a PUBLIC COMPANY (q.v.) the directors' dates of birth must also be given.

register of directors' interests. A record required to be kept by a company. It gives details of any INTEREST (q.v.) in the company or of any SUBSIDIARY COMPANY (q.v.) in the form of shares, debentures or options thereon held by the directors, their spouses or minor children.

register of members. A record required to be kept by a company. It lists the shareholders of the company by name and address and records the number of shares which each holds. An entry in the register of members is conclusive evidence of the ownership of shares.

registrar. That officer of a company whose responsibility it is to maintain the REGISTER OF MEMBERS (q.v.).

Registrar of Companies. A public official charged with the responsibility of receiving and holding prescribed information about companies registered under the Companies Act 1985. Every company is required to make an ANNUAL RETURN (q.v.) to the Registrar and to file a copy of its accounts. It is also the Registrar of Companies who deals with the initial registration procedures and issues the company's CERTIFICATE OF INCORPORATION (q.v.).

registration. A legal process by which a company may come into being. It has to be registered with the REGISTRAR OF COMPANIES (q.v.).

regressive tax. A tax which bears more heavily on those with low incomes than those with higher incomes. An example of a regressive tax would be a purchase tax on the basic necessities of life. These form a bigger proportion of the expenditure of persons on low incomes. Most tax in the UK is PROGRESSIVE TAX (q.v.) and where a tax proves to be regressive this is usually not by design. For example duty on cigarettes tends to be regressive because it so happens that smoking is significantly more prevalent amongst lower income earners.

regulation. The process of controlling some industry. It may be organised by the industry itself, self-regulation, or it may be set up by statute.

regulatory body. A body set up under the terms of an Act of Parliament or voluntarily to achieve the REGULATION (q.v.) of some industry or activity.

reimburse. To repay to a person amounts paid by him or her on behalf of someone else. Thus a person who travels on behalf of an employer may be reimbursed for the expenses of so doing.

reinsurance. The process whereby an insurer transfers some of the risks which have been accepted to another insurer. It is a mechanism whereby insurers can maintain a balanced PORTFOLIO (q.v.) of risks.

reinvestment. The immediate investment of funds released from the realisation of some other investment. A stockbroker may charge a reduced COMMISSION (q.v.) when asked to reinvest funds.

related company. A company in which the company to which it is related holds equity shares on a long-term basis for the purpose of securing a contribution to that company's own activities by the exercise of control and influence arising from that interest. A 20 per cent holding of shares is presumed to create a related company status unless the contrary can be shown. The concept of a related company was introduced in the Companies Act 1981 (now the 1985 Act).

related parties. Persons who, whilst apparently acting independently, are actually acting together. Comparatively small shareholdings, for example, may be held by related parties. Collectively they may, therefore, have an unexpectedly large influence in the affairs of the company.

relevant cost. A cost which would be charged were a proposal under consideration to be implemented but not otherwise. It is relevant costs only which should be considered in decision making.

relevant income. That income of a CLOSE COMPANY (q.v.) which may be deemed to be distributable for the purpose of making a SHORTFALL ASSESSMENT (q.v.) to tax. Since 1980 it consists of the company's DISTRIBUTABLE INVESTMENT INCOME (q.v.) plus 50 per cent of its property income. The relevant income may be reduced below this figure if the company can prove that it was unable to distribute the money because it was needed for a business purpose.

remit. To send money by some carrier, e.g. by post.

remittance. An amount of money sent by one person to another.

remittance advice. A document accompanying a REMITTANCE (q.v.) which explains to what the payment relates.

remuneration. An amount paid in consideration for services rendered by an employee. The major part of remuneration is in the form of WAGES (q.v.) or SALARY (q.v.) but it may also include benefits such as a free pension scheme, health insurance or the provision of a car.

renewals. Purchases of minor items of plant and equipment to replace those lost or worn out. If a renewals basis is used for accounting for such items, as opposed to providing for their DEPRECIATION (q.v.), the cost of renewals will be charged in the profit and loss account at the amount actually spent during the accounting period.

renounce. To give up rights. A LETTER OF ALLOTMENT (q.v.) for shares may be renounced in favour of a person other than the one to whom the letter was addressed and this is done when the shares embodied in the letter are sold to that other person.

rent. An amount paid for the use of land or buildings. It is quoted as a certain sum for a defined period of time. Rent is commonly paid in advance of the period to which it relates.

rentier. A person whose income arises from the ownership of property or investments rather than from personal labour.

reorder quantity. A quantity set with the intention that when stocks fall to that level the procedure for reordering will be set in motion. The reorder quantity should be set so that enough stock then remains to cover requirements between the ordering and the delivery of fresh supplies.

reorganisation costs. The costs directly attributable to the reorganisation of a business or of a part of it. Such costs should be treated in the profit and loss account as EXCEPTIONAL ITEMS (q.v.).

replacement. The process of purchasing an asset to take the place of a similar asset which has been consumed. The necessity of replacement is a justification for using REPLACEMENT COST (q.v.) as a basis of valuation.

replacement cost. The cost of replacing an asset with another which is identical or equivalent. Replacement cost is an important basis of valuation and is used as part of

CURRENT COST ACCOUNTING (q.v.). It may be argued that replacement cost is a more realistic measure of the value of an asset than its original cost.

reported profit. The amount of profit shown by the profit and loss account of a business. The amount depends in part on the bases of accounting which have been used in preparing the account.

reporting accountant. An accountant who prepares a financial report for some defined purpose. For example, a reporting accountant might prepare figures for inclusion in a PROSPECTUS (q.v.).

reporting currency. The currency in which final accounts are expressed. They may originally have been prepared in some other currency which has subsequently been translated such as in the case of a UK company having foreign subsidiaries.

repossession. Action taken by a lender to take possession of a property given as security for a loan when the debtor is in default. If a person buying a house fails to maintain the mortgage repayments the building society may repossess the house. This will then be sold to repay the debt.

required rate of return. The rate of return on a project involving the investment of capital which a company will require before it regards the investment as worthwhile. It thus acts as a criterion in the making of such investment decisions. The required rate of return would normally be equal to the COST OF CAPITAL (q.v.) of the company.

requisition. A document requiring and authorising some action. A material requisition, for example, requires and authorises the issue of material to production.

resale price maintenance. An agreement between a retailer and the manufacturer of a product sold by the retailer that the product will be sold only at a price set by the manufacturer. This has the effect of standardising prices by eliminating price competition between retailers. Such agreements are not now legal in the UK except in the case of books. Even in this field agreements are being disregarded by some retailers.

research and development expenditure. Expenditure not related to current production but to the creation of future opportunities. It is the subject of a standard, SSAP 13. Research expenditure is expenditure on general research not related to the development of any specific product. It should be written off in the year in which it is incurred except for expenditure on fixed assets used in research (e.g. laboratory equipment) which should be written off over the period of their useful lives. Development expenditure is expenditure on the development of specific products. It, too, should be written off when incurred unless it meets certain criteria, in which case it may be carried forward as an asset. These criteria are:
   (a) there is a clearly defined project;
   (b) the expenditure on development of that project can be identified;
   (c) successful completion of the project is both technically and commercially possible;
   (d) the total of all development cost is expected to be met by future revenues from the project;
   (e) adequate resources exist to fund completion of the project.
The rules in the Companies Act 1985 concerning research and development expenditure are met by adherence to SSAP 13.

reservation of title. A condition attached to the supply of goods that title in them will not pass from the seller to the buyer until payment has been made in full. Normally a creditor for goods supplied would rank below many prior interests in the event of the BANKRUPTCY (q.v.) of the customer. With reservation of title, however, the supplier has the legal right to repossess the actual goods in such an event.

reserve. An amount retained by a company other than as a PROVISION (q.v.) for a known liability or for DEPRECIATION (q.v.). A reserve may be a CAPITAL RESERVE (q.v.) such as the SHARE PREMIUM ACCOUNT (q.v.), in which case it is not distributable but may be used to pay up BONUS SHARES (q.v.). Alternatively, it may be a REVENUE RESERVE (q.v.) which may be distributed. The profit and loss account is the usual source of revenue reserves.

reserve capital. That part of the NOMINAL CAPITAL (q.v.) of a business which has not yet been called up. It is thus a reserve which can be drawn on in case of need.

reserve price. A price set in advance of a sale by AUCTION (q.v.) below which a sale will not be concluded. The function of a reserve price is that a seller can be assured thereby that the object of the sale will not be sold at too low a price because of lack of interest at the sale. If the reserve price is set unrealistically high no sale will be achieved so its level needs to be determined carefully.

residence. The place where a taxpayer usually lives. Residence may change from one tax year to another and the main criterion is the amount of time spent in one place. Residence in the UK determines liability to tax on income arising abroad.

residual income. That part of the income of a segment of a business which remains after all costs, including the cost of the capital employed in the segment, are taken into account. The concept of residual income is one which has an application in the measurement of divisional performance.

residual value. The value left in a fixed asset after it has reached the end of its useful life. It would be taken into account in determining the recurrent charge for DEPRECIATION (q.v.).

residue. That which is left from the estate of a deceased person after all specific bequests have been fulfilled. It may often be the major part of the estate and be left to a named individual.

resistance level. A level of prices in the stock market at which it is believed that there is a tendency for price movements to halt or reverse. Resistance levels may, however, move from time to time. The concept is used by CHARTISTS (q.v.) in the process of MARKET ANALYSIS (q.v.). If a resistance level is breached decisively by a price movement it is usually believed that the movement will then continue in the same direction until another resistance level is encountered. If it exists a resistance level reflects the consensus opinion of an appropriate level of prices.

responsibility centre. An area of business activity under the responsibility of a defined person or group of persons. If a BUDGET (q.v.) is prepared for a responsibility centre its manager can be made fully accountable for any VARIANCE (q.v.) which occurs.

restock. To replace STOCK (q.v.) after it has been depleted either by sale or by loss or destruction.

restructuring costs. The costs involved in making substantial organisational changes to a business. They would normally not be expected to recur and might, therefore, be discounted in predicting future profits from an analysis of current accounts.

results. The outcome, in terms of profit and EARNINGS PER SHARE (q.v.), of the activities of a company during a trading period.

retail banking services. Banking services provided to individual members of the public as opposed to those provided to businesses and institutions.

Retail Price Index. An index which measures the general level of retail prices. It is calculated and published monthly under government auspices. Its importance is as a measure of inflation and as a yardstick against which index-linked investments and pensions are adjusted.

retained earnings. A synonym for RETAINED PROFIT (q.v.).

retained profit. That part of the profit of a company which has not been distributed to the members in the form of dividends. It is a cumulative amount and each year's retained profit, if any, increases the total. Retained profit is a REVENUE RESERVE (q.v.) and will appear as such on the balance sheet. It will often be described there as profit and loss account. Retained profit is an important source of finance for the expansion of a company. It may also be used to support a dividend where current profit is inadequate to do so.

retention of title. A form of the sale of goods whereby the seller retains the property in them until payment has been made. The more usual contract for sale has the effect that title passes when the goods are delivered. Retention of title has the advantage for the seller that, if payment is not made (e.g. because of INSOLVENCY (q.v.)), the goods may be reclaimed. Under a conventional contract of sale they would be available for the benefit of all creditors equally.

retirement. Withdrawing from employment because of age. A secure retirement requires that proper provision has been made for a PENSION (q.v.).

retirement pension. A PENSION (q.v.) paid to a person who has retired.

retrospective. Taking effect as though it had occurred at an earlier date. Normally legislation is not made retrospective as this would imply uncertainty as to the legality of any action which might be taken.

return on capital employed. Profit related to the investment of capital required to produce it. It is used as a measure of performance but is subject to distortion due to difficulties in determining both profit and capital employed.

revaluation. The process of placing a different valuation on an asset from its current recorded value. Revaluation is a comparatively rare event in accounting on the basis of HISTORICAL COST (q.v.) and is used only where balance sheet values have become conspicuously misleading. Revaluation should be properly done by independent valuers. If CURRENT COST ACCOUNTING (q.v.) is used, regular revaluation of all assets will take place.

revaluation reserve. A RESERVE (q.v.) to which is credited surpluses arising on the revaluation of assets. A particular application of a revaluation reserve is in connection with CURRENT COST ACCOUNTING (q.v.) where regular revaluations of assets to current cost are required. A revaluation reserve is technically a REVENUE RESERVE (q.v.) in so far as the revaluations have been realised, and is a CAPITAL RESERVE (q.v.) in so far as unrealised revaluations are concerned.

revenue. Literally, amounts received. The term is, however, commonly used to refer to all items appearing in the profit and loss account whether incoming or outgoing. Thus revenue expenditure is to be contrasted with capital expenditure.

revenue reserve. An amount withheld from profits otherwise available for distribution. It is a term used in company accounts. A company may have a single revenue reserve (designated either profit and loss account or retained profit) or it may have designated reserves made for specific purposes, e.g. debenture redemption reserve, plant replacement reserve, general reserve, etc. By law, all transfers to and from reserves must be disclosed.

reverse takeover. A situation where a company which was threatened by takeover responds by taking over the prospective bidder.

reversion. The return of property which was the subject of a lease to the freeholder at the expiration of the lease.

revolving credit. The facility to borrow money up to a certain specified amount and to replace one borrowing with another as the former is paid off so long as the overall limit is not exceeded.

reward. Amount offered or paid to a person rendering some special service. A reward might be paid, for example, to someone who gave information which led to the recovery of property which had been stolen.

rigging a market. Acting in a market in such a way that the prices established bear no relation to those which would have been produced by a free interplay of supply and demand. This might be done by large buying or selling or by supplying false information to the market.

rights issue. An issue to the existing shareholders of a company of the right to subscribe for additional shares *pro rata* to their existing holdings. Where a relatively small amount of extra finance is required a rights issue represents an economical way of raising it. Shareholders not wishing to invest more in the company may sell their rights on the market.

ring. A group of persons who agree not to bid against one another at an AUCTION (q.v.). The property is thus sold at a low price and members of the ring share in the profit achieved on its subsequent resale. Taking part in a ring amounts to a conspiracy against the seller of the property.

risk. The probability that events will differ from what was predicted. The effects of risk may be either favourable or adverse. The definition implies only that they were unforeseen. All business activity involves an element of risk and those activities which are potentially the most rewarding often carry the highest risk of failure. Risk should be allowed for in all business plans. It may sometimes be reduced by a policy of DIVERSIFICATION (q.v.).

risk aversion. A characteristic imputed to business managers whereby they are deemed to seek to avoid risk except to the extent that it is rewarded. It is an important component of PORTFOLIO THEORY (q.v.). This argues that there is a trade-off between the risk attaching to an investment and its rate of return. Given a certain level of return, an investor will seek the minimum risk. Given the level of risk the maximum return will be sought.

risk capital. Capital such that its remuneration and ultimate repayment depend entirely upon the outcome of a business activity as opposed to being dependent on a contract. Shares in a company and a sole trader's investment in a business are both examples of risk capital. Persons are induced to contribute to risk capital by the hope of rewards more substantial than those available from a risk-free investment.

risk-free rate of return. The rate of return which may be obtained from an investment in which there is no risk whatsoever, i.e. the return is known with complete certainty. It is usually regarded as equal to the rate of return on government securities. The significance of the risk-free rate of return is that it is the datum from which the returns attributable to risk can be measured. A risky investment may be expected to have a yield made up of a combination of the risk-free rate of return and a risk premium to compensate the investor for the risk which is taken.

ROCE. Letters standing for RETURN ON CAPITAL EMPLOYED (q.v.).

rolling budget. A BUDGET (q.v.) which, having been established at the beginning of a period, is then constantly amended to take account of developing circumstances. The advantage of a rolling budget is that it should prevent a VARIANCE (q.v.) arising from external and uncontrollable circumstances. This gives a more powerful meaning to the variances which remain. They are fully attributable to management effort.

rollover relief. A postponement of CAPITAL GAINS TAX (q.v.) given to a business which reinvests the proceeds of the sale of an asset on which a gain is made. Without rollover relief businesses would have a powerful disincentive to replacing such assets.

EXAMPLE. A business bought a building for £200,000 and sold it for £400,000, replacing it with another, larger building at a cost of £600,000. Without any relief the business would have to pay tax on its gain of £200,000 at the same time as making the investment in the new building. This would impose a severe strain on its cash resources. Rollover relief would allow it to deduct the gain from the cost of the new asset rather than immediately paying the tax. The cost of the new assets for capital gains tax purposes when this is ultimately sold is thus £800,000.

Romalpa case. A leading case concerning RETENTION OF TITLE (q.v.). The full name of the case was *Aluminium Industrie Vaassen BV* v. *Romalpa Aluminium Ltd.* and it was decided in 1976. It established that the property in goods sold subject to a retention of title remained with the seller until they had been paid for.

roulette. A game of chance in which a winning number is indicated by a ball which falls into a slot in a horizontally spun wheel.

round figures. Approximations or estimates.

round lot. A quantity of shares in a company which is a round figure, e.g. 1,000 or 10,000. It is usually cheaper to deal in round lots but events such as SCRIP DIVIDENDS (q.v.) and BONUS ISSUES (q.v.) may mean that some investors do not hold round lots.

royal charter. A legal document emanating from the Crown and creating a corporate entity. Examples exist in history of trading companies which were incorporated by royal charter (e.g. the Hudson's Bay Company, which still operates in Canada today), but in modern times the procedure has been reserved for such institutions as universities and professional bodies. All of the main professional bodies of accountants in the UK are incorporated by royal charter.

Royal Mail Steam Packet case. Popular title of a leading case on false accounting, *R* v. *Kylsant and Morland* (1931). Lord Kylsant, the chairman, and Morland, the AUDITOR (q.v.) of the Royal Mail Steam Packet Co. Ltd, were charged with issuing false annual reports to the shareholders. The facts were that trading losses over a number of years had been concealed by undisclosed transfers from reserves. Under the Companies Act 1929, the legislation in force at the time, there was no explicit obligation to disclose these transfers and the defendants were acquitted (although Lord Kylsant was convicted on a different charge of falsifying a PROSPECTUS (q.v.)). The case aroused considerable controversy and was probably very influential in the decision to introduce, in the Companies Act 1948, the requirement that all movements on reserves were to be disclosed.

royalty. Payment made for the use of some right. A publisher, for example, will pay royalties to authors in respect of sales of their books. A manufacturer may pay a royalty to the owner of a patent for an industrial process which is being used. The total amount of the royalties is based on the quantity of the product which is sold.

running cost. The recurrent cost of operating a particular activity. It is to be contrasted with CAPITAL COST (q.v.). The running costs of a factory include raw materials, wages, fuel, light and heat, etc.

running yield. The yield on a fixed interest security having regard only to its current market price and to its COUPON RATE (q.v.) of interest. Thus a 5½ per cent DEBENTURE (q.v.) now on sale at £55 per £100 nominal, but redeemable at par in 10 years' time, has a running yield of 10 per cent per annum. There will be an additional yield to an investor in the form of an increase in the market value as the date of redemption approaches but this will not form part of the running yield. *See also* YIELD TO REDEMPTION.

S

S and P. Letters standing for STANDARD AND POOR (q.v.).

safe deposit. A safe owned and protected by a company, usually a bank, which can be hired by a person wishing to deposit therein valuable articles, such as jewellery, cash or documents. The hirer of the safe deposit has a private key and is not usually required to declare the articles which have been deposited.

salary. Remuneration paid under a contract of employment involving non-manual work. Salaries are usually paid on a monthly basis.

sale and leaseback. A type of agreement whereby a business sells a major asset to a finance company and then continues to use it under a leasing arrangement. The purpose of the agreement is to release the capital tied up in the asset and is an alternative to borrowing and using the asset as security.

sale or return. Goods supplied on the basis that if they are not sold or used they may be returned to the supplier. If a business acquires goods on sale or return it does not undertake the risk that it will not be able to find customers for the goods. In accounting for such an item the company supplying the goods should treat them as stock at cost until the sale is confirmed. The profit on them does not, therefore, figure in its profit and loss account until that time.

sales. The total value, at selling prices, of the goods sold by a business in a period of time. It will appear as the first item on the TRADING ACCOUNT (q.v.). It is also a useful measure of the level of activity.

sales account. That account in a DOUBLE ENTRY SYSTEM (q.v.) in which is recorded the amount of the sales of a business. Its function is to collect together all such items for an accounting period at the end of which the total is transferred to the TRADING ACCOUNT (q.v.).

sales analysis. A statement showing how the sales of a business may be attributed to certain categories. There may, for example, be a sales analysis by types of goods supplied or by the geographical area of residence of the customers.

sales day book. Synonym for SALES JOURNAL (q.v.).

sales forecast. A prediction of the level of sales to be achieved in a forthcoming period. The forecast will be based on trends which appear to have been established in the past and on expectations about conditions likely to prevail in the future. The order books of sales representatives may also give valuable information. A sales forecast is fundamental to the preparation of a BUDGET (q.v.).

sales invoice. Document prepared by the supplier of goods and sent to their recipient. The invoice will identify the goods sent and quote the price and the total charge. It is, in effect, the bill for the goods.

sales journal. A BOOK OF PRIME ENTRY (q.v.) in which is recorded the sales made by a business on a day-to-day basis. Individual items in the sales journal would be posted to the accounts of debtors and the totals would be posted to the sales account.

sales ledger. A portion of the LEDGER (q.v.) containing all the accounts of persons to whom sales on credit have been made. The sales ledger thus contains the records of debtors of the business.

sales mix. The proportion of total sales which each of the range of products bears to the whole. The significance of the sales mix is that some products are likely to produce a larger gross profit than others. The overall gross profit rate will, therefore, depend on sales mix.

sales returns. Goods sold to a customer and then accepted back. This may be because they are damaged or because the customer has been permitted to cancel the sale as a gesture of goodwill. Sales returns are accounted for as a reduction to sales.

sales returns journal. The BOOK OF PRIME ENTRY (q.v.) in which are recorded the SALES RETURNS (q.v.) as they occur.

salvage. A person who rescues abandoned property, for example, by taking in tow a vessel which has been left unattended in a storm, is entitled to some fraction of the value saved as a payment for the service even though not explicitly contracted to give it.

sampling. A method of drawing conclusions about a whole by examining portions of it selected at random. Its main financial application is in the field of auditing. It would be impracticable for an AUDITOR (q.v.) to examine in full detail every transaction in which a business had engaged. By examining a sample of transactions, however, it will be possible to form an adequate opinion on the care and accuracy with which the recording process as a whole has been undertaken.

sanctions. Actions which can be used to bring pressure to bear on some party to perform some desired action. A sanction which may be used against a recalcitrant debtor, for example, is to refuse to supply more goods until the existing account has been paid. Sanctions are sometimes exercised by the government against undesirable foreign regimes, for example those with poor human rights records, by refusing to trade with them.

Sandilands Committee. The Inflation Accounting Committee which reported in 1975. It was so-named after its chairman Mr (later Sir) Francis Sandilands. The committee's report recommended that companies and nationalised industries should adopt a system of accounting known as CURRENT COST ACCOUNTING (q.v.). It was left to the ACCOUNTING STANDARDS COMMITTEE (q.v.) to embody this principle into practical proposals which, in the event, enjoyed little success.

satisficing. Adopting a policy of achieving satisfactory results without necessarily achieving the best which might be possible. Such a course of action is a recognition that a policy of optimisation is very difficult to operate and involves special costs and risks of its own. To achieve a satisfactory position is much easier and may be more secure.

save as you earn. A savings scheme instigated by the government and operated by National Savings and by some banks and building societies. The saver agrees to pay a certain monthly sum into an account for 5 years. After five years the amount saved may be withdrawn with accumulated interest or it may be left for a further 2 years (without any further monthly contributions) to qualify for a bonus. The income earned under SAYE, as it is termed, is not taxable.

savings. Amounts of money withheld from spending and thus conserved for future use. Normally they are invested in some way and there is a considerable industry involved in creating opportunities for this.

SAYE. Letters standing for SAVE AS YOU EARN (q.v.).

scale. A table of charges associated with different levels of service. A bank may, for example, make a charge which is based on a scale relating to the value of the transaction involved (as opposed to the actual cost of the work done).

scam. A fraudulent activity usually such that a relatively small amount of money is obtained from a large number of people. In this way the activity is either undetected or is not worth action by the individual.

EXAMPLE. Badegg plc publishes a directory of business names and addresses. No permission to include businesses in this list was sought and the directory is available only on request. As it is not advertised, requests are not received and there is no circulation. The company then bills all those businesses listed with a charge for the entry in a way which implies that the entry was ordered and that it confers substantial benefit. Many businesses will pay the amount without query, because of inadequate control procedures, and are thus cheated into paying for a worthless service. This operation might be termed a scam.

schedule. A supporting statement showing how figures in a main document have been determined.

schedules of income tax. The categories into which income is classified for the purposes of INCOME TAX (q.v.). The same rates of tax apply in each case, but there are different rules concerning the timing of payments and the expenses which may be charged in arriving at taxable income. The schedules and the types of income which they cover are set out below:

Schedule	Type of income
A	Income from land and buildings
B	Income from woodlands
C	Income from GILT-EDGED SECURITIES (q.v.)
D Case I	Income from a trade
Case II	Income from a profession
Case III	Interest and annual payments
Cases IV and V	Overseas income from certain types of investment
Case VI	Miscellaneous income not included elsewhere
E	Wages and salaries from employment
F	Dividends paid by companies

scheme of arrangement. An agreement between a company and its creditors which will allow an insolvent business to continue. It will be made where creditors are persuaded that their interests are likely to be better served by a continuance of the business than by a WINDING UP (q.v.).

scrap. Unwanted material emanating from an industrial process. Scrap may sometimes be sold for use by someone else but may sometimes involve a cost in its disposal. In either case the proceeds or costs should be treated as varying the cost of operating the process rather than as a separate item of revenue or expenditure.

scrap value. A realisable value possessed by a FIXED ASSET (q.v.) at the end of its useful life. Scrap value, if it can be predicted accurately, may be taken into account in calculating DEPRECIATION (q.v.).

scrip dividend. A dividend given in the form of extra shares instead of cash. It thus represents a capitalisation of part of the profit and loss account. A scrip dividend is often offered as an alternative to cash at the option of individual shareholders. For them it has the advantage that they can increase the size of their holdings in the company without incurring dealing costs. For the company it enables it to make a permanent retention of profit to provide funds for expansion.

scrip issue. Synonym for BONUS ISSUE (q.v.).

scripophily. The activity of collecting share and stock certificates for their inherent interest or attractiveness rather than out of any concern for their underlying investment value. The subjects of collections are usually certificates issued by defunct regimes or companies, e.g. pre Boxer uprising Chinese bonds, Tsarist bonds or UK railway companies' share certificates.

seal. A disc of wax or paper embossed and affixed to a document or an impression formed on the paper by a press. A seal is an essential part of a DEED (q.v.). Every company must have a seal which is embossed on documents to which it is a party, i.e. it amounts to the company's signature. A SHARE CERTIFICATE (q.v.) will bear the company's seal.

SEAQ. Letters standing for STOCK EXCHANGE AUTOMATED QUOTATIONS (q.v.).

season ticket. A pass giving unlimited access to some service for a specified period of time. A person undertaking a daily rail journey, for example, may acquire a season ticket which entitles him or her to travel the journey as many times as wished during the period of currency of the ticket as opposed to purchasing a fresh ticket for every journey. A season ticket will save money for heavy users of a service.

secondary auditor. One who has the overall responsibility for an AUDIT (q.v.) but who has to rely on the work of another auditor, at least in part, when assuming that responsibility. The auditor of the HOLDING COMPANY (q.v.) of a group may, for example, have to rely on audits undertaken by others for figures deriving from SUBSIDIARY COMPANIES (q.v.).

secondary stock. Shares in a company which is smaller or less actively traded than the giants of the stock market.

second class. An inferior and, therefore, cheaper service. Letters sent by second-class mail, for example, cost less to send but are likely to take longer in transit.

second mortgage. A MORTGAGE (q.v.) on a property which is already the subject of a mortgage. Provided that the value of the property is sufficient it may provide security in this way for more than one loan. In the event of a default the claim of the holder of the second mortgage ranks behind that of the first mortgage holder.

second preference shares. An issue of preference shares which rank for dividend after a pre-existing issue of preference shares. They may well command a higher maximum rate of dividend in order to compensate for the slightly higher risk.

secretary. An officer of a LIMITED COMPANY (q.v.) having specific statutory duties. Every company must, by law, have a secretary.

secret reserve. A RESERVE (q.v.) which does not appear on the face of the balance sheet. It is made by writing down assets to below their true value.

EXAMPLE. Stock which has cost £40,000 was written off in the profit and loss account as part of COST OF SALES (q.v.) although expected to be realised at a profit in a subsequent trading period. This action has the same effect as the making of a reserve but does not show up on the balance sheet. For a company to make a secret reserve is, nowadays, illegal.

sector. A part of the Stock Exchange concerned with shares of one type. Oil shares, for example, represent one sector of the market.

secured creditor. A creditor who has a legal claim against some asset of the business in the event that payment is not made at the due time. A secured creditor is thus in a stronger position than an unsecured one. It would be unusual for an ordinary trade creditor to require security against the supply of goods.

Securities and Exchange Commission. An official body in the USA having the responsibility of overseeing the operation of the New York Stock Exchange.

Securities and Investments Board. An official body in the UK having responsibility for the orderly and fair running of the financial services industry.

securitisation. The process whereby a loan by one person to another may be made divisible and transferable, i.e. like a debenture. This enables the lender to realise the investment without having to call in the debt.

security. 1. An asset against which a creditor has a legal claim in the event of non-payment.

2. A negotiable claim against a company's assets or activities such as a share or debenture. Securities in this sense are thus held as income bearing investments.

segment. A distinguishable portion of a whole. Thus a segment of a business's activity will be one which can be clearly identified and for which figures can be prepared.

segmental reporting. Reporting on segments of a business's activity. It is useful for a business in its management processes to make use of these techniques. It is not, however, always easy to separate one segment of activity clearly from its effects on another.

self-assessment. A method of administering taxation such that the taxpayer is responsible for calculating the amount of tax due. This is used in the USA but not, currently, in the UK.

self-employed. Description of a person who is in business independently of any employer, i.e. as a sole trader or a partner.

self-insurance. The consequence of a decision that it is more economic to stand the risk of a loss than it is to pay a premium to an insurer to take it.

self-regulation. The process whereby an industry imposes upon itself codes of practice and other rules of conduct and polices them. It is an alternative to regulation by statute.

sellers' market. A market in which the seller is in a stronger bargaining position than the buyer, usually because there are few sellers and many potential buyers. In a sellers' market, e.g. for property, prices are likely to rise sharply.

selling costs. Those costs associated with the selling effort made by a business. It would include advertising and the salaries and COMMISSION (q.v.) paid to travelling sales people.

selling short. Selling shares or commodities which are not actually owned by the seller. They will have to be bought subsequently to complete the deal by which time the seller hopes that the price will have fallen. Selling short is a form of speculation. It carries the risk of loss if the price of the security or commodity rises.

semi-variable cost. A cost which cannot properly be classified as either a FIXED COST (q.v.) or a VARIABLE COST (q.v.). Semi-variable costs may be encountered in different forms. One item of such costs may, for example, vary with production but in a nonlinear way. Another may be 'stepped' so that it is fixed over narrow ranges of production. Yet another may appear to have a mixture of fixed and variable components.

sensitivity analysis. An analysis of the components of a BUDGET (q.v.) with a view to discovering which of the forecasts on which it is based are most critical. It may, for example, be found that results are much more sensitive to variations in material prices than they are to wage rates. This would occur where a product had a relatively high material content. Sensitivity analysis is a part of the assessment of overall RISK (q.v.).

sentiment. Instinct and feeling. The sentiments of those involved in a market will often have a big influence on prices particularly in the absence of any objective information.

separable assets. Those assets of a business which can be sold independently of one another without necessarily impairing the continued existence of the business. They are to be distinguished from GOODWILL (q.v.) which, by definition, is not a separable asset.

separate assessment. A form of tax arrangement whereby the total assessment on the joint income of a married couple could be divided between the husband and wife so that each paid their own share of the tax. Couples are now taxed as separate individuals so that this arrangement is now obsolete.

sequestration. The process of seizing the funds of a particular organisation or individual. It is done under an order of and powers given by a court of law. Sequestration may be ordered, for example, if a company refuses to pay a fine which has been imposed on it by a court.

SERPS. Letters standing for STATE EARNINGS RELATED PENSION SCHEME (q.v.).

service charge. A charge added by such establishments as hotels and restaurants to the total bill as an amount to be distributed to staff. It takes the place of a GRATUITY (q.v.) and removes the voluntary element from the process of recognition by a customer of good service.

service contract. A contract of employment. The term is usually applied to contracts between a company and its directors.

service cost centre. A COST CENTRE (q.v.) for a service provided internally for other parts of the business. A good example of a service cost centre is the maintenance department. The costs from the centre have to be reapportioned, after determination, to other cost centres on some equitable basis.

servicing of finance. The payment of interest on loans and dividends on shares. Such payments are required to be identified on a CASH FLOW STATEMENT (q.v.) by FRS 1.

set-off. The setting off of an amount owed by a person against an amount owed to that person. The net amount only is then recorded or paid. If a supplier of one kind of goods to a business is also a customer for another kind of goods it will figure in both the business's debtors and creditors. One amount may be set off against the other so as to determine the net position.

settlement. 1. The process of paying an outstanding account.
2. The process of creating a trust, other than by means of a will, for the benefit of named persons. A person might create a settlement for the benefit of his or her grandchildren. Such a person is described as the settlor.

settlement day. The day on which, every two weeks, Stock Exchange accounts for the previous period fall to be settled.

settlor. One who creates a trust, other than by means of a will, for the benefit of named persons.

several liability. Legal liability falling on members of a group as individuals. It is in contrast to JOINT LIABILITY (q.v.) although both may exist at the same time. If a group of people are indebted to another party and have several liability, the creditor may pursue any one member of the group in an action to recover the amount due. There does not need to be any regard for the interests of the others. Thus the creditor may choose to sue the most wealthy one or the one most vulnerable to pressure.

severe disability allowance. A social security benefit paid to persons who suffer from a severely disabling condition.

shadow price. The OPPORTUNITY COST (q.v.) of using an item of stock or other asset.

share. Individual unit of capital in a limited company. A share must have a NOMINAL VALUE (q.v.) but this has no necessary relationship to its market price. Shares in a company may be of different types carrying different rights. The most common types are ORDINARY SHARES (q.v.) and PREFERENCE SHARES (q.v.).

share capital. That part of a company's financing which is represented by the total nominal value of the shares which it has issued. Share capital may be in the form of both ORDINARY SHARES (q.v.) and PREFERENCE SHARES (q.v.). It does not include either RESERVES (q.v.) or LOAN CAPITAL (q.v.).

share certificate. A document evidencing the ownership of shares in a limited company. It will bear the name of the shareholder and the number and type of the shares. It will also bear an impression of the company SEAL (q.v.). The share certificate is issued by the company at the time that a member's shareholding is registered with it. The certificate does not give conclusive proof of the ownership of the shares which can only be given by the entry in the REGISTER OF MEMBERS (q.v.).

shareholder. One who is registered as a MEMBER (q.v.) of a company, i.e. one who owns shares in that company.

shareholders' equity. That which remains of a company's value after all prior claims against its assets have been met. The balance sheet value of shareholders' equity is the total value of SHARE CAPITAL (q.v.) and RESERVES (q.v.).

share premium. The amount by which the issue price of a share exceeds its nominal value. It is common practice for a company issuing shares subsequent to its first issue to issue them at a premium in order to allow for the increase in the value of the business which has taken place. First issues may, however, also be at a premium in order to allow different persons to subscribe for shares at different prices. The amount of the premium must, by law, be carried to a SHARE PREMIUM ACCOUNT (q.v.).

share premium account. A statutory CAPITAL RESERVE (q.v.) required where a company issues shares at a price in excess of their nominal value. The premium amounts to a profit to the company on the sale of the shares and thus is to be held for the benefit of all the shareholders. It is not, however, regarded in law as distributable and may not be paid to them as a cash dividend. Where a share premium account exists it must be shown on the face of the balance sheet. Permitted uses of a share premium account, which would cause it to be depleted or to disappear, include paying up a BONUS ISSUE (q.v.) of shares or meeting the preliminary expenses of the company or its expenses connected with the issue of the shares.

share shop. An establishment to which members of the public may go for the trouble-free buying and selling of shares. The shop does not normally hold the shares in which it arranges dealing but acts like a STOCKBROKER (q.v.).

share split. The action of dividing shares in a limited company into a larger number of shares of a lower NOMINAL VALUE (q.v.). Thus a company which has in issue 10 million shares of £1 each might split these into 100 million shares of 10p each. The object is to make the shares more marketable by bringing down the stock market price for a single share. It has a psychological rather than financial effect.

Shearer* v. *Bercain. An important case which seemed to confirm that the MERGER METHOD (q.v.) of preparing consolidated accounts was illegal. It was, in fact, a tax case and not a company law case. The effect of the decision so far as merger accounting is concerned, however, was reversed by the Companies Act 1981 (now in the 1985 Act) which allows merger accounting in appropriate defined circumstances.

shell company. A company whose shares are listed on the Stock Exchange and which is taken over by some person or organisation in order to obtain the benefit of that listing. There is no intention to maintain or improve the existing activity of the business but to use it as a vehicle to commence some other type of business.

shilling. A pre-decimalisation unit of currency in the UK. Twenty shillings made up one pound.

short-dated. Approaching maturity. The term is applied to redeemable fixed-interest securities. Such a security which was to be repaid in, say, 1 year would be described as short-dated. The market value of such securities is likely to be very close to the redemption value and be influenced to a relatively small extent by fluctuations in rates of interest.

shortfall assessment. An assessment to income tax made on a CLOSE COMPANY (q.v.) which has distributed less than its RELEVANT INCOME (q.v.) during a chargeable period. The object of the legislation is to prevent the company form of organisation from being used as a device to avoid a higher rate of income tax. The shortfall assessment allows the Inspector of Taxes to apportion the undistributed income amongst the shareholders and to tax it as though it had been distributed to them.

short lease. A LEASE (q.v.) which has only a short period to run before expiry. It is likely to have very little value.

SIB. Letters standing for SECURITIES AND INVESTMENTS BOARD (q.v.).

sickness benefit. A social security benefit payable to those who are prevented by illness from working.

sick pay. Payments made by an employer to workers who are temporarily unable to work because of illness. There are usually terms in the contract of employment which set down the entitlement of an employee in this respect.

signatory. One who has attached his or her SIGNATURE (q.v.) to a document.

signature. The name of a person written in that person's own handwriting and appended to a document with the intention of giving authority to the contents. A signature often has financial implications such as on a CHEQUE (q.v.), a WILL (q.v.) or a CONTRACT (q.v.).

significant influence. The influence by a company over the activities of another company which thereby falls to be treated as an ASSOCIATED COMPANY (q.v.). The term is used in SSAP 1 Accounting for Associated Companies. It is defined as being participation in the financial and operating policies of the company without necessarily having full control of them.

simple interest. A method of calculating INTEREST (q.v.) such that the rate of interest is always applied to the original principal sum. It thus contrasts with COMPOUND INTEREST (q.v.). Simple interest is normally applied in cases where interest is paid at regular intervals, e.g. for government securities or commercial debentures.

simplex method. A mathematical technique for resolving problems in LINEAR PROGRAMMING (q.v.).

sinecure. A salaried position where the work required is very little in relation to the remuneration received.

single premium endowment policy. An ENDOWMENT POLICY (q.v.) in which a large single premium is paid at the outset but none thereafter. It is a long-term investment and has the benefit that the ultimate proceeds will be received free of income tax.

sinking fund. A device used to accumulate liquid funds over a specified number of years in order to meet a known need for cash at the end of that time. The cash will be required for some such purpose as the redemption of a loan or the replacement of a fixed asset. Sinking funds are comparatively rarely encountered in the business world nowadays as there are generally more efficient ways of achieving the same purpose. Occasionally, however, the establishment of a sinking fund for its repayment may be a condition of granting a loan. To operate a sinking fund a calculation is made of the amount which must be invested annually so that it will, with accumulated interest, amount to the total sum required at the expiry of the prescribed period. This amount is then charged annually to the profit and loss account. If the sinking fund is being used for the replacement of a fixed asset the annual charge will be shown as an expense. If it is for the redemption of a loan it will be shown as a transfer to reserve. Simultaneously with the annual entry in the profit and loss account the corresponding amount will be invested in interest bearing but liquid securities outside the business. It will be a feature of the balance sheet of a business operating a sinking fund that amongst its liabilities will appear the sinking fund account and amongst its assets will be the sinking fund investments and that the balances on these two accounts will be equal in amount.

sleeping partner. A person who is technically a member of a PARTNERSHIP (q.v.) but who takes no active part in the operation of the business.

slump. A state of the economy of a country in which economic activity is at a very low level. It is characterised by high unemployment and, usually, falling prices.

slush fund. A fund of money held in an organisation for which the persons administering it are not made fully accountable, that is, they have informal discretion over its use.

small claim. A claim which one person has against another for a small amount of money. If disputed this can be settled by a small claims court with the minimum formality and cost.

small companies' rate of corporation tax. A special, lower rate of corporation tax which is charged on companies whose total profits do not exceed prescribed limits.

small company. A category of company specified in the Companies Act 1985. It is relieved of some of the disclosure requirements of the Act. A small company must meet at least two of the following criteria both for the current year and for the previous year:
 (a) Turnover not over £1.4 million.
 (b) Balance sheet total not over £0.7 million.
 (c) Average number of employees not greater than 50.

smart card. A form of CREDIT CARD (q.v.) with built-in electronics such that it can store and amend information. Fraudulent use of such a card can be made very difficult.

smoothing. The adoption of accounting policies designed to smooth out apparent variations in profit. The smoothing of profits is often hypothesised as an important motivation for management policies but evidence for the practice is inconclusive.

smuggle. To take concealed goods past some checkpoint illegally with the intention of avoiding the payment of import duty. The term might also be used about goods taken illegally from a factory and taken past security guards.

snake. A precursor of the EUROPEAN MONETARY SYSTEM (q.v.) in which the rate of exchange between the major European currencies and the US dollar were controlled within fairly tight bands.

social responsibility accounting. A form of accounting in which the benefits and costs to society, and not just to itself, of a business's activities are reported. It has not to any extent been given practical expression and exists as an idea rather than as a set of practical techniques. Recent concern with environmental issues has given some boost to developments in this field.

social security. Name given to the collection of legal provisions designed to offer financial and other help to persons who have an inadequate income.

Société Anonyme. The equivalent, in France, of the JOINT STOCK COMPANY (q.v.) in the UK.

soft currency. A currency, associated with an ailing economy, whose value and convertibility into other currencies is unreliable.

software. A collective term for programs available for use on a computer. In selecting a computer it is important to be assured that an appropriate range of software will be available. The equipment itself is known collectively as hardware.

sole trader. A person operating an unincorporated business alone. The law does not recognise the business of a sole trader as being distinct from the proprietor him or herself and a sole trader is therefore liable personally for business debts. Accounts may be prepared for the business as if it were a separate entity, however. This is an example of the ENTITY CONCEPT (q.v.) in accounting.

solicitors' accounts. Accounts prepared under the Solicitors' Accounts Rules. The main legal requirement for solicitors' accounts is that all money held on behalf of clients should be kept separate from the firm's own money and placed in a designated bank account. Thus a solicitor is not permitted to make use of a client's funds (e.g. the proceeds of the sale of a house) temporarily in his or her hands. This protects the client from loss in the event that the solicitor encounters financial difficulty.

Solomons Report. A report on the education and training of accountants in the UK. It was published in 1974 under the title *Prospectus for a Profession*. The report followed an inquiry undertaken by Professor David Solomons from whose name the popular title of the report is derived.

solvency. The state of owning assets with a total value exceeding the total value of liabilities. It is illegal for a company which is not solvent to continue trading. An individual may remain insolvent for a time and then recover from that position particularly if it can be concealed from others. There is, however, the danger for an insolvent person that BANKRUPTCY (q.v.) will occur.

SORP. Letters standing for STATEMENT OF RECOMMENDED PRACTICE (q.v.).

source and application of funds statement. A statement showing the main sources of funds arising during a period of time and the application of those funds. Companies were until recently required to produce such a statement as part of the annual accounts under SSAP 10. This has now been replaced by FRS 1 which requires the preparation of a CASH FLOW STATEMENT (q.v.).

sovereign. A gold coin of ancient origin having a face value of 1 pound. At one time it was freely used in transactions. Because of the gold content its actual market value is nowadays much higher than 1 pound and it does not circulate as currency. It is held by collectors or by investors in gold. Sovereigns are still minted today, sometimes to commemorate special occasions.

Special Commissioners. A body of officials of the Inland Revenue constituted in order to hear appeals against tax assessments.

special meeting. A meeting of the members of a company at which a SPECIAL RESOLUTION (q.v.) is to be put. Three weeks' notice of such a meeting is required.

special range investments. Holdings of investments held by a TRUST (q.v.) which are permitted under special powers of the trustees conferred by the terms of the trust. These may go outside the ranges of investments allowed by the Trustee Investments Act 1961.

special resolution. A resolution of a meeting of the members of a company which requires a three-quarters majority of those voting before it is passed. The law defines what matters fall to be decided by special resolution. They include a change in the MEMORANDUM OF ASSOCIATION (q.v.) of the company, e.g. to amend its OBJECTS CLAUSE (q.v.). In contrast to a special resolution is an ORDINARY RESOLUTION (q.v.).

special situation. The situation relating to the shares of a company which make it likely that its share price will move differently from the market as a whole. Investors seek special situations with a view to making a profit from them.

speculator. One who enters a market with the sole intention of making a profit out of its price movements. In order to be successful a speculator will have to predict price movements. Speculators are found in all kinds of market. Some examples are the stock market, the foreign exchange market and commodities markets. Speculators take high risks and, although they are seen by some as parasites on the system, they can be regarded as providing a valuable contribution to the smooth running of markets.

split capital. A dual issue of shares having different rights issued by some INVESTMENT TRUSTS (q.v.). One type of share, for example, might be entitled to any income earned by the fund and other entitled to any capital appreciation.

split depreciation. A device whereby, under CURRENT COST ACCOUNTING (q.v.), DEPRECIATION (q.v.) is split between that attributable to the original cost of the asset, which is charged to the profit and loss account, and that which is attributable to the increase in valuation, which is charged to the REVALUATION RESERVE (q.v.). The device is not justifiable if current cost accounting is being used as a method of accounting for inflation as it fails to charge the full current cost of depreciation in the profit and loss account. It is now outlawed under SSAP 12 Accounting for Depreciation.

sponsor. One who agrees to lend his or her name to and support, usually financially, some activity. A company may, for example, sponsor a sporting event or an artistic endeavour. The ultimate intention will be to promote its own name.

spot rate. The rate of exchange between one currency and another which applies at the present time. It is to be contrasted with the rate which would be quoted for future delivery of the currency, which is the FORWARD RATE (q.v.).

spot transaction. A transaction for immediate completion at the SPOT RATE (q.v.).

spread. The difference between the price offered for a share by a market maker and the price asked for it. The amount of the spread will vary according to the activity and volatility of the market.

spreadsheet. A form of computer program, very widely used in processing financial information, which provides the user with a large grid in which to enter values. Some values may depend on others and these are automatically calculated by the software. The great value of a spreadsheet is that changes to it can be made very readily and all the effects of those changes noted as the computer undertakes all of the associated arithmetic.

SSAP. Stands for STATEMENT OF STANDARD ACCOUNTING PRACTICE (q.v.).

stag. One who subscribes for a new issue of shares with the intention of selling any allotment immediately as opposed to holding it as an investment. Stags are sometimes regarded as a nuisance. They may apply in large numbers, and sometimes with MULTIPLE APPLICATIONS (q.v.), if permitted, to already oversubscribed issues where they can expect to make an immediate profit. They tend, however, to avoid less glamorous issues where, of course, more applications would be welcome. Stagging cannot be prevented but many companies present all cheques sent for applications for shares before proceeding to allotment and this may deter applicants where the prospect of an actual allotment seems low. Multiple applications, the hallmark of the stag, may also be outlawed.

stage payments. Payments made under a long-term contract, e.g. for the erection of a building, at defined stages in its completion. This avoids the necessity for the contractor to finance the whole of the work.

stake. A deposit or investment in a particular situation.

stakeholder. 1. One having an interest in the activities of a company. It is thus a wider group than that of shareholders. It includes also debenture holders, employees and creditors.
2. One who holds a sum of money on behalf of negotiating parties until the outcome of the negotiations is determined. Where a person pays a deposit on the signing of a contract to buy property, for example, this may be held by the vendor's solicitor as stakeholder pending completion of the sale.

stale cheque. A cheque which, whilst otherwise valid, has passed the date by which it should have been presented for payment. A cheque must normally be presented for payment within 6 months of the date on which it was drawn.

stamp. An adhesive or embossed design signifying that some payment has been made. A postage stamp, for example, is fixed to a letter to signify that payment has been made for its delivery. A stamp is embossed on a deed to signify that the duty has been paid.

stamp duty. A tax, the payment of which is evidenced by the affixing or embossing of a stamp on a document. An important example of stamp duty is that which has to be paid when land and buildings are conveyed. Stamp duty was payable on every cheque until decimalisation of the currency in 1971, when this was abolished.

stamp duty reserve tax. A charge relating to certain transactions in securities not otherwise subject to stamp duty (q.v.).

Standard and Poor. A US company which provides detailed information relating to investment through the Stock Exchange.

standard cost. The targeted or planned cost of a unit of production. A standard cost is calculated from an underlying BUDGET (q.v.) and it depends, amongst other things, on the planned level of activity. Standard costing is a valuable form of financial control. In operation actual costs of production are compared regularly with the standard cost. Any VARIANCE (q.v.) is calculated and analysed with a view to locating controllable sources of inefficiency.

standing order. An instruction to a bank by a customer to make a fixed payment regularly on stated dates to some third party. The regular payments may be monthly or annually or at any other convenient interval. Standing orders are commonly used by customers to make payments of their mortgage or annual subscription to societies. Where the regular payments are of differing amounts a DIRECT DEBIT (q.v.) may be used.

starting price. A term used in horse and dog racing. It states the odds that were on offer at the start of the race and its significance is that it is the basis of settlement of most off-course betting.

State Earnings Related Pension Scheme. A scheme, now abolished, whereby part of the pension payable to a retired person by the state would bear a relationship to what they had previously earned. This was paid for with higher contributions from persons having incomes above a certain level.

statement. A document giving details of a financial position or of financial dealings. Thus both the balance sheet and the profit and loss account are statements. The term is most commonly applied to a copy of an account sent by one person to another, e.g. a bank will send regular statements to its customers and a supplier will send statements to debtors.

statement in lieu of prospectus. A statement containing the same information as would have been contained in a PROSPECTUS (q.v.) where the share issue is made not requiring a prospectus. The document is delivered to the REGISTRAR OF COMPANIES (q.v.).

statement of affairs. A document prepared in BANKRUPTCY (q.v.) setting out all of the assets owned by the bankrupt and the claims against him or her.

Statement of Recommended Practice. A statement previously issued by the ACCOUNTING STANDARDS COMMITTEE (q.v.) or by some other body. It recommends a practice in a particular industry. The ACCOUNTING STANDARDS BOARD (q.v.) has announced that it does not propose to issue statements of recommended practice on its own initiative.

statement of source and application of funds. Synonym for SOURCE AND APPLICATION OF FUNDS STATEMENT (q.v.).

Statement of Standard Accounting Practice. A prescribed method of accounting for a particular type of transaction or situation. Issue of these has now ceased following the replacement of the ACCOUNTING STANDARDS COMMITTEE (q.v.) by the ACCOUNTING STANDARDS BOARD (q.v.), but they will remain current unless and until replaced by FINANCIAL REPORTING STANDARDS (q.v.). Standards were formulated by the Accounting Standards Committee and then simultaneously promulgated by the Councils of the participating professional bodies. Although it does not have legal force an SSAP (the usual abbreviation) is binding on members of the bodies issuing it under sanction of disciplinary procedures. SSAPs are to apply to all financial statements intended to give a TRUE AND FAIR VIEW (q.v.). They are mainly applicable to the published accounts of limited companies.

statute barred. A matter, usually a debt, which can no longer be the subject of legal action because the time limit decreed by the STATUTE OF LIMITATIONS (q.v.) has been exceeded.

statute of limitations. Legislation designed to place a time limit on the right of legal action. For example, a person wishing to sue for the recovery of a debt must do so within 6 years of the most recent acknowledgement of the existence of the debt or the right is lost.

statutory apportionment. An apportionment of the receipts of a TRUST (q.v.) between capital and income so that the rights of the beneficiaries of the trust can be preserved.

statutory books. Records which are required to be kept by a company under the Companies Acts. These include the Register of Members and the Register of Directors' Interests.

statutory company. A company incorporated by its own special Act of Parliament. It is thus to be distinguished from a registered company which is merely registered under general company legislation. Statutory companies are normally established to provide some public utility such as water supply.

statutory declaration. A written declaration, made at the time that registration of a limited company is sought, that all legal formalities have been observed. It may be made by a solicitor dealing with the formation of the company, or other responsible person, and it is delivered to the REGISTRAR OF COMPANIES (q.v.) along with the MEMORANDUM OF ASSOCIATION (q.v.) and ARTICLES OF ASSOCIATION (q.v.).

statutory instrument. A detailed rule or set of rules issued by government under the authority of an Act of Parliament. Many details of legislation which are complex or which need revision from time to time are dealt with in this way.

statutory reserve. A RESERVE (q.v.) in the balance sheet of a company which is required to be created by the Companies Acts 1985–9. These include the SHARE PREMIUM ACCOUNT (q.v.) and the CAPITAL REDEMPTION RESERVE (q.v.).

statutory sick pay. Amounts paid to an employee who is absent from work due to sickness prescribed by statute.

step-by-step acquisition. The assumption of control of one company by another where the shareholding giving control is acquired in a number of steps. These may not initially have given full control. The process has implications for the preparation of CONSOLIDATED ACCOUNTS (q.v.).

sterling. The general term used to describe the currency of the UK. Thus the announcement that sterling fell in world money markets would signify that the value of the pound fell as compared with other currencies.

sterling silver. Silver of a defined standard of purity. It will bear a HALLMARK (q.v.) as a guarantee of this.

stewardship. The state of responsibility for the property of others. The directors of a company, for example, exercise stewardship over the assets of the company. With stewardship goes ACCOUNTABILITY (q.v.) and many accounting formats are designed to enable a judgement to be made on the effectiveness of the stewardship function.

stipend. Remuneration for the services of certain types of employee such as the clergy.

stock. 1. An undivided but infinitely divisible block of some SECURITY (q.v.). Government stock (e.g. CONSOLS (q.v.) and WAR LOAN (q.v.)) is extensively issued and companies will commonly issue loans in the form of debenture stock. Equity stock, although sometimes encountered, is much less usual in the UK and most companies' equity is in the form of SHARES (q.v.). Stock can be transferred between holders in any required amount (e.g. £978.37 nominal of debenture stock). Shares, on the other hand, must be transferred in whole numbers (e.g. 1,000 shares of £1).

2. A collection of physical materials held by a business to support the flow of its activities. A manufacturing business will maintain a stock of its RAW MATERIALS (q.v.) so that the continuity of production will not be held up while fresh deliveries are awaited. Trading businesses will maintain stocks of FINISHED GOODS (q.v.) so that customers can be supplied on demand. Stock is classified on the balance sheet as a CURRENT ASSET (q.v.).

stockbroker. A member of the Stock Exchange who buys and sells securities on behalf of clients. Unlike a MARKET MAKER (q.v.) a stockbroker does not deal on his or her own account. Remuneration comes from the COMMISSION (q.v.) which is charged to clients.

stock control. The process of controlling the usage and cost of stock. It will include the physical security of stock (protection from pilferage and damage) and the administrative procedures necessary to ensure that adequate but not excessive quantities of stock are held. In a typical stock control system all purchases and issues to production of stock will have to be properly authorised by responsible people. Stock security and stock levels will be constantly monitored by a storekeeper.

stock exchange. An organised market in securities. The Stock Exchange in the UK is governed by a Council and imposes rigid rules of conduct on its members. It also imposes reporting requirements on the companies in whose shares it deals. The Stock Exchange in London is situated in Throgmorton Street and is one of the leading financial markets of the world. Stock Exchanges also exist in other major cities.

Stock Exchange Automated Quotations. A computer operated by the Stock Exchange which displays information about the market, e.g. latest share prices, and records all trading done on the Exchange. It came into use on 27 October 1986, the day of the so-called BIG BANG (q.v.).

stockholder. 1. A business which makes its profits by holding stocks of a wide variety of raw materials, e.g. steel. This allows its customers to operate with much smaller stocks.

2. A person holding a security which is in the form of STOCK (q.v.).

stock in transit. STOCK (q.v.) which at a balance sheet date is in transit from one business to another with the consequence that it is included in the assets of neither. Stock in transit is met as an accounting problem in connection with CONSOLIDATED ACCOUNTS (q.v.) when it is in transit between two members of the group. On consolidation its value must be included in the group total for stock.

stock relief. A relief against taxation given from 1975 to 1984. It allowed for the effect of inflation by permitting increases in the value of stock to be charged against taxable profit. It applied both to companies and to unincorporated businesses. Stock relief was abolished from 12 March 1984.

stock split. The process of reducing the nominal value of the shares of a company by dividing one share into two or more parts. Thus shares of £1 each may be split into ten times the number of shares of 10p each. The object of a stock split is to increase the amount of trading in the shares. This is likely to follow where more are available at a lower market price.

stock-taking. The process of making a physical count of the types and amounts of STOCK (q.v.) on hand at a particular date with the object of determining its total quantity and, ultimately, value. Stock is frequently a large item on the balance sheet and its periodic verification is, therefore, important. It will be a part of an AUDIT (q.v.) that the auditor attends the stock-taking.

stock turnover. The relationship between COST OF SALES (q.v.) and the average level of stock. It is thus a measure of how quickly stock is moved through the profit making process.

stock warrant. An agreement which entitles but does not require the holder to purchase a certain number of shares at a stated price during specified time periods. It is thus a form of option.

stop loss. An order given to a stockbroker to sell shares on behalf of a client if and when their price descends to a stated level. The object of a stop loss order is to place a limit on the possible loss on an investment if it does not succeed as expected.

stopped cheque. A cheque which a bank has been ordered not to pay by the person drawing the cheque. A cheque can only be stopped before payment has actually been made. The circumstances in which the action is appropriate may be where the cheque has been lost or stolen or where its issue was induced by misrepresentation. It is a criminal offence to stop a cheque merely in order to withdraw the promise to pay implicit in the original issue of the cheque.

straight line. A method of calculating the annual charge for the DEPRECIATION (q.v.) of an asset. It is applied by dividing the total cost of the asset into equal portions over its useful life. If it is expected that the asset will have SCRAP VALUE (q.v.) this may be taken into account to reduce the total amount of depreciation. The straight line method is by far the most common method of depreciation in the UK. An important advantage is that it is simple to operate and to understand.

striking price. The price at which securities originally offered for TENDER (q.v.) are sold. All those tendering at the striking price or higher should receive the amount of the security for which they applied. Having regard to the prices which have been tendered the striking price will be established at a level which enables the full issue of the total amount of the security available.

subjective goodwill. The difference between the value placed on an asset by its owner and the value placed on it by the market. It is the existence of subjective goodwill which explains why the owner of an asset should retain it rather than sell it.

sub-lease. This arises where the LESSOR (q.v.) of property leases it again to some third party.

subordinated loan. A loan which does not have priority of repayment as compared to other loans.

subscription. The payment of money for a particular purpose. A person may make a subscription for shares in a company, a subscription to charity or a subscription to a journal.

subsidiary company. A company which is controlled by another company. The control is commonly gained by the acquisition of a shareholding in excess of 50 per cent. *See also* GROUP; HOLDING COMPANY.

subsidy. A payment intended to relieve some loss. A loss making bus service, for example, may receive a subsidy from the local council because it is seen to have a value to the community.

substance. The reality of a transaction or situation as opposed to its form. A FINANCE LEASE (q.v.), for example, is in form the rental of an asset. In substance it is the borrowing of funds which are then used to purchase the asset. In accounting substance should normally take precedence over form in deciding how a particular transaction should be recorded.

sum. A total of a number of component values.

sum of the years' digits. A method for calculating the DEPRECIATION (q.v.) of an asset. It is more commonly used in the USA than in the UK. It is a method which charges a greater proportion of the asset's cost in the early part of its life than it does in the later part. To operate the method, each year of the asset's life is numbered with 1 for its final year, 2 for its penultimate year and so on. The depreciation for any year is that year's number divided by the sum of all the years' numbers applied as a fraction to the total cost of the asset.

sunk cost. Expenditure which has given rise to an unrealisable benefit. Investment in the development of a new product, for example, will be a sunk cost if the only way to recover it is to market the new product. Investment in a building is not a sunk cost because it can be recovered by selling the building.

superannuation. An amount paid by an employee towards the provision of a PENSION (q.v.).

super profit. Profit in excess of a fair rate of return on recorded assets. The concept is used in one method of valuing GOODWILL (q.v.). The super profit is attributed to an unrecorded asset, interpreted as being goodwill, the value of which can be determined by attributing a rate of return to it.

supplies. Material goods not directly incorporated into a product. Maintenance materials are a good example of supplies.

supply and demand. The twin factors which determine the price in any market, whether it be for vegetables or shares. Supply is the quantity of the subject of trading which is made available at a given price and it normally increases with price. Demand is the quantity taken from the market at the given price and it normally decreases as the price increases. The price in the market is established at a level at which supply and demand are equal.

surcharge. A charge superimposed on and added to some other charge in recognition of some special circumstance. A person paying for the carriage of goods, for example, may be surcharged if they are badly packed or if they have to be delivered to an address outside the mainland.

surplus. An excess of revenue over expenditure. The term is usually used in connection with organisations which are not set up with the intention of earning a profit. The surplus will very probably, therefore, be extinguished in the long run by DEFICITS (q.v.) in other years. A surplus should be transferred to the ACCUMULATED FUND (q.v.).

surplus advance corporation tax. ADVANCE CORPORATION TAX (q.v.) which cannot be set off against the corporation tax liability of the period in which it arises because of the operation of a statutory restriction. Such surplus advance corporation tax may be carried back to be relieved against any liability arising in the 2 years preceding the distribution which gave rise to the surplus or it may be carried forward indefinitely until it can be relieved in the future.

surrender value. The amount which would be paid by a life assurance company to the holder of an ENDOWMENT POLICY (q.v.) or WHOLE LIFE POLICY (q.v.) if this were to be surrendered. The surrender value of any policy is likely to be extremely low in the early years and may not rise above the amount paid in premiums until it is a substantial part of the way towards maturity.

surtax. A form of taxation, now abolished, under which persons having a high income were required to pay a special supplementary income tax over and above the normal rates.

Survey of UK Published Accounts. A survey published annually and intended to highlight important matters of accounting practice exemplified by currently issued accounts.

suspended quotation. A stock market quotation which is temporarily withdrawn. This is done where some major event or uncertainty has made it impossible for a fair market in the shares to be maintained. This might occur, for example, if some fraudulent use of the company's funds has come to light. The suspension is imposed for no longer than is necessary.

suspense account. An account opened to record an amount whose correct treatment is not immediately apparent. This may be because further information has to become available or because the person making up the accounts is unsure of how to proceed with it. A suspense account may sometimes be used to balance a set of books pending the explanation of a DIFFERENCE (q.v.).

swap. Exchanging a loan contract with a fixed rate of interest for one with a variable rate. The intention is to profit from forecasts of the movement of interest rates.

switching. Moving resources from one investment to another with the object of maximising long-term gains. Switching would be expected to take place as circumstances change so that investments which previously seemed appropriate no longer seem so.

syndicate. A group of companies working together on a project with an agreement as to how costs and profits should be shared.

syndicated loan. A loan made by a group of persons acting as a syndicate.

synergy. The phenomenon whereby a whole has greater power or a greater value than the sum of its parts. GOODWILL (q.v.) is an example of synergy arising when a collection of assets is brought together under common control. Synergy is often stated as the rationale underlying the formation of groups of companies by takeovers and mergers.

systematic error. An error which is recurrent and accumulates to a large error over a number of items. An example of a systematic error would be the consistent rounding down of figures.

systematic risk. A RISK (q.v.) which pervades the whole of a set of investment opportunities. The risk that all share prices will fall on a major market setback is an example of a systematic risk. The importance of systematic risk is that it cannot be avoided by DIVERSIFICATION (q.v.).

T

Table A. A table appearing in the Companies Act 1985. It is a model set of ARTICLES OF ASSOCIATION (q.v.) for a limited company and may be adopted in place of an individual set of Articles if desired. Table A will in any case apply unless its provisions are expressly excluded by the company's own Articles.

T account. A rough form of account commonly used to calculate accounting quantities, particularly by students in undertaking exercises. It takes its name from its form which resembles a letter T. The debit entries are recorded to the left-hand side of the stem and the credit entries to the right.

take home pay. The amount of pay left to an employee after income tax, national insurance and other deductions have been made.

takeover. The acquisition of control of a company by another company. This is usually achieved by the purchase of the majority of its shares.

Takeover Panel. A panel set up under the auspices of the Stock Exchange to ensure that takeovers are conducted in a proper and orderly manner.

takings. The amount of cash received by a retail business in a certain period of time. The physical handling of takings, including security, may be a problem to many retailers.

Talisman. The mechanism organised by the Stock Exchange whereby shares can be transferred between seller and buyer.

tangible asset. An asset having physical existence. Plant and machinery is a tangible asset. Goodwill, on the other hand, is an intangible asset.

tap stock. An interest bearing government security which is issued progressively to match the need for funds. It thus contrasts with the issue of other securities where a given amount is issued all at the same time. It gets the name from the fact that, as with a tap, its supply can be switched on and off.

target. A plan such that an effort will be made to achieve it. A business might, for example, establish a target for its sales during a forthcoming period. There may be incentives or penalties incorporated into the remuneration of employees to motivate them towards achieving a target.

tariff. A tax levied on specified goods imported into a country.

TAURUS. A system of electronic recording of transfers and ownership of shares which is intended to have been introduced by the Stock Exchange. It should have given a paperless share transfer system, dispensing even with share certificates. In March 1993 it was announced that the system had been found unworkable and had been abandoned.

tax avoidance. The arrangement of a taxpayer's affairs so that his or her tax liability is legally reduced. An example of tax avoidance is the phasing of the sales of securities over a number of years so as to make maximum use of the exemptions to capital gains tax. Tax avoidance, which is legal, should be contrasted with TAX EVASION (q.v.) which is not.

tax code. A number issued each year to every employed person by the Inland Revenue. In conjunction with TAX TABLES (q.v.) it enables the employer to deduct the correct amount of tax from each payment of wages or salary. The tax code is determined by adding together all the ALLOWANCES (q.v.) to which the employee is entitled and then dividing the result by 10. Thus the higher the code the less tax is deducted. Where a person turns out to have paid too little tax in a particular year this may be recovered over the following year by an appropriate adjustment to the tax code. The letter, such as H or L, which also appears as part of the code, signals certain components of the code. H means that the code contains the married person's allowance, L means that it does not. This makes changes in codes brought about by tax legislation easier to implement. There are some special, all letter, codes. BR, for example, means that tax is to be deducted at the basic rate (because allowances are given against other income). NT means that no tax is to be deducted.

tax credit. The amount of tax imputed to a dividend paid by a limited company. A taxpayer may use the tax credit to discharge basic rate (but not higher rate) liability to income tax. A person who does not pay tax, because of low income, may reclaim the amount of the tax credit.

tax efficient. Description applied to any procedure for achieving a desired objective which at the same time minimises any tax liability. Use of a PERSONAL EQUITY PLAN (q.v.), for example, is a tax efficient method of building up an investment in shares.

tax evasion. The escape from the payment of tax which is legally due. Tax evasion usually takes place by a failure to make a full declaration of income. Tax evasion is fraud and, if detected, is punishable as such.

Tax Exempt Special Savings Account. A designated account offered to private individuals by banks and building societies under rules established by legislation. A person may invest cash in such an account within prescribed limits and, subject to leaving the fund untouched for a minimum of 5 years, may receive all interest free of income tax. An individual may not hold more than one such account.

tax haven. A location where business enterprise or individuals are subject to favourable tax treatment. The Channel Islands are, in some respects, a tax haven. A tax haven will be attractive to a wealthy person, particularly if retired, who wishes to retain a more substantial proportion of income than is possible in the UK.

tax holiday. A period of time, established under statute, during which a business will pay no taxation. Typically this might be offered during its early years to a business setting up in an area where such developments are socially desirable.

tax liability. An amount which a business or individual has become obliged to pay in taxation, e.g. because an income has been earned, but which has not yet been paid, perhaps because the due date has not arrived.

taxpayer. One who pays tax.

tax planning. Planning financial operations and arrangements so as to take full account of the incidence of taxation. A large aim of tax planning will be to minimise total liability to tax to the extent that this can legally be done.

tax point. The date of a transaction for the purposes of VALUE ADDED TAX (q.v.).

tax return. A statement of financial circumstances required to be submitted to the Inland Revenue annually by each taxpayer. There is a legal obligation on any individual having taxable income or capital gains to submit a tax return whether or not asked spe-

H

cifically to do so. The return is made on a special form and relates to a period of 1 year ending on 5 April. It requires disclosure of the taxpayer's income under a number of separate categories including chargeable capital gains. It also enables tax allowances to be claimed. There are substantial penalties for knowingly submitting an incorrect or incomplete tax return. Persons who have no income other than a wage or salary and who pay the correct tax by deduction from this money may, as a matter of administrative convenience, not be required formally to submit a tax return.

tax shelter. Some mechanism whereby a transaction is legally protected from taxation which might otherwise be due. A PERSONAL EQUITY PLAN (q.v.) provides a tax shelter for some investments in shares.

tax tables. Tables issued annually by the Inland Revenue to all employers. These are tables used in operating the PAY AS YOU EARN (q.v.) system for collecting income tax. By reference to an employee's TAX CODE (q.v.) and to cumulative pay to date the employer can see from the tax table how much tax should be deducted in the current pay period. For people on unchanged incomes this will be a constant amount on each occasion.

technical adjustment. A movement of share prices which occurs as a reaction to a previous movement which has been overdone rather than to a change in the underlying situation. If the market has been rising strongly for a period there is likely to be a technical adjustment whereby the price rise is temporarily reversed before it resumes.

teeming and lading. A fraudulent activity allowing the MISAPPROPRIATION (q.v.) of cash without detection. It is undertaken in the following manner. An amount of cash is received from a debtor and misappropriated by the cashier. This would normally come to light when the debtor was asked to pay a second time. A second debtor pays and this money is applied to meeting the *first* debtor's account. Thus discovery of each misappropriation is progressively deferred. In order to prevent teeming and lading, debtors should be encouraged to pay by cheque or to receive an official receipt for cash. The cash records and SALES LEDGER (q.v.) should also be maintained by different people.

teller. A counter clerk at a bank.

temporal method. A method used for the TRANSLATION (q.v.) of foreign currency. By this method all values are translated at rates determined by the rate of exchange obtaining at the time of the original transaction underlying them.

tenancy. The state of renting a property by one person from another.

tenancy in common. A form of joint ownership of land and buildings. It is often used where a residential property is owned jointly by a married couple. One consequence of a joint tenancy is that on the decease of one party the property automatically vests in the other.

tenant. One who rents a property from another.

tender. A competitive QUOTATION (q.v.) for a contract. Businesses working for the government and for local authorities frequently have to tender for work which is then normally offered to the one tendering the lowest. Issues of shares or other securities are sometimes offered on a tender basis. Instead of subscribing at a fixed price the applicant states the maximum he or she is willing to pay. A STRIKING PRICE (q.v.) is determined and this is paid by all successful applicants.

terminal bonus. A BONUS (q.v.) paid on maturing policies of life assurance. It is given at the option of the company issuing the policy and is paid out of profits. It is given in addition to any other bonuses which may have accrued to the policy.

terminal loss. A loss made by a business in its last year of trading. A terminal loss has significance in the calculation of the business's liability to tax. It may be set off against the assessment of profits for the previous 3 years, thus reducing the tax due on them.

terminal value. Value at the end. Many capital investments have a terminal value, i.e. some value which may be realised when economic operations are no longer possible. This terminal value, along with other returns accruing, must be taken into consideration in assessing whether or not a project is worthwhile.

terminated activity. The activity of a business segment which has ceased operating. Costs associated with the termination of an activity (as opposed to its operating costs before termination) fall to be treated under FRS 3 as EXTRAORDINARY ITEMS (q.v.).

term life assurance. An assurance which provides a stated benefit on the death of the assured during a specified period of time. Since the policy becomes valueless at the end of this time the premiums paid are less than they would be on ENDOWMENT (q.v.) or WHOLE LIFE (q.v.) policies.

TESSA. Letters standing for TAX EXEMPT SPECIAL SAVINGS ACCOUNT (q.v.).

testator. A man who makes a WILL (q.v.). A woman would be termed a testatrix. Although the will is generally drafted in appropriate legal terms it will embody the wishes of the testator in respect of the disposition of his estate after death.

testatrix. The feminine form of TESTATOR (q.v.).

test check. A check undertaken by an AUDITOR (q.v.) on the basis that a proportion only of the items will be examined. In the case of any large audit it would be impracticable for an auditor to check every single transaction in complete detail. Test checking is a useful method of forming an opinion of the quality of the recording process without this necessity. Ideally, if quantifiable conclusions are to be drawn, the test check should be on some scientific basis, such as RANDOM SAMPLING (q.v.).

test data. Data introduced by an auditor into an accounting system, particularly a computerised system, to verify that it is working correctly.

theft. The crime of taking property without the permission of the owner and with the intention of depriving the owner of the property permanently.

Theft Act 1968. The Act of Parliament which defines theft and prescribes the punishment for it.

thin market. A market in which very few transactions take place. The shares of a named company might be said to trade in a thin market on the Stock Exchange. The consequence of a thin market is that substantial price movement may be triggered by an unusual increase in activity.

third market. A market in shares operated under the auspices of the Stock Exchange for companies which did not qualify for full listing nor for the UNLISTED SECURITIES MARKET (q.v.). It no longer operates.

third party. A person who is not a party to a contract but who has to be referred to in the contract. A policy of insurance, for example, may give the insured protection against a claim by a third party, i.e. by a person who is not a party to the contract of insurance.

Threadneedle Street. The street in London where the Bank of England is situated. The bank is sometimes referred to colloquially as the Old Lady of Threadneedle Street.

threshold. A level of price or income at which some provision comes into effect. Income above a certain threshold, for example, will be subject to national insurance contributions.

Throgmorton Street. The street in London where the Stock Exchange is situated. The name is sometimes, therefore, used colloquially to refer to the Stock Exchange.

ticket. A small piece of paper or card evidencing that a payment has been made for a service not yet provided. An example is a ticket for air travel or one for a theatre seat.

tight money. A situation in which it is difficult to borrow money, often because government policies are in place to restrict the level of debt in an economy.

till. A mechanical or electronic device used in retail shops where large amounts of cash are handled. It will keep a running record of the transactions entered into and provide a safe receptacle for the cash taken.

time and a half. A common method of calculating the payment for OVERTIME (q.v.) working. The number of hours actually worked is paid for at one and a half times the normal rate.

timeshare. A form of shared property ownership whereby the purchaser of the timeshare has the right to occupy the property for a given number of weeks at a prescribed time in each year. Timeshare is used, therefore, for holiday accommodation, particularly in the form of apartments in large buildings. The total amount realised for a property sold on this basis is likely to be considerably higher than if the whole property had been sold outright to a single purchaser. The advantage for the purchaser is that the price payable for the holiday accommodation becomes immune to inflationary increase. The high-pressure sales techniques used by some unscrupulous operators have given rise to some anxieties about timeshare.

time value. The value which attaches to the use of money for a period of time and for which INTEREST (q.v.) is payable. Because money has a time value any proposed investment must give a yield which pays at least this time value if it is to be worthy of consideration.

timing difference. A difference between accounting profit and taxable profit caused by difference in the timing of income or expenditure. The most important example arises from the discrepancy between DEPRECIATION (q.v.) and CAPITAL ALLOWANCES (q.v.). Timing differences are referred to in SSAP 15 and prima facie will give rise to an adjustment for DEFERRED TAXATION (q.v.).

tip. A small amount of money given voluntarily to a person who has given a service which is paid for separately. In origin a tip represents an acknowledgement of an exceptional level of service but in many fields it is now regarded as customary, regardless of the quality of the service. It is usual to give a tip to, for example, a waiter in a restaurant or a taxi driver.

tithe. An archaic form of tax, levied by the church or a landowner, which took the form of a tenth part of the produce of the land. Tithe barns, which can still be seen in certain parts of the UK, were originally constructed to hold this produce.

title. A right of ownership. Thus a landowner is said to have a title to the land.

token. Small object, often made of metal, which represents a certain amount of money. It may be purchased for use in operating certain types of machine and is, in effect, a coin with a limited range of uses.

toll. A charge made for the use of a road. Toll roads are common in some parts of Europe. In the UK, apart from a very small number of privately owned roads, tolls are restricted to certain tunnels and bridges. The toll is intended to defray the cost of construction of the road and to provide a return on the investment.

tontine. An agreement amongst a number of people that a certain property shall accrue to the final survivor of the group.

tools and equipment. A fixed asset on which depreciation is often charged on a renewals basis, i.e. the amount charged as depreciation is equal to the amount spent on renewals.

TOPP. Letters standing for Training Outside Public Practice. It is now possible for a chartered accountant to undertake some of his or her training in this way.

total account. An account containing the totals of values which have been posted in detail to other accounts. A total account is a form of CONTROL ACCOUNT (q.v.).

totalisator. A mechanism for betting on horses or greyhounds in which the total staked is placed into a pool and then divided, after a deduction to allow a profit, amongst those holding winning bets.

tout. A person who applies unsolicited pressure on individuals to buy some high-priced commodity in short supply. The term is frequently applied to those who obtain tickets for a popular event and then seek to resell the tickets to others at inflated prices.

trade creditors. *See* CREDITORS.

trade debtors. *See* DEBTORS.

trade discount. A discount given by one business to another which is making a purchase for resale to an ultimate customer. In effect it is a device for selling at wholesale rather than retail prices in these circumstances. Trade discount is not normally available to the private consumer.

traded option. An option to purchase or sell shares at a specified price which can be bought and sold in its own market. The options thus themselves have a market value.

trade gap. The difference between the value of exports and the value of imports of the country during a specified period of time. The gap may be either favourable or unfavourable.

trade investment. An investment held by a company for the benefit which this might give to its trade. An investment in a supplier or in a customer, for example, may give some influence which will improve the relationship between them.

trademark. A symbol used by a business to represent itself or its products in a quickly recognisable way. Trademarks have to be registered and are then available for use only by their registered owners. A trademark is a valuable property which may be sold. If it appears on a balance sheet it is classified as an INTANGIBLE ASSET (q.v.). An example of a trademark is the famous Bass 'Red Triangle' which was the first trademark ever registered.

trade union. An association of workers with the function of protecting and improving the rights of its members collectively and as individuals. A trade union is governed by legislation which includes accounting requirements.

trading account. An account which determines the GROSS PROFIT (q.v.) of a business. Its main components are SALES (q.v.) and COST OF SALES (q.v.).

training contract. A contract between an accountant in practice and a student whereby the accountant undertakes to provide the student with experience which will fit him or her for membership of a professional body.

training office. An office of a professional chartered accountant which has been approved as being able to provide acceptable training to recruits.

tranche. An instalment in the progressive issue of a security. The government might, for example, make an issue of a fixed interest security in a number of tranches as the funds are required.

transaction. A financial event of a nature that is recorded in the accounting system. The following are all examples of transactions:
    (a) The sale of goods to a customer.
    (b) The payment of a creditor.
    (c) The payment of a dividend.
    (d) The receipt of the proceeds of an issue of shares.

transfer deed. A deed which effects the transfer of property from one person to another.

transfer fee. An amount paid to the employer of a sportsperson in exchange for the transfer of his or her contract to another. It is commonly encountered in football where clubs frequently have to 'buy' good players in this way.

transfer value. The value placed on stocks or work in progress for the purposes of their transfer from one department of the business to another.

translation. The conversion of values expressed in one national currency into values expressed in a different currency. SSAP 20 deals with this topic. The two main methods available are the TEMPORAL METHOD (q.v.) and the CLOSING RATE METHOD (q.v.).

travellers' cheque. A document issued by a bank having a value specified in some currency which can be exchanged to that value at another bank. The travellers' cheque is signed by the bearer when issued and again when cashed. It is thus a safer way of carrying funds than is actual currency.

treasurer. A person responsible for the care and deployment of funds. In the UK the term is usually applied to a person acting in that capacity, often on a voluntary basis, for a club or similar organisation.

treasure trove. Valuable items which are found accidentally after having been hidden for many years. They are legally the property of the Crown although the finder will usually be rewarded by a sum equal to the value of the objects discovered.

Treasury. That government department responsible for administering the financial affairs of the country. It is headed by the Chancellor of the Exchequer.

treasury operations. Those activities carried out by a business in order to manage efficiently its short-term variations in cash balances. This would lead for example to investing temporarily surplus funds so that they will earn interest.

trend. A general direction predicted from past movements. Prices on the Stock Exchange may, for example appear to be following an upward trend because they have been moving upwards for some time in the past. Trends can be a dangerous guide to future behaviour as there can be no guarantee that they will be maintained.

trial balance. A list of the balances contained in a complete set of books, showing debit and credit balances in separate columns. The summing to the same total of each set of balances is an important verification of the arithmetical accuracy of the records. A trial balance is frequently used as a summary of a set of books from which to prepare the FINAL ACCOUNTS (q.v.) of a business.

tribunal. A court constituted for a special purpose, e.g. an industrial dispute. Its procedures are often less formal than those of a normal court of law.

truck. A method of paying workers in goods rather than cash. In earlier centuries this was popular with employers but was outlawed when it became too widely abused.

true and fair view. A view which accurately conveys the situation it seeks to portray. Accounts prepared under the requirements of company law are subject to the overriding necessity that they present a true and fair view although this is not statutorily defined. The AUDITORS' REPORT (q.v.) is required specifically to express an opinion on the truth and fairness of the profit and loss account and the balance sheet. The concept of a true and fair view dates from the Companies Act 1948 and is restated in the Companies Act 1985.

Trueblood Report. A report on the *Objectives of Financial Statements* published in the USA in 1973. It was named after the leader of the study group which prepared the report, Robert Trueblood.

trust. A legal arrangement whereby assets are owned and managed by one or more persons (trustees) on behalf of others (beneficiaries). There is a legal obligation on trustees to act wholly for the benefit of the trust and to render proper accounts of their actions. The terms of reference under which trustees act will be set out in a formal DEED (q.v.) establishing the trust.

trustee. A person responsible for administering a TRUST (q.v.). Legal ownership of the property of the trust will be vested in the trustee (or trustees) but they are bound to administer it in the interest only of the BENEFICIARY (q.v.). Unless the DEED (q.v.) setting up the trust makes provision for remuneration (which it commonly does) a trustee must act free of charge. When a trustee dies his or her EXECUTOR (q.v.) takes his or her place as trustee.

Trustee Savings Bank. A major high street bank dealing mainly with personal, as opposed to business, customers. It was formed originally from the progressive amalgamations of small savings banks governed by boards of trustees. It has now been made into a public limited company with shares quoted on the Stock Exchange.

Tsarist bonds. Securities issued by the Russian government prior to 1918 when the country was ruled by a Tsar. In that year the Tsar and his family were murdered as an element in the revolution and existing commitments were dishonoured. The bonds retained some value as hope persisted that eventually they would be repaid or that interest payments would resume.

turf accountant. Synonym for BOOKMAKER (q.v.).

turn. The difference between an OFFER PRICE (q.v.) and a BID PRICE (q.v.) for a security. Turns are met both on marketable securities and on UNIT TRUSTS (q.v.). In each case the function of the turn is to give an income to the dealer, i.e. a MARKET MAKER (q.v.) or unit trust manager, by making it possible to sell at a higher price than that paid when buying.

turnover. The total value of the goods or services provided in a given period of time by a trading organisation. It is an important measure of the volume of business undertaken. For a company the amount of turnover is required to be disclosed. This requirement was first introduced into the Companies Act 1967.

U

uberrimae fidei. A legal term meaning of the utmost good faith. Certain types of contract are invalid if the utmost good faith is not shown by the parties to it. This means that each has made full disclosure of all the facts and circumstances known to him or her which might have a bearing on the other's decision on whether or not to enter into the contract or regarding the terms on which to do so. Examples of contracts which are *uberrimae fidei* are PARTNERSHIP (q.v.) and INSURANCE (q.v.).

UITF. Letters standing for URGENT ISSUES TASK FORCE (q.v.).

ultra vires. A legal term meaning outside the power of. If a person acts *ultra vires* it means that he or she is exceeding his or her authority and that the action may be challenged and possibly revoked. The concept is of most importance to the accountant in connection with limited companies. The powers of directors are constrained by general law and by the ARTICLES OF ASSOCIATION (q.v.). Similarly a company's activities are bound by the OBJECTS CLAUSE (q.v.) in its MEMORANDUM OF ASSOCIATION (q.v.) and it may not legally carry on any activity not allowed by that clause. The opposite of ULTRA VIRES is INTRA VIRES (q.v.) (i.e. within the power of).

unbundling. The breaking up of a large and complex business into clear components each concentrating on a narrow range of activities.

uncertainty. Synonym for RISK (q.v.).

uncirculated coin. A brand-new coin which has not been used as currency. It is of interest to collectors of coins.

uncleared lodgement. An amount paid into a bank which has not yet been cleared to the account to which it is to be credited. Its accounting significance is that it may be one of the items which has to be taken into account in preparing a BANK RECONCILIATION STATEMENT (q.v.).

undated security. A security which has no date for redemption. The presumption may be that it will never be redeemed but that the holders will continue to receive an income at a rate of interest determined when the securities were first issued.

underabsorbed overhead. OVERHEAD (q.v.) which has not been charged to production because the actual level of activity was lower than the anticipated level. It may be regarded as the cost of underutilised capacity.

undercapitalised. The condition of having too little capital invested in the business. It will show itself by the frequent short-term cash crises which the business has to meet and by the inability of the management to undertake any investment in profitable opportunities.

underfunded. Having an insufficient budget to allow for fully effective operations. The term is usually applied to public services and is often an expression of disappointment that more cannot be done. Underfunding would show itself by a shortage of staff or other requirements, an inferior quality of service or long waiting lists for service.

underinsurance. That state where an asset is insured for an amount considerably less than its true value. Where the true value has been wilfully concealed from the insurer that would be grounds for declaring the contract of insurance void. An alternative is that, in the event of a claim, an AVERAGE (q.v.) could be applied so that a portion only of the claim will be met.

undersubscription. A situation which arises when fewer than the full number of shares offered in a PROSPECTUS (q.v.) are applied for. If the undersubscription is very substantial the issue may fail because the MINIMUM SUBSCRIPTION (q.v.) has not been reached. In other cases it may merely mean that the company raises rather less money than it had hoped. Undersubscription can be guarded against by having the issue underwritten, i.e. insured.

undertaking. A business organisation.

under the hammer. For sale at an AUCTION (q.v.). The expression derives from the hammer used by the auctioneer to signal the conclusion of the sale of an item.

underwriting. The acceptance of a financial risk in consideration for the payment of a premium or commission. A new issue of shares in a company may be underwritten. The underwriter agrees to take up any shares which are not applied for by the public and thus guarantees the success of the issue.

undivided profit. Profit which has not yet been distributed to the shareholders. In the simplest case this will be the balance on the profit and loss account but it may also include other REVENUE RESERVES (q.v.).

undue influence. An influence exercised over a person executing a legal document which goes beyond the influence expected of informed advice. Where undue influence exists there is a presumption that the contents of the document were influenced improperly.

unearned income. Income acquired other than by the provision of personal effort. Thus it includes dividends, interest and rental income. A PENSION (q.v.) or the ROYALTIES (q.v.) paid to an author are regarded as earned income even though the activity from which they arise took place in the past. The concept of unearned income is important in tax law where traditionally it is treated less favourably than earned income.

unemployment benefit. A social security benefit given to persons who, whilst unemployed, are actively seeking employment. It is intended to enable them to survive until they do so.

unencumbered. In the state of being free from any charge such as a mortgage. The existence of unencumbered property is an important element in the long-term solvency of a business.

unexpired expense. An expense the full benefit of which has not yet been received at the relevant date. An example might be an insurance premium paid for 1 year in advance before the end of the preceding accounting year. An unexpired expense may be recorded in the balance sheet as a CURRENT ASSET (q.v.).

unfavourable variance. Synonym for ADVERSE VARIANCE (q.v.).

unfranked SORP. A STATEMENT OF RECOMMENDED PRACTICE (q.v.) which has not been formally endorsed by the ACCOUNTING STANDARDS COMMITTEE (q.v.).

uniform accounting. A system whereby a number of businesses in a similar line of activity prepare accounts on a uniform basis so as to aid comparison. Uniform accounting is normally organised through a trade association which circulates averages to its members. Thus they are able to gain useful information about their competitors but confidentiality is preserved for the individual.

uniform business rate. A form of property tax levied on business premises, the proceeds of which are to support local authority activities.

unincorporated business. A business which does not have the status of a corporation. Examples of unincorporated businesses are those operated by sole traders and by partnerships. An unincorporated business cannot enjoy the benefit of LIMITED LIABILITY (q.v.) and its life does not exceed those of its proprietors.

unitary tax. A tax which is all-embracing so that taxpayers do not have to pay a number of different taxes.

unit cost. The cost of making a single unit of production. Because of FIXED COSTS (q.v.) unit cost will depend on the level of production as well as on the quantities of material and labour used. A calculation of unit cost is helpful in determining the price which needs to be charged for a product in order to sell it at a profit.

unit of account. A currency unit when it is being used to keep a record of business transactions rather than being used as a medium of exchange.

unit trust. An institution set up to enable the small investor to invest in a wide spread of securities. The trust sells units to investors and repurchases from them as required. The fund thereby built up is invested through the Stock Exchange according to the stated policy of the trust. A trust might for example invest only in food manufacturing businesses, or in those shares giving a high income or which are expected to have above average capital growth. It will quote a daily offer price (at which it will sell units) and bid price (at which it will repurchase them). The offer price is always higher than the bid price to give the trust a TURN (q.v.). The prices are, however, based on the underlying market value of the securities held by the trust.

unlimited company. A corporate body, i.e. company, the members of which do not have LIMITED LIABILITY (q.v.). Such bodies are very rarely encountered as trading concerns but their activities are governed, like those of limited companies, by company legislation.

Unlisted Securities Market. A market organised similarly to the Stock Exchange and under its auspices for shares not quoted on the main exchange. It is used by smaller companies having ultimate aspiration to a full quotation. The advantage for them is that there are less stringent criteria applied for admission to the market. The Unlisted Securities Market has not been greatly used recently and it has been suggested that it be discontinued.

unpresented cheque. A cheque which has been issued and is valid for payment but which has not yet been presented for payment. There is always likely to be a proportion of cheques unpresented when a bank statement is received and this will be one of the factors causing a discrepancy between the statement balance and the cash book balance. Unpresented cheques will, therefore, be an element of a BANK RECONCILIATION STATEMENT (q.v.).

unquoted investment. A holding of a security which does not have a Stock Exchange quotation. Companies are required in their balance sheets to show separately the value of quoted and of unquoted securities and in their profit and loss accounts to distinguish between the income from each.

unrealised loss. A decrease in the value of an asset which has not been sold or used up in making a product. It is generally regarded as good accounting practice to reduce the balance sheet valuation of such assets to their realisable value and to write off the loss in the profit and loss account. This treatment contrasts with that accorded to UNREALISED PROFITS (q.v.).

unrealised profit. An increase in the value of an asset which has not been sold or used up in making a product. It is generally regarded as good accounting practice not to take any account of unrealised profit, but where, exceptionally, it is recognised in a balance sheet it should be taken to CAPITAL RESERVE (q.v.) where it will not be available for distribution.

unsecured creditor. A creditor whose claim is supported only by the agreement that payment should be made. The position of an unsecured creditor should be distinguished from that of a SECURED CREDITOR (q.v.). In the event of the BANKRUPTCY (q.v.) of an individual or the WINDING UP (q.v.) of a company an unsecured creditor may be forced to accept less than the full amount due. A secured creditor will normally be paid in full.

unsystematic risk. The risk applying to a single investment and not affecting other investments. It is to be contrasted with SYSTEMATIC RISK (q.v.). Unsystematic risk is a concept relevant to PORTFOLIO THEORY (q.v.) and it is possible to reduce or eliminate it by DIVERSIFICATION (q.v.).

Urgent Issues Task Force. A subcommittee of the ACCOUNTING STANDARDS BOARD (q.v.) set up to deal urgently with situations where conflicting interpretations of accounting standards seem to be emerging. Its pronouncements resolve the conflict and, pending any amendment to the standard itself, have the same authority as the standard.

usage variance. A difference between the amount of material used for making a quantity of product and the amount budgeted for that quantity. The quantity of material making up the usage variance is valued at the STANDARD COST (q.v.) in order to determine the overall financial effect of the variance.

EXAMPLE. Production has been planned on the basis that each unit of a product will use 2 kg of a material priced at £2 per kg. During a particular period of time 1,000 units of product were made and 2,100 kg of the material used. There is an adverse usage variance of £200 (i.e. 100 kg × £2).

useful economic life. The length of time for which a FIXED ASSET (q.v.) can be used before a deterioration in its condition or developments in technology elsewhere makes this unprofitable. The useful economic life will be an important factor in deciding the rate of DEPRECIATION (q.v.) for the asset.

user friendly. A term used of any mechanism or system, e.g. a computer or an accounting system, which is easy to use. It requires, therefore, a minimum of training before it can be operated effectively.

user group. A group of persons having a definable common characteristic who have a legitimate interest in published accounts. The term was used in the CORPORATE REPORT (q.v.). The user groups specified in that document were:
  (a) The equity investor group.
  (b) The loan creditor group.
  (c) The employee group.
  (d) The analyst-adviser group.
  (e) The business contact group.
  (f) The government.
  (g) The public.

USM. Letters standing for UNLISTED SECURITIES MARKET (q.v.).

usury. A charge for lending money which, in principle, is like INTEREST (q.v.) but which is at unreasonably high rates. This occurs because the borrower is in desperate need of money and not in a good negotiating position.

utility. An industry providing a service of universal need such as water, electricity or gas.

V

valuation. The process of attaching a monetary value to some asset or, less usually, liability. A valuation may derive from a particular accounting convention, e.g HISTORICAL COST (q.v.), or CURRENT COST (q.v.). Alternatively, it may be an *ad hoc* exercise such as the valuation of a building prior to offering it for sale.

valuation certificate. A document whereby a person declares that an authoritative valuation has been made and states what that value is. The directors of a company, for example, might provide a valuation certificate for the stock of the company.

value. A measure, in terms of money, of the usefulness or desirability of an asset.

value added. The value which a business adds to a bought-in product by its own efforts. It consists of the difference between the selling price of the product and the cost of the bought-in component. It thus equates with the total of manufacturing and administrative costs, interest payments and profit. A statement of value added as an addition to the other reports produced by a company was suggested in the CORPORATE REPORT (q.v.).

value added tax. A tax charged to the final consumer on the total value of a wide range of goods and services. It is commonly abbreviated to VAT. The method of collection of VAT gives it its name. Every business is accountable to the Customs and Excise for VAT charged on its output but is allowed to set off against this the VAT which it pays on its inputs. Thus a business will always pay over the tax on the value which it has added by its own activities although it then recovers this from its own customers.

value analysis. A careful examination of a product and the way that it is manufactured with the object of producing it more cheaply without reducing its usefulness or general quality.

value-based company. A company which holds investment properties or securities and relies on changes in the value of these for a substantial part of its profit.

value for money. A concept of business operation under which all expenditure is scrutinised to ensure that the maximum possible benefit is being obtained for the money spent.

value to the business. A concept of value which values an asset at the maximum which a business would be prepared to pay in order to retain the asset. It will be the lower of two values. These are (a) REPLACEMENT COST (q.v.) and (b) the higher of ECONOMIC VALUE (q.v.) and REALISABLE VALUE (q.v.).

variable cost. A cost whose total varies proportionately with the level of production. MATERIAL (q.v.) and LABOUR (q.v.) are good examples of variable costs.

variable overhead. OVERHEAD (q.v.) which varies in total amount directly with the volume of the production to which it relates. Maintenance of the machines used in production (where its cost is a function of usage) and supervisory wages are examples of variable overheads. Most overhead is FIXED OVERHEAD (q.v.).

variable rate. The rate of interest charged on a mortgage or similar loan on terms such that the rate of interest charged will be varied from time to time in line with fluctuations in the market rate of interest. It is to be contrasted with a loan carrying a fixed rate of interest.

variance. A divergence of actual results from those planned. It is thus a term met in connection with BUDGETING (q.v.) and STANDARD COSTING (q.v.). A variance should be explained by being attributed to causes. There may be a combination of causes so that analysis of the variance may be necessary.

vendor. A seller, usually of a substantial asset such as a building.

vendor placing. A device whereby a company may take over another company in what is effectively an acquisition in a form which technically qualifies it to be defined as a merger. This enables the more favourable MERGER METHOD (q.v.) of consolidation to be used rather than the ACQUISITION METHOD (q.v.). The merger method requires that the SUBSIDIARY COMPANY (q.v.) is acquired by the issue of shares in the HOLDING COMPANY (q.v.) to its shareholders in exchange for their existing holdings. When a vendor placing is used, the shares are issued to a merchant bank which purchases the subsidiary's shares for cash and passes them to the holding company. In effect, therefore, if not in form, the holding company has made an issue of shares for cash and used the cash to acquire its interest in the subsidiary.

venture capital. Funds which are invested in a business on the basis that the investor receives a share in the outcome of the enterprise rather than an agreed fixed rate of return. It is thus capital which is at risk.

verification. The process of assessing the truth of a statement. An AUDITOR (q.v.) will be concerned with the verification of the information contained in a company's accounts.

vertical integration. The merger of businesses involved in sequential stages of production and distribution. The acquisition of a bakery by a shop selling bread is an example of vertical integration. It should be contrasted with HORIZONTAL INTEGRATION (q.v.).

virement. The power sometimes given to a BUDGET HOLDER (q.v.) to transfer sums from one budget heading to another. This gives more flexibility than there would be without this power as money saved by economies in one direction may then be spent in another. The argument against giving the power of virement is that it prevents higher management from considering priorities in the use of funds which have been saved.

virus. A computer program illicitly introduced into a system with the intention that it should cause inconvenience or damage. These can be very hard to trace and to deactivate. They are the creation of persons trying to show off a skill or by those with malevolent intentions.

Visa. One of the main world-wide organisations under which a CREDIT CARD (q.v.) operates.

visible earnings. That element in the earnings from the international trade of the country which derives from tangible goods. It should be distinguished from INVISIBLE EARNINGS (q.v.).

void. Of no effect. If a contract is void this means that it does not, in effect, exist. This may occur if, for example, it is a contract for an illegal purpose.

voidable. Description of a contract which can be voided by one party to it but not another. A contract entered into following misrepresentation is voidable by the deceived party.

230

volatile securities. Securities the price of which is liable to frequent substantial movements. A SPECULATOR (q.v.) in securities will make use of volatile securities where, in the event of success, the profit is likely to be greatest. There is also the greatest risk of loss.

volume of trading. A measure of how many deals have been concluded in the Stock Exchange in a given period of time, usually 1 day. The volume of trading is believed by some to be as important a predictor of future performance as is the movement of prices.

volume variance. A VARIANCE (q.v.) brought about by deviations of the actual volume of production from the budgeted volume.

voluntary winding up. A WINDING UP (q.v.) instigated by the company itself. It will take place when the company which is to be wound up is nevertheless solvent (*see* SOLVENCY).

voting rights. The rights which attach to ordinary shares and some other securities whereby the holder may vote at a meeting of the company. The voting power of the shareholder is in proportion to the size of the holding. Sometimes securities will acquire voting rights in specific circumstances. Cumulative preference shares, not normally having voting rights, may acquire them when the dividend is in arrears.

voucher. A document providing evidence of some transaction. Many examples exist. PETTY CASH (q.v.) should be paid out only against a voucher signed by the person claiming the money and bearing an explanation of what it was used for. A person paying a sum of money after deduction of tax will issue a tax voucher to enable the recipient to evidence the deduction to the Inland Revenue. An AUDITOR (q.v.) will make extensive use of vouchers of various kinds in the work of verifying the accounting records.

vouching. Verifying a transaction by the examination of a VOUCHER (q.v.).

voyage accounting. A form of accounting used in the shipping industry where a profit or loss is computed for each voyage made by a ship. The account will contain all revenues and expenses relating to the voyage including a provision for depreciation on the ship.

W

wage. Amount of remuneration paid to a manual worker. Wages are usually paid weekly.

wage earner. One who is in receipt of a WAGE (q.v.). The term is often applied more generally to identify that member of a household on whom the others rely for income.

wage freeze. A situation where the wages of a group of workers are held constant for a period of time. This may be done by their employer or may be imposed by a government. The motive for imposing a wage freeze is to limit costs for a company, or to control inflation for a government.

wager. A bet.

wages council. A body whose function it is to determine the level of wages within a specified industry.

waiver. The action of disclaiming some benefit to which there is an entitlement. If the directors of a company hold shares they might exercise a waiver in respect of dividends due to them as shareholders as a gesture of goodwill to other shareholders.

Wall Street. Colloquial way of referring to the New York Stock Exchange. This is located in Wall Street, New York.

war loan. A marketable government security issued originally to raise funds required for the conduct of the war. It pays a rate of interest of 3½ per cent and is an IRREDEEMABLE STOCK (q.v.). For many years it has therefore stood in the market at a substantial discount.

war pension. A PENSION (q.v.) paid to an ex-service man or woman and arising out of wartime activities.

warrant. A document giving some right. A company may issue warrants which give the option to their holder to subscribe for a defined number of shares at a defined price on specified future dates. Such warrants may be traded on the Stock Exchange. Their value will depend on the relationship between the price at which the shares may be obtained under the option embodied in the warrants and expectations about the market price of the shares themselves.

warranty services. Service of a consumer product carried out free of charge under what is commonly called a guarantee. The total cost of warranty services is an expense of the business which must be recovered in the price charged for the product.

wasting asset. An asset which is a natural resource physically consumed in the process of use. A mine or a quarry is an example of a wasting asset. Its accounting significance is that DEPLETION (q.v.) should be charged in the profit and loss account according to the amount of the resource consumed. A useful concept is to regard a wasting asset as a once and for all acquisition of a stock of raw material. A wasting asset is, however, categorised as a fixed asset on the balance sheet.

watchdog. General term applied to any body which has been set up to safeguard the interests of a particular group, e.g. the consumers of a product or service.

watered stock. Shares in a company whose nominal value exceeds the actual market value of the underlying assets.

way leave. The right, and hence the amount paid for the right, to make use of part of a person's land for providing transit for persons or goods. An electricity company might pay a way leave for the right to erect pylons on land it does not own.

ways and means. The processes whereby money will be raised for a particular objective, The term is often applied to a committee (i.e. Ways and Means Committee of the House of Commons) set up to look into the raising of finance.

weak market. One in which there is very little interest in buying so that prices tend to fall and business to be at a low ebb. The description is often used in connection with the stock market.

wealth. Material possessions.

wealth tax. An annual tax on the total amount of wealth which an individual possesses. There is currently no wealth tax in the UK but it is a possibility which is considered from time to time. One of the difficulties involved in the imposition of such a tax is valuing a person's wealth, much of which may be in the form of property which could not easily be realised.

weighted average cost of capital. The COST OF CAPITAL (q.v.) taking into account the various sources in use and the proportions in which they are employed. The importance of the measure is in its use in the process of INVESTMENT APPRAISAL (q.v.). A company is taken to have an optimum CAPITAL STRUCTURE (q.v.) which ought to be preserved. It follows from this that capital should be taken to have a cost, whatever its immediate source, equal to the weighted average cost of capital.

white knight. A company which volunteers to take over another company to rescue the latter from an unwelcome takeover bid from some third party.

whole life policy. A form of ENDOWMENT POLICY (q.v.) where the proceeds of the policy are paid out at the death of the assured whenever that occurs. It is a useful way for a person to accumulate savings for the benefit of a surviving dependant.

wholesale price. The price charged by a supplier of goods to a person who is not the ultimate consumer but who will resell the goods to other persons. A wholesale price is usually available only to a business and often carries the requirement to accept delivery of a fairly substantial supply of the goods.

wife's earned income allowance. An income tax allowance, now withdrawn, which was at one time given to a couple in respect of EARNED INCOME (q.v.) of the wife. It was equal in amount to the PERSONAL ALLOWANCE (q.v.) or to the whole of the wife's earned income, whichever was the less.

wife's earnings election. An option, now withdrawn, which used to exist in income tax law whereby a couple could elect for the wife's EARNED INCOME (q.v.) to be treated as if it were that of a separate person. Without the election the couple's income would be treated as that of a man. The wife's earning election was worthwhile only where the income of the couple rose above a certain amount as under it the married man's allowance was forfeit although some higher rates of tax might be avoided.

will. A document drawn up by a person, known as the testator (or, if a woman, testatrix) to give expression to his or her wishes for the disposal of his or her property after death. The will should name an executor who is responsible for carrying out the terms of the will. It must be signed by the testator and the signature witnessed by two persons who are not beneficiaries under the will. The terms of a will may be overruled by a court of law if it can be shown that the testator was not of sound mind at the time it was made.

windfall. A wholly unexpected gain or, sometimes, loss. A company stocking a raw material which suddenly becomes very valuable because of an acute shortage would make a windfall gain for having bought the material at a lower price.

winding up. The process of bringing to a conclusion the life of a company. It involves the realisation of all assets and the payment of creditors and other obligations out of the proceeds. Any surplus funds are then returned rateably to the shareholders. A winding up may occur because a company has become insolvent, in which case shareholders will receive nothing, or because its original objects have been fulfilled or no longer seem appropriate to pursue.

window dressing. The practice of bringing forward or delaying financial transactions or of recording artificial transactions with the intention of presenting a more favourable position in a set of accounts. Examples of window dressing are as follows:

(a) Including in the current year sales invoices relating to the early part of the following year so as to boost reported profit.

(b) Delaying the write-off of bad debts until after the year end so as not to reveal losses from that source in the current profit and loss account.

(c) Repaying a loan immediately before the balance sheet date and borrowing the money again immediately afterwards so as to give a false picture of the company's indebtedness.

Window dressing is not to be regarded as a legitimate accounting technique. It clearly offends against the TRUE AND FAIR VIEW (q.v.) principle which accounts are supposed to embody.

window tax. An obsolete form of taxation in which the payment depended on the number of windows found in a building. This was a crude method of assessing the value of the building and led to the bricking in of windows in order to avoid the tax.

withholding tax. A tax deducted from dividends before they are paid. In the UK dividends are not subject to a withholding tax but such taxes are common in other countries.

without profits policy. A policy of LIFE ASSURANCE (q.v.) which gives the holder no right to share in the profits of the company issuing the policy. Premiums are much lower than for a WITH PROFITS POLICY (q.v.) although the latter is usually the better investment.

without recourse. A right to receive money which does not carry any rights against previous holders of the right.

EXAMPLE. Smith holds a PROMISSORY NOTE (q.v.) from Jones for £2,000 payable in three months' time. Because he requires the money urgently Smith sells the note to Robinson for £1,500 'without recourse'. This means that Robinson will collect the £2,000 from Jones. If Jones defaults on payment the loss will be stood by Robinson who, on the terms on which the note was bought, has no claim against Smith who would otherwise have become liable.

with profits policy. A policy of LIFE ASSURANCE (q.v.) which gives the holder the right to share in the profits of the company issuing the policy. Effect is given to this right by allocating to the policy annual bonuses which increase the amount of the sum assured but do not increase the premium. The bonus is determined by the company after an actuarial valuation of the fund and of its liabilities for claims. Policies of life assurance are also available on a without profits basis when the premium will be lower.

witness. One who observes an event and can provide evidence that it actually took place. The signature of certain documents such as a DEED OF COVENANT (q.v.) or a WILL (q.v.) requires to be witnessed before the document is valid. The witness also signs the document in the presence of the chief signatory to evidence that the signature is that of the person which it purports to be.

working capital. The net assets which circulate as an essential part of the profit earning process. Working capital is usually calculated as CURRENT ASSETS (q.v.) less CURRENT LIABILITIES (q.v.).

working papers. Papers outside the main accounting records produced in support of some task, such as an AUDIT (q.v.), in relation to those records. An auditor's working papers will include details of checks made and notes on key facts about the business. They will also include calculations of the main quantities appearing in the accounts. It is established in law that an accountant's working papers are his or her own property even though they relate to a client's accounting affairs and contain information drawn from the client's records.

work in process. The US synonym for the UK WORK IN PROGRESS (q.v.).

work in progress. Partly completed production or services. Its importance is that it is a valuable asset which is, however, very difficult to value with any accuracy. The normal basis of valuation is cost but the cost of a partly finished product is hard to determine.

worksheet. A sheet laying out the effects of particular transactions on a financial position. The worksheet is more likely to be used by a student in working an exercise than it is to be used by a practitioner.

write back. To restore a balance in a set of books by reversing a previous entry made to WRITE OFF (q.v.) or WRITE DOWN (q.v.) the balance. This might occur if an asset which had suffered a depletion in value was later found to have had its value restored by a change in circumstances.

write down. To reduce the value of a debit balance in the books of account, normally to reflect a diminution in value. Thus a debtor might be written down because only a part of the balance owed is expected to be recoverable.

write off. To extinguish or reduce a balance existing in a set of books by an entry designed for that purpose. The term is normally used for the writing off of debit balances which no longer represent value. Thus a debtor may be written off as a bad debt. An amount may be written off stock because it has deteriorated and can no longer be sold at a normal price. The term is used by an insurer to mean property which is so badly damaged that the cost of repair is not justified.

writing down allowance. A form of CAPITAL ALLOWANCE (q.v.) given by tax legislation. It applies to an asset following the deduction of the FIRST YEAR ALLOWANCE (q.v.). The writing down allowance is at a rate set by the legislation and is expressed as a percentage to be applied to the reducing balance of expenditure year by year.

wrongful trading. Trading by a limited company which is insolvent. It is illegal for it to do this.

Y

yearly plan. A scheme whereby national savings certificates can be purchased over 1 year by means of a monthly subscription ranging between £20 and £200. Once the subscription has commenced the terms of the certificate are guaranteed. It matures 4 years after the payments are complete.

yen. The unit of currency in Japan. Japan has considerable importance industrially and financially so the fate of the yen is of world-wide concern.

yield. The amount, expressed normally as a percentage on the capital invested, of income created by an investment. Thus if £160 interest is paid to an investor of £2,000 in a building society the yield to the investor is 8 per cent per annum.

yield gap. The gap between the average yield on shares and the average yield on fixed interest securities. At one time the fixed interest yield was traditionally the lower of the two. This arose from the supposition that it was more secure. Now the gap is reversed so that equities yield less on average.

yield to redemption. The effective YIELD (q.v.) on a redeemable security, taking into account any gain or loss due to the fact that it was purchased at a price different from the redemption value.

EXAMPLE. A £1,000 debenture with a COUPON RATE (q.v.) of 10 per cent per annum can be purchased for £900. It is redeemable at PAR (q.v.) in 5 years' time. The RUNNING YIELD (q.v.) on this debenture is:

$$\frac{10\% \times £1,000}{90} = 11.1\%$$

The yield to redemption takes account of the £100 additional gain arising because the debenture has been purchased at below its redemption price. It is 12.84 per cent per annum.

yo-yo stock. A quoted security whose price fluctuates widely and rapidly so that it seems to be moving up and down all the time.

Z

zero base budget. A BUDGET (q.v.) constructed on the basis that the inclusion of every item has to be justified and none is taken for granted. It differs from the more usual approach to budgeting where the practice is to take the budget for a previous period as the base and then amend it allowing for known or anticipated changes in circumstances. An advantage claimed for zero base budgeting is that it avoids building on established inefficiencies and requires a thoroughgoing reconsideration of all expenditure at the beginning of each period.

zero coupon. A security having a COUPON RATE (q.v.) of interest of 0 per cent. Such securities are issued at a discount and later redeemed at par so that the investor's reward is the difference between these two amounts. The advantage of zero coupon is that the gain to the investor may be taxed as a capital gain rather than as income. The issuer has the benefit that no cash has to be found until the end of the life of the security.

zero rating. The attachment to the supply of goods or services of a rate of VALUE ADDED TAX (q.v.) of 0 per cent. A zero-rated supply is not the same as an exempt supply. If the supply is zero rated the supplier, if registered, may recover the VAT which has been paid on the inputs. If the supply is exempt this may not be done. Important examples of zero rated supplies are food, books and transport, but there are many others.

APPENDIX 1

The contents of a company's annual report and accounts (required by law except where otherwise stated)

1. *Chairman's report* (optional)
   A narrative report on the activities of the year and proposed future developments.

2. *Director's report*
   A formal report giving statutorily required financial and other information.

3. *Auditors' report*
   Confirmation by the independent auditors that the accounts give a true and fair view and comply with the law or an explanation of how they depart from this.

4. *Statement of accounting policies*
   Originally required by SSAP 2, but since the Companies Act 1981 it has been a legal requirement.

5. *Profit and loss account*
   One of four prescribed formats must be selected. Its form is also influenced by the requirements of FRS 3.

6. *Balance sheet*
   One of two prescribed formats must be selected.

7. *Cash flow statement*
   Required by FRS 1.

8. *Notes to the accounts*
   Containing amplification of items in the accounts and some other additional statutory information.

APPENDIX 2

Accounting Standards issued up to 31 December 1992

SSAP	Subject
1	Accounting for associated companies. *Amended by FRS 2.*
2	Disclosure of accounting policies.
3	Earnings per share. *Amended by FRS 3.*
4	Accounting for government grants.
5	Accounting for value added tax.
6	Extraordinary items and prior year adjustments. *Now withdrawn.*
7	Accounting for changes in purchasing power. *Now withdrawn.*
8	The treatment of taxation under the imputation system in the accounts of companies.
9	Stocks and long term contracts.
10	Statements of source and application of funds. *Now withdrawn.*
11	Accounting for deferred taxation. *Now withdrawn.*
12	Accounting for depreciation.
13	Accounting for research and development.
14	Group accounts. *Now withdrawn.*
15	Accounting for deferred taxation.
16	Current cost accounting. *Now withdrawn.*
17	Accounting for post-balance sheet events.
18	Accounting for contingencies.
19	Accounting for investment properties.
20	Foreign currency translation.
21	Accounting for leases and hire purchase transactions.
22	Accounting for goodwill.
23	Accounting for acquisitions and mergers.
24	Accounting for pension costs.
25	Segmental reporting.

FRS	
1	Cash Flow statements.
2	Accounting for subsidiary undertakings.
3	Reporting financial performance.

APPENDIX 3

Highlights in the development of company law relating to accounting and finance

Companies
Act

1844	Incorporation by registration
	Books of account to be kept
	Annual balance sheet provided to shareholders
	Audit of records and balance sheet
1855	Limited liability
1856	Compulsory reporting becomes voluntary
1900	Compulsory audit reintroduced
1908	Balance sheet to be filed with Registrar of Companies
1929	Annual profit and loss account compulsory but form not specified
1948	Transfer to and from reserves to be disclosed
	Minimum information in profit and loss account specified
	Group accounts required for holding companies
	Auditors to be professionally qualified
	True and fair view requirement for accounts
1967	Disclosure of turnover
	Disclosure of payments to political parties
1976	Auditors to be reappointed annually
	Term 'books of account' changed to 'accounting records'
1980	Distributable profit clearly defined
1981	Detailed prescribed format for accounts
	Right to redeem or purchase own shares
1985	Consolidation and re-enactment of legislation contained in Companies Acts 1848–81
1989	Adding provisions required under EC Directives on consolidated accounts and company auditors